FAMILY LIFE IN

NATIVE AMERICA

FAMILY LIFE IN

NATIVE AMERICA

JAMES M. VOLO AND
DOROTHY DENNEEN VOLO

Family Life through History

GREENWOOD PRESS
Westport, Connecticut • London

Library of Congress Cataloging-in-Publication Data

Volo, James M., 1947–
  Family life in Native America / James M. Volo
and Dorothy Denneen Volo.
      p. cm.—(Family life through history, ISSN 1558–6286)
  Includes bibliographical references and index.
  ISBN–13: 978–0–313–33795–6 (alk. paper)
  1. Woodland Indians—Social life and customs.   2. Woodland Indians—History.
3. Family—East (U.S.)—History.   4. Kinship—East (U.S.)—History.   5. Social
structure—East (U.S.)—History.   6. East (U.S.)—Social life and customs.   7. East
(U.S.)—History.   I. Volo, Dorothy Denneen, 1949–   II. Title.
E78.E2V66   2007
306.85089'97—dc22   2007029710

British Library Cataloguing in Publication Data is available.

Library of Congress Catalog Card Number: 2007029710
ISBN–13: 978–0–313–33795–6
ISSN: 1558–6286

First published in 2007

Greenwood Press, 88 Post Road West, Westport, CT 06881
An imprint of Greenwood Publishing Group, Inc.
www.greenwood.com

Printed in the United States of America

The paper used in this book complies with the
Permanent Paper Standard issued by the National
Information Standards Organization (Z39.48–1984).

10   9   8   7   6   5   4   3   2   1

Contents

Preface

The pre-contact cultures of native America were as remote from 16th-century Europeans as they are from us today—possibly more so because modern researchers have the advantages of archeology, historiography, hindsight, and computer-based Internet information. Nonetheless, the Indian nations residing in the woodlands of the northeast quadrant of the North American continent and those living in the adjacent coastal and piedmont regions almost certainly came into intimate contact with European explorers, settlers, and fishermen before the arrival of Christopher Columbus. These Native Americans were also among the most familiar to Euro-colonials for more than two centuries. From the tribes of the northeast woodlands came "great hunters, fishermen, farmers and fighters, as well as the most powerful and sophisticated Indian nation north of Mexico [the Iroquois Confederacy]."[1]

In aboriginal times, the woodlands universe of broad-leafed trees, towering evergreens, lakes, streams, and rivers was home for a half million or more men, women, and children to whom it gave protection, sustenance, and the raw materials of the culture. Estimates of the total population of the North American continent north of Mexico remain controversial, but they certainly hover between 1 and 2 million persons. The lowest estimates have some 900,000 living within the present-day limits of the contiguous United States and Alaska and 250,000 in present-day Canada. In the 17th and 18th centuries, little or nothing was known of the nations of the plains, the deserts, or the western mountains. Then, in the first decade of the 19th century, the explorations of Lewis and Clark opened the

Louisiana Territory. By the beginning of the 20th century, the U.S. government estimated that the Native American population of the continent had been reduced by approximately 65 percent through starvation, exposure, fevers, epidemic diseases, and wholesale massacres.

As with people across the world, the Native American family was the primary mechanism by which children passed to successful adulthood acquiring the skills, the values, and the philosophies of their forebearers. The knowledge gained by the experiences of childhood, the acquisition of formal or informal skills, and the formation of adult values were all intimate functions of the family. The family served to transmit cultural ideals, societal standards, and tribal awareness through succeeding generations. A well-ordered family also helped to mitigate the sometimes wild fluctuations in the levels of agricultural output; success at hunting, fishing, and gathering; and the level of personal security that effected family members in an organized and distinctive way. The family functioned to allow each member to adapt to the outside world and overcome the peculiar challenges of life that they faced. In this way, the family life of Native Americans was remarkably similar to that of people all over the world, but it was considerably different in outward appearances from that of the Europeans who came among them.

Family Types

From the sociological perspective, families can take on many functional and acceptable forms, and a wide diversity of familial structures could be found in native America. While each family has discrete characteristics, in general they can be condensed into a handful of archetypes with real families falling into a gray region between the black and white features of particular types. In this regard, it is necessary to define some terms before continuing. Of all the general forms of family structure, social historians normally include these four among them: *nuclear families, extended families, stem-nuclear families,* and *clan-like families.* Each of these familial structures has its own peculiar characteristics.

The true *nuclear family* was composed of a married couple living with their children under the same roof and apart from all other relatives. A *stem-nuclear family* occurred when a son married, moved with his bride (or vice-versa) into their parents' home, and raised the next generation there creating a multi-generational home. An *extended family* structure was less a matter of living arrangement than a kinship network among blood relatives living within the same community but in discrete households. Only in old age were parents likely to move in to live with a married child. In the *clan-like family* structure, the members of each group claimed a common ancestry, usually carried a common name, and, most importantly, recognized a common identity beyond the bounds of the nuclear family, which was largely unaffected by any daily living arrangement. It was the acknowledged continuity and maintenance of ancestry that defined the clan.

It is clear that Native American families rarely exhibited nuclear or stem-nuclear family characteristics in the pre-contact and early contact periods. All Indian nations were clearly clan-like to a large degree, but the extent to which their living arrangements were like those of a large extended family rather than a clan in the European sense is unclear. The characteristics of communal living were certainly much more prominent among Native Americans than they were in any white settlement in America at the same time. Nonetheless, Algonquians tended to live in discrete family dwellings within a tribal unit, while Iroquoians were clearly clan-like, not only in their living style, but also in their social, military, economic, and political structure. The specific characteristics of terms defining kinship groups and political organizations, such as *tribes, bands, villages, chiefdoms,* and *clans,* will be discussed later in the text.

These terms do not relate well to the structure of American-style families having mother, father, and some decimal number of children, but real families in white American history rarely fit that picture. Among the Indians, gender and kinship roles with respect to family and childrearing often overlapped, especially among adult brothers and sisters. Consequently, the discrete functions of Indian fathers, mothers, children, or grandparents, as seen in the light of white expectations, are often blurred beyond the ability of researchers to disaggregate them. Certainly, the idea that it takes a village to raise a child might be more appropriate and relevant than other formats for studying the family life of the American Indian. With this in mind, the author has chosen to analyze the Native American family in a different manner from his former studies, which focused generally on nuclear families.

A Note on Sources

Native American sources of information regarding their history, culture, or way of life are available and interesting, but they must be used with certain qualifications. While generally accurate as to the description of events, the sources are widely scattered chronologically and limited in absolute number. Moreover, Indian sources have proven to be imprecise with regard to the order and chronology of events. Events were more important to Indian traditions than dates, and it is left to the modern historian to delineate dates from events rather than vice-versa. Unlike the scholar Sequoia of the Southeastern Cherokee, the Indians of the northeast woodlands developed no system of narrative writing that might have catalogued a reliable description of their pre-contact culture in their own words. Almost all the surviving impressions of their lifestyle in the 17th and 18th centuries were recorded through the backward-looking and not-so-unbiased filter of European observation.

Nonetheless, the descriptive literature that was created by these Europeans was remarkable. It ranged from personal letters and private diaries first scribbled in the forests or written aboard ships to adventure journals and captivity narratives published for the consumption of a mass of 19th-century readers. Unfortunately, the catalogue of observations also includes a number of questionable documents dictated in the boudoirs of Europe and illustrated with more imagination than factual detail often by persons who had never visited America. Certainly, those writers closest to the events deserve the most attention from historians and researchers. Yet, even the most careful of the on-site observers were biased in their reporting. "Indeed, to later observers the interpretations offered by members of one society for the practices of another can appear ludicrous."[2] This book will attempt to work through the centuries of distortions and stereotypes in order to expose the truth.

Notes

1. James A. Maxwell, ed., *America's Fascinating Indian Heritage* (Pleasantville, NY: Reader's Digest Association, 1978), 111.
2. Richard White, *The Middle Ground, Indians, Empires, and Republics in the Great Lakes Region, 1650–1815* (New York: Cambridge University Press, 1991), 56.

Introduction: First Contacts with Native America

Skraelings and the Norse

The earliest recorded observations of Native Americans in their own environment were thought to have been made by the Norse. There are a number of extant Norse chronicles—including those known as the sagas—that provide important information concerning these Native American residents of the Canadian Maritimes. They include the *Hauksbok Saga,* the *Book of Icelanders,* the *History of Norway,* and the *Icelandic Annals.* Like the sagas, which were based on verbal accounts, the other chronicles were not written by contemporary eyewitnesses. Rather, they were transcriptions of oral traditions set down almost two centuries after the events that they described.

Norse mariners made contact with and attempted settlement on the North American continent (Vineland) almost 500 years before Columbus was born, and it is possible—but less certain—that individual Norsemen or small groups ascended the St. Lawrence River to the Great Lakes region in the 11th or 12th centuries. These explorers, if they existed, may have spawned some of the Indian legends of white men with blonde hair and light eyes that are common as far west as Minnesota. Optimistic researchers in the field of early Norse (Viking) exploration of America point to a scattering of runic and other Scandinavian artifacts to support their case. Nonetheless, the compendium of Norse chronicles are silent concerning trips into the interior, while they record that the Norse failed to have peaceful relations with the natives of the Canadian Maritimes whom they called *skraelings.*

Although the Norse were noted and capable warriors in their own right, they considered the skraelings fierce and worthy opponents, and the most remarkable descriptions of them are from accounts of friction between the two peoples rather than from any record of peaceful coexistence. The Norse term *skraeling,* when used in a derogatory manner, can mean scared or scruffy, but it can also be used in a positive sense when referring to the act of gliding smoothly, as in moving silently through the water or forests—a characteristic Europeans commonly applied to all forms of Indian warfare.

Norse interactions with the American Indians were often so fraught with difficulty that they quickly degenerated into conflict and open warfare. In a famous skirmish between the Norse aboard their ship and the Indians firing arrows from their canoes, Leif Erickson's brother, Thorvald, was mortally wounded by a skraeling arrow to his bowels. This battle—the first face-to-face encounter to be recorded between American Indians and Europeans arrayed for battle—ended in a draw when the Indians ran out of arrows and retired to the shore. The hard-pressed Norse were glad to see them go. The continued enmity of the skraelings for the Norse—engendered largely by blatant European aggression and prejudice—may have been one of the reasons for the abandonment of early Norse settlements in Newfoundland and Maine (see Map 1).

Other Norse pioneers led by Thorfin Karlsefni, an early explorer of North America, settled at a place they called Straumfiord, which may have been in the Kennebeck River area south of Bath, Maine. Here, in 1011 or 1012, they began peacefully trading furs and skins for milk and cloth with the local Indians. However, Karlsefni considered the skraelings great thieves and viewed them with contempt. The Indians would seemingly pick up and attempt to keep unattended tools and other items—a cultural difference with respect to the concept of the ownership of material objects that caused no end of trouble between Europeans and Native Americans throughout the centuries.

The peaceful economic exchange was broken when a Norseman and an Indian began to argue over a metal ax, and the Norseman killed the Indian. The other natives in the trading party paddled away in fear, but three weeks later a fleet of "several hundred canoes filled with armed warriors" appeared at Straumfiord. The *Hauksbok Saga* relates that the skraelings sprang from their boats with loud cries and met the defending Norse in open battle. The Norse used their swords, axes, and shields to great effect. Even the Norse women took up weapons. The Indians reportedly fought with stone axes and slings made of hide that projected stones a great distance producing "a fierce shower of missiles" that forced the Norse to retreat. In the battle, 4 Indians and 2 Norsemen were killed, but more than 30 Europeans and an untold number of natives were wounded. The following autumn, the Norse abandoned their settlement and returned to Greenland.[1]

A geography written independent of the sagas in 1075 by Adam of Bremen, a German, confirms Karlsefni's stay in Vineland, and modern archeology has supported the sagas with material evidence of Norse attempts at settlement in North America and their early association with Indians.

Contacts with skraelings were also recorded in the *Book of Icelanders* thought to have been written shortly after the founding of a settlement in Greenland by Ari the Wise in the early 12th century. Ari reported that human dwellings, fragments of skin boats, and stone artifacts found in parts of Greenland were identical to those seen in Vineland. The skraelings seemingly crossed to Greenland from the Maritimes in leather boats to make a series of attacks on the coastal Norse settlements. The next early reference to skraelings comes from the late 12th century *History of Norway.* Here, the skraelings were called "little people" (meaning short), and they were described as having no knowledge of iron. It was also reported that their weapons and missiles were made of walrus tusk and stone. Some historians believe that these descriptions relate to Eskimo, Inuit, or other sub-arctic peoples.[2]

Finally, an important report on skraelings comes from the *Icelandic Annals* of the early 14th century referring to the experiences of the crew of a small Norse vessel returning to the Greenland settlements from North America with a load of timber and firewood—a common occupation for the wood-starved Greenlanders into the 14th century. The *Annals* included detailed descriptions of native encampments, such as wooden troughs filled with grain, cups of marrow mixed with blood, flailing staves, skin boats, and stone axes—all suggesting a culture much more like that of the sub-arctic Beothuk or Inuit peoples rather than that of the woodland Micmac, Maliseet, or Montagnais of eastern Canada in the historic period.

Post-Columbian Contact

The natives living in the Canadian Maritimes in the 15th century were almost certainly Micmac or so closely related to them as to be culturally indistinguishable from them using descriptions found in contemporary sources. They traded with Portuguese and Basque fisherman harvesting cod on the Grand Banks and drying their catch on the Canadian shoreline. European mariners generally kept the existence of these bountiful fishing grounds an open secret from the rest of the world, and they may have been visiting the upper latitudes of North America decades before Columbus supposedly discovered the islands of the Caribbean in 1492.

Much of what was reported of Native American life in the 16th century was based on the observations of Indians living in the warm waters of the Caribbean. This may help to explain engravings of woodland Indians with palm trees in the background based solely on verbal accounts. A great number of reliable contemporary documents relative to Indian culture are available, but each is limited in its own way. The primary difficulty is that the

Indians themselves were in transformation—largely due to the invasion of whites and their European culture, but also due to a changing natural environment and an unusually long period of climatic cooling. The problems associated with this climate anomaly were universal, even affecting the early colonists. The Indians, perforce, were in varying stages of a complex system of adaptation throughout much of the 17th and 18th centuries, and observers saw them at different points during their transformation.

Moreover, the effects of contact were also largely a product of geography with the coastal tribes and those nations living on navigable rivers being effected first, and those in the interior remaining largely unaffected. For instance, the Erie, who populated the region around the lake named for them, seemingly had no European visitors prior to their dissolution as a viable nation in the 1650s at the hands of the Iroquois. Therefore, nothing of their cultural pattern, or lifeways, is known with certainty, although they appear to have been a highly numerous nation. Historians have been forced, therefore, to assume much about the Erie culture from the lifeways of their neighbors.[3]

The early accounts of Euro-Amerindian interactions are interesting and varied. The immediate result of an encounter between Native American and Europeans remained unpredictable. In 1508, a French ship's captain named Aubert captured three Beothuk on the shores of Canada and shipped them to Paris to be put on display. John Cabot had perpetrated a similar kidnapping a decade earlier. This tendency to capture natives as samples for exposition in Europe created an "inveterate malice" toward European sailors among some coastal tribes. Many natives would not venture aboard a European vessel unless a sailor was held ashore as hostage for their safe return, and others immediately attacked any party that came ashore without warning.[4]

The Italian explorer Giovanni de Verrazano sailed the New England coast as early as 1524 stopping in Narragansett Bay to trade trinkets for furs with the local inhabitants and leaving behind a record of some of the earliest descriptions of the Indians of the region. Verrazano noted, "We spent many days with the natives, who were friendly and generous, beautiful and civilized. They excel us in size, and are of a bronze color, some inclining more to whiteness and others of tawny color...The women are very handsome and fair. Some wear very rich skins of the lynx. Their hair is adorned with ornaments and hangs down before both sides of their breasts. We saw many of the men wearing breast-plates wrought of copper." Verrazano was less positively impressed with the natives of the Maine coast where he and his men were "shot at" with arrows and were "showed all signs of discourtesy and disdain, as was possible for any creature to invent."[5]

Bartholomew Gosnold, an English sailor entering the river at Portsmouth, New Hampshire in 1602, was greeted by Indians wearing waistcoats, breeches, stockings, shoes, and hats who spoke "Christian words" mixed with their native Algonquian. Gabriel Archer, a crewman on Gosnold's vessel, noted that these Indians were "of tall stature, with black swarthy complexions, but their eyebrows were painted white." On Martha's Vineyard, Gosnold was greeted by "olive skinned" natives "with dark hair." Hundreds of men, women, and children came out to meet him. "They were armed with bows and arrows...wore deerskins and [were] of a tall stature. Their Indian pipes were steeled [reinforced] with copper, and one wore a copper breast-plate. They were exceedingly courteous, gentle of disposition, and well conditioned, exceeding all others we have seen in shape and looks." It was also noted that most of the Indians wore copper jewelry. "Some of the copper is very red and some of a paler color, none of them but have chains, earrings, or collar of this metal."[6]

In 1603, two vessels under the command of Martin Pringe visited the Cape Cod region of Massachusetts, where he was welcomed by Indians described as "somewhat taller than we, strong and swift, wearing feathers in their knotted hair, and aprons of leather and bear skin, like an Irish mantle, over one shoulder." Once again there were a few natives—mostly men—wearing breastplates of copper. Crewman James Rofier described the native bodies as "painted with black, and their faces, some with red, some with black and some with blue." After several weeks of peaceful trading, Pringe's shore base was suddenly attacked by "seven score savages, armed with six-foot bows and arrows." These were frightened off with several discharges of the ship's cannon. The Indians that attacked Pringe may not have been from the same group that had traded with him. Other natives known to him urged him not to leave or abandon his base before he set sail.[7]

In 1608, Captain John Smith of Jamestown, Virginia undertook an exploration of Chesapeake Bay in an open boat with 25 other Englishmen. In their first encounter with the natives of the region they spied two men fishing in the shallows with "long poles like javelins, headed with bone." These fishermen invited the explorers to their village where they were treated kindly. The English next ran afoul of an unidentified group of Indians that showered them with arrows forcing their retreat to mid-river, but they were soon befriended by Nanticoke fishermen who traded with them and gave them helpful information concerning the geography of the bay. Smith was also surprised to find metal tools and hatchets of European manufacture in a Tochwogh village in present-day Maryland. These, he was told, had come by way of trade from the Susquehannock, a mighty tribe that lived to the north.[8]

The Pequot and Wampanoag tribes of Southern New England were observed by Dutch sailors under the command of Adriaen Block in 1613 and 1614. Block Island is named for this explorer who spent some time exploring the coastline of Long Island Sound. He recorded the existence of the Norwalk Archipelago, Martha's Vineyard, and many small islands, the position of the Thames and Connecticut Rivers, and the location of Narragansett Bay. Yet, Block made scant contact with the Indians.

Regular contact with the Pequot and Wampanoag did not begin until the 1630s. The Wampanoag resided in Narragansett Bay, and the Pequot seemingly occupied the Thames River drainage basin some time before European contact. The dividing line of their influence was approximately at the present border between Rhode Island and Connecticut. By historic times, the Pequot had extended their holdings through intertribal warfare with their neighbors to parts of Long Island.[9]

The Montagnais traded with the French at Tadoussac at the mouth of the Saguenay River where it flowed into the St. Lawrence as early as 1601, and it was probably they that Samuel de Champlain saw at Quebec in 1608. Champlain was a great explorer, and he traversed with a small group of friendly Indians much of the St. Lawrence Valley to the west and the lake that bears his name to the south. Here he inserted himself into an intertribal battle on the side of his Algonquian-speaking guides against an Iroquoian-speaking opponent—most likely the Mohawk. This signal act of interference in intertribal affairs resulted in the death of three Iroquoian warriors at the hands of the French and set the stage for many of the relationships between the French and the Indians thereafter.

Meanwhile, both the Europeans and the Indians carefully observed each other, and while the conclusions reached by the Indians with respect to whites went largely unreported—unless recorded by the Europeans themselves—the opposite was not the case. European observers had every reason to emphasize the richness of the land, the health of the environment, and the good will of the Native Americans. In this respect, the Norse chronicles describing the exploration and settlement of Vineland are an exception in that they detail the inextricable hatred and violence to be expected of the skraelings. The generally favorable reports of later European explorers were crafted to generate colonization and investment so that they might lead to increased wealth for trading company proprietors, land speculators, and their sovereigns.

In his book concerning the conversion of the natives of New France to Catholicism, written in 1610, French author Marc Lescarbot was the first to refer to the Indians as "noble savages." Herein, Lescarbot considered the Indians savage "only in that they were not formally Christian." English observers and authors tended to use the word *heathen* to describe the lack of Christianity among the natives, but the sobriquet *noble savage* stuck mainly because the Indians had shown that they were willing to battle both their neighbors and the Europeans when their natural rights concerning land or culture were endangered. This made them noble in the eyes of most observers because it set them apart as warriors the way knights and men-at-arms were separated from peasants in European society.

European descriptions of the Indians rendered in the early contact period were generally positive, and the appearance of individual natives—both men and women—was categorized as healthy, handsome, and approaching the physical perfection accorded to the classical Greeks or Romans.

Ironically, the greatest drawback that the English, in particular, found among the Indians was their near-classical "nakedness," which varied greatly with the 17th-century penchant for Europeans to cloth themselves from throat to heel in woolens and velvets even in the most intolerable extremes of heat and humidity. Nonetheless, John Smith's initial descriptions of the natives of Virginia were extraordinarily positive, and Thomas Morton viewed the Indians of New England as so highly principled that they "would not lie nor steal."[10]

Although considered savage and heathen, there was also a grudging concession that native society was highly developed (for an uncivilized people) and that the native warriors should be regarded as a force to be reckoned with even in the absences of firearms. Hostility and stealing were expected constantly, and when an Indian was too friendly, Europeans usually expected treachery or imminent attack.[11]

Whites considered Indians unstable, unreliable, and unpredictable to the point of being fickle, if not erratic. The least signs of friendliness from the natives were described as admiration, love, or even reverence, while cordiality, cooperation, and hospitality were reported as childlike submission. These anecdotal reports generally strayed from reality.[12]

In much the same way that Indians sought to affect the world of plants, animals, and spirits by appealing to the good will of the manitou, so it seems they sought to gain the benefits of the social, economic, and technological world of Europe by appealing to the egos of their visitors.[13] On the other hand, Jesuit Father Pierre Biard noted the "confusion, discord, rage, and uproar" that was produced in friendly Indians by an unusual manifestation of the Aurora Borealis in 1612 as it turned the sky "blood-red...spreading, little by little, in vivid streaks and flashes...directly over the village." Biard reported that the superstitions of the Indians caused a great anxiety among the small band of Frenchmen, but no violence. "I do not doubt that a cursed band of furious and sanguinary spirits [the Indians] were hovering about all this night, expecting every hour and moment a horrible massacre of the few Christians who were there."[14]

Although the Dutch produced some of the earliest formal records of their experiences among the Indians in the valleys of the Hudson and Delaware rivers, such documents, while numerous, were largely the product of the business interests of the Dutch West India Company, not the ethnographic impressions of American Indian tribes or their way of life. Even these were systematically destroyed in the 19th century before interested historians could amass a significant body of research from them. Historical researchers were thereby primarily left with French and English sources describing the Native Americans of the northeast quadrant of the continent. On these copious volumes, historians have relied for decades. Nonetheless, the few surviving letters, diaries, and journals authored primarily by Dutch ministers and traders can provide a meaningful footnote into 17th-century America.[15]

The formal reports that the black robed Jesuit fathers sent home to France are particularly important. The Jesuit devotion and self-sacrifice, the hardships they endured, and their triumphs or martyrdom were all set down in meticulous detail. In the 19th century, the individual reports were combined into 70 massive volumes known as *The Jesuit Relations.* Full English translations of the *Relations* can be found in most college libraries or on the Internet. They make fascinating reading for devotees of the early colonial period. Although written with the obvious bias of Christian churchmen serving among people they considered heathens, pagans, and savages, the *Relations* serve, nonetheless, as a major source of information about Indian life in early America. There are also numerous reports written by the officials of the Crown in New France. However, these tend to deal with the political environment of the French colony rather than Native American life.[16]

Pierre Esprit Radisson, famed for opening the fur trade with the Indian nations of the north country surrounding Hudson's Bay, was a prodigious writer. Unfortunately, Radisson was also considered an equally prodigious liar, rogue, and fabricator of tall tales by many of his contemporaries. Nonetheless, some of his more extraordinary experiences have found verification through a careful reading of the *Jesuit Relations.* Several of Radisson's manuscripts were included in the papers of Samuel Pepys, secretary of the British Admiralty who granted the fur trader a pension of £300 per year for life in recognition of his service in Hudson's Bay. The reports of Radisson's early life among the Indians fill no fewer than six volumes titled *Voyages.* Five of these were published in English and the last was published in Radisson's native French.

In the first of these volumes, Radisson described his time as a captive among the Mohawk, his adoption into the tribe, his Indian foster family, his part as a member of a small war party, and his return to white society by way of Albany. This volume covers the important years of 1652 and 1653 when the Iroquois, and the Mohawk in particular, were at the height of their power among other nations in the northeast woodlands. His other volumes detail his trips to Onondaga with the Huron, his embassy to the Cree and Chippewa with his brother-in-law Medard Chouart des Groseilliers, and his discovery of a practical route to Hudson's Bay. Here he helped to establish the Hudson's Bay Company that traded with the Micmac, the Cree, and another tribe known only as the Sorcerers.

Jolicoeur Charles Bonin, a soldier of the French and Indian War period, has also left a vivid journal of his time in the northeast woodlands. As a private soldier who fought beside the Indians at the Monongahela against the British under Edward Braddock, his observations of the French allied Indians of the 1755–1763 period are invaluable due to their perspective. Published many years after the fact, Bonin's journals include several additions to his observations credited only to J.C.B., who most historians believe to be the same Jolicoeur Charles Bonin.

The published papers of Sir William Johnson, Conrad Weiser, George Croghan, and other agents of the British crown; the notices and articles abstracted from colonial newspapers; and the government documents of the various Anglo-American colonies all serve as important sources of information about Indian life from the English perspective during the Colonial Wars Era (approx. 1690–1763). Johnson's papers are particularly revealing of Iroquois culture in the 18th century because he lived closely among them in his younger years, married a Mohawk "princess," and served at times as a war party leader. Croghan wrote two journals concerning the treaty transactions carried out with the Indians in 1765. One of these was prepared for the English officials and magistrates in London. The other was evidently prepared for colonial land speculators, emphasizing the fine topography, fertile soil, numerous trees, and constant availability of game in western Pennsylvania and the Ohio country. It has been noted that "No paragraph in one [journal] is the same as any paragraph in the other, yet there is nothing contradictory in the two."[17]

The reports authored by most Europeans in the 17th and 18th centuries generally cut across the more overt forms of prejudice and racism that came with the later work of historians, such as Francis Parkman, but they were parochial and biased in their own way. Europeans expressed many of the most unique features of Native American life in terms more appropriate for the English, Dutch, and French of the 17th and 18th century than for those doing an analysis in today's society. Because of the lack of readily available parallels for the complex structure of Indian family life, for instance, Europeans often misrepresented the sexual relations among husbands, wives, and their lovers as some sort of free-love. Reports were made in ways that were often mutually contradictory—one observer complaining of a man's coercive authority over his wife or sister and another chiding women in the same circumstance for being adulterous or wanton. European conceptions of marriage, adultery, sexual inhibitions, or the lack thereof, simply could not encompass the actual variety of interpersonal relationships allowed under the scheme of Native American mores.

The descriptive literature that flowed from these voyagers, explorers, journalist, trappers, traders, and government officials was also filled with references to antiquity where imperial Romans, democratic Greeks, barbaric Germans, fierce Celts, and ancient Britons—all ancestor models of early 17th-century Europeans—had been depicted as strong, admirable, or capable of establishing flourishing societies. Village leaders were rendered as kings, emperors, chiefs, or queens often without regard to political or cultural realities.[18]

Yet, between the lines of high praise for Native American life, health, and society could be read a program of propaganda endorsing the idea that the riches, the free land, and the climate of North America were capable of supporting a European lifestyle.

Notes

1. Robert Ellis Cahill, *New England's Viking and Indian Wars* (Danvers, MA: Old Saltbox Publishing, 1987), 12–13.

2. Cahill, 13.

3. William A. Starna, "The Pequots in the Early Seventeenth Century," in *The Pequots in Southern New England, The Fall and Rise of an American Indian Nation,* ed. Laurence M. Hauptman and James D. Wherry (Norman: University Press of Oklahoma, 1990), 34.

4. Cahill, 27.

5. Cahill, 15–16.

6. Cahill, 21–22.

7. Cahill, 23–24.

8. Philip J. Webster and Christopher Cerino, "Exploring The Chesapeake Bay with Captain John Smith: 1608 and 2007," *Sea History,* no. 118 (Spring 2007): 28.

9. Starna, 33–34.

10. Winfield Ross, "Coming to America," *Early American Life* (April 2007): 52.

11. Karen Ordahl Kupperman, *Indians and English, Facing Off in Early America* (Ithaca: Cornell University Press, 2000), 9.

12. Kupperman, 9.

13. See White, 51–52.

14. Harold F. McGee, *The Native Peoples of Atlantic Canada, A History of Indian-European Relations* (Ottawa: Carleton University Press, 1983), 29–30.

15. Walter D. Edmonds, *The Musket and the Cross, the Struggle of France and England for North America* (Boston: Little, Brown and Company, 1968), 82.

16. See Reuben Gold Thwaites, ed., *The Jesuit Relations and Allied Documents* (Cleveland: Burrows Brothers, 1898).

17. Albert T. Volwiler, *George Croghan and the Westward movement, 1742–1783* (Lewisburg, PA: Wennawoods Publishing, 2000), 183n. Also see indexed collections such as Almon W. Lauber, ed., *The Papers of Sir William Johnson* (Albany: University of the State of New York, 1939); Paul A. W. Wallace, *Conrad Weiser, Friend of Colonist and Mohawk: 1696–1760* (Lewisburg, PA: Wennawoods Publishing, 1996); Armand Francis Lucier, ed., *French and Indian War Notices Abstracted from Colonial Newspapers,* vols. 1–4 (Bowie, MD: Heritage Books 1999); or E. B. O'Callaghan, ed., *Documents Relative to the Colonial History of the State of New York* (Albany: Weed, Parsons and Co., 1855).

18. Kupperman, 30.

I

An Overview of the Native American World

1

An Environmental Geography of the Northeast Woodlands

The wood was so thick, that for a mile at a time we could not find a place of the size of a hand, where the sunshine could penetrate, even in the clearest day.

—Conrad Weiser, Colonial Indian Agent

A New World

Transatlantic explorers from Europe were initially upset to find a vast continental barrier to the westward navigation to China and the Far East, yet in just a few years they had explored and claimed a vast portion of the New World called America. In less than a century, Spain had conquered all that is present-day Mexico and had raped the Inca and Aztec empires of their treasures. The Spanish treasury, in particular, was made the recipient of a far greater portion of this wealth than other European powers because it was the first to sack the largest, richest portions of Central and South America. Moreover, by the 1540s, Spanish mariners had a general idea of the broad outlines of North America. Six decades before the English had established their first permanent settlement at Jamestown or the French their first outpost in Canada, the Spanish priests had established and closed a mission in Virginia, and Spanish soldiers had overrun the largest islands in the Caribbean. By the end of the 16th century, Spanish explorers had also journeyed through present day Georgia, South Carolina, North Carolina, Alabama, Mississippi, Arkansas, parts of the Tennessee River valley, the Appalachian Mountains, and much of the great desert

Southwest. Their record of exploration and conquest was not only incredible, it was unrivaled. "In a single generation the Spaniards seized more new territory than Rome could acquire in five hundred years."[1]

Yet, the woodlands of the Northeast quadrant of North America and the fertile and temperate lands along the Atlantic coast seemingly held little attraction for the Spanish. Although they had seen forests, rivers, animal life, and fertile soil to rival all that was in Europe, they did not covet the natural wealth of the region. This is understandable when one considers the mighty empires, monuments, temples, and treasures the Spaniards had found elsewhere in the Americas. A Spanish courtier wrote, "What need have we of what is found everywhere in Europe? It is toward the south, not toward the frozen north, that those who seek their fortune should bend their way; for everything at the equator is rich." With such sentiments in mind, Spain seemingly abandoned the Northeast woodlands to its European rivals—chiefly the English, French, and Dutch—to do with as they pleased.[2]

This circumstance essentially left the seafaring nations of western Europe to compete for much of the North American woodlands. Nonetheless, as the 16th century closed, none of these nations had established a single successful colony in the New World, and Spain was still busily exploiting its claims in Latin America, the Gulf Coast, and Florida. Not until 1607–1608 did the English or French establish a successful colony— one in Virginia and one in Canada. The Dutch first sailed up the Hudson River in 1609, and they quickly set up trading posts at Fort Orange (Albany) and on Manhattan Island. They also quickly extinguished the bright ember of initial Swedish colonization in the Delaware Bay through force of arms. Thereafter, the aggressive and business-like expansion of the Dutch colony was remarkable, but it was short circuited by their own defeat in the Anglo-Dutch wars of the 17th century. The Dutch residents of New Netherlands survived both the name change to New York and the English-speaking colonial managers appointed by the Duke of York in 1664. The Dutch, thereafter, focused on their possessions in the sugar-rich Caribbean, leaving only England and France to contend over much of the North American woodlands. "The one [to] rest content with the country east of the Alleghenies and the other with the forests, savages, and beaver skins of the northern lakes."[3]

The Northeast Woodlands

A woodland, rather than a purely prairie culture, embraced the native population of almost the entire Northeast quadrant of North America from the Mississippi River to the Atlantic coastal region and Canadian Maritimes, and from the watershed of the Tennessee River to the frozen waste of Hudson's Bay. This region can be thought of as shaped like a giant Valentine's heart with its stem rooted in the Tennessee and Ohio

River valleys, and its cleft being Hudson's Bay. The right lobe of the heart encompassed much of present-day Pennsylvania, New York, New England, and the Eastern Canadian provinces quite to the Arctic Circle, and the left lobe surrounded the Great Lakes states and Canada's prairie provinces to a general western boundary along the course of the Upper Missouri River. Much of this region was heavily forested and well-watered by numerous rivers, streams, and lakes.[4]

The geographical center of this region was somewhere near the present location of Niagara Falls, which lies between Lakes Erie and Ontario. Yet, the population density center of the region was skewed well to the west near Lake Superior by the extremely populous Ojibwa peoples (aka, Chippewa, Ottawa, etc.) and the Canadian Cree, who were loosely aligned politically but almost identical in their culture to the Ojibwa. These western tribes combined may have numbered in excess of 70,000 persons. The term Chippewa is a synonym for Ojibwa, the last sound of which refers to a puckered seam common to their way of making moccasins. European grabbled the name into Chippewa, and it stuck so persistently that many Ojibwas today called themselves Chippewa. In a conservative estimate, the Ojibwa, Cree, and Ottawa nations alone—the last to come into contact with whites—may have represented half the Indian population characterized as Northeast Woodland Indians.[5]

In the middle of the 17th century, the rough outline of the Northeast woodlands was known only to within a few days journey on foot of a navigable water source. On most European maps the region was surrounded by the words *Terra Incognita* (unknown lands) or some such written admission that the white man had not yet successfully penetrated the forest wilderness. A 19th-century map reproduced in a children's history text noted the entire region between Quebec City and Lake Superior as "Forested, rough, Lake-rock-muskeg country" (see Map 5). The vast area to the north and east of Hudson's Bay was sparsely populated by the Wabanaki (People of the Dawn) who formed the "hoop of seven great nations." These included the Micmac, Maliseet, and Montagnais of eastern Canada; the Passamaquoddy, Penobscot, and Abenaki of Maine, New Hampshire, and western Massachusetts; and several small sub-arctic bands such as the Naskapi. The sub-arctic Indians had followed the caribou that drifted north with the retreating tundra of an earth warming after the last ice age. Several of the smaller tribes were on the periphery of subsequent historical events, which eliminates them from inclusion in most discussions of the woodlands culture. Others, like the Abenaki, were critical players in the frontier wars of the 18th century.[6]

The Atlantic coast of southern New England was well-populated until the residents were ravaged by diseases of epidemic proportions. In the historic period, it was the home of the Pequot, Wampanoag, Mohegan, Narragansett, and other subsidiary nations. The region enjoyed warm summers and delightful autumns, but the winters were more severe than presently. Beginning about 1620, the entire earth fell into a century-long period of cooling known as the Little Ice Age (aka, the Maunder Minimum). Indians had to be especially hardy, alert, and adaptable to equip and feed themselves in this suddenly changing environment. At the time that English and Dutch colonials intruded into the region, the climate had just deterio-rated with remarkably harsher winters and shorter growing seasons than the natives had experienced in their own lifetimes. This put stresses on the native family and their kinfolk that we can only surmise.

The lowlands and marshes of Long Island Sound, Narragansett Bay, and southeast Massachusetts would have been the areas least effected by any adverse change in average temperature. In the leafy forests along the margins of these lowlands, moose and deer were the largest herbi-vores to be found as a food source. Bears, themselves a source of food for humans, competed with the Indian hunter–gatherer for berries, small animals, and fish. Nonetheless, the Indians of New England had learned to farm. Beginning about A.D. 1000 the cultivation of maize, beans, and squash by means of hoeing small hillocks became a common practice along the coast. These garden vegetables clearly "provided only dietary supplements, rather than economic staples." The difference seen by a simple hunter–gatherer family would have been a seasonal abundance of harvested crops and the addition to the family's winter larder of foods that could be dried and stored.[7]

As the name suggests, the Northeast woodlands region was generally covered with trees ranging from conifers in the Canadian North to decidu-ous trees in the American Midwest. Meadows, flatlands, and treeless (sub-arctic) regions could be found, but only in the western sections were there significant patches of open plain that might be classified as prairie. The re-gion north of the Great Lakes was covered mostly in pine and spruce. From Illinois to southern New England there was a wide belt of predominantly oak and hickory trees; from Wisconsin to central New York was a band of northern hardwoods, such as birch, beech, maple, and ash. The distribution of these species was not uniform, and individual examples could be found almost anywhere that environmental conditions proved favorable.

Local native culture was greatly affected by the type of woodland and its distribution in the immediate area. Also important was the availability of berries, nuts, roots, fish, and the variety of animal resources that each type of woodland supported. Few mountains in the Northeast were of such high elevation as to be above the tree-line, but open rocky escarpments formed during the last period of world-wide glaciation were not infrequent. The Great Lakes themselves were remnants of the last Ice Age 25,000 years ago.

Wilderness

Many Europeans described America as a wilderness, but most areas of the world that are considered wilderness today are remote, inhospitable, or bereft of natural resources. Regions filled with wildlife, timber, fresh water, and fertile soil, as was America, generally do not evoke the necessary quality of desolation associated with a wilderness tract. Yet, for most 17th-century Europeans, the very concept of wilderness was heavily freighted with a myriad of personal meanings and symbolic devices.[8]

When the pilgrim leader William Bradford stepped off the *Mayflower* in Plymouth, Massachusetts in 1620, he described himself as entering "a hideous and desolate wilderness filled with evil and capable of making man revert to savagery."[9] Bradford's wilderness was intimately tied to his religious concepts of good and evil, or even of rectitude and witchcraft. For many early immigrants like Bradford, the American wilderness was seen from this religious perspective not as a remote and desolate expanse, but rather as "a sanctuary from a sinful and persecuting society…[a] wild country…in which to find and draw close to God…a testing ground where a chosen people were purged, humbled, and made ready for the land of promise."[10] The wilderness drew to itself a self-righteous people, like the Pilgrims, precisely because it was harsh and forbidding. Like John the Baptist, Moses, and Elijah in the Bible, they sought out the wilderness as a place to pray and be nearer to God. On the other hand, in Europe, inaccessible mountain peaks and craggy cliff sides were the only landforms that had not been put into production by the 16th century. Possibly for these reasons, many Europeans tended to link the concept of wilderness with uncultivated land that was rocky, heavily wooded, and inhabited only by wild beasts, sorcerers, and savages—an area of black forests, formidable crags, and fearsome cliffs. In these characteristics, many areas of the Americas were very close to being absolute wilderness.

By comparison to Europeans, Native Americans exhibited little antipathy toward the concept of wilderness. Indian religions accepted a relationship between man and the natural regions of the world that bordered on love. They recognized humans as one with all other living things. Moreover, for them, the wilderness did not have connotations of evil and disorder, but rather those of natural order and the very essence of deity. It should not be surprising, therefore, that European explorers, missionaries, and settlers failed to understand the native American's close relationship with, and deep regard for, the land.[11]

Wilderness had long been associated with savagery, and the nakedness and lawlessness of the Native Americans, in the eyes of Europeans, seemed to justify the conclusion that America was a wilderness populated by savages or wild men. Yet, "as a wild people," the Native Americans should have presented themselves as "nomads ranging over the land in search of game." They should have "resembled the beasts that they hunted." However, "no one who actually came to America and described personal experience of Indians ever projected such an image."[12] Not only did native societies exhibit permanence and civil order, they also had traditions, ceremonies, political and familial hierarchies, and social distinctions that were obvious to even the casual observer. "So close were the Indians to European norms, in fact, that commentators assured their readers that only a series of short steps...separated them from achieving full [European-style] civility."[13]

For the Europeans, the thought that North America was a wilderness populated with wild men and savages was a great advantage to the newcomer who wished to establish his own claim in the New World. Land and its legal disposition were of no small regard to the first settlers in America, and they took the legalities of property transfer and tenure quite seriously. Just how wild a region had to be to qualify as a wilderness in the minds of colonial settlers is not certain. Some small amount of previous settlement seems to have been tolerated as a sign of ownership, while any form of civilization that failed to demonstrate its influence in European terms seems to have been dismissed. Nonetheless, agreements made with a single village elder were thought to bind an entire Indian nation as though he were a potentate or ambassador of a European principality. Ambivalence, therefore, shaped the context in which some Native Americans were viewed. The more experience Europeans had with the Indians, the more complex became their descriptions of them and the more varied became their understandings of Indian society and order.

To the European mind of the 17th century, the concepts of wilderness and civilization were at opposite ends of a spectrum with a scale in between suggesting a thorough shading or blending of the two in the center, which was marked *the frontier*. The frontier was possibly best described in European terms as "ploughed"—a balance between man's needs and God's clockwork nature.[14] "The frontier [was] the outer edge of the wave—the meeting point between savagery and civilization." The greatest cities of Europe were small and unsophisticated by comparison with those of today, yet London or Paris were certainly well along toward a synthetic condition of life remote from the fields and pastures of the 17th-century peasant. On this scale, the modest New World settlements of the 17th and 18th century, even those highly urbanized ones in New Amsterdam and Quebec, were nothing but outposts on a wilderness frontier.[15]

Inland Waterways

Rather than being a trackless wasteland, the woodlands region was actually crisscrossed by a network of well-established water routes. Just as surely as the Appalachian Mountains stood as a barrier to easy entry into the interior of North America from the English colonies on the Atlantic coast, the St. Lawrence River served the French of Canada as a convenient water route to the Great Lakes and the whole center of the continent. French control of this vital waterway is often cited by historians as a key to the continent. In the fur trade period, the French used the Ottawa River, the St. Maurice River, and the Saguenay River to travel from the interior to Montreal, Trois Riviers, and Quebec, respectfully. Although a simple survey of a map would suggest that the French had an advantage, the available water routes to the interior actually used by the French and the English were nonetheless approximately equivalent.

On the St. Lawrence River, medium-sized ships were able to sail a considerable distance inland to the limits of navigation. One of the most important obstacles to navigation was at the narrows between Montreal and Lake Ontario. Here, the La Chine rapids prevented the passage of large vessels, while at the other end of the lake the great cataract of Niagara Falls stalled even the passage of canoes. The Hudson-Mohawk River system served the English in somewhat the same manner as the St. Lawrence River served the French. The limit of navigation for sailing vessels on the Hudson River was at the falls near Albany. Thereafter, goods and passengers were transferred by hand to canoes, or bateau, capable of being operated by human power on the Mohawk River or on the streams and lakes of the Adirondack region. Both routes led to Lake Ontario. Thereafter, French and English explorers faced similar geographic and topographic obstacles to their further progress into the interior.

Yet, the French are commonly thought to have started the quest for a North American empire with an advantage because of their early exploration of the region. Before the end of the 17th century, Samuel de Champlain journeyed up the Ottawa River to the west of Montreal, then northward toward Hudson's Bay, westward to Lakes Ontario and Huron, and along the Richelieu River southward into the lake that bears his name in north-central New York. Only chance kept the French explorers that followed him from descending further into the Hudson River valley and planting a colony on the Atlantic Ocean somewhere near Manhattan Island. All this could have been done before the Dutch made a claim on the area.[16]

The geography of North America, available to any school child by simply opening an atlas or searching on the Internet, was hidden from early explorers and missionaries. Their knowledge of the interior was often sketchy, superficial, and uncertain. Captain John Smith took more than six months during 1608 to record the basic outline of Chesapeake Bay and the major tributaries that flowed into it—an open boat voyage of 2,500 miles. During this voyage, he was informed by the natives that the eastern shore of the bay was actually a peninsula between the Chesapeake and Delaware Bays and the Atlantic Ocean. Smith's map was published in London in 1612.[17]

For most of the continental interior, there were no reliable maps at all until the beginning of the 19th century. Even the most successful explorers had no inkling of the details of most of the topography of the continent. A voyage of 500 miles from the mouth of the St. Lawrence took French explorers to the La Chine rapids near Montreal. Another 500 miles by canoe brought them only to Detroit with 500 more miles of unexplored lakes before them. It would take Europeans hundreds of years to record the actual contours of the continent on maps, while Native Americans simply carried the interlocking pattern of streams, rivers, and lakes in their heads.[18]

From the early part of the 17th century, the French tried to penetrate the interior of the continent and comprehend its geography. French interest in the topography of the continent was not rooted in exploration for its own sake. Indeed such a concept was "alien to Europeans before the onset of the Romantic movement of the nineteenth century. Pious Europeans explored for souls; the rest explored for riches." Within three decades of the founding of the French post at Quebec City (1608), Etienne Brule traveled to Lake Erie, and the Jesuit missionaries de Brebeuf and Chaumont wintered with the Indians west of Lake Ontario. In 1679, Robert de la Salle sailed up the St. Claire River and passed through Lake St. Claire at Detroit. Each of these early explorers reported the richness of the Great Lakes region in terms of furs, and the reports, spreading rapidly across Europe, insured that the French would not be alone in coveting control of the region.[19]

At a time when the line of mountains was the boundary between the English settlements and the wilderness interior, there were three significant water routes open to them through the mountains into the interior. Besides the Hudson River, the major rivers of the northeastern Atlantic seaboard in this region were the Delaware and the Susquehanna. All three rivers found their headwaters in the mountains east and southeast of the Great Lakes. The tributaries of the Delaware and Susquehanna rivers are almost completely entangled in this region. This headwaters region was occupied by the Five Nations Iroquois Confederacy, and the river banks to the sea were lined with the homes of many sub-tribes of the Delaware, Shawnee, and Susquehannock nations, making the watershed one of the most densely populated centers of Native American life east of the Mississippi River. Major centers of Native American settlement were located near these water courses in the present-day states of New York, Pennsylvania, and parts of Maryland, Delaware, and Virginia. It would be impossible to describe in detail the many nations that peopled this vast region. Suffice it to say that they resembled their neighbors to the north, for whom there were many descriptions by contemporary observers, and that they shared many of their religious and cultural characteristics.

The Susquehanna River gave the indigenous populations of this region the best water route from central New York to the Chesapeake Bay and the South. The Delaware River gave access to southeastern Pennsylvania, western New Jersey, and the lower part of New York. The latter river continued through the Delaware Water Gap to form the boundaries between the colonies of Delaware, Pennsylvania, and New Jersey and exited into

Delaware Bay. For almost their entire length the Hudson, Delaware, and Susquehanna rivers were navigable by canoes with only short portages between entering and exiting points around small falls and rapids.

Nonetheless, the canoe did not guarantee unimpeded passage at all seasons of the year. Streams swollen by melt water and heavy rains were just as impassable as those that turned into a long wet puddle of boulders in the dry seasons. Travelers often had to exit their vessels and drag them through shallow water and across bars of gravel and sand. Such circumstances were hard on both the paddlers and the canoes, which were often scraped so badly as to warrant repair on the stream bank. Fortunately, the materials needed to accomplish the repairs were easily available from the forests along the route. It should be remembered that these canoes, unlike the recreational craft used today, were almost always fully loaded with either trade goods, furs, or passengers.

Jesuit Father Louis Hennepin left a vivid impression of the obstacle posed by the falls and rapids known as the Long Sault in the Ottawa River. "[A] dreadful encounter of water that beats so furiously against the rock, continues about 2 leagues [four miles], the waters spurt about 10 or 12 yards high, and appear like huge snowballs, hail, and rain, with dreadful thunder, and a noise like hissing and howling of fierce beasts; and I do certainly believe that if a man continues there a considerable time, he would become deaf, without any hope of cure."[20]

Portages

The key to the inland waterways of North America proved to be a pattern of short land bridges where goods and boats could be manhandled overland from one water route to another known in French as *portages*. The Native Americans had discovered these interconnections through centuries of travel. East of the Mississippi River, the important portages could be divided into three distinct systems. Those that went east–west along the St. Lawrence Valley and through the Great Lake region gave access to the furs of the western plains. Other portages gave a north–south passage from Hudson's Bay through the Great Lakes to the Mississippi River and its tributaries, such as the Ohio and Tennessee Rivers. It was possible to enter the Bay of St. Lawrence near Newfoundland, travel the St. Lawrence River, enter and exit the Great Lakes, enter the Ohio–Mississippi River system, and exit at New Orleans into the Gulf of Mexico by utilizing the numerous short portages that existed. This was essentially the method used by Robert de la Salle during his expedition of discovery in 1679. Finally, there was a series of portages leading northward from the Hudson River valley through the Lake George–Lake Champlain valley and the Richelieu River to the St. Lawrence River.

For the French, the major stumbling block to easy movement of trade goods to the west was the great falls in the Niagara River as it flowed between Lake Erie and Lake Ontario. The portage around the falls required a torturous route along the Niagara River gorge of more than a dozen miles. The location of the outlet of the river into Lake Ontario was strategically important, and the French built a fortified trading post there. The passage of Niagara Falls, taken together with the numerous rapids in the St. Lawrence, made French navigation into the interior more difficult than it seemed at first glance.

For the English, the major difficulty in moving west lay in the four- to five-mile distance between the headwaters of the Mohawk River and the westward flowing Wood Creek near present-day Rome, New York. This almost flat land bridge between water courses was called the Great Carrying Place. Here the British built a series of forts during the French and Indian Wars. The carry from the Mohawk was not difficult, and the mild current of Wood Creek swept travelers first to Oneida Lake, then to the Oswego River, and finally into Lake Ontario. Once in Lake Ontario the English faced the same difficulty in moving further west that was posed to the French by Niagara Falls. The outlet of the Oswego River into Lake Ontario was also fortified by the British.

The Hudson–Richelieu Corridor

The English settlements at New York and the French settlements in Canada were connected by water through the Hudson River–Richelieu River corridor (sometimes called the Mahican Channel). In the 18th century, both England and France found that they were being funneled by geography into this same region of the continent, fated to come into conflict in what would later become the capital region of New York state near Albany. Of course, the same water route that promised the English easy access to Canada afforded the French the same access to the New York frontier. Both sides raced to control the significant portages along this route, and some historians consider it the most heavily fortified and important strategic route in North American military history. The Hudson–Richelieu route was used many times in the colonial period by both French and English armies.[21]

There was a portage from the upper reaches of the Hudson River that gave access to the North into Canada through Lake George. This portage of more than a dozen miles was also called the Great Carrying Place. The water exit from the Hudson was at present day Fort Edward, New York, and the entrance was at the South Bay of the Lake Champlain system. The latter place was called Wood Creek, and it is very closely associated with the present-day city of Whitehall.

Finally, there was a particularly important portage at the falls in the La Chute River through which Lake George emptied into Lake Champlain. Nearby was a peninsula of land known as Ticonderoga. Ticonderoga was to become one of the most sought after strategic positions in all of

North America. No fewer than four critical military operations took place there. Ironically, the French left the position unfortified for more than a century and a half. Thereafter, it passed from the French to the British during the French and Indian Wars; from the British to the Americans in the Revolution; back to the British for a brief period, and finally back to American hands.

Indian Trails

Frontier exploration and settlement was greatly influenced, and somewhat eased, by the existence of a relatively well-articulated network of Indian trails and paths. These provided ready access to the major river valleys, stream crossings, portages, and mountain passes of the region. Paths led to many of the best agricultural lands in the interior where the open nature of the woodlands—especially in the major river valleys—made the land rather more favorable for early settlement than the virgin woodlands and forested hillsides.[22]

The Indians are often berated for not developing the wheel, although there is evidence that they knew the technology but chose not to employ it on an everyday basis.[23] They dragged or carried their goods and household items from place to place because they did not have roads or draft animals capable of pulling carts or wagons. Before the advent of bulldozers and other mechanized earth-movers, cutting roads through the forests by hand was generally viewed as an onerous and backbreaking task to be avoided if at all possible. The first Europeans found that the native solution to land transportation—much like that of the canoe for water transport—was generally superior to their own, and major road building projects were not undertaken until the second half of the 18th century. Indian trails rendered the heavily forested areas less of a barrier than they might have otherwise posed. Although the Native Americans, lacking wheeled vehicles, failed to develop wide roads, settlers found that they could use the well-beaten Indian footpaths to "ride on horseback without inconvenience in the woods, and even with a cart in most places."[24]

Many Indian routes were two to three feet wide, worn into the ground by centuries of use, and easily located. The regular traffic of the indigenous population—which seems to have been quite far-reaching and common—kept the major trails from one region of the country to another fairly clear throughout the year. However, the native population tended to walk in single file, and many minor paths were difficult to locate or seemingly disappeared over rocky or wet ground. Moreover, the entrance of whites into certain regions caused many of the less frequented paths to become obscured by brush or obstructed by wind falls as the Indians withdrew and discontinued their use. Some of these trails came to be known to whites as "blind Indian paths" that seemingly led nowhere. The true course of these paths and their interconnections were known only to the few Indians that had not left the locality. Nonetheless, Indian paths continued to be used by the whites to define the boundaries of purchases and land grants, sometimes creating difficulties in future years when assessing the legitimate limits of ownership between those who had conflicting legal interests.[25]

The region just west of Albany contained an important hub of Indian trails that served the entire northeastern colonial frontier. Here, near the confluence of the Mohawk River and Schoharie Creek (Fort Hunter, NY), was one of the principal population centers of the powerful Mohawk nation known as Teantontalogo, or the Lower Mohawk Castle. The Upper Mohawk Castle, at Canajoharie (named for the large sinkhole there) some 30 miles further inland, had a larger Mohawk population. Onondaga in the Finger Lakes region of western New York was the practical seat of Iroquois government in the Northeast. While a trail from Albany along the bank of the Mohawk led to the great council fire of the Iroquois at Onondaga, the most important trail in the region was the north–south Onondaga Trail, which followed the course of the Susquehanna River. The Susquehanna route (whether taken by foot, horseback, or canoe) was the route most commonly used by Native Americans traveling between central New York and Delaware Bay on the coast.[26]

Finally, there was the Warrior's Path that followed the Shenandoah River valley through the back country of the English settlements to the southern colonies. Every year parties of Iroquois from New York descended the Warrior's Path to the south to attack their traditional enemies among the Cherokees. In the 18th century, colonial preachers from Pennsylvania traveled the Warrior's Path south through Maryland and the valley of the Shenandoah River making converts as far south as the Carolinas and Georgia. Other than the Braddock and Forbes roads built by British armies in Pennsylvania between 1755 and 1758, no land route was more important than the Warrior's Path in bringing settlers to the frontier.

Mound Builders

Although most of the Northeast woodland region was dominated by a type of lifestyle characteristic of its post-contact forest residents, the presence of physical evidence suggests the existence of a prehistoric and mysterious mound building culture that may have been significantly different. The lack of any written record among these pre-contact residents has obscured the actual pre-history of this region and the motivation behind raising so many large and small mounds.

In 1775, one of Anglo-America's first naturalists, William Bartram, could not fathom why the natives had raised such "heaps of earth." Yet, he understood that the mounds, taken as "public works" projects, could not have been completed without a stronger central governing force among the natives than either he or his predecessors had observed among the 17th- or 18th-century native inhabitants of the region. There may have been more than 200,000 mounds in the eastern woodlands representing a total amount of work greater than the sum of all that done on all the pyramids in ancient Egypt. The peoples of the Ohio Valley had an abundance of plant and animal life to serve as food, and this gave them something that other native tribes lacked—a permanent, or semi-permanent residence and the free time to plan and move millions of baskets of earth. Evidence suggests that mound building continued into the 15th century and then suddenly stopped. However, we do not know why the woodland peoples built mounds because researchers have not found any evidence of a written language to enlighten them as to the Indian purpose.

The evidence of a prehistoric people in the region tempted many 19th-century historians to conclude that there was a political or cultural connection between the mound builders of Ohio and Mississippi and the temple-building Meso-American civilizations of Mexico and Central America with their step pyramids. This connection is now generally discounted in favor of a distinct and separate culture generally known as the Adena, Hopewell, or Mississippian culture. The Mississippian culture, of which the Hopewell and Adena may have been either branches or precursors, seems to have developed on its own separate from Aztec, Inca, or any other identified influence.

Today, anthropologists generally refer to the last prehistoric culture to dominate North America before European contact as the Late Mississippian culture. Thriving from about A.D. 800, the Mississippian culture seemingly spanned a huge region from Wisconsin and Minnesota in the north, through Georgia to the south, and westward into the Great Plains. Divided into three distinct cultural periods Early (A.D. 800–1200), Middle (A.D. 1200–1500), and Late (A.D. 1500–1700), the Mississippians may have introduced the cultivation of maize (corn) throughout the eastern woodlands, but Indian traditions recorded after European contact seem to bolster the idea that the practice of extensive agriculture was imported from outside the region rather than developed from within it.

Major sites at Cahokia (Illinois) and Moundville (Alabama) appear to be at the core of the classic Mississippian cultural area, which extended through the lower Ohio River valley including western and central Kentucky, western Tennessee, and northern Alabama and Mississippi. This culture was characterized by large, man-made effigy and platform mounds, the latter of which probably served as bases for temples or council houses. None of the tribes existing in the historic period retained such a tradition.

The city at Moundville was second only to Cahokia in size. In fact, Cahokia was the largest city in the geographic footprint of the contiguous states before they became the United States. Greater in area and population than many major cities in Europe, Cahokia was a walled city surrounded by a timber stockade 1 foot thick and 20 feet high covered in places by a coating of mud-based stucco or plaster. The extensive stockade suggests that all was not peace and harmony in pre-contact America. Nonetheless, it is generally accepted, based on the evidence of artifacts, that the society of the mound builders was based on agricultural fertility rather than on widespread warfare—the latter being more common among historic peoples.

The largest earthwork generally credited to the Mississippians is Monks Mound at Cahokia, which is thought to have been a chiefdom center controlling a small specific area (possibly 50 square miles) of the nearby river floodplain rather than the vast regions of political or military dominion that were characteristic of the Aztecs or the Incas. Monks Mound was 10 stories high and covered 14 acres. It was the largest pre-contact earth work attempted in the western hemisphere. It is believed that the house of the "chief" atop Monks Mound covered more than 5,000 square feet.

Twentieth-century excavation has found evidence of the use of Monks Mound by historic Indians that included burials during the historic period. However, these were clearly intrusions. Moreover, materials have been recovered suggesting that the site may have been used as a French colonial mission between 1735 and 1752. Indian remains, house remains, and evidence of a small French chapel have been found on the first terrace of the mound. There are also indications that a group of Trappist Monks, who owned the area and provided the inspiration for its name, built a monastery on a nearby mound and farmed the terraces of the larger mound in the first decade of the 19th century.

One of the most remarkable archeological finds at Cahokia was evidence of postholes set in a number of discrete arcs of circles in an entrenchment. There may have been as many as five discrete, if incomplete, circles (suggesting circles of 24, 36, 48, 60, and 72 posts, respectively aligned with a center post). The circle had great ritual meaning among most North American Indians, and Theodor De Bray has left an often referenced engraving of an Algonquian village from 1590 with a small ceremonial circle of carved wooden totems used as a ceremonial area. Yet, the much larger Mississippian circles are theorized to have also served as a sort of celestial calendar, or woodhenge.

Evidence, including radioactive dating, suggests that these circles were built and revised over a period of 200 years (A.D. 900–1100), but no reason has been proposed for their ever-increasing radius other than that the area inside the perimeter may have served as a ceremonial or festival site for an increasing population. Fragments of wood taken from the excavations show that only red cedar posts were used during these constructions. It has been proposed that the red cedar, 15 to 20 inches in diameter and about 15 feet high, may have been considered a sacred wood. The posts may also have been painted with red ocher. Although there is evidence of dozens of posts, only three, besides the center one, are considered to mark out crucial astronomical positions. These indicate the winter solstice, the summer solstice, and the autumnal and vernal equinoxes. The post that aligns with the equinoxes also aligns with the front of Monks Mound, but the significance of this may be purely conjectural as other features in the city also make such an alignment.

The development of an archaic culture from independent roots is less of a problem for historians than explaining its sudden collapse. The disappearance of the mound building people, or their absorption by other tribes, has been variously credited to a continued series of crop failures or other natural disasters that weakened the stability of the chiefdom. Yet, this could not have destroyed all the people. So where did the survivors go?

The existence of a series of distinctive motifs done in shell, ceramics, and stone among extent artifacts, along with elaborate objects of hammered natural copper, which are similar to the work of a dozen local cultures from the historic period, adds strength to the theory that the mound builders were absorbed by other tribes. Furthermore, burial sites found in Mohawk territory containing items with distinctive mound builder characteristics show that there was a considerable Adena-like occupation of New York around A.D. 400. Nonetheless, the Indians who first came into contact with Europeans in the region claimed no knowledge of the identity of the mound builders and claimed no relationship to them.

Some historians look to the effects of diseases introduced by Europeans as a cause of the collapse of Indian culture in the Ohio Valley. It is quite likely that in a population lacking immunity, illnesses would spread faster through the Amerindian populations than did the explorers themselves, reaching the Midwest and South almost as fast as word of the white intrusion on the Atlantic coastline. This may help to explain why some regions of America were virtually devoid of native populations when first visited by whites. Yet, it is almost too convenient to blame European contact for any unexplained downturn in Indian fortunes, and conflicting hard evidence clouds the actual history of the period and its people.

This is particularly true as more sophisticated analytical methods are brought to bear. The archeological record reveals a sharp decline in mound building around A.D. 500, well before the beginning of Euro-Indian contact and coinciding with an apparent disruption of long-distance trade in exotic materials and artifacts among various tribes. Moreover, the Late Mississippian period (beginning about A.D. 1500) seems to have remained quite dynamic. Bow and arrow technologies seemingly improved, hunting efficiency increased, and maize, beans, and squash were introduced to supplement native seeds, nuts, and roots as sources of food. These factors tend to give a view of the Mississippian culture as one in expansion, not one in collapse. Once again, the Indians first contacted by Europeans seem to have been as much in the dark as they with regard to the identity of these people.

The Mississippians seemingly practiced head-flattening, a custom shared with a number of southeastern tribes from the historic period. In this process, an infant was bound to a cradle board with a bag of sand pressing its forehead into a permanent backward slant. Partly for this reason ethnologists believed that the Creek people of the Southeast (who continued the practice) were descendants of the mound builders. Archaeologists classify the pre-contact Creek culture as late Mississippian (A.D. 1500–1700), but Creek intrusion into the region may have come as early as the Middle Mississippian period some 300 years earlier. Tribal legend has it that the Creek came to the Southeast by way of the Red River, but their actual origin is obscure.

If the Creek were invaders, as their traditions suggest, they either destroyed, dispersed, or incorporated the Mississippians into their own number without leaving a tradition of victory behind them. None of these explanations for the disappearance of the mound builders is undisputed, but the last remains a "distinct possibility" because Indian tribes tended to increase their numbers by incorporating the survivors of the peoples that they conquered. Anthropologists usually classify the Creek as Muskhogean-speaking, but it has been suggested more recently that they may be more closely related by genetics to the northern Algonquian. Such evidence tends to make the question of what happened to the mound builders even more complex.[27]

Notes

1. Robert Leckie, *A Few Acres of Snow: The Saga of the French and Indian Wars* (New York: John Wiley & Sons, Inc., 1999), 33.

2. Peter Martyr as quoted in David J. Weber, *The Spanish Frontier in North America* (New Haven: Yale University Press, 1992), 38. See also p. 56.

3. Francis Parkman, *LaSalle and the Discovery of the Great West* (New York: The Modern Library, 1999), 84.

4. Robert E. Ritzenthaler and Pat Ritzenthaler, *The Woodland Indians of the Western Great Lakes* (Garden City, NY: The Natural History Press, 1970), 7.

5. See William Brandon, *Indians* (Boston: Houghton Mifflin Company, 1987), 155–156.

6. Evan T. Pritchard, *No Word For Time, The Way of the Algonquian People* (Tulsa, OK: Council Oaks Books, 1997), 240.

7. Dena F. Dincauze, "A Capsule Prehistory of Southern New England," in *The Pequots in Southern New England, The Rise and Fall of an American Indian Nation,* ed. Laurence M. Hauptman and James D. Wherry (Norman: University Press of Oklahoma, 1990), 30–31.

8. Roderick Nash, *Wilderness and the American Mind* (New Haven: Yale University Press, 1971), 1.

9. Louis B. Wright, *The Atlantic Frontier, Colonial American Civilization, 1607–1763* (New York: Alfred A. Knopf, 1951), 124.

10. Nash, 16.

11. Paul A. W. Wallace, *Conrad Weiser, Friend of Colonist and Mohawk: 1696–1760* (Lewisburg, PA: Wennawoods Publishing, 1996), 80–82. See also Louis M. Waddell and Bruce D. Bromberger, *The French and Indian War in Pennsylvania, 1753–1763: Fortification and Struggle During the War for Empire* (Harrisburg, PA: Pennsylvania Historical and Museum Commission, 1996), 46.

12. Karen Ordahl Kupperman, *Indians and English, Facing Off in Early America* (Ithaca: Cornell University Press, 2000), 78.

13. Kupperman, 76.

14. Nash, 6.

15. Frederick Jackson Turner, *The Significance of the Frontier in American History* (New York: Henry Holt & Co., 1920), 2.

16. John Keegan, *Fields of Battle, the Wars for North America* (New York: Alfred A. Knopf, 1996), 92.

17. Philip J. Webster and Christopher Cerino, "Exploring the Chesapeake Bay with Captain John Smith: 1608 and 2007," *Sea History,* no. 118 (Spring 2007): 25.

18. Keegan, 89–90, 76.

19. Keegan, 96–97.

20. Quoted in Stanley Vestal, *King of the Fur Traders, The Deeds and Deviltry of Pierre Esprit Radisson* (Boston: Houghton Mifflin Company, 1940), 146.

21. Keegan, 93. This same route was used by both American rebels and British troops during the American Revolution.

22. Peter O. Wacker, *The Musconetcong Valley of New Jersey: A Historical Geography* (New Brunswick, NJ: Rutgers University Press, 1968), 30–37.

23. Winfield Ross, "Coming to America," *Early American Life* (April 2007): 53.

24. Edward Armstrong, ed., *Good Order Established in Pennsylvania and New Jersey in America by Thomas Budd* (New York: Williams Gowans, 1865), 44.

25. Peter O. Wacker, 27.

26. Wallace, 25–26, 35, 78.

27. David H. Corkran, *The Creek Frontier, 1540–1783* (Norman: University of Oklahoma Press, 1967), 4.

2

The Structure of Woodland Society

Beside the lakes and rivers, in the occasional park lands and in the long reaches of unbroken forest of the Northeast, a people lived, multitongued, of great diversities and many samenesses [similarities], who at the Europeans' arrival still traveled the worn paths of all [the] accumulated ages.

—William Brandon, historian[1]

The Organization of Native Society

No single set of material characteristics has been found to unite the diverse nations that made up the Native American residents of the Northeast woodlands. As these Native Americans left no written records of their own prior to the 19th century, much of what is known about them was reported by missionaries, explorers, government officials, soldiers, and fur traders, none of whom can be considered unbiased and objective sources of information. It was not unusual for whites to form strongly held opinions of Indian life "that were somewhat wide of the truth."[2] In fact, the archaic native world, as the Indians knew it, had in many respects disappeared before any white man saw or recorded it because of the transmission of European ideas and goods inland from the Atlantic coast. The historical reality of pre-contact native societies is largely unknowable, and its study, therefore, remains inexorably linked with the anecdotal histories recorded by the European intruders who first saw the Indians. It is important, therefore, for students of Native American family life during the early contact period to recognize the conjectural nature of much of what is, or has been, written about native peoples. It is equally fruitless to involve oneself in endless arguments concerning the proper or improper use of terms such as *tribe, band,* or *nation* as if the Indians of a former time might suffer insult through their improper use. The Indians used none of these, and in their own language they usually referred to persons of their own kinship group as "the people" or "the real People" as did the Lene Lenape of the Delaware Nation. These terms are simply white attempts to bring order and structure to their study of Native American life.[3]

In addition, modern archeological researchers recognize three ancient and mysterious native *civilizations* or *cultures* in the Midwestern heartland: the Adena, the Hopewell, and the Mississippian (Early, Middle, and Late). Yet, all three were gone by the time of European contact, and their disappearance remains one of the mysteries on which researchers have focused in recent decades. Evidence suggests that the region left vacant by these older cultures was inhabited at one time or another in the historic period by the tribal remnants fleeing the Iroquois during the dispersal, but these were fleeting intrusions into the region rather than any long-term migrations.

Confederacies

The geographical center of the Northeast woodlands was inhabited at the time of white contact by the Iroquois Confederacy to the east and the Hurons and their related cantons to the west. All of these were Iroquoian-speaking peoples who lived in centralized villages and stockaded towns (sometimes called "castles" in Dutch and English documents). The several confederated tribes of Iroquois that inhabited present-day central New York were possibly the most influential natives in the history of the region (see Map 2).

Generally known as "the Iroquois," the Iroquois Confederacy included the Seneca, Cayuga, Onondaga, Oneida, Mohawk, and later the Tuscarora. These tribes were formed into the strongest of the political and military confederacies in the region, known either as the Five Nations, or Six Nations (after 1722). Through the alliances that it made, or refused to make, the Iroquois Confederacy unintentionally determined which European nation would rule the region.

The Iroquois Confederacy also changed the face of native America in the 17th century through their use of trade agreements, diplomacy, and unrelenting warfare against both Iroquoian and Algonquian rivals. The intertribal conflicts of the mid-17th century, known as the Great Dispersal, were total wars prosecuted with means that often bordered on genocide primarily by the Mohawk and Seneca. The result of this series of conflicts radically shifted the pre-contact mix of indigenous peoples in the region and in many cases restructured it beyond our ability to know what it had been.

Recent historians and modern Native Americans recognize several loosely confederated groupings of Indians that existed in the Northeast region in the 17th century other than the Iroquois. These were based on the political or defensive alliances they formed during the nascent contact period or during the Great Dispersal (1649–1653). They included the Wabanaki (or Northeastern) Confederacy, the New England Confederacies (separated by three dialects: Pequot, Wampanoag, and Narragansett), the Delaware Confederacy, the Illinois Confederacy, the Ojibwa (or Three Fires) Confederacy, and a loose confederacy of Iroquoian-speakers generally formed around the Huron survivors of the dispersal. In the late decades of the 17th century, a strong alliance of confederated tribes from the Great Lakes region was formed at the instigation and with the continued support of the French. This Algonquian alliance was essentially anti-English and anti-Iroquois, and more will be said of its organization later.

Bands

Unlike the Iroquois, who seem to have formed a strong sense of central governance and tribal integrity, the Algonquian peoples were most often divided into many small *bands* or *villages* throughout the region. Bands were small groups with limited lines of shared descent that lived and traveled together. They were often patrilineal, and they rarely came together with other bands for group activities. Documents from the period refer to both villages and bands promiscuously, and the true nature of any tribal organization among the Algonquians in the early contact period remains uncertain. Such small bands existed among the Chippewa and the Cree sub-groups of the Ojibwa of the western Lakes region that they exhibited little in the way of overall leadership or tribal organization. Their cousins, the Ottawa, seem to have had more settled villages and a better organization than other Ojibwa peoples. Yet, the actual level of isolation among the Algonquian groups is almost impossible to determine because they generally lacked a political structure with coercive and long-lasting institutions similar to the Central Council of the Iroquois at Onondaga. Rather, they lived in a society in which obedience to central authority was neither a societal expectation nor a cultural virtue. Nonetheless, if a particular native community was under a definite political leadership, the term *band* seems more appropriate in sociological parlance than either *tribe* or *village*. This observation has "stirred some controversy" among anthropologists, but "it has a certain general validity."[4]

Tribe

The Europeans who made early contact with the native population noted unique differences among the *tribes*—a term commonly used by anthropologists with regard to Indian societies. The *tribe* may be defined as the constellation of small communities, or bands, composed of major groupings of kinspersons who came together with some regularity for the social or religious purposes of the group. Descent groups within these communities—what most people would call *family trees, kinship groups,* or *clans*—often comprised the nucleus of a tribe. They provided a framework for social organization and bound persons together into a self-conscious body that was self-sufficient, self-sustaining, and politically independent. Tribes could be groupings with a strict class structure and hierarchy like a *chiefdom,* or they could be less stratified and conglomerate—exhibiting an absence of clearly defined social strata with separate and distinct, but unequal levels. The Delaware of the Northeast woodlands region were generally organized into chiefdoms based on consensus and compromise rather than authority or mandate.

Such classless societies tend to stress the gender roles, status positions, and rank of their individual members rather than the continuation of a royal house or the permanent subservience of the populace. In a tribal society, there were usually few high ranking or high status positions, and the vast majority of the tribe were simply ordinary members who found their place within the kinship group through everyday living. The latter were often ranked by their abilities or their reputations, but in no case were they considered lower class or inferior persons.[5]

A Mutual Infancy of Language

Some of the Native peoples were alike in virtually every visible material characteristic save language, and it has been estimated that in North America alone there were from 500 to 1,000 mutually unintelligible languages and dialects. The widest diversity of these were among the nations of the West. Midway through the 16th century, Europeans had no inkling of the vast diversity that would greet them 100 years hence, and the majority of New World nations had received no word of the collision of cultures that had taken place.[6]

Among other particulars concerning Native Americans, early European writers attempted to precisely represent Indian speech patterns and language both because of their anthropological interest in the topic and because of the purely practical aspects of improving cross-cultural communications and trade. Yet, the nature of Native American speech made the recording of it difficult. Most Indian dialects were polysynthetic; that is, many stem words were fused together into one until the thought was transmitted. Sometimes words of 10 to 15 syllables were needed to determine a single thought. This may be illustrated by the Algonquian word *takusar-iartor-uma-galvar-nerpa* (Do you think he really intends to go to look for it?) The phrase is made of several elements: *takusar* (he looks after it), *iartor* (he goes to), *uma* (he intends to), *galvar* (he does so, but), and *nerpa* (do you think?) Such a language, composed of up to 2,000 stem words such as these, has a fathomless number of derivatives.[7]

The 17th-century distribution of Algonquian dialects is uncertain because most of them were scantily or poorly recorded. The language reached out to the Blackfoot, Cheyenne, and Arapaho nations of the Great Plains, and had two widespread geographical vernaculars in the Northeast woodlands. In the central portions of the woodlands, the following dialect groupings can be made: Cree-Montagnais-Naskapi, Fox-Sauk-Kickapoo, Peoria-Miami, and Ojibwa-Ottawa-Algonkian-Salteaux. The following tribes spoke discrete dialects: Shawnee, Potawatomi, Delaware, Menomini, and Powhatan. In the eastern woodlands of New England were found Natick-Narragansett, Mohegan-Pequot, Penobscot-Abenaki, and Passamaquoddy-Malcite. The Micmac had a distinct dialect of their own. Iroquoian was much less diverse with only minor changes in dialects being spoken by the Tuscarora and the Cherokee. These language relationships should be kept in mend when considering the direction of historical events as they unfold.[8]

As early as the 16th century, Thomas Harriot was able to learn the basics of Algonquian speech from two Indians taken to England by the expedition of Sir Walter Raleigh in 1584. The two Indians, identified as Manteo and Wanchese, also learned English from Harriot and returned to Virginia with him in 1585. How fluent the participants became in a single year is an open question. Nonetheless, settlers arriving on the coast of Massachusetts in the 1620s were surprised to find natives who spoke or understood both English and Spanish. Squanto (Tasquanto), a Pawtuxet (aka, Patuxet, Pawtucket) Indian famed for his early contact with the pilgrims of the Plymouth Plantation, was an accomplished English-speaker due to several years spent in England. Moreover, many coastal New England tribes had made contact with European fishermen attracted to the Grand Banks, and some Indians were found who could speak words and phrases in English, French, Spanish, Portuguese, or Basque.

French-speaking Franciscan Recollet friars accompanied Champlain on his earliest explorations, but with a scarcity of secular priests, the French were compelled to rely for their religious ministries on their missionary orders, particularly the Jesuits. All Jesuit priests were supposedly literate having studied their own language as well as Latin and Greek as part of their theological preparation. Many of them were learned men who attempted a practical knowledge of Native American dialects in order to make converts and service their flocks.

Jesuit Father Pierre Biard, writing from Port Royal (Acadia/Nova Scotia) in 1612, bemoaned his own lack of understanding of the native tongue, but seemingly blamed the Indians for his inability to learn it. Herein, he bares his own prejudices and the many faulty preconceptions he held about the Indian. "As the Savages have no definite religion, magistracy or government, liberal or mechanical arts, commercial or civil life, they have consequently no words to describe things they have never seen or even

conceived. Furthermore, rude and untutored as they are, all their conceptions are limited to sensible and material things; there is nothing abstract,
internal, spiritual, or distinct. *Good, strong, red, black, large, hard,* they will
repeat to you in their jargon; *goodness, strength, redness, blackness*—they do
not know what they are. And as to virtues you may enumerate to them,
wisdom, fidelity, justice, mercy, gratitude, piety, and others, these are not
found among them at all except as expressed in the words *happy, tender,
love,* [or] *good heart.* Likewise they will name to you a wolf, a fox, a squirrel, a moose, and so on to every kind of animal they have, all of which are
wild, except the dog; but as to words expressing universal and generic
ideas, such as *beast, animal, body, substance,* and the like, these are altogether too learned for them. Add to this, if you please, the great difficulty
of obtaining from them even the words that they have...We are compelled
to make a thousand gesticulations and signs to express to them our ideas,
and thus to draw from them the names of some of the things which we can
not point out...The first things the poor Savages learn are oaths and vile
and insulting words; you will often hear the women Savages, who otherwise are very timid and modest, hurl vulgar, vile, and shameless epithets
at our people, in the French language, not that they know the meaning of
them."[9]

Meanwhile, unbeknownst to these white observers, it seems that the
Indians, rather than being "untutored" or "in a perpetual infancy as to
language or reason," had taken the practical expedient of simplifying
their language for their European contacts.[10] Modern linguistic analysis
of surviving documents, grammars, and dictionaries from the early contact period show that the natives were deliberately fashioning a *pidgin
dialect,* or over-simplified language, that allowed for communications and
facilitated trade. It seems certain that in this regard, the Indians were treating the Europeans as children, or simpletons, incapable of mastering the
many nuances and subtle qualities of their native tongue.

Jesuit Father Jean de Brebeuf, an accomplished linguist himself,
noted in 1636 that the Huron tongue (an Iroquoian language) had as
many tenses and as many numbers as ancient Greek, with which ancient language he drew a favorable comparison of Iroquoian speech. The
Mohawk language was described as a work of art, reasoned and accurate in its structure. Rather than being childish and concrete as Biard
thought, Indian language was capable of expressing the most refined ab-
stractions concerning spirituality, loyalty, honor, and other feelings. De
Brebeuf considered it possible that a complete Iroquois grammar might
be as extensive as one for Latin or Sanskrit. Some Europeans realized
that they were being offered something less than a full knowledge of the
language spoken among the natives themselves, and others assumed that
the natives wished to keep the Europeans largely in the dark so that they
could speak freely in front of them without their understanding what
was said.

Many early observers tried to write down the Indian languages phonetically using the contemporary English, French, Dutch, or Spanish manuscript renderings for vowels, consonants, and combinations thereof that they thought they heard. This led to a multitude of wildly different spellings and pronunciations for the same words. One of the fundamental obstacles to making a usable written record of a native language was that the pronunciations of many European languages themselves were not yet standardized, and many colonials and explorers spoke with regional dialects that were themselves subtle and complex and lacked simple discrimination or reproduction in written form.

Many contemporary linguists accepted the false concept that no race that had not as yet attained a sophisticated civilization could create one at such a late date in human development as the 16th century. Only the Aryan, Semitic, and Chinese races were thought to have reached this state of development, and all languages discovered thereafter were attributed to being adaptations, adoptions, or syntheses of one or more of these three. It was widely and incorrectly reported that Native American languages were related to Welsh, Gaelic, Hebrew, or other remote dialects. Shortly after the establishment of Jamestown (1607), Captain Peter Wynne, a native of Wales, was engaged to interpret the Indian speech of regional tribes incorrectly thought to be related to Welsh. He quickly found that he understood none of what the Indians spoke. Yet, it was not until the 19th century that the unique origins and individual excellence of the Iroquoian, Algonquian, and other native foundational languages were recognized as being separate from Semitic, Chinese, and other tongues.

While several Indian grammars were contemplated at the time, no complete textbook of the Huron-Iroquois language was forthcoming for 200 years. An Iroquois (Onondaga) dictionary and a grammar of the Huron tongue, vaguely attributed to Jesuit missionaries of the 17th century, may have been available among their contemporaries, but they were not published until the 19th century. On the other hand, Jesuit Father Sabastien Rasles (sometimes spelled Rale') spent more of his life among the Algonquian-speaking Abenaki nation than he did in European society. He learned their language, and in the early 18th century he completed an Abenaki dictionary with entries in French and English that is preserved at Harvard University.

Sign Language

The Reverend Jonas Michaelus, a prolific Dutch journalist from New York, understood that Europeans were generally being given only enough knowledge of native language to supplement the many gestures (known as *sign language*) used in trading and negotiations. He noted (1628) that the Algonquian-speaking tribes on the Hudson did as much trading by signs made with the thumb and fingers as by speaking. The use of sign language remained in evidence among the Sauk, Fox, Potawatomi, and other Great Lakes tribes into the 1800s. The general continuance of signs and gestures in the place of speech declined thereafter because of a growing acquaintance with European languages among the Indian nations. As a mode of communication, sign language may have been a simple expedient to which Indians turned when whites lacked a comprehensive knowledge of a spoken native tongue. Nonetheless, Jean-Bernard Bossu, a French observer traveling in the Louisiana territory in the middle of the 18th century, remained for two years with an Indian party that also resorted to gestures (pantomimes) to communicate with other tribes whenever language posed a problem.

A number of 19th-century scholars assumed that a universally accepted set of gestures tied the native peoples of all the regions of America together in an unspoken common language of signs that allowed Indians of different tribes to communicate in situations where speech was impractical or inconvenient. Eminent anthropologists of the 19th century proclaimed signing a common medium of conversation from Hudson's Bay to the Gulf of Mexico, and it was certainly a common medium among the tribes of the Great Plains at that time. Although there is some question of just how prevalent signing was among the Native Americans of the Northeast woodlands, a number of accounts of its use between Indians and whites were recorded in the 17th and 18th centuries. A number of early-contact observers began or published guides to Indian signing and other nonverbal forms of communication that they related to similar gestures in common use among public speakers in Europe.[11]

Linguistic Stocks

Although Jean de Brebeuf's comparison of native languages to Greek remained strikingly attractive to many 19th-century linguists, in the 1830s, ethnologists, believing that they had a better understanding of native speech patterns, settled on a commonality of language as a gauge to determine lineal relationships among the tribes of North America. There were several linguistic stocks of native peoples identified at this time: Iroquoian, Algonquian, Muskhogean, Timucan, Siouan, and Caddoan among them. Nonetheless, tribes related by language could be found on either side of any hypothetical geographic or regional divide between political or tribal entities.[12]

Such simplifications seemingly satisfied 19th-century anthropologists, historians, and a general public following in the newspapers the forcible removal of the Plains Indians or the Apache from "public lands." Some of these traditional language classifications have changed or remain in dispute today. Historians have very little information as to how many of the five different language groups were spoken among the native peoples of the Southeast woodlands, for instance; but their distribution, as with those of the Northeast, exhibited no simple geographical or socio-political pattern. Suffice it to say that the tribes of the Southeast well-resembled their neighbors to the north in their nonconformity. Other language groups have been hyphenated, as in Hokan-Siouan, which includes Muskhogean and Iroquoian as sub-dialects, or as in Algonquian-Wakashan, one of the most widespread linguistic stocks comprised of more than 50 distinct tribal languages.

Algonquian was spoken by major tribes such as the Delaware, Shawnee, Abenaki, Mahican, Ojibwa, and many other nations; Muskhogean was the foundation language of the Creek, Choctaw, Chickasaw, Timuca, Natchez, and Seminole nations, who occupied most of the southeastern region of the present United States. The Siouan language was most commonly associated with the Osage, Dakota, and Crow on the western plains, but it was also the linguistic stock of many eastern tribes such as the Tutelo, Catawba, and Yuchi in far away Georgia and Alabama. The Cherokee and Tuscarora of Tennessee, northern Georgia, and the Carolinas spoke an Iroquoian tongue that marked them as recent invaders like their brethren in central New York. Finally, Caddo was spoken by the peoples of Arkansas, Louisiana, and parts of east Texas in sharp contrast to the variations of an Aztec-Tanoan language spoken by the Zuni, Hopi, Apache, and Comanche of the Southwest.

Recent studies have suggested that there may have been up to 500 distinct native languages (not dialects) used north of present-day Mexico. A single band or village might limit their everyday speech to a small number of dialects in common use among local tribes speaking the same root language. Due to the patterns of intermarriage, trade, and politics, however, it seems reasonable that many native communities were multilingual as often as they were language-specific.

The Two-language Concept

One of the long-standing paradigms dominating the study of the Northeast woodlands was that there were only two great linguistic stocks of native peoples who were in constant conflict over control of the region: the Algonquian and the Iroquoian. Henry Rowe Schoolcraft, in 1839, noted of these two groups, "Regard [them] in whatever light we may, it is impossible to overlook the strong points of character in which they differed. Both were dexterous and cunning woodsmen, excelling in all the forest arts necessary to their condition, and having much in their manners and appearance in common. But they spoke a radically different language, and they differed scarcely less in their distinctive character and policy. The one was mild and conciliating, the other fierce and domineering... The Iroquois... interposed themselves between New England and the Algonquin sub-types, and thus cut off their communications with each other. This separation was complete."[13]

The popularity of 19th-century authors, such as James Fenimore Cooper and Francis Parkman, who relied on estimates like Schoolcraft's in their work, helped to cement as facts many questionable ideas and stereotypes concerning native peoples. The two-language concept fostered by Schoolcraft, Cooper, Parkman, and others was made part of the fabric of Amerindian ethnology by John Wesley Powell, in 1891, when he introduced to the world of native research the term *Algonquian* (Algonkian), meaning *first people.* This term became a linguistic catch-all for all the related tribes of the Northeast who were thereafter distinguished by their tongue rather than their material culture or political organization.

Contemporary observers over-simplified the complexity of native America and advanced the concept that the Iroquoian-speaking nations had pressed back the Algonquians to the north and northeast from the Ohio River valley (or the southeast) some time before the period of European contact, but certainly not too far removed from the end of the 15th century. The resulting fragmented pattern of Indian villages exposed each to dissension with their warlike neighbors and left pockets of conflicting ethnicities throughout the region. The whites used these geographical and linguistic boundaries to undermine Indian solidarity by setting one group against the other. Colonials of the 18th century quickly found, however, that simply because certain tribes spoke similar language it did not mean that they were allied in a political or economic sense.[14]

There is general agreement among anthropologists that the eastern Algonquians first discovered by whites were probably not the first inhabitants of the Atlantic coastal region, and that the Algonquian language spoken in the eastern and central portions of the Northeast woodlands probably originated among the peoples of the western Great Lakes. Many ceremonies, rituals, and myths seem to have migrated in the same west-to-east direction. This suggests a movement of Algonquian-speaking Indians from the Northwest to the Atlantic coast, but it is equally clear that there was no grand exodus of tribes to the east as with the Iroquoians because there is no similar tradition among the Algonquians. Rather, the Algonquian migration seems to have consisted of several cells or small groups of people coming into the area in succession over a long period of time and settling in the quiet niches of archaic America. Archeological evidence suggests that the Algonquians of the Carolinas may have arrived beginning as early as the 1st or 2nd century A.D., while those residing in Delaware, Maryland, and Pennsylvania came some 600 to 700 years later.

Iroquoians

Archeological evidence indicates that the several nations resident in central New York at the time of European contact, known collectively as the Iroquois, were once a single people possibly subject to the Algonquian-speaking Adirondacks of the St. Lawrence Valley. The

Adirondacks were an archaic people long gone by the time of European contact. They may have introduced the Iroquoians to the dynamics of an extensive agricultural technology in place of the simple gardening they may have relied on earlier. An alternative hypothesis, supported by Iroquois tradition, claims that the larger mass of Iroquoian-speaking peoples (including the cantons of Huron, Petun, Erie, and Neutrals) migrated from the geographical center of the region east of the Mississippi River valley as invaders of the Northeast woodlands, pushing aside the more numerous but less fierce Adirondacks and leaving their cousins, the Susquehannock, Cherokee, and Tuscarora, to split off and push down the coastal plains of Maryland, Virginia, and the Carolinas. The Huron and their associated cantons, thereafter, moved into the inter-lake region of present-day Ontario, while the Five Nations settled in the Finger Lake region of central New York. It has been noted that "the Five Nations Iroquois were traditionally hostile toward most of these surrounding Iroquoian peoples." Of course, they were also hostile to the surrounding Algonquian peoples and the members of their own league before its founding. Tribal legends lend support to the existence of warring factions among the Iroquois in the late prehistoric period.[15]

It has been suggested that the Iroquoian-speakers were "the most divergent" of all the language groups residing in the Northeast woodlands. Not only was their linguistic foundation different from that of the other resident nations of the region, but they practiced a more extensive form of agricultural, followed a different method of determining familial lineage (essentially matrilineal vs. patrilineal), and practiced a number of unique ceremonies, including ritual cannibalism. The name *Iroquois* is a French form of the Algonquian word for *rattlesnake,* suggesting that there was no love lost between the two language groups.[16]

The Iroquoian League

The foundation of the Iroquois-speaking social, political, and religious culture was the formation of a grand Iroquoian League sometime in the 2nd millennium A.D. This should not be confused with the Five Nations of the Iroquois Confederation. The traditions suggest that before the formation of the League, the Iroquoian-speaking peoples had fallen into a pattern of internecine wars, blood feuds, and revenge killings that threatened their way of life. The peace among them was saved by the appearance of Deganawida, a Huron holy man known as the "Peacemaker." Deganawida brought a message of brotherly peace that won the support of Hiawatha (Hayehwatha), described as an Onondaga by lineage who had somehow become a Mohawk chief through marriage. Deganawida brought consolation (ritual condolence) to Hiawatha, who was mourning the death of three of his daughters at the hands of an evil enemy. With considerable effort, the two men were able to convince the many Iroquoian-speaking cantons to form a league of mutual support, which held the peace for many generations.

There is no doubt that an Iroquois League was fully established sometime between A.D. 900 and 1570 and that it was composed of four major confederacies led by the Attiwandaronk (Neutrals), Susquehannocks, Hurons, and Iroquois, respectively, and supported by their sub-groups. Legend has it that Deganawida blotted out the sun as part of his program to convince recalcitrant cantons to join the league. A total solar eclipse visible in the region in 1451 may set the actual date of the formation of the Iroquois League to the later part of this range. Native tradition suggests that at the time of the league's creation most of the individual tribes were residing in those regions in which whites found them during the period of initial European contact.

European observers were told that the Iroquoian-speaking nations had pressed back the Algonquians to the north and northeast from the Ohio River valley some time before the period of European contact, but certainly not too far removed from the end of the 15th century. The Iroquoian-speaking Hurons apparently formed the northern wing of this migration, and their four cantons, or phratries (Bear, Cord, Rock, and Deer), passed north of Lake Erie and Lake Ontario ultimately settling in the Georgian Bay–Lake Simcoe area of the present-day Canadian province of Ontario. Meanwhile, the Attiwandaronk (Petuns, Eries, and so-called Neutral cantons) sandwiched themselves among the three easternmost of the Great Lakes (Lakes Erie, Ontario, and Huron). The five closely related cantons of Iroquois passed to the south of the lakes to occupy present-day central New York state. The Susquehannock, Cherokee, Tuscarora, and other minor tribes of Iroquoian lineage either found homes flanking the southeastern Atlantic seaboard by displacing the original inhabitants, or they had already been resident there for several generations.

The Susquehannock (sometimes called the Savannah by Anglo-colonial authorities) were late arrivals to the coastal plain probably moving there from central Pennsylvania after the initial contact period. It seems certain, however, that the Cherokee, who resided in the southernmost Appalachians, and the Tuscarora of the north central portions of the Carolinas had been separated from the Iroquois of New York for a very long time. Nonetheless, the Tuscarora maintained much better relations with their Iroquois cousins in New York than with any other Iroquoian-speaking tribe in the Southeast.

In the middle Atlantic and the Carolinas, Algonquian-speaking tribes inhabited the coasts and sounds at the time of contact; the Iroquoians occupied the coastal plain; and Siouan-speakers (Catawba, Tutelo, and others) remained on the Atlantic slope of the piedmont. Some scholars believe that these Siouan peoples originally came from the Ohio Valley or the Alleghenies and may have been the original inhabitants of that region. There is evidence of an extended dry period in this area at the end of the 1st millennium A.D. that may have served as a mechanism for this migration, but it seems certain that the Algonquian-speakers had been in possession of the coastline, the bays, and the sounds for at least 1,000 years before white contact. The Iroquoians seemingly formed wedges of invasion among the other tribes about A.D. 800 pushing the Algonquians onto marginal farming lands along the coast and forcing the northern-most Muskhogean-speakers south into Georgia and Alabama. The out-numbered Siouan peoples simply retreated into uninhabited pockets in the woodlands to hunt and fish.[17]

In the 1970s, certain archeologists uncovered a number of sites near St. Johnsville, New York belonging to an Indian culture called the Owasco. These people seemingly maintained a material culture that may have affected the New York Iroquois. The Owasco were almost certainly the first natives in the region to cultivate corn. Moreover they produced cord-marked pottery, triangular projectile points, clay elbow pipes, bone har-poon points, and other items similar to those found among the Iroquois at the time of contact. One of the most convincing pieces of evidence in this regard were posthole marks that showed that the Owasco lived in large oblong or rectangular houses similar in size and structure to the long-houses of the Iroquois. Nonetheless, anthropologists have recently regis-tered strong reservations concerning any cultural continuity other than a casual one between the Owasco and the Iroquois.

Before the Iroquoian invasion, the region between the Cumberland and Ohio Rivers had seemingly been an empty land for many genera-tions. Comprising parts of the present states of Tennessee, Kentucky, Ohio, Indiana, and Illinois, the tribal identities of the pre-contact occupants of

The longhouse, with various roof styles, was closely associated with the Iroquois, but it was also used by many groups in the Northeast. It was a permanent, multi-family residential structure that usually housed a single clan or kinship group. The number of longhouses and their placement in a village was often a measure of the kinship structure of the community.

this lush region have been in dispute among researchers and ethnologists for centuries. By the 18th century, the only native peoples living permanently in the southernmost portion of the area (Tennessee) were the Cherokee and the Siouan-speaking Yuchi, but there is no archeological or historical evidence that they used the area for anything other than hunting. The Shawnee and the Creek briefly occupied small parts of the region, but they did not establish a permanent presence. The minimal evidence of four different language groups occupying this key region of the Northeast woodlands has led researchers to propose each language group as its original residents at one time or another.

The Haudenosaunee

Five Iroquoian tribes of central New York—the Seneca (Great Hill People), Cayuga (People of the Landing), Onondaga (People of the Mountain), Oneida (People of the Stone), and Mohawk (People of the Flint)—formed a confederacy of their own that was a vast extension of kinship groups. These five confederated nations (later six with the addition of the Tuscarora in 1722) were known in the customary frame of reference as the Iroquois, but they called themselves *Haudenosaunee*. These Iroquois were so strongly entrenched in central New York and northern Pennsylvania that the entire region from Lake Champlain in the east to the Genesee River in the west was generally known as *Iroquoia*.

Most historic accounts regard the St. Lawrence River and Lake Champlain as the northern and eastern boundaries of Iroquoia, respectively, leaving most of the present-day provinces of Quebec and Ontario, the Canadian Maritimes, and all of New England in Algonquian possession. However, when Jacques Cartier visited the St. Lawrence Valley in 1535 and again in 1541, he found at least 11 well-established villages of Iroquoian-speaking natives there. The village of Hochelaga, which he visited, on the site of present-day Montreal was certainly Iroquoian with its longhouses and stockaded walls, but it has not been determined if it was of Huron or Mohawk origin. Both groups made claims to white observers that these had been their ancestors, and because the Huron and the Mohawk were cousins in the familial sense, they could both have been correct.

These same villages had all disappeared seven decades later when Samuel de Champlain explored the area, which was later replaced by roving bands of nomadic Algonquian-speaking hunters such as the Montagnais and the Nipissings. Champlain benefited from the peaceful access afforded him by finding a surprisingly vacant, but immensely rich, region when he established his small wooden stockade at Quebec on the former site of the village of Stadacona in 1608.

For lack of a better name, historians have called these missing natives the Laurentian Iroquois. While both Huron and Mohawk traditions claim the Laurentian as their own, neither has a legend that convincingly explains their disappearance. An aged Indian who claimed to have been a resident of the island of Montreal in the period before the French regime was reported to have told a Jesuit of a memory passed down from his father. "The Huron, who were then our enemies, drove our forefathers from this country. Some went toward the country of the Abenaki [southeast], others toward the country of the Iroquois [southwest], some to the Huron themselves [west], and joined them." This version of events would also help to explain the documented migration of the Algonquian-speaking Pequots and Mohegan into southern New England at this time and the almost simultaneous outbreak of skirmishes among the Mohawks, the Mahicans, and the Pocumtuc in western New England.[18]

An alternative tradition suggests that the Laurentian were actually an early alliance of Mohawks and Oneidas who drove the mysterious Algonquian-speaking Adirondack from the range of mountains named for them around 1570. Ultimately, the Algonquian-speaking tribes of eastern Canada and Vermont so harassed the Mohawks and Oneidas that they retreated to more peaceful residences near their cousins, the Onondaga, in central New York. Samuel de Champlain may have witnessed one of the subsequent battles between the Mohawk and the Algonquians at the lake that bares his name in 1609. With regard to the case of the missing Laurentian or of the nebulous Adirondack, oral traditions may be accurate as to the menu of separate verifiable events, but inaccurate as to their order, their cause, their relation to one another, or their ultimate resolution.

It is certain that in central New York the Iroquois practiced an extensive form of communal agriculture in the rich valleys that fed the Mohawk River. Another tradition suggests that the Onondaga, at least, had been residents of the region for many generations, and that the other tribes of the Five Nations joined them there because of the longer growing season and a more pleasant climate. There is presently no way of verifying this tradition. Yet, it seems certain that the Mohawk and Oneida, at least, came late to the region. Less is known of the pre-contact migratory history of the Seneca and Cayuga. The Five Nations controlled a vast portion of New York centered at the *Great Council Fire* on Lake Onondaga, but they did not occupy all of it. At first the Mohawk and Oneida united in the eastern part of the region, while the Seneca, Cayuga, and Onondaga combined in the western region among the Finger Lakes. Evidence supports the idea that the initial purpose of the Five Nation Confederacy was defensive. They took great pains to strengthen their villages with stockades and to bind the people together politically. They made Iroquoia a bastion against attack from without and a society generally free of division from within. As their strength and confidence grew, the member nations of the confederacy spread out to occupy the places where whites found them.

European observers of native life saved their choicest superlatives for the Iroquois, but they were also especially prone to note the warlike nature, hostile ferocity, and utter cruelty of the Mohawk as an enemy.

It should be noted, however, that the Mohawk were the most easterly and, therefore, the most closely observed of the Five Nations. Early records, especially among the Jesuits, referred to all Iroquois indiscriminately as Mohawk, and Anglo-colonial officials, especially William Johnson, were intimately familiar with them. The modern historical record indicates that the Seneca were probably as ferocious and capable in war as the Mohawk, if not notoriously so. The Cayuga and Oneida usually allied with one or the other of these two when the occasion pleased them. Among the members of the confederacy, only the Onondaga seem to have restrained themselves somewhat in favoring diplomacy over warfare, but even they sent out raiding parties and allied with their cousins in large campaigns. There is no question that fear of concerted Iroquois retaliation kept much of the region surrounding Iroquoia almost free of non-Iroquoian habitation.

In the 17th century, the Iroquoian-speaking Susquehannock of central Pennsylvania were seemingly more willing to ally themselves with French interests and their Algonquian-speaking neighbors than they were to form a subsidiary alliance with the Iroquois of New York. It seems certain that at a time not too far removed from European contact, the Seneca (possibly with Cayuga aide) drove the Susquehannock from central Pennsylvania down the Susquehanna River valley toward the head of Chesapeake Bay where they settled. Here the Susquehannocks traded with the Dutch and the Swedes throughout the 17th century and formed alliances with the Algonquian-speaking Delaware (Lene Lenapi), the Shawnee, and other refugees from Iroquois aggression in Maryland and Virginia. Seneca warriors, in particular, showed an amazing willingness to raid among the Susquehannock. The Conestoga, a small remnant of the Susquehannock, returned to their traditional residences in Pennsylvania in the 18th century to live under Iroquois domination as a "conquered" people.

To the northwest of Iroquoia, there was established a wide-ranging economic alliance of the Algonquian-speaking peoples with the Huron of the Lake Simcoe–Georgian Bay region. The Hurons seem to have outnumbered the New York Iroquois at this time and to have broken with them politically. Nonetheless, an uncomfortable status quo ensued between Huron and Iroquois until white Europeans, specifically the Dutch at Albany, upset the balance in the 1640s by arming the Mohawks. This set off a series of aggressive moves carried out principally by the Seneca and Mohawk known as the Great Dispersal. The Iroquois decimated their Huron, Erie, Petun, and Neutral relations during the winters of 1649–1650 and 1650–1651, and they scattered the remnants of their victims to the west and south. Many of these landless refugees became known to whites on the frontier as Mingo (a Delaware name suggesting *treachery*) or Wyandot (an Algonquian word for the Huron meaning *villagers*).[19]

The five Iroquois nations of New York were also noted for their chronic hostility toward several tribes that lived great distances from them. Among these were the Catawba of the Southeast and the Ojibwa and Illinois of the western Great Lakes. The Mohawk also never ceased attacking to the east in Abenaki territory, and the Seneca maintained an internecine feud with their Susquehannock relations in the Southeast until they were dispersed. The Seneca would also spend more than 30 days on the Warrior's Path through the Shenandoah Valley to raid into Cherokee territory in the Carolinas or Georgia. The Cherokees suffered greatly from these Seneca raids.

The members of the Five Nations modeled their confederacy for some time on the traditional dwelling known as a *longhouse*. The Mohawk were the keepers of the eastern door. The Seneca that of the western door. These two were the most numerous and warlike of the confederated tribes. The Onondaga were the mediators and keepers of the great central fire, while the less numerous Cayuga and Oneida were the younger brothers who lived among them. The Tuscarora, fearing increased aggression by white Carolinians in the 18th century, removed to Iroquoia to ally themselves in a subsidiary role with the Five Nations (who became the Six Nation Confederacy about 1722). The Tuscarora seemingly formed a strong association with the Oneida with whom they allied in 1776 to support the patriots during the American Revolution. This split the confederacy into pro-British and pro-Patriot factions. The blood shed between them during the Revolution destroyed Iroquois unity and peace for the first time in more than a century.

Algonquians

The Algonquin-speaking peoples were active and transient in the pre-contact period, roaming and hunting in the great wilderness forests of present-day Canada, the Great Lakes, New England, and the eastern seaboard of the Atlantic. In winter they hunted and foraged in small bands but came together annually for fishing, summer encampments, or religious ceremonies. Unfortunately, the Algonquian peoples of the Atlantic coastal region were largely destroyed or dispersed by war and disease in the late 16th or early 17th century. Almost nothing of their material culture has survived that had not been drastically changed by early European contact, and the surviving reports of their lifestyles made by ethnocentric and biased European observers remain highly suspect as to their accuracy in portraying Indian culture and social organization.

The Algonquian-speaking peoples can be grouped in a number of ways. With some obvious exceptions, most tribal societies consisted of just a few thousand persons. Geographically, it has been estimated that the major eastern Algonquian tribes in descending order of their population at the time of European contact included the Massachusetts (13,000), Delaware (8,000), Montauks (6,000), Narragansett (5,000), Abenaki (3,800), Micmac (3,500), Mahican (3,000), Wampanoag (3,000), Pequot (2,200), Pennecock (2,000), Montagnais (2,000), Naskapi (2,000), and Malecite (800).

The Abenaki of Maine were closely related in language to Algonquian peoples hundreds of miles to the west among the Great Lakes, and it has been pointed out that the name Abenaki stems from an Algonquian root meaning *easterner*. The Indians of the Canadian Maritimes, including Nova Scotia, Cape Breton, and Prince Edward Island, known to the French as the Souriquois and to most researchers today as the Micmacs, seem to have been set-off from the rest of the Algonquian-speaking tribes to the west so long before the period of contact as to lose a common dialect with the neighboring nations in the province of Quebec and in New Hampshire and Massachusetts. While the Micmacs could understand the language common to the mainland, the opposite was not true. The natives of the continent found the maritime dialect unintelligible without resorting to the language of signs.

The Naskapi were a sub-arctic tribe that had little contact with Europeans or other Native Americans except their neighbors the Montagnais. The little-known Beothuk of Newfoundland were even further removed from their Algonquian relations in dialect and culture. Whether this isolation was the result of invasion or simply geographic separation has not been determined.[20]

The lake region Algonquian tribes included two sub-groups commonly distinguished as Forest Tribes and Prairie Tribes. The Forest Tribes were the most numerous of all the Indian nations in the Northeast because of the size of the Ojibwa family: the Ojibwa/Chippewa (50,000), the Cree (20,000),

The Indians of the cold north country lived in small kinship groups or as nuclear families. Many of the sub-arctic tribes were so remote that they remained on the periphery of historic events during the 16th, 17th, and 18th centuries.

and the Ottawa (4000). Other tribes included in the Forest sub-group were the Potawatomi (4,000) and Menominee (3,000). Among the Prairie Tribes, the most numerous were the Miami (4,500). They were closely followed by the Peoria (4,000), Illinois (4,000), and Mascouten (4,000); the Winnebago (3,800); the Sauk (3,000) and Fox (3,000); the Kickapoo (2,000); and the Piankashaw (1,000). Some researchers include the Shawnee (3,000) in this sub-group although they make their first entrance into the historical record in the East (Maryland and Virginia) in the 1660s.[21]

These major subdivisions could be further divided into minor tribes, villages, and bands; but such a process is largely a meaningless academic exercise because of the many anomalies that are present in the data. The Winnebago, for instance, lived among their Algonquian-speaking neighbors, but they were actually Siouan-speaking migrants from a non-woodland upper Mississippi riverine culture. The Nipissing, actually eastern Ottawa numbering about 1,000, received their individual tribal name from their residence along the shores of Lake Nipissing and their close proximity to the French in Montreal who were well aware of them.

In New England, the Wampanoag were a defensive confederacy of more than 30 villages formed from many small bands gathered together politically for protection from the English. The Narragansett, likewise, were composed of eight separate villages. On Long Island (New York), besides the numerous Montauks, there were at least a dozen minor tribes that dealt regularly with the Dutch in New Amsterdam, including the Canarsee, the Shinnecock, the Wyandach, and the Massapequa (aka, Marsapeaque). In the Hudson Valley could be found the Hoboken, the Hackensack, the Nyack, and the Wappinger, among other Algonquian-speakers. Many modern place names still reflect the residence of these tribes from the 17th century.

Notes

1. William Brandon, *Indians* (Boston: Houghton Mifflin Company, 1987), 151.

2. George T. Hunt, *The Wars of the Iroquois, A Study in Intertribal Trade Relations* (Madison: University of Wisconsin Press, 1972), 5.

3. Archeology and historical ethnology suggest that both linguistic groups built their cultures on a pre-contact Mississippian or "temple mound" civilization of which the earliest Europeans to enter the interior may have seen the dying remnants.

4. Robert E. Ritzenthaler and Pat Ritzenthaler, *The Woodland Indians of the Western Great Lakes* (Garden City, NY: The Natural History Press, 1970), 47.

5. William A. Starna, "The Pequots in the Early Seventeenth Century," in *The Pequots in Southern New England, The Fall and Rise of an American Indian Nation*, ed. Laurence M. Hauptman and James D. Wherry (Norman: University of Oklahoma Press, 1990), 40–41.

6. Alvin M. Josephy, Jr., ed., *The American Heritage Book of Indians* (New York: American Heritage Publishing, 1961), 110.

7. Loomis Havermeyer, *Ethnography* (Boston: Ginn and Company, 1929), 265–266.

8. Harry Hoijer, "Indian Languages of North America," in *The North American Indians, A Sourcebook,* ed. Roger C. Owen (Toronto: Collier-Macmillan Limited, 1971), 79.

9. Harold F. McGee, Ed., *The Native People of Atlantic Canada, A History of Indian-European Relations* (Ottawa: Carleton University Press, 1983), 24.

10. McGee, 24.

11. See Karen Ordahl Kupperman, *Indians and English, Facing Off in Early America* (Ithaca: Cornell University Press, 2000), 83–84.

12. The most widely accepted classification of Native American languages for the continental United States was suggested by Edward Sapir in 1929. These included six groups of unrelated linguistic stocks.

13. Henry Rowe Schoolcraft, *Algic Researches, North American Indian Folktales and Legends* (Minneola, NY: Dover Publications, Inc., 1999; reprint of the 1839 edition), xix.

14. Ethnologists feel more secure in their knowledge of the Indians of the Desert Southwest or the Great Plains because of their long contact with them, but it is difficult to say whether or not their lifestyle in the 18th or 19th century closely resembled that of earlier centuries. Both groups underwent radical changes in their traditional lifestyles because of contact with Europeans. The development of a horse culture among the Plains peoples can be directly associated with the reintroduction of horses to the North American continent in the 16th century.

15. Brandon, 180–181.

16. Ritzenthaler and Ritzenthaler, 6.

17. Ritzenthaler and Ritzenthaler, 25.

18. Ian K. Steele, *Warpaths: Invasions of North America* (New York: Oxford University Press, 1994), 63; Francis Jennings, *The Ambiguous Iroquois Empire, The Covenant Chain Confederation of Indian Tribes with English Colonies from its Beginnings to the Lancaster Treaty of 1744* (New York: W.W. Norton and Company, 1984), 28–29, note 8.

19. Jennings, 321.

20. McGee, 103.

21. Ritzenthaler and Ritzenthaler, 4–5.

II

THE INDIAN FAMILY AS VILLAGERS

3

Native American Kinship Systems

The women caught hold of the captive's hair, combed it with her fingers, stroked his face, and sang to him, smiling and making signs of friendship. She tied a bracelet about his wrist...Old women were much respected and their opinions deferred to...He hoped she might save him from death when the time came.

—Pierre Esprit Radisson, 17th-century fur trader

Village Living

Much has been written concerning the lifestyle of the Iroquois because of their close alliance with the English in the final struggle for empire with the French. Less is known for certain of the Huron and their associated cantons (tribal groups) because of their great dispersal at the hands of the Iroquois in 1649.[1] The Algonquian nations were numerous and widespread and much that has been written concerning them is a compilation of various observations of distinct bands who just happened to speak the same language.

Although the Indians left few records of their daily life, they were visited by a large number of fur traders, priests, missionaries, and soldiers who took careful note of their day-to-day behavior. Moreover, there were a number of white captives and adoptees among the tribes who recorded the details of family life among the Indians of the Northeast woodlands. Among these were Harmen van der Bogaert, Peter Kalm, Jolicoeur Charles Bonin, Henry Timberlake, Pierre Pouchot, Pierre Esprit Radisson, William

Johnson, John Williams, Mary Jemison, Mary Rowlandson, Elizabeth Hicks, and many more.

Nonetheless, standard population demographics for the residents of the Northeast woodlands, such as family size, the number of pregnancies, infant mortality, life expectancy, and other statistics, completely elude the researcher. The estimates—really guesses—that can be made from surviving anecdotal accounts or colonial documents are so far-ranging as to be useless except in the broadest of comparisons. It might be safe to say that one tribe was larger than another, that Indian women were pregnant about as often as white women, or that native babies survived into their teens at about the same rate as white children; but such comparisons are of little use. Starvation, exposure, snakebite, farming and hunting accidents, lack of medical attention, bad water, and attack by enemies added to the list of common diseases that made continued life tenuous. Accidents and common childhood diseases claimed nearly half of all white children before the age of five, and it is safe to assume a similar standard for Indian children.

Kinship Groups

Woodland society and village living throughout the Northeast was based largely on kinship groups. Interpersonal relationships, marriage, politics, hunting, trade, and warfare relied almost exclusively on kinship ties. Kinship formed the bonds between bands and villages; set apart clans, phratries, and moieties (if there were any); and sometimes defined the tribe itself. Kinship obligations required certain patterns of behavior on the part of the individual toward others and toward the wider community, and vice-versa. Respect, deference, support, education, counsel, revenge, and loyalty all originated in kinship.

The discussion of Native American kinship systems requires the use of some unfamiliar terms that are quite specific. The *clan* was a kinship group that claimed descent from a common ancestor even if that ancestry could not be proven. If the supposed common ancestor was non-human, the term *totem* might be used, but this was rarely done as the word had other meanings as with small sacred objects. A *phratry* was a kinship group consisting of two clans claiming a common ancestor. There could be several phratries in a societal structure, and in some cases, one of the foundational pair may have extinguished itself leaving a single clan as a phratry. The term *moiety* (from a French word for *half*) was used to describe societies that were divided exactly into two and had only two descent groups. Sky–earth and peace–war moieties were not uncommon.

The Iroquois system of kinship, know as *bifurcated merging*, stands out as one of six basic types identified by Louis Henry Morgan in his foundational work titled *Systems of Consanguinity and Affinity of the Human Family* (1871). Four of these types were based on Morgan's studies of North American

Indians (Iroquois, Eskimo, Crow, and Omaha), essentially a woodland, a sub-arctic, and two plains tribes, respectively. None of the tribes of the Northeast woodlands, other than the Iroquois, fit into their own discrete kinship type, but many exhibited Crow or Omaha characteristics to greater or lesser extent.[2]

Among the Iroquois, descent was determined through only one parent *(unilineal)*, the mother. All other relatives, including the biological father, were considered "in-laws." It was common under this system to link the birth-father's brothers to the concept of fatherhood, and the birth-mother's sisters to the concept of motherhood. All the birth-brothers of one's father were referred to as father by his son, and likewise for one's mother and her birth-sisters, who were called mother. The children of these parallel fathers and mothers were *parallel cousins,* and they were considered the person's brothers and sisters just as surely as a full-blooded sibling having the same discrete pair of birth parents. The children of the other-gender relations of a person's parents, a mother's brother or a father's sister for instance, were considered *cross cousins.* These distinctions were important in determining possible marriage partners and kinship duties.

Carved representations of clan animals and birds may have been placed over the entrance doors of longhouses associated with that clan, and the wearing of carved figurines of clan animals (totems) or the painting or tattooing of them on the breast may have occurred. Vague references were made to such in the available record. Nonetheless, the clan animal or bird never figured as part of the name of an individual.

The distinctive traits of the Iroquois clan system can be summarized as follows: (1) the clans were exogamous, marriage within the same clan was forbidden; (2) each clan had its own set of names for individuals, and these were used over when one person died and another was born; (3) the majority clans claimed the right to select and to seat a leader at the tribal council; (4) the clan owned a burial ground and at least some communal territory or regional rights; (5) one clan occupied or predominated in each longhouse; (6) the clan had a right to adopt members from among outsiders; (7) the clans selected their leaders for ceremonial purposes; and (8) in ancient times before the formation of the confederacy the clan structure was somewhat different and may have been associated with discrete villages.

Family Living

All the material wealth of the Indians belonged to the women, including the fields, gardens, dwellings, and the village itself. For this reason many historians believed that the more settled tribes gave greater political and social power to females. Certainly among the Iroquois, the clan or lineage was accounted through the female line. Such a situation is known as *matrilineal*, but it was far removed from a political matriarchy in which the women actually ruled the tribe. The Iroquois man usually moved in with his wife after marriage making the family *matrilocal* (living with the mother's kin). This may also have been true of the Iroquoian-speaking Huron, but there is simply not enough available information about their customs to make a definite determination. The Huron of the historic period were so mixed by intermarriage with the Algonquians (to whom they ran for refuge during the dispersal) that they seem to have lost some of their cultural identity and social character as Iroquoians.

Algonquian-speaking peoples seem to have been *patrilineal* (through the father's line) in reckoning ancestry, inheritance, and marriage duties. However, the patrilineal emphasis did not automatically translate into *patrilocal* living (residing with the father's kin) because it seems they could be, and often were, matrilocal in their living arrangements. In some cases, even when the lineage was counted through the father, an adult man moved to live with his maternal uncle. This type of living was known as *avuncular*. In these cases, men took to their maternal uncles in much the same way as patrilineal men took to their fathers. In cases where the traditional living arrangements were not strictly adhered to—known as *bilocal*—adult men were free to leave their own village to reside with near relatives on either side of the family, or they could live as they had before marriage. Among many patrilineal kinship groups all parallel cousins were grouped as equal siblings, while cross cousins on the paternal side were raised a generation and those on the maternal side were lowered a generation making them the equivalent of one's children.

While matrilocal and avuncular living were thought to emphasize the authority of women in the wider society, bilocal living patterns generally indicated a weakened position of influence for women. Jolicoeur Charles Bonin noted of the Algonquians, "Perhaps no nation in the world scorns women more than these savages usually do." It has been pointed out, however, that Algonquian women lived as well as the situation of any primitive people allowed.[3] Yet, under the matrilineal principle, the women of the Iroquois nations, at least, enjoyed a good deal of authority and influence. It was the senior clan matrons who chose the next leader from among the available males of the same matrilineal line as their predecessor, and they could bring pressure to bear to remove him when a poor choice had been made.[4]

Those tribes with more permanent villages, such as the Iroquois, tended to be matrilineal, calculating clan lineage through the biological mother. On the other hand, the more mobile tribal villages with small family-size and less permanent domiciles, such as the Algonquians, tended toward patrilineal descent. This association between the two concepts of lineage and living style may be viewed as an oversimplification that masked deeper social relationships. Nonetheless, the clan structure played an important role in the socialization of native American youth, and it was the basis for village organization and tribal politics. "As a rule of thumb the number of longhouses in a village indicated the emphasis placed on the clans."[5]

Village Organization

The Iroquoian-speaking peoples were more settled in their village lifestyle than their Algonquians neighbors who tended to wander from campsite to campsite. Iroquoian culture was organized around an annual cycle of extensive agricultural activity, established political institutions, and permanent, fortified villages. The daily life of most woodland Indian women centered on the production of their three main crops—maize, beans, and squash. The fields and gardens that surrounded the village were cultivated by the women. An observer noted "a considerable Indian town inhabited by the Senecas...The low lands on which it is built, like all the others, are excellent, and I saw with pleasure a great deal of industry in the cultivation of their little fields. Corn, beans, potatoes, pumpkins, squashes appeared extremely flourishing."[6]

Although the Iroquois may have traveled annually to hunt in the grasslands or fish in waters far removed from their homes, they were much more sedentary than the Algonquians, who tended to roam over large areas in small bands of 8 or 10 marital units. It should be noted, however, that as with most Indians of the Northeast woodlands, even the "permanent towns" of the Iroquois were moved about every 10 years because the fields became too depleted of nutrients to warrant further cultivation.[7]

An entire village might take to the trail with all its belongings moving single file as the natives frequently did. Rather than moving in the distance consuming dog-trot of a war party, the villagers trudged along the trail under heavy loads of skins and furs, slabs of bark used for shelters, baskets and gourds filled with foodstuffs, cooking utensils and tools, and blankets, clothing, and extra weapons. The women carried much of this on their backs and supported it with a tumpline, a wide, woven band that lay across the forehead and attached to the load behind for support. During these moves, dogs were often fitted with small packs, and larger dogs might pull a *travois,* a crossed set of poles that dragged along the ground. The travois could be loaded with bulky items but not overloaded in terms of weight. Unlike their prairie cousins, who were sometimes known as the People of the Horse, the woodlands Indians generally did not keep horses, draft animals, or livestock other than dogs throughout the 17th century. Children helped in the move in proportion to their age or ability, and they were strictly admonished to remain on the trail with the group. The men and older boys served as scouts and protectors marking out the trail, flanking the line of march, and remaining on alert against attack.

The Iroquoian-speaking peoples lived in villages having substantial populations, sometimes numbering in the hundreds. These settlements were usually built near a lake or a riverside, but they were set back far enough from the water's edge to prevent surprise attacks by canoe-borne raiders. Major villages (often called castles by Europeans) were designed to serve as places of refuge and were always located near a source of fresh spring water. They were surrounded by as many as four concentric rows of palisades topped with a scaffold from which the perimeter could be defended. At the beginning of the 17th century, Champlain found some criss-crossed stockades that were 35 feet high. It seems that the Huron built much more imposing structures than the Iroquois of New York. Some contemporary observers suggest that this was due to fear of the Iroquois, but this is probably not true. Rather formidable stockades were a common defensive strategy used by many nations, including the Iroquois themselves.[8]

Harmen van der Bogaert was one of the first to leave a description of a Mohawk (Iroquois) village after he visited several in the winter of 1634–1635. Here, he saw both fortified castles and unfortified villages. Bogaert's report was obviously colored by his European roots. "We came into their first castle [a stockaded village] that stood on a high hill. There were only 36 houses, row on row in the manner of streets, so that we easily could pass through. These houses are constructed and covered with bark of trees, and are mostly flat above. Some are 100, 90, or 80 steps long; 22 or 23 feet high. There are also some interior doors made of split planks." Bogaert reported a number of iron artifacts in these longhouses suggestive of the continued trade between the Mohawk and the Dutch. "These houses were full of grain that they call *Onesti* and we corn; indeed, some held 300 to 400 Skipples [each about 3/4 of a bushel]."[9] In another village, Bogaert noted, "In each house there were four, five, or six places for fires and cooking. There were many Indians at home here so that we caused much curiosity in the young and old; indeed, we could hardly pass through... There is considerable flatland around and near the castle, and the woods are full of oak and walnut trees."[10] The next morning, Bogaert came to a village of nine houses without a stockade within a half mile of the place he had just left. He discovered that a person of importance had moved here to escape a recent threat of disease in the more densely populated castle. It seems certain, however, that in times of war the populations of the outlying settlements may have moved to the better fortified position afforded by the castle.

The Laurentian Iroquois at the village of Hochelaga (Montreal) was described by Champlain in 1608 as surrounded by cultivated lands and fields of maize, beans, and squash.

The town [was] round in shape and enclosed with three rows of timbers in the shape of a pyramid crossed on top, having the middle stakes perpendicular, and the others at an angle on each other, well joined and fastened in their fashion. It is the height of two lances [25 feet] and there is only one entrance through a gate which can be barred. There were in the town about fifty houses, each fifty steps

[100 feet] or more in length and twelve or fifteen [25 to 30 feet] wide, all made of wood covered with bark and strips of wood as large as a table, sewn well together artificially in their way. Within there were several rooms [sleeping alcoves]. In the center of the house there was a large space used as a fireplace, where they eat in common, each man retiring afterwards to his rooms with his wife and children. Likewise they have lofts or granaries in their houses, where they store their corn, out of which they make their bread.[11]

Algonquian peoples were much less sedentary than the Iroquois and were still roaming in extended family groups of about 20 persons in the historic period. They were most active when hunting in winter, and they came together as a tribe when the warmer planting season approached to make maple sugar and to plant their family gardens, which were less extensive than the communal fields of the Iroquois clans. Because of their seasonal cycle of living, the Algonquian tribes generally failed to establish permanent cities or large-scale villages with extensive stockades, choosing to live in small groups of family-style dwellings, known as wigwams (*we-gi-was*). Many Indian families chose to return each season to a convenient rock shelter. This was usually an overhanging rock ledge facing away from the prevailing wind that afforded protection from wild animals and was near a source of potable water. A small central fire and a few boughs properly arranged about the shelter could make a warm and cozy habitation, even in a rock crevice. Evidence unearthed by archeologists suggests that some rock shelters were used continuously for several generations.

Algonquian bands tended to favor remote family-sized shelters, but in times of crisis they seem to have gathered together in defense. Samuel de Champlain noted a large, fortified Penobscot village at Saco (Maine) in 1604 that may have been built to ward off Indian enemies from the Canadian provinces. Moreover, Captain John Mason noted, during the Pequot War (1637), a stockaded village of 70 wigwams built upon a high hill between the Mystic and Thames estuaries with a palisade of tree trunks 10 feet high enclosing a space of two acres. The stockade was fitted with loopholes for Indian marksmen and had only two entrances. Captain Benjamin Church also observed a major stockaded "fort" built by the Narragansett during King Philip's War (1675) at South Kingston in Rhode Island. This village held a remarkable 500 family-sized wigwams and was placed on a five-acre island in the midst of a great swamp that could be reached only by a single bridge.

Over the years, a great number of earthworks and ditches have been termed Indian forts by local antiquarians and historians in New England, but many of these structures may have been of Anglo-colonial origin. It seems unlikely that Indians undertook any considerable amount of ditching with their stone- or bone-based picks and shovels. Nonetheless, two lightly stockaded and ditched Algonquian villages were reported at Agawam opposite Springfield, Massachusetts, and three others were reported at Penacook near Franklin, New Hampshire. There were from 50 to 100 wigwams scattered about each of these semi-permanent towns with their rudimentary fortifications of upright saplings set in banks of earth. These fortified Algonquian villages may have been wartime expedients built specifically to ward off the English.

Jolicoeur Charles Bonin left a detailed description of an Algonquian village in his memoir of the French and Indian War:

An Algonquian village has no plan. It is a group of cabins of various shapes and sizes. Some are as long as a shed. They are all built and covered with tree bark, with the exception of a strip in the roof about two feet long, to let out the smoke from a fire of the same size. On each side of a cabin, there are beds made of bark spread on sticks and raised seven or eight inches above the ground. The exterior of these cabins is sometimes covered with a mixture of earth and brush to keep out the wind. The doors are likewise of bark hung from the top like blinds, or fastened on one side with wooden withes, making a swinging door. In general, [the natives] fortify better than they house themselves. Villages may be seen stockaded like redoubts, making provision for water and stones. The piles and the stones used to build them have battlements able to withstand a siege. But they must live near their enemies and fear being surprised, if they entrench themselves in this manner.[12]

The coastal Algonquian-speaking peoples seemingly favored small villages of 10 to 20 dwellings (wigwams) with a circular or oval floor plan occupied by smaller groups or single families. The Northeast coastal nations had semi-permanent dwellings much like those of the north-central peoples, but the mid-coastal tribes and the nations of the south-central woodlands seem to have favored a more permanent scaled-down longhouse between 25 and 50 feet in length with straight sides and a dome-capped roof. These were arranged in orderly rows on a central plaza with extensive gardens all around. If the village was stockaded the longhouses were more tightly bunched together.

In southern New England there were also longhouses of a decidedly different profile. These structures were the basis for the Quonset huts used in World War II by American forces. "Instead of vertical sides and a rounded roof, the saplings forming the sides were bent in a continuous arc." These "half-cylinders" were shingled with bark or reed mats, and they held six to eight families. The northern Algonquians seemingly built permanent Iroquois-style longhouses and used more temporary cone-shaped dwellings (teepees) covered with birch-bark shingles that could be carried when moving from place to place.[13]

Clans

The Iroquois clan was a female-oriented institution. It offered a structure to aboriginal society that was organized around common female ancestors and female relations. Among these, sisterhood was recognized as a very strong bond. When an Iroquois man married, he moved in with his wife and her relatives—usually her sisters and their husbands. These matrilineal relatives—who might be full sisters or female parallel cousins—would join together to build a large clan-oriented longhouse, to clear and tend the outlying fields, and to care for and educate the young. All male parallel cousins—the sons of actual sisters—were recognized by other male parallel cousins as siblings, either younger or older brothers depending on their relative age or generation. In the case of female parallel cousins, they were looked upon as younger or older sisters.[14]

Outside of marriage, ceremonial adoption provided the most common mechanism for extending kinship to outsiders. Such adoptions were largely misunderstood by European observers. Both friends and former enemies (usually captives), but never a relative, could be adopted into a family and granted certain kinship rights in the clan. Along with these rights came obligations. Yet, the adoptee remained the person that he was, retaining his own family, clan identity, and kinship network along with those he gained through adoption. Filling all these various kinship niches simultaneously could be difficult and sometimes frustrating.

One of the principles of the League of the Iroquois was the absorption of conquered peoples. This was most often accomplished on an individual basis through the adoption of captives. The person selected for adoption was often unaware of his status, initially being bound or even tortured as a prisoner. However, he might be separated from other captives and offered a seat near the fire and some food. He was often brought into the presence of "dignitaries" or other persons of importance who sat and smoked their pipes while they "looked him over." Ultimately, an elder woman of the household would "address him as a son" and provide him gifts such as a blanket, leggings, or moccasins. Radisson's adoptive family provided a feast for 300 persons on the occasion of his adoption. His new "sisters" decorated him with bracelets and garters, and his "brothers" painted his face and arranged his hair with feathers and beads. During the feast, his new "father" made a mighty speech, presented him with a hatchet, and climaxed the ceremony by naming him after a dead son, who Radisson was replacing through adoption.[15]

The clans took names from among a number of animals, birds, plants, and even mythical beings; but wolves, bears, foxes, elk, deer, hawks, and eagles predominated. Some Algonquian peoples, as discussed earlier, separated their clan-based tribal structure into moieties along "sky" and "earth" divisions. The "sky" clans were named for birds and were dedicated to the pursuits of peace, the adjudication of blood feuds, and the promotion of harmony; while the "earth" clans were devoted to preparations for war, defense, and policing the tribe. The political leaders of the tribe were chosen from "sky" clans, and the war chiefs were from the "earth" clans. This dual division of power among the clans was found in diverse forms in many Algonquian communities, and it was thought to provide a sort of checks and balances within the governance mechanism of the tribe.[16]

Among many nations, moieties were used to regulated the availability of marriage partners. The Winnebago, Menominee, and Miami were divided into earth and sky moieties with the sky/animal clans forming one moiety and the land dweller/water dweller clans forming the other. Other tribes assigned the moiety by order of birth, alternating through one or the other starting with the first-born child who usually assumed the moiety of its mother. Husband and wife had to come from different moieties. This tended to limit the ill effects of consanguinity in an otherwise narrow gene pool. Many tribes also used the moiety as an organizing factor for games, hunting, warfare, or other rivalry.

Individual Iroquois tribes were usually divided into three clans: Turtle, Bear, and Wolf. Each clan was headed by a clan mother and a group of clan matrons. The Seneca, like their Huron cousins, initially had eight matrilineal clans. Before the formation of the Iroquois confederacy, Turtle, Bear, and Wolf were in one phratry, and Hawk, Deer, Snipe, Crane, and Eel were in another. Phratries were super-groupings of clans used for ceremonial and social purposes. After the confederacy, the Turtle-Bear-Wolf phratry remained, but the other changed to Hawk, Little Snipe, and Great Snipe. The Deer, Duck, and Eel clans disappeared and may have been absorbed into others. No representatives of them appeared at any council after the time of confederation.

All of the original Huron clan names have been lost in the dustbin of history, but they are thought to have paralleled those of the Seneca. The Huron also organized into phratries, and the names of these have survived: Bear, Cord, Rock, and Deer. Each of the Huron phratries encompassed one or more clan, and those of just one clan usually retained the same single name. The dramatic dispersal of the Huron in the late 1640s extended and mixed their clan structure with those of other peoples, such as the Petuns, the Neutrals, and the Algonquian. Nonetheless, something approximating the clan in function seems to have remained the political, familial, and cultural unit among these mixed peoples.[17]

The clan elders (or clan matrons) determined the social and familial functions of the kinship group and helped to determine the diplomatic and military attitudes taken by the wider community. They also oversaw the allocation, distribution, and use of tribal resources and controlled the trade practices of its members to some extent. Access to important food sources, hunting grounds, firewood, or raw materials outside a clan's normal territory was usually assured by a formalized agreement between the elders or leaders of the clans involved. Social and economic stability were reinforced by such agreements. The role of the head of the clan, or clan mother, in this exchange system should not be underrated.

Chieftainship

The word *chief* has been used loosely in the context of this discussion because it has become part of the modern concept of Indian-ness. However, it is doubtful that the term was used by the Indians themselves. Chieftainship was not a generally accepted political concept among Native Americans. Before the arrival of whites, a chain of separate but interrelated Algonquian-speaking communities flourished along the Atlantic seaboard from Chesapeake Bay to the Gulf of St. Lawrence. These groups rarely achieved anything beyond local unity, but the relative weakness of the early European settlements made local native leaders, such as Metacomet, Uncas, or Massasoit, seem like potentates. European observers, in cases like these, often impressed their own ideas of chieftainship on the political structure of the Indians that they faced.

The term *chief* was not altogether inappropriate. The clans of Scotland, Wales, and Ireland had recognized *chieftains,* and Native American governance was seemingly characterized by a personal and interactive relationship between the political head and the people that was very similar to the Celtic understanding of the role of a chieftain. Moreover, like the Celts, the Indian relationship between ruler and ruled was established (rather than defined) in the oral tradition of the people; and, like the Celts, the Indians took great pains to observe the traditional decorum of their oral-ceremonial system of governance.

It seems certain that it was the French who first brought the concept of *chieftainship* into use when dealing with the nations of the woodlands. Frenchmen often used the concept of a chief as a "generic tag for any Indian who shows signs of having influence in his own society." French gallic traditions, such as those of the Scots, Welsh, and Irish, also recognized chiefs such as the Gallic war leaders Alaric and Vercingetorix. Louis de Bougainville noted that among all the tribes in the region "the Abenaki is that in which the young men have the least submission to the old men and the chiefs, either in peace or war." Notwithstanding these similarities, the Europeans—who had generally developed monarchies rather than clan chiefdoms—relied on written codes and constitutions that were open to interpretation by persons who had not been present when they were originated. This idea of *chieftainship* was foreign to most Indian concepts of leadership, law, and military or political organization.[18]

Only among the Miami of the Midwest and the Powhatan of Virginia did Indian leaders actually possess the powers of a monarch in European terms. Even in these cases, the reports of king-like or emperor-like tribal chieftains among the woodlands tribes were always those of whites filtered through the mechanism of European thinking. The English seemingly adopted the practice of recognizing chiefs only after the Native Americans had made a grudging acceptance of the idea in the 18th century.

On the other hand, the Indians tended to place European leaders in a hierarchy that fit into their own cultural logic. The French governor of Canada, for instance, was considered the leader of his people in an Indian way, *as a father to his people,* not as a representative of a king in far-away Europe. Neither the Indians nor the Europeans had any concept of the real power, capabilities, or authority of their opposite number. This caused no end of misunderstandings, recriminations, and bloodshed.

The hierarchical nature of the Powhatan political organization of coastal Virginia was as much a reflection of John Smith's understanding of the social and political structure of England as it was a true picture of Powhatan culture. It included a royal family with retainers and servants, a council, a sub-structure of district chiefs, a sacred priesthood, and a sophisticated system for collecting tribute from among as many as 200 separate villages. The paramount chief of the Powhatan (known to the English as Powhatan, but actually named Wahunsonacock) had extensive powers of punishment over his subjects and seems to have been imbued with a tinge of divinity and some degree of aristocratic heredity. Yet, his power was not unlimited and seems to have been restrained by the need to follow the advice of his relatives who acted as counselors. "Thus the political organization of the Powhatan was that of a ranked, kin-oriented society in which the number of status positions was limited and the status and administrative structure was arranged in a hierarchy of major and minor leaders governing major and minor subdivisions of the group."[19]

Among the Iroquois there was an arrangement of clans at councils that suggested a superstructure among chiefs. The Mohawk and Seneca leaders formed the senior (elder brother) group, the Cayuga and Oneida formed the junior (younger brother) group, and the Onondaga were clearly in charge of the proceedings. There was a similar tripartite arrangement among the clans of the Seneca when they met in council with the Turtle and Little Snipe leaders in charge, the Turtle-Bear-Wolfe leaders in the senior group, and the Hawk-Great Snipe leaders in the junior group. A lesser Little Snipe leader was also represented in the junior group. Exactly how this organization came to pass was unrecorded, but it may have its origins in the virtual disappearance of some Seneca clans during the formation of the confederacy. Among the Mohawk there were only three clans. This was also true of the Oneida, but the Oneida recognized three sub-divisions of each clan making a total of nine chiefs. The remaining facets of Iroquois political organization were not recorded at the time, but the ones presented were verified through the analysis of Iroquois genealogies.[20]

The Algonquians of the Great Lakes region did recognize an *okama* as a village civil leader, and elder women were respected as clan matrons. Yet, these persons had little influence outside the circle of their own neighbors and kin. Only war leaders on campaign could command the activities of other Native Americans. Even then they could not act without the consent of their counsels or, depending on the tribe, the clan matrons. As persons of influence they tried to mediate quarrels and shape village decisions, but no one was required to obey.

The Indians of New England and Long Island recognized villages leaders called *sachems*, or *sagamores*—the latter name made more common by its use in the 19th-century novels of James Fenimore Cooper. This leadership role among the Algonquians was usually hereditary and may have moved through matrilineal generations with both men and women holding political power. Anthropologists have also identified among the tribes of southern New England a true hereditary social stratification and something similar to a class structure. The social organization of the Wampanoag, for instance, placed the sachem and his extended family at the top of the tribe; ordinary members of the group, both men and women, in the center; and the resident non-members of the tribe (refugees, captives, and slaves) at the bottom. There is "little compelling evidence" that such stratified organizations existed elsewhere in the Northeast.[21]

Large concentrations of natives, as in villages or fortified towns, were often marked by levels of *sub-chiefs* and *war-chiefs*. Among the New England tribes, the position of *pniese* (advisor or counselor) was given to individuals who claimed to have had special supernatural visions during a physical ordeal. Such persons often acted as members of a sachem's council. Also important were the *shamans*, "magico-religious specialists" sometimes called *powwows*, who acted as intermediaries between the physical and spiritual worlds. "Power came from the manitou, who gave it to individuals or to ancestors of the group."[22] Nonetheless, the spiritual role of shaman and the political role of sachem did not generally come to rest in the same person. Most Native Americans listened to their leaders as a mark of respect even if they disagreed with what was being said, and many Indians chiefs acquired a type of non-coercive political power that many Europeans failed to understand.

Complicating the matter of chieftainship was the issue of leaders designated by European observers as *half-kings*, or *viceroys*. These men were supposedly delegated by the Iroquois council to handle the diplomatic relations among their subject tribes, particularly those who resided far from the central council fire at Onondaga, as in the Ohio country or the Carolinas. It is unclear whether these men were directly appointed by the Iroquois council or were selected by the people whom they represented. Some of these half-kings were the product of mixed marriages between members of their own tribe and the Iroquois. The Catawba-Seneca Tanacharison, half-king of an Ohio Valley village composed mostly of Shawnees and Mingos, seems to have successfully promoted himself as a mediator between his neighbors and Onondaga although neither of his parents had strong kinship ties among the villagers.[23]

While the family served as the fundamental unit of life and the clan served as the basis for kinship, the *village* served as the basic face-to-face unit of politics. A fully functional form of governance that balanced the desires of the village while respecting the needs of the individual or the clans was difficult when the conditions of life were sometimes spartan or inadequate. Father Pierre de Charlevioux found internal native politics puzzling. The Indians were "eternally negotiating" among themselves, and they always "had some affairs or other on the table such as the concluding or renewing of treaties, offers of service, mutual civilities, making alliances, invitations to become parties in a war, and lastly, compliments of condolence on the death of some chief or considerable person."[24] The added effects of inter-clan rivalries, hostile neighbors, and competing colonial governments made the whole sociopolitical process a troublesome one for many Indian communities.

Peace Medals and Gorgets

Presentation medals (peace medals) were the visible marks of chieftainship to which the French resorted to designate those persons they considered chiefs, and they became such a characteristic part of Euro-Indian politics that they were adopted by the British as a sign of alliance and by the Americans in later decades as symbolic of peace. Most Indian leaders welcomed the medals because they bestowed influence on the recipient

These photographs of a pre-1809 presentation Peace Medal from the authors' collection clearly show the profile of King George II (left) and a calumet ceremony between an Indian and a white man under the tree of peace with the date 1757 (right). The medal reads, "Let us look to the most high who blessed our fathers with peace." The diameter of the pewter disk is approximately 2 inches (5.0 cm).

within his village. The chiefs so designated became a conduit for the gifts given by the French to the Algonquians, and according to Indian logic, a good chief was recognized for his liberality in distributing presents. "Accumulating wealth meant little to Algonquians, but the status and influence that came from bestowing goods on others meant much."[25]

Nonetheless, some chiefs received special gifts—European clothing, muskets, and presentation items such as metal tomahawks and swords— that they were not expected to distribute, especially if they came as part of official delegations to Montreal or Quebec. Moreover, some of the young men who had gained status and reputation through war or other deeds were overlooked as the medals were distributed to the elders of the tribal council. This tended to create a fragile and unnatural political struc- ture within the village or tribe that the French needed to control through careful management and constant compromise.

The French diffused this situation somewhat by distributing brass and silver *gorgets* to warriors in recognition of their high military reputations. The gorget was a metal plate worn by most European officers as a part of their uniform. It had a lima bean or kidney shape, was four to eight inches long, and was suspended below the throat from a cord or ribbon worn around the neck. The gorget mollified the warriors somewhat without confirming the status of chieftain upon them. Through the use of gifts, medals, and other material symbols, the French created an alliance that was a blend of Algonquian and European understandings. The human center of these understandings were the alliance chiefs with whom the French were able to establish a network of ties, maintain the peace, and forward their economic and political objectives.

Although they may not have been recognized as such at the time, historians have accorded certain Native American leaders the designa- tion of an Indian *chief*. Unfortunately, many of these Indian leaders were associated solely with the military aspects of Native American leader- ship or with the violent protests against losing their land to white incur- sions. Opechancanough, brother and successor to Wahunsonacock (the Powhatan of John Smith), for instance, figured prominently in the earliest history of Jamestown and led the massacre of English colonials in 1622. Tiyanogo, a Mohawk war leader known as *King Hendrick* among the English, was influential in marshalling the power of his tribe on the side of the British during the French and Indian War, but he did so through the force of his personality rather than through any innate political au- thority. He died fighting for the British at the Battle of Lake George in 1755. Pontiac, the Ottawa leader known in Algonquian as Obwandiyag, led a serious uprising of Great Lakes tribes against the British in 1764 although he was only a warrior of considerable reputation. Joseph Brant (Thayendanegea) was initially a minor war leader among the Mohawk, but he was able to rally a majority of the Iroquoian-speaking tribes to the side of the British during the American Revolution.

Red Jacket (Sagoyewatha) and Cornplanter (Gyantwahia), were equally influential elder politicians of the Seneca nation. Red Jacket was a supporter of the British known for the bright red military coat given to him by the Royal Army. Red Jacket openly opposed Cornplanter and his half-brother Handsome Lake (Ganijahdiyah or Skaniadariyo) after the American Revolution. Cornplanter counseled a policy of reconciliation with the United States, and Handsome Lake, a pacifist prophet, wanted to wean the Iroquois away from European ways. Handsome Lake claimed a series of visitations from messengers sent by the Creator who led him up the Sky Path where he was shown the punishments that awaited the wicked. He used the Indian belief in the relevance of dreams to affect the behavior of his people. He preached a code of conduct (*Gaiwiio,* or the Good Word) that required the Iroquois to renounce alcohol, witchcraft, promiscuity, quarrelling, gambling, and the secret poisoning of their enemies. He also denounced the Christian missionaries that had come among his people. Within just a few years, Handsome Lake had revived the old Indian religion, especially among the Seneca.

Finally, there were native American leaders who became influential by opposing the young American Republic in the 19th century. Highly regarded among these was the Shawnee leader Tecumseh who, with his brother Tenskwatawa, known as the Prophet, confronted the future president of the United States, William Henry Harrison. Their face-to-face confrontations during a treaty negotiation in 1809 were to become the stuff of political propaganda and cultural prejudice later in the century. Tecumseh and his brother utilized the Indian concept of leadership as coming from the spirit world to take their place at the head of their people.

Clan Mothers

Among native American traditions was that of the Mother Peacemaker, *Jikonsahseh,* who as leader of her clan in the Iroquois Confederacy supposedly codified the powers and obligations of Iroquois women, particularly the clan mothers and clan matrons. Jikonsahseh was also known as New Face, or the Great Peace Woman. Among the duties expounded by Jikonsahseh were the power to make proposals, choose male chiefs, guide and help male leaders, and replace bad leaders with new ones. Upon the death of a chief, word would be brought to the women of his matrilineal "side." These women would then select a replacement from their own men and send their choice to the women of the lineage of his other "side" to be confirmed. If confirmed, the candidate was sent to the confederacy council to be ratified and seated.

Women officials planned and superintended a number of festivals: the harvest, the strawberry, the raspberry, the mid-winter, and the Green Corn festivals. They could order and organize the planting and harvesting, the cooking and arranging of feasts, and the placement of housing within the village. Women were thought to be wise and hard working, and the elder matrons were accorded respect in their persons and served as spiritual heads of their clans.

The clan matrons took their role seriously as the following historical account demonstrates. When the French attempted to move the Wyandots (Huron-Petuns) to Montreal in 1742, the Indian women vetoed the clan council's decision. So strong was their influence that the French opened secret talks restricted to the men of the tribe in an unsuccessful attempt to bypass the influence of the clan matrons. With no consensus emerging among the elders of the council, the entire power structure of the tribe shifted to some of the younger men who had initially supported the clan matrons in their refusal to move. Thereafter, the council elders became unwilling to act without first consulting both the mass of younger men and the clan matrons.[26]

It is certain that among the Shawnee there were female chiefs, both for war and for peace. These were almost always related to the principle chiefs of the band or village, usually either their mother or sister. The female chiefs had the general responsibility of superintending the female affairs of the village. These duties of office were usually slight, but the office of *peace woman* was employed to prevent the unnecessary effusion of blood. Through this method, the women of the village might make entreaties to the war chief if some military undertaking was not countenanced by the wider community. The peace woman would go to the war chief and, sitting before him, would set forth the cares and anxieties felt by the women of the tribe. This usually took the form of appeals that he spare the innocent and unoffending against whom his hand was raised.[27]

Among the Algonquian peoples of Pennsylvania was a woman known as Madame Montour. Born in Canada about 1667, her father was a French trader named Pierre Couc. In 1709, she became an interpreter for Governor Robert Hunter in New York where she met and married an Oneida chief named Carandowana. Her husband was killed in 1729 during a raid against another tribe in the Southeast. Madame Montour lived near Shamokin with her niece French Margaret and her son, Andrew (André). This clan mother was described as a distinguished women with an engaging personality. Her son, Andrew, performed a number of diplomatic errands for both the Pennsylvania and New York colonies, and he held a commission in Virginia as one of William Johnson's native captains. He was killed in 1772 by a Seneca warrior.

Queen Esther was reported to be the daughter of French Margaret, along with her sisters Mary (Molly) and Catherine (Kate), each of whom were influential in her own right. Esther lived in a settlement near Tioga Point known as Queen Esther's Town. Of course, the designation as queen in reference to this clan mother was merely a British sobriquet. History assigns Esther the dark role of executioner of white women and children taken during the Wyoming Valley raid of the Revolutionary War.

Warned of the approach of an avenging American army, Esther reportedly took her people into hiding in a ravine thereby saving them from destruction. After the Revolution, she married a Tuscarora warrior and moved to Cayuga Lake.

The older sister of Joseph Brant, Mary (Molly) Brant was one of the most influential Native American women during the 18th century. Known in Iroquoian as Konwatsitsiaienni, Molly Brant married Sir William Johnson, by Mohawk rites, some time during the 1760s. As the sister of a Mohawk leader and the wife of a powerful and influential British trader, agent, and Baronet, she enjoyed a higher status than most Indian matrons. Even after the death of Sir William in 1774, Molly wielded immense power and authority within the traditional matriarchal structure of Iroquois government as a diplomat and stateswomen at the head of a society of Six Nations matrons. Whenever Iroquois loyalty to the Crown wavered, she was able to convince most of the Confederacy, and the Mohawks in particular, to continue their support of the British. Only the Oneida and Tuscarora sided with the Americans. Unfortunately, the Iroquois (the pro-American Oneida and Tuscarora excepted) were forced to leave their lands in central New York and flee to Canada at the end of the war. Molly, her seven children, and her female black slave became the subject of blood revenge enacted by the Oneida. Chased from New York to Niagara to Carleton Island in the St. Lawrence River, Molly was finally placed under the protection of the Governor of Quebec, Sir Frederick Hamilton, who arranged that a house be built for her at Cataraqui (Kingston) in 1783. Besides protection, Molly was given a pension for life and received compensation for the lands that she had inherited from her husband that were abandoned during her flight. Molly Brant has been described as a woman of high intelligence and remarkable ability who was at ease in two cultures. She personified the dignity and influence accorded to respected matrons among the Iroquois people.

Feasts

There were a number of occasions on which formal feasts might be held. These were divided into private and tribal affairs. Jesuit Father Jean de Brefeuf, when visiting the Huron, noted of the private feasts among friends. "When they are not with their fields, hunting, fishing, or trading, they are less in their own houses than in those of their friends... If they have something [food or game] better than usual, they make a feast for their friends, and hardly ever eat it alone."[28] It was also the custom for a private person to invite his friends and the leading persons of his village to a feast if he wished to make an announcement regarding his affairs (marriage, divorce, childbirth, adoption), or if he simply wished to win renown by telling of his exploits. No negative connotation was seemingly connected to bragging.

The second category of feasts were those held at general assemblies or councils at which representatives of the political entities or villages gathered. This was done to renew friendships or plan for activities of common interest. Such feasts were often given for the representatives of European powers. At a feast there was food, dancing, and the exchange of presents between the various groups involved. Father de Brebeuf noted of these gatherings, "The day of their arrival they erect their huts; the second [day], they hold their councils and make their presents; the third and fourth, they trade... when this is over they take one more day for their last council, for the feast... and the dance; and early the next morning they disappear like a flock of birds."[29]

Music

Indians used music in a great many settings, but their songs were generally lullabies, gambling songs, songs associated with tales, or incantations sung during rituals. The warrior's death song was one written for himself with the help of his spirit guide and saved for the time of his impending demise.

Not all Native American music was the same, and ethnomusicologists have developed the study of native music by creating geographic *musical areas* for its study. In order to attain the designation of a musical area, a geographical territory must show musical styles that are common in one or more traits. These include identical forms, scale types, or melodic ranges. The science of enthomusicology is painstaking and difficult. It is difficult to decide the specific level of homogeneity of a music that has not been heard or recorded and is only known through Native American traditions and oral anecdotes.

Nonetheless, certain generalities can be made with confidence. Native American music usually had a single voice, a single meter, and a short range of notes. The melodic movement ranged from the undulating changes of the sub-arctic tribes to the pendulum-like sweeps of the tribes of the Northwest Pacific coast leaping in broad intervals from one limit of the range to the other. The drone was in use in many instances, but antiphonal (sung by two groups) and responsorial (answering back and forth) forms were also used. Pulsation characterized the style of the singing, and extremes of vocal extension were used to produce contrasts, ornamentation, and rhythm. This was sometimes, but not always, accompanied by drumming, rattles, or the twitter of simple flutes and whistles. Sudden accents were not unusual even during one sustained note, and there may have been sharp contrasts between very long and very short tones. Typical pulsation schemes included an incomplete repetition beginning and ending with the same phrase as in ABC-BC-AABC-ABC. This was then repeated sometimes with extra emphasis on the third element during the second rendition. Often the first rendition was composed of meaningless syllables, and the second was sung with a meaningful text.[30]

The rise was often in evidence, and the nature of its inclusion was often dispositive of the musical area of origin. The rise usually contained new melodic material made distinct through the use of a greater number of the high-pitched tones. It is found in 20 percent of songs from the Northwest Pacific coast, about 15 percent of that from the Southeast, and in only a few songs from the Northeast. The proportion differed slightly among tribes in the same region.

The music of the Northeast woodlands, in particular, is not well-documented except along the Atlantic coast and along its southernmost boundaries. By extension from what is known of their relatives, the Cherokee and Susquehannock, it has been proposed that the music of the Iroquois was highly complex when compared to that of their Algonquian neighbors. Yet, the music of the Ojibwa and Menominee exhibited some of the widest range of musical tones used anywhere on the continent. The Siouan Winnebago also evidenced a wide tonal range. All three resided around the Great Lakes. The Delaware and Penobscot, largely coastal peoples, had much simpler forms; and the Shawnee, who moved from the Great Lakes to the coastal region in historic times, were somewhere in between the extremes of complexity.

The main musical traits of the Northeast woodlands were short phrases; the use of shouts before, during, and after songs; simple rhythmic and metric organization; and a great number of antiphonal and responsorial elements. A moderate amount of pulsation and vocal tension was present. The Northeast was the least varied of all the recognized musical areas, and its western parts seem closely tied to the musical patterns of the plains. The diversity of musical traits was greater in the West than in the East. This type of arrangement was the general rule throughout the continent.

It should be noted that the limited sampling of Native American songs available to researchers that have been authenticated to represent the period may lead to inaccurate conclusions. The conclusions reached by researchers, therefore, are highly tentative and open to revision. The only really close association among linguistic stock, geographic location, and musical style seems to be found among the Native Americans speaking Athabascan, the root language of many of the tribes of the Southwest (Navajo, Pueblo, Apache, etc.), and the coastal California tribes. This style is characterized by limited durational value, the use of falsetto voice, pulsations, and a nasal sound that is especially distinctive of its type.

No Word for Time

Anthropologists have formed their concepts concerning Indian time into a descriptive model known as a *temporal orientation*. Indian time seems to have been oriented into two types: *reckoned time,* as in determining duration or place in time, and *social time,* the purposeful scheduling of both optional and obligatory community activities. In simple societies the demands of social time were usually well articulated with one another, and individuals were rarely torn by mutually exclusive temporal commitments. On the other hand, reckoned time was generally unimportant to the functioning of day-to-day Indian life.[31]

It has been pointed out that there is no word in the Algonquian tongue for time, or for the reckoning of it, and the concept of duration was based solely on a relative separation between visible events that would have made a man like Albert Einstein pleased. There simply was no description of time in isolation from events. "There are words for day (*nagwew*), and night (*depkik*), one for sunrise, sunset, for the lunar cycle, one for the yearly cycle, youth, adulthood, and old age, but no word for absolute time which measures the universe from outside of it." Indians reckoned time in cycles like the passing of the seasons, of which they recognized several: Spring, Summer, the Earing of the Corn, Harvest, the Fall of Leaves, and Winter. The concept of *when* could be expressed in images, as in "the winter of the deep snows," but not in numbers, as in "7 years ago." There were no birthdays, no anniversaries, and no holidays in the European sense. Feasts were organized to celebrate things in the *now,* or *neegeh.* A new year, for instance, was determined by the first new moon after the freezing of the local creek—an actual event that happened earlier in the north than it did in the south—or by the moving of a village as in the case of the Ceremony of the Dead.[32]

Social time among the tribes was either *compact* or *diffuse,* and each of these was largely determined by annual ecological factors, such as the run of salmon, the ripening of wild rice, or the migration of waterfowl. *Compact time* corresponded to those seasons of the year when members of the tribe gathered together at certain traditional places and spent several months gathering and preserving large quantities of fish, fowl, or grain. This was a period that required group effort, but it also allowed for celebration, ritual, feasting, the recitation of genealogies and war honors, and the arrangement of marriages among the bands and clans. This was strongly contrasted to *diffuse time,* during which the extended family groups or bands dispersed throughout the tribal territory to hunt and gather or to trap furs.

There remains an ongoing controversy as to whether or not the woodland Indians kept celestial calendars to mark the Summer and Winter Solstices, or the twice yearly Equinoxes. Certainly other Indian peoples in North America did so, but there are few structures or evidences that the peoples of forests followed a similar astronomy. Nonetheless, the Algonquian year was broken into full-moon lunar cycles that were largely descriptive of the weather or of the tasks that needed to be performed periodically.

A loose analogy can be made with our own calendar as an illustration. January was the Hard Times Moon of biting winds and long nights.

February was the Snow Blinder Moon when hunting families, their food reserves dwindling, spent a part of their time on the trail hunting in the winter forest. March was the Sap Moon that brought maple sugaring, and April brought the great runs of smelt, bass, salmon, and sturgeon during the Spearfish Moon. May was the Planting Moon, and June's Strawberry Moon brought the first of the juicy red fruit. The ears of corn appeared during July's Ripening Moon when the children were posted on scaffolds in the field to scare off birds and deer. August was the Green Corn Moon that brought festivities and games, and September's Harvest Moon needs no further description. The Hunter's Moon of October brought the first group hunt of the year, and November's Beaver Moon began the prime time for trapping fur bearing animals. Finally, there came the Tom Cod Moon when Indians spent a great deal of time fishing through holes in the ice. Of course, there were many other names for the full moons among tribes that had different seasonal habits, but each, like these, remained descriptive of the chores associated with daily life and the struggle to survive.[33]

Temporal Changes in Indian Life

Christianity, the fur trade, and alcohol changed the traditional rhythm of native life. Christianity generally retained the overall time dimensions of both compact and diffuse time for the Indians, while the quest for furs substantially changed their purposeful use of diffuse time. Alcohol, on the other hand, simply suspended time for many Indians in a pseudo-religious context, but the Indians who became dependent on liquor could not break free of its effects. It devastated the Native American community, broke apart families, and caused uncounted deaths, both directly and indirectly.[34]

Christian sacraments and religious obligations gradually replaced or became part of many tribal rituals and ceremonies, but they required no structural changes in the framework of population concentration and/or dispersal. This was especially true of the Algonquian-speaking tribes who came into contact with Jesuit missionaries who carefully chose to celebrate Christian feast days from the Roman Catholic Liturgical Calendar so as to coordinate with the height of traditional Native American festivals. The almost continuous warfare among the French, the English, and the various tribes that characterized the 18th century, however, convinced many Indians to gather together in the protection of the Christian missions. These were both Catholic and Protestant, but the Catholic missions penetrated further into native America and were more numerous and more densely populated. This changed the demographic face of the region somewhat with novel forms of intertribal living, mixed marriages, the formation of new clans, and a reliance on Euro-centric concepts of time.

The trapping of fur-bearing animals, which had supplemented the acquisition of food as the primary purpose of hunting, quickly became an overriding pursuit bordering on an addiction. By the middle of the 17th century, Father de Brebeuf noted that the Indians seemingly "spent the entire year in the act of [fur] trading or in preparing for it." Although this development failed to change the alternation of compact and diffuse times significantly, it changed radically the nature of the tasks carried out by families when separated from their tribal groups as a whole. Family units became fixated on trapping and accumulating furs. The enforcement of tribal hunting boundaries and the need to pass down certain rivers became, for the first time, major stumbling blocks to native cooperation and the cause of violence, murder, and war.[35]

Traders amassed great profits by trading alcohol to the Indians for their furs. Although many native peoples made a weak sort of beer from maple syrup or spruce buds, none of the western or northern tribes had discovered the process of distillation. They, therefore, had developed no tolerance for strong drink. Moreover, some historians propose a physiological cause related to the sugar content of their blood that might theoretically explain the almost immediate reaction that many Indians had when exposed to strong drink. Others relate it to a synthesis of a lack of social stigma, spiritual beliefs, and spirits of a more organic type. Regardless of the cause, Native Americans exhibited an extraordinary susceptibility to the effects of alcohol consumption, which was utilized and exploited by most fur traders to the detriment of the Indian population.[36]

Whether physiological, spiritual, or cultural, the effect of alcohol on Native American behavior was reported by contemporaries as pathological and devastating. "The liquor made them more than quarrelsome; it literally drove them mad." There seemed to be no limit to the senseless violence to which a drunken Indian might resort, and the women were equally effected. "Their habitual modesty evaporated," and they were capable of violent acts that they would not have considered in a sober state. Robert Juet, a sailor on the Dutch vessel *Half Moon*, noted in 1609 that "there is scarcely a savage, small or great, even among the girls and women, who does not enjoy this intoxication, and who does not take these beverages when they can be had, purely and simply for the sake of being drunk."[37] While the Indians quickly learned what alcohol would do to them, they seemed powerless to resist it, and in many individuals, it is certain that they experienced a physical addiction. Ultimately, alcohol shattered the structural and familial foundations of many native cultures.

Notes

1. See George T. Hunt, *The Wars of the Iroquois, A Study in Intertribal Trade Relations* (Madison: University of Wisconsin Press, 1972), 39.
2. The six were Hawaiian, Eskimo, Sudanese, Crow, Omaha, and Iroquois.
3. Paul A. W. Wallace, *Indians of Pennsylvania* (Harrisburg: The Pennsylvania Historical and Museum Commission, 1986), 31.

4. Andrew Gallup, ed., *Memoir of a French and Indian War Soldier, Jolicoeur Charles Bonin* (Bowie, MD: Heritage Books, Inc., 1993), 216.

5. C. Keith Wilbur, *The Woodland Indians, An Illustrated Account of the Lifestyles of America's First Inhabitants* (Guilford, CT: The Globe Pequot Press, 1995), 78.

6. Albert E. Stone, ed., *Letters from an American Farmer and Sketches of Eighteenth-Century America by J. Hector St. John de Crevecoeur* (New York: Penguin Classics, 1986), 377.

7. Wilbur, 55.

8. Hunt, 39.

9. Charles T. Gehring and William A. Starna, eds., *A Journey into Mohawk and Oneida Country, 1634–1635: The Journal of Harmen Meyndertz van der Bogaert* (Syracuse, NY: Syracuse University Press, 1988), 4.

10. Gehring and Starna, 7.

11. Elizabeth Metz, *Sainte Marie Among the Iroquois* (Syracuse, NY: Midgley Printing, 1995), 22.

12. Gallup, ed., 223.

13. Wilbur, 77–78.

14. Gehring and Starna, 64.

15. Stanley Vestal, *King of the Fur Traders, The Deeds and Deviltry of Pierre Esprit Radisson* (Boston: Houghton Mifflin Company, 1940), 19–20.

16. Wilbur, 55–56.

17. Alexander A. Goldenweiser, "Iroquois Social Organization," in *The North American Indians, A Sourcebook,* ed. Roger C. Owen (Toronto: Collier-Macmillan, Limited, 1971), 567.

18. Colin G. Calloway, *Dawnland Encounters: Indians and Europeans in Northern New England* (Hanover, NH: University Press of New England, 1991), 170.

19. Stephen R. Potter, *Commoners, Tribute, and Chiefs, The Development of Algonquian Culture in the Potomac Valley* (Charlottesville: University Press of Virginia, 1993), 18.

20. Goldenweiser, 568–569.

21. William A Starna, "The Pequots in the Early Seventeenth Century," in *The Pequots in Southern New England, The Fall and Rise of an American Indian Nation,* ed. Laurence M. Hauptman and James D. Wherry (Norman: University of Oklahoma Press, 1990), 40.

22. Richard White, *The Middle Ground, Indians, Empires, and Republics in the Great Lakes Region, 1650–1815* (New York: Cambridge University Press, 1991), 38.

23. White, 225.

24. Quoted in White, 148.

25. See White, 183–185; quote on 183.

26. White, 194.

27. Paul A. W. Wallace, *Indians in Pennsylvania* (Harrisburg: Pennsylvania Historical and Museum Commission, 1986), 121.

28. Quoted in Mary W. Herman, "The Social Aspects of Huron Property," in Owen, ed., 584.

29. Quoted in Herman, 587.

30. Bruno Nettl, "American Indian Music," in Owen, ed., 113.

31. Harold F. McGee, ed., *The Native Peoples of Atlantic Canada, A History of Indian-European Relations* (Ottawa: Carleton University Press, 1983), 154.

32. Evan T. Pritchard, *No Word For Time, The Way of the Algonquian People* (Tulsa: Council Oaks Books, 1997), 11–12.

33. See Michael McCurdy, *An Algonquian Year, The Year According to the Full Moon* (Boston: Houghton Mifflin Company, 2000).

34. McGee, 154.

35. Quoted in George T. Hunt, *The Wars of the Iroquois, A Study in Intertribal Trade Relations* (Madison: University of Wisconsin Press, 1972), 63.

36. Walter D. Edmonds, *The Musket and the Cross, the Struggle of France and England for North America* (Boston: Little, Brown and Company, 1968), 49.

37. Quoted in Edmonds, 48.

4

Child Rearing from Birth to Marriage

Nowhere on earth was a young man better treated than in the camps of warlike Indians. Life as he knew it there was without restraint.
—Pierre Esprit Radisson

Child Birth

Indian families highly valued their children, and a couple greeted the birth of their first child with a welcoming feast at the mother's family home. The couple stayed there a few days and then returned to their own residence if it were a different place. Sons were always welcomed because they ultimately brought hunters to the family and a strong arm for defense; but among the Iroquois, daughters were somewhat more highly prized than girls elsewhere because their society was matrilineal.

Birthing took place in a hut located outside the village, and as her time drew near the mother-to-be and a few other women withdrew to the hut and remained there until a few days after the birth. The mother used this time to purify herself through the performance of simple ceremonies and rituals. Babies spent their days outside of the family living quarters secured to a cradle board until they were able to walk, and the mother would often hang this from a tree while she worked in the fields.

Thomas Morton noted of native women in 1637: "Very apt are they to be with child, and very laborious when they bear children. Yes, when they are as great as they can be, yet in that case they neither forbear labor, nor travail…Their women are very good midwives, and the [mothers] very lusty after delivery, and in a day or two will travel or trudge about."[1]

Childlessness, unless planned or caused by a physical disability, was implausible in a society that had few sexual taboos. Most Indian women were probably exposed, therefore, to the rigors of almost continuous pregnancy, interrupted only by a painful and dangerous labor, and months of nursing. So frequent were these bouts with nature that many women, conceiving again before fully recovering from a previous pregnancy, gave birth to underweight or physically weakened children who were prime candidates for an early death. Even in a society where large families were the norm and were valued and wanted, at least some women must have dreaded the prospect. Many women took steps through ritual or through the use of amulets and charms to prevent miscarriages, but others seemingly relied on essentially the same useless expedients to bring on abortions.

Child Rearing

The education of Indian children was "a family concern and their instruction was constant, given at any waking hour and so deeply implanted that the history of [their] race, tribal politics and warfare, economics, religion and medicine were memorized faultlessly and adhered to without deviation." Each child among matrilineal tribes belonged to the clan of his mother and lived in a clan house or a group of wigwams with his mother's relations. While this did not disqualify the father from taking a critical role in the life of his children, the most important males in a boy's upbringing were undoubtedly his mother's brothers, or his maternal uncles. These would be the ones who instructed him in the skills that he would need as an adult, and it was they who would decide if he was ready to move forward through the events that led to adulthood, such as the vision quest. This freed the father from having to make life altering decisions in his son's life and insured a more unbiased judgmental process.[2] Nonetheless, Indian fathers cared for the children. Roger Williams noted in 1643, "I have known a father take so grievously the loss of his child that he hath cut and stabbed himself with grief and rage."[3]

The rest of a child's education, apart from that which he gained from personal experience, was obtained by watching the activities and listening to the discourse of adult warriors and other elders who had gained the respect of the people by the services they had rendered to the tribe in the past. Elderly women were also a source of cultural and historical information, which they related through narratives and traditions "of which they [were] by the consent of custom the unerring and sacred depositories."[4]

These older persons were venerated by all, and the listeners paid great attention to their narratives even though the conversations, speeches, and plots they repeated were so often used as to risk their being mere tautologies. Children of even tender years could often recite these stories and traditions with little or no error. No tale ended in a moral point that was not justified by the narrative; and there were no unlooked-for features connected to the subject that did not reinforce the concepts being taught.

Henry Rowe Schoolcraft, a 19th-century observer of Indian lore, noted, "The value of these traditional stories appeared to depend, very much, upon their being left, as nearly as possible, in their original forms of thought and expression....Judged by this test, most of the tales are of the era of flint arrowheads, earthen pots, and skin clothes. Their fishnets are represented as being made of the bark of trees. No mention is made of blanket, gun, knife, or any metallic instrument." These particulars, as Schoolcraft called them, indicated the antiquity and the importance of continuity given to these narratives; and they separated ancient tales from those of a later era when modern compounds, such as the names of European domestic animals, guns, compasses, or wagons inhabit the stories.[5]

Jolicoeur Charles Bonin has left a description of the child-rearing practices among the French Indians. Because of its remarkable detail, his depiction is important even though the observations were sometimes ethnocentric, chauvinistic, and otherwise indifferent to the feminine or native point of view.[6]

The women bear children, usually unattended and without pain but always away from their dwellings,[7] in a little shelter built for this purpose forty or fifty days previous in the woods, or sometimes in their fields....These mothers nurse their own children...care for them, and carry them on their backs with a small board twenty-five or thirty inches long, bent at the upper end....[T]his is fastened with straps, and carried with the child's head upright under the plank's curved end.... [T]he child is changed when necessary.

When it leaves the cradle[board], the child is not interfered with in any way. He is given complete liberty to roll about on his feet and hands, in the woods, in the snow, and even in the water, when he is strong enough. He learns to swim like a fish. All this helps a great deal in making these children strong, supple, and agile. Ordinarily, when they are three or four years old, their mother leave them to themselves; not through harshness and indifference, but because they believe nature must be let alone and unhampered.

Bows and arrows are put in the hands of children at an early age, and they become expert in their use in a short time. They are made to fight each other, and, sometimes, one would be killed if care were not taken to separate them. The losers are so ashamed, that they do not rest until they have revenge. For this reason they seem born with a desire for glory.

The only education children receive is by hearing their mother and father tell the brave deeds of their ancestors and their tribe. They become enthusiastic over these stories, and grow up and imitate what they have been taught to admire. Kindness is used in correcting them, never threats ...

The giving of a name ends the period of early infancy. The ceremony is carried out with a feast attended only by persons of the same sex as the child that is to be named. He is held on his mother's knee, and given the name of a dead warrior in his family. Children are usually thought of as belonging more to the mother than to the father. Since they are brought up with this notion, they respect their father only as the master of the dwelling.[8]

Should the child be a boy, his mother would take him with her on all of her visits and witness his "playfulness" with his "infantile fellows." The children were seldom together long without quarrelling, and they generally made a pretty bold fight among themselves if it was allowed to continue. The mother would feel great mortification should her child evidence any ignoble traits, such as cowardice or subservience, during this play; and she would feel great pride to find the innate character of courage and leadership unfolding in her child. A disappointed mother might discipline her child away from others by placing a stick in his hands and forcing him to beat a dog, or any other animal that happened to be convenient. He was thereby encouraged to enforce his mastery over others and to tolerate no insult to his person even to the point of retaliating against his own mother. A second lesson was rarely needed, if the mother was to ever be successful.[9]

Young boys were physically hardened and taught to be self-reliant. They were also taught a pattern of emotional restraint, social inhibition, and diplomatic reserve when they interacted with the world outside their own kinship group. It was from early reports of this characteristic among all woodland nations that the stereotype of the stoic, stone-faced, and detached Indian was formed. A Jesuit observer noted in 1710, "Whenever misfortune may befall them they never allow themselves to lose their calm composure of mind, in which they think that happiness especially consists." Yet, there were also consistent reports of great laughter, joking, and a keen sense of humor in the villages, and the individual's personal relationships were marked by gentleness, humanity, and genuine sociability. Such traits, common throughout the Northeast woodlands tribes, appear to have been culturally determined and transmitted through a careful program of education.[10]

When their uncles determined that it was safe to do so, boys were made to jump into a river, lake, or pond in any weather, even if the ice needed to be broken in winter. Each boy was rigorously trained in woodcraft, weapons, and personal survival. At about the age of 10, a boy was usually put to his first test of personal endurance. He was sent into the forests with his bow and told not to return until he had shot something to eat. His face was blackened with charcoal as a sign that he was under a test and was not to be helped nor hindered. Undergoing such an ordeal might take a few hours or several days, but if he managed to shoot some small animal with his arrow he returned to his family increased in the pride of having passed a hurdle on the way to being considered a man. As he matured, he would pass through several such episodes that would lead to his vision quest, of which more will be said later.

Nowhere in white society could a young man in his teens experience the freedom and lack of restraint common to their Indian counterparts.

The Native American youth was viewed as the foundation and future support of his tribe. Pampered by his mothers and sisters, petted by all his relations, envied by the young children, and praised by his uncles and brothers, a young man spent his time training in arms, hunting, fishing, dancing, singing, feasting, and wandering about the country alone or in a small group of friends. If he were a bloodied warrior, a young man might enjoy a distinction and importance beyond that normally accorded one of his years. This circumstance often gave the young man an air of pride and confidence that was mistaken by whites as conceit and arrogance.

Female children received no special lessons, taking their education by the example and advice of their mothers and the other clan women to whom they were exposed. No other tasks was set for her beyond the normal fetching, cooking, sewing, and repairing that were the common tasks of all women. Young girls applied themselves industriously to the mastery of their decorative work using beads or porcupine quills. Older girls were often set to collecting firewood and water or to overseeing the small children in their play, but it was common for all the women in a kinship group to care for all the children of the clan.

A researcher of Algonquian ways has noted, "The important activities of the culture were centered around the male. The boys were given names of the most powerful beings, while the girls were given protective names. The boy's first game kill was recognized by a formal ceremony, while the excellence of performance shown in any task by a girl was never celebrated. Special celebrations were held for young males victorious in war, while their sisters stood by and accepted the scalps." The women were, in the main, forced to be spectators of many of the most important events in Native American life.[11]

The Vision Quest

Puberty was an important time in the life of a child because it marked, more distinctly than it does for teens today, the passage from childhood to the status of an adult. The search for a protecting or guiding spirit through the experience of a metaphysical vision was an important part of this transition. The vision quest was common to most Native American peoples, but unlike the nations of the Southwest, the tribes of the Northeast woodlands seem to have eschewed the use of mind altering drugs in favor of fasting. However, tobacco may have been burned as a ceremonial offering to ensure success.

Puberty marked a girl's acceptance into adult membership in the kinship group. On the occasion of her first menses, a girl would retire to an isolation hut (*wetuomiemese*) for the duration of her period. Here she would fast, denying herself food and drink, until her unseen guardian would make a dream visitation and give her directions for her duties as an adult in the form of a vision. She would repeat this program many times in her lifetime because all menstruating women were isolated at their time of the month. During menstruation, she was prohibited from eating certain foods or from making contact with hunters, warriors, and children for fear of stealing their power or even causing death. Foods that she might prepare endangered the guiding spirits of men, who would vomit them out should they accidentally be made "unclean."[12] At the end of her term "she washeth herself and all that she hath touched or used, and is again received to her husband's bed or family."[13]

Young men generally embarked upon their vision quest when their maternal uncles thought that they were fit in terms of physical and behavioral maturity. The preparation for this was often extensive and was usually undertaken when his voice began to change. The boy's uncles would find a secluded spot, and the boy would build a shelter in which he might live for up to a year. He ate sparsely and filled his time with physically demanding exercises, such as running, climbing, and swimming, even in winter. Among the hardest lessons to learn was overcoming long periods of isolation. The purpose of this extended period of isolation was to inculcate a sense of self-reliance. An old man or woman would sometimes be set to oversee his well-being during this period, and his uncles would visit periodically to assess his progress.

When his uncles thought the proper time had come, the boy would retire to some rock formation, cliff side, or mountaintop of mystical importance to himself and fast alone there for up to 10 days. The rite of fasting was one of the most deep-seated of Indian rituals. The physical stress created by the denial of food and water usually brought on an hallucination or vision. In this state, he would search for a guardian spirit, usually represented by an animal totem that he would follow for his entire life. During his quest, the young man might put together a small bag of totems or special items of meaning only to himself. Upon his return, his uncles would authenticate the quality of the vision quest. After a successful vision, the young man usually painted his head red as a sign of having reached adult status.

Young persons of both genders might be favored with visions that conveyed a clear meaning, but the experience might leave them with an unclear or confused message. In such a case, they might have to consult with a shaman, or wiseman, who would attempt to interpret a clear meaning—usually in consultation with the child's parents or guardians. By this means, the adult relations of youngsters could effectively direct their efforts throughout their adolescence. Young persons favored by many spirit helpers in their visions were considered fortunate, and in some tribes young men, and sometimes women, might themselves become shaman.

While Indians believe fasts to be meritorious, there is no evidence of prescribed fasts or regular fasting days among the Indians as there were in Christian theology. In their subsequent life adults fasted for clarification of the precepts learned during the vision quest, or for a renewal of the powers and virtues gained during the initial vision when adolescents. These fasts rarely lasted for more than seven days. Nonetheless, there seems to have been a general fasting season in the spring when the common store of preserved food had diminished. Fasts may have been observed more frequently by those who were striving to preserve an altered state, such as shamans or magicians; by those who wished to assume the austere habits of an ascetic for the purpose of gaining influence in the tribe; or by those preparing for war or some extraordinary feat.

Games

Games and physical contests were important as a means of teaching children the need to be cooperative and skillful. Besides practice with the bow or throwing tomahawks and knifes, which was done with great perseverance and zeal, Indian children played a number of games. In good weather, running, jumping, wrestling, and climbing contests abound as they would among any group of children. Nonetheless, marksmanship and playing with a hoop or other simple toy also filled much of their free time. Lance and spear casting games were popular. These were often played with a wooden hoop. The players faced each other in two parallel lines about 20 yards apart with spears in hand. A third party rolled the hoop between the opponents who tried to stop it with a cast of their spears. Once stopped, the opponents must hit the motionless hoop or lose a spear. The game went on until one side or the other was stripped of spears. The game could also be played with bows and arrows, but a smaller hoop and larger field was required.

A remarkable development was the vigorous and unrestrained game known to the Jesuits as Lacrosse. Played with a long handled net and a leather ball, Lacrosse pitted two teams in a contest to score the ball through a goal. The game could cover many acres of ground and might involve many hundreds of players at any time of the year. Winter games included a form of ice hockey without skates and a game known as Indian snakes in which a long stick was propelled along an icy trench. The stick that went the greatest distance won.

Women and older girls played a version of Lacrosse called double ball. The double ball was itself composed of two oblong buckskin bags joined together by an eight-inch thong. The players were equipped with three- to four-foot long sticks. During the game the double ball was picked up and carried or thrown with the sticks. The point of the game was to hit the opponent's goal with the double ball. The goals were placed some 300 feet apart. The girls, like the boys, were urged to compete to win in all these activities.[14]

Girls and women were often included with the boys in some of their games and amusements, but they generally did not play among the men in physically demanding situations. Those amusements in which they most

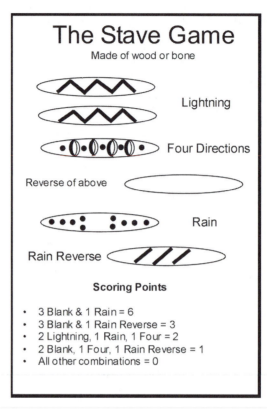

The stave game was played both for entertainment and as a form of gambling. The pieces were a hand width in length and made from flattened wood strips or bone. They were shaken in the cupped hands and thrown on the ground or onto a blanket or skin. The game could be played to any number.

frequently engaged generally involved dancing, which they soon learned to perform with accuracy and grace. Games ranged from public contests to quiet diversions that could be played indoors by the fire. A form of jack-straws using reeds was played, and there was a similar game called *puum* played with short sticks. A feat of individual skill was the cap and pin game where a player swung a string of perforated bones into the air and tried to slide a thin pin or dart into the perforations. Other quiet games utilized dice, cherry stones, grains of corn, and flattened sticks.

The elders encouraged and promoted these sports and games because they were an important means of preparing young bodies and minds for the important offices of war, hunting, and daily living. Many games involved men, women, and children of both genders playing together in teams or in individual events. Judges were often appointed to determine who was victorious and to whom prizes should be awarded. These could be a beaver pelt or a deer skin, or articles of clothing, such as moccasins or leggings. More usually, however, the prize consisted of shells, nuts, fruit, or other trifles. A council was usually held after a team game so that the opposing sides might leave without regret or recrimination. These councils were observed with great gravity because the integrity of the tribe was held in the highest esteem.[15]

Indians of all ages were great gamblers. Among the gambling games played was the hand game, a simple guessing game involving the hiding of small objects in the hand and guessing which hand held which object. A more sophisticated form of the hand game was the moccasin game, which was played on a blanket by several persons at once. Four moccasins, tokens, and scoring sticks were used. A great pretense was made of hiding tokens under one or more of the moccasins, and the opposing team tried to correctly identify their location. Many forms of dice were popular. The game equipment usually consisted of a bowl and several unique circular counters (dice) made of the cross section of animal rib. These were usually colored on one side and left white on the other. One or two might be inscribed on the white side with the picture of a horse's head, turtle, or owl. The bowl was held with the counters in it, shaken to mix them, and flipped onto a blanket or animal skin. The scoring followed a rubric depending on the number and distribution of face-up sides. As an example:

All of a similar color except 2	1 point
All of a similar color except 1	3 points
All of a similar color except turtle	5 points
All of a similar color	8 points
All of a similar color except horse	10 points

Scoring and winning, of course, varied with the way individuals played the game, and beans, sticks, or stones may have been used as score counters. Games pieces and other paraphernalia could be made of many materials including deer horn, colored stones, or wood. The plum stones of fruit were often employed, and these were sometimes carved to represent objects from the Indian's everyday surroundings, such as a canoe, dog, or man.[16]

Marriage

In many cultures, marriage between persons who were too closely related by blood usually fell under an incest taboo. Parallel cousins were not generally considered appropriate marriage partners in most unilineal societies, while the cross cousin was the preferred potential spouse even though the two relationships were often no further separated in terns of genetics. While the "mother's brother's daughter" might be the symbolically perfect cross cousin marriage partner for a man in a matrilineal society, the offspring of any man having the relationship of "brother" to one's mother would fall into this classification, even if he did not share the same discrete pair of birth parents. In a patrilineal society, following a similar paradigm, a "father's sister's daughter" would have the same preferred status.

Iroquois men generally deferred marriage until they were in their mid-twenties in order that they might become accustomed to the hardships of the hunt and the warpath. The time of his marriage was generally decided by his mother. When she considered that her son was ready, she would look around for an appropriate woman as a candidate. A suitable bride had to exhibit a good disposition and mild temperament. She might be of any age, even an older widow, but most couples were of an approximately equal age. A negotiation between the mothers of the couple would then take place and an agreement reached. Sometimes the tribal elders would be consulted at this point, but the fathers would never interfere. The fathers considered marriage arrangements the prerogative of the mothers and to interfere would bring public disapproval on them.[17]

Although many marriages were arranged by Indian parents, the parties concerned do not appear to have been forced to marry without their own consent. Promiscuity among teenagers was common,[18] and among some tribes the girls were not urged to marry at an early age "for they are permitted as many trial marriages as they wish."[19] The only social barrier to premarital intercourse was pregnancy, which might make it difficult to attract a high-ranking husband.[20] Nonetheless, there was a formal courtship procedure that was dictated by tribal traditions. These customs seem to have changed from tribe to tribe, but they usually involved the giving and receiving of presents. It was customary upon the announcement of an impending marriage for the female relations of the groom to bring gifts to the female relations of the intended bride. Afterward, the groom's female relations would return the compliment. The gifts often included beads or baskets of meal.

Among the Algonquians, a prospective husband presented a tumpline halter, a kettle, and a fire log to his intended. The symbolism of these gifts was based in practical considerations and represented very little in the way of romance. The woman's acceptance of these gifts signified her acceptance of her role as a wife. The tumpline, worn across the forehead and used to help support loads carried on the back, showed that she would carry; the kettle, that she would cook; and the fire log, that she would not only provide the firewood, but would do everything else required to establish a household. She was also expected to cultivate the fields, help to carry home game from the hunt, transport the bark sheets used to make wigwams and shelters, and to make and repair moccasins and other items of clothing.[21]

The woman gave her intended husband only a bag of Indian tobacco and sweet sumac leaves. As Indian men almost always had a pipe in their mouths or hands, the tobacco may have signified their position as husband. An observer noted, "the men glory in their idleness." Certainly the prospective husband's duties were limited "save for hunting, fishing, and war."[22] The men seemed to "despise the value of time; and this has appeared so constant a trait...that it might be regarded as the probable effect of a luxurious effeminacy," which was "the first impression made upon strangers from the Old World."[23]

On the day of the wedding, the bride was escorted to the marriage dwelling with great ceremony where she was received by her new husband and his relations. Thereafter, the couple was left alone, and a great feast was celebrated. Among the Algonquians, the husband was also required to build and repair the initial family dwelling, while among the Iroquoian nations he moved into an established dwelling with his wife's relations, and it is unclear whether or not he was required to help them in maintaining it.

Daily Life of an Iroquois Wife

In the Native American world there was a generally fair division of labor between men and women. Men attended to the more strenuous and dangerous duties of life because of their physical strength and freedom from the burden of child rearing and nursing. He cleared the land; felled the trees; built and repaired the communal shelters; made the canoes and all the hunting, trapping, and fishing gear; and fought the wars. He left the management of the home and village to his wife and the women of her lineage and listened to their advice in matters of war, peace, and leadership.

In the midst of the French and Indian War (1758), 15-year-old Mary Jemison was captured by the Shawnee near Gettysburg, Pennsylvania. Shortly thereafter she was traded to a Seneca family and adopted into their clan. In the first year of her adoption she was married to a Delaware warrior who was living among the Seneca. One year later her first son died almost immediately after birth. In the fourth year of her captivity she had a second child, Thomas. Although free to return to her white community at the end of the war, she chose to spend the rest of her life as an Indian wife living in an Iroquois village. Her description of the daily labors of the women in this village is detailed and interesting. It is even more important because the Iroquois women, themselves, left no written records of their daily lives.

I...had become so far accustomed to their mode of living, habits and dispositions, that my anxiety to get away, to be set at liberty and leave them, had almost subsided. With them was my home; my family was there, and there I had many friends to whom I was warmly attached...

Our labor was not severe; and that of one year was exactly similar, in almost every respect to that of the others without that endless variety that is to be observed in the common labor of white people. Notwithstanding that Indian women have all the fuel and bread to procure, and the cooking to perform, their task is probably not harder than that of white women, who have those articles provided for them; and their cares certainly are not half as numerous nor as great. In the summer season, we planted, tended and harvested our corn, and generally had all our children with us; but had no master to oversee or drive us, so that we could work as leisurely as we pleased. We had no ploughs... but performed the whole process of planting and hoeing with a small tool that resembled, in some respects, a hoe with a short handle.

Our cooking consisted in pounding our corn into samp or hominy, boiling the hominy, making now and then a cake and baking it in the ashes, and boiling or roasting our venison. As our cooking and eating utensils consisted of a hominy block [mortar] and pestle, a small kettle, a knife or two, and a few vessels of bark or wood, it required but little time to keep them in order for use... In the season of hunting, it was our business, in addition to our cooking, to bring home the game that was taken by the Indians, dress it, and carefully preserve the edible meat, and prepare or dress the skins... One thing only marred my happiness... and that was the recollection that I had once had tender parents, and a home that I loved. Aside from that consideration... I should have been contented in my situation.[24]

Alternative Marriages

Polygamy was common among many tribes with an Algonquian man sometimes marrying several or all the sisters in a family, "a custom based on the notion that sisters get along better with each other than with strangers." Nonetheless, the Algonquians also recognized two types of wives, one of whom was subservient to the other. It was into this class that many white women captives were placed if they married a native warrior. In some tribes, consanguity was scrupulously regarded. One did not marry a relative or a member of one's own clan. However, a widower might marry his dead wife's sister or some other female relation. This person might be chosen for him by the clan matrons, and the process insured that the children of the previous marriage would be brought up in the clan tradition. A widow might be required to do the same thing with regard to her dead husband's brothers. However, if she had no children and was still young, she might be allowed to seek a husband elsewhere.[25]

It would be a mistake to think that these concepts concerning matrimony were hard and fast rules. Even within a single clan there were many variations. Among the Iroquois, for instance, both polygamy and polyandry (many husbands for one woman) were practiced. Among some nations men had wives at every place where they hunted, yet there were some clans that recognized marriages only among themselves. Divorce was accomplished in different ways. Couples might agree to stay together only as long as they were happy; others agreed to separate only for good cause. A man who abandoned his wife might have to face retaliation by her rela- tions, and a woman who left her husband for another man without her husband's consent and the approbation of the clan matrons could "have a bad time of it." In this regard the clan matrons often served in place of a divorce court, deciding if the cause warranted the separation.[26]

Adultery among some nations, as opposed to promiscuity, merited ex- treme punishment. Jealousy not only disturbed the peace of the family but also sent shudders of unrest throughout the clan. A disgraced hus- band might cut off the nose of his straying wife, while two husbands might agree to exchange wives "to increase their happiness." The women of the Iroquois, Mahican, and Shawnee nations were reported to be exces- sively jealous. "When a woman discovers that her husband loves another, her rival had better beware; especially as the faithless husband dare not defend her in any way without dishonor."[27] Even among the Algonquian a woman's subordination to her husband was not complete. She could call on her brothers and other male relations to protect her, and she could leave her husband at any point in their relationship.

Among most tribes open promiscuity apparently ended with marriage, but some women never married, not because of a lack of husband- making material, but because they chose to remain unattached. A class of unmarried women known as *Ickoue ne Kioussa,* or Hunting Women, argued, according to European observers, that they could not endure the conjugal subordination of men and that they were incapable of bringing up children. These women were too impatient to spend winters alone in the village while the men went out to hunt. Some of them accompanied the hunters, sleeping with them or otherwise expressing their sexual freedom. It was from this facet of their behavior that they obtained their sobriquet. These sexual favors were ostensibly extended to European hunters and traders as well with equal freedom from attachment. These women did not solicit customers, as did European prostitutes, but they did make a general agreement to do the work expected of an Algonquian wife. European observers were hard pressed to understand the nature of these relationships. The Jesuits, in particular, incorrectly attributed them to prostitution, lewdness, and temporary marriages. The appeal of such relationships may have been due to an imbalance in the number of avail- able men. As a result of a generation of warfare with the Iroquois, the proportion of women to men among their enemies may have reached as high as four to one.

This behavior and the general acceptance of polygamy were particu- lar targets of the Jesuit missionaries, whose battles with their converts seemingly increased in proportion to the number of French coureurs de bois living among the Indians. In the 1670s, the Jesuits were successful at Michilimackinac in having a number of Algonquian men put aside all but their first wife, but this simply increased the number of women cohabitating with Frenchmen. Furthermore, in the 1690s, the French government abandoned many of its western posts and created a sudden rise in interracial marriages—according to the Algonquian custom and lacking solemnization by the missionaries. By this means, the French coureurs de bois and voyageurs hoped to establish family ties that would ensure their continued safe access to furs through their Indian relatives.[28]

Antonine de la Moth, Sieur de Cadillac and governor of the French post at Detroit, actively promoted marriages between soldiers and native women. He explained, "Marriages of this kind will strengthen the friendship of the tribes, as the alliances of the Romans perpetuated peace with the Sabine through the intervention of the women whom the former had taken from the other." Although the Jesuits fumed at the suggestion, the Indians seemingly saw these relationships in a similar light, especially because the women seemed more than willing.[29] Louis-Armand, Baron de Lahontan, who spent a good deal of time among the Algonquian-speaking tribes, regarded all such talk of women's personal choice in matters of marriage and intercourse an excuse for sexual lewdness and promiscuity, but he did note that such women were not censured by their parents or others in authority in their communities. The children that these women bore were considered legitimate issue and members in good standing of their mothers' clan.[30]

The Algonquian sense of an unmarried woman's autonomy over her own body appears to have been absolute, and her family seems to have been more interested in her choice of a permanent partner than in any casual liaisons. Marriage created an alliance between families that concerned a wider group of people than just the two marriage partners, and it established kinship relationships and obligations that demanded a response to calls for aid, protection, and blood revenge.

It has been pointed out that "all human societies attempt to control human sexual behavior; and if heterosexual behavioral patterns are everywhere regarded by the majority as the normal, the desirable, the ideal, human cultures must also deal with at least one other human potential— homosexuality." Some societies permit and accept homosexuality among men, women, or both genders. Others hide, deny, or even persecute those that practice same-gender sex. Some native cultures regarded homosexuals as deviant or humorous. Others permitted homosexuals to express themselves openly, accepted the relationships formed between same-gender partners, and, at times, allowed homosexuals to rise to important social positions. Most parents attributed homosexual tendencies in their children to the action of spirits or dreams during pregnancy, and they took no steps to alter the sexual orientation of their children.[31]

Mixed Race Persons

Samuel de Champlain, while serving as governor, reportedly proposed a policy of intermarriage between young Frenchmen and the daughters of the Algonquians. The Indian nations, deprived of their young men through disease and intertribal warfare, were eager to have their widows and daughters married off to Frenchmen who could guarantee their supply of European goods and weapons. Moreover, the French Crown was suspicious of sending its citizens to the New World and hoped that intermarriage with the indigenous population would produce a corps of on-the-spot Frenchmen to populate its colony. Indian wives taught their European husbands, and later their mixed race children, the ways of the forests, and the Frenchmen advanced a paternalistic relationship between himself and his new-found kinship group.

Not wholly European nor wholly Native American, the children of these unions often rose to great power, derived from ability, persuasion, and kinship, but generally not from hereditary authority. Through marriage the European trader gained entry to the Indian kinship group and became directly related to those with whom he did business, and his children often took an active role in their father's business by being absorbed into their mother's clan. The children of Indian men with white women were endowed with the same status as their mother, be she slave, prisoner, or adoptee, but most found the Indians kinder to their predicament than were whites. The vast majority of mixed race persons who rose to prominence in the native community had Indian mothers.

Sexual relations between native women and Frenchmen created a great deal of unease among the Jesuits and the officials of government, but the priests considered marriage between the parties only a partial solution. They considered all mixed race offspring of unmarried couples *metis batards*, even if they were married according to Indian rites. Those that were married under the auspices of the Church were considered *metis legitimes.* The Jesuits noted that the *metis batards* invariably followed the Indian way of life and were loyal to their mother's tribe, while the *metis legitimes* became French in their outlook, culture, and loyalty. "Metis batards may have become Indian, and metis legitimes French, but both, nonetheless, represented significant ties between the two peoples…Priests and officials in France feared betrayal and corruption, but local commanders realized that such connections could be useful."[32]

One of these mixed race children was Charles Langlade, born to a French trader at Michchilimackinac named Augustin de Moras (known as Langlade) and an Ottawa woman known as Domitilde. Charles' mother was the daughter of an Ottawa chief named LaFourche by the French. As a young man, Charles first gained a military reputation when his maternal uncle included him in a war party sent against the Chickasaw. Here he was successful, winning the title Aukewingeketawso, or defender. Augustin de Moras thereafter purchased a French commission for his son, and Charles became a cadet. In 1748, the young man became involved in a dispute with a pro-British Miami chief known as La Demoiselle. Blood was spilled on both sides, and Charles vowed revenge. Around

1750, he married an Ottawa woman named Agathe, and they had a son. In 1752, Charles made friends with the Ottawa warrior, Pontiac, and the two men led a raid against the Miami at Pickawillany in the Ohio Valley with 250 Ottawa and Chippewa warriors. The village was surprised, and LaDemoiselle and an English trader were captured, killed, and eaten by the warriors. The raid brought high praise to both leaders from among the Indians.

Charles Langlade was made Indian Agent by Governor Duquesne, but he realized that his marriage to an Ottawa women might hold back his career among his father's people. Therefore, he left Agathe, and in 1754 he married Catherine Bourassa of Montreal whose father was a well-to-do trader at Michchilimackinac. His new wife was remarkably beautiful, but ironically she was terribly frightened of Indians. Nonetheless, the new couple had two children, Charlotte (born 1756) and Louise (born 1758). Although not in overall command, Charles Langlade was generally given credit for the success of the Native American attack on Edward Braddock's column of redcoats and Virginia militia at the Monongahela River in 1755. After the French and Indian War, and during the American Revolution, he served the British as an Indian Agent and native contingent commander.

Daniel and Chabert Joncaire were the sons of Chabert Joncaire (Jonquiere), a French trader adopted into the Seneca nation, and his native wife. Through his intercession with his Indian relations, in 1720 the elder Joncaire built a trading post near the present site of Fort Niagara were the Niagara River empties into Lake Ontario. The French made Niagara a fortified outpost in 1726. Joncaire became the official portage master controlling all the goods and furs that passed through the 17-mile long trail around Niagara Falls. Joncaire employed hundreds of his Indian kinsmen to help carry the cargo up and down the escarpment at present-day Lewiston, New York.

Using both the influence of their father and the kinship ties of their mother, Daniel and Chabert Joncaire (the sons) became greatly successful in persuading the Seneca to remain neutral to British overtures. Chabert Joncaire, the younger, accompanied Captain Pierre Joseph de Celeron on his expedition through the heart of the Northeast woodlands on a tour of inspection of the French king's land claims in the Ohio River valley during 1749. He was a good guide and interpreter and had become an important intermediary between the French and the Indians. Celeron carried a series of lead plates engraved as a token of the renewal of French possession of all the lands drained by the Ohio. These he buried at strategic locations as proof of his monarch's claim. Oddly, Celeron and Joncaire passed through the point where the Allegheny and Monongahela rivers join the Ohio without laying claim to the spot. This is the present location of Pittsburgh (Fort Dusquesne/Fort Pitt), the occupation of which was the proximate cause of the Seven Year's War and the location of the worst defeat of a British colonial army by Native American forces in history (Braddock's defeat, 1755).[33]

Within the Ohio watershed there were literally thousands of Native American residents who, despite the lead plates and French claims of ownership, knew precisely to whom the land belonged. It was Indian land, and they had no intention of giving it up. Celeron found that he could only request the obedience of these tribes that the government had ordered him to command, and he dared not evict the British traders that he found in the Ohio country without their support. Partly for this reason the Indians that he encountered were suspicious of him. Joncaire better understood Indian psychology than Celeron. He awarded medals to the chiefs, gave them sizable presents to distribute among their people, and attempted to mediate some of their outstanding quarrels. This policy of reconciliation proved more successful than Celeron's threats and demands for submission.

During the 1750s, both Joncaire brothers, Daniel and Chabert, moved throughout the Indian nations doing everything in their power to convince the Seneca to reopen their long-standing enmity with the Catawba tribes of South Carolina in order to keep the English frontier settlements in turmoil with war parties going back and forth on the Warrior's Trail. Under these circumstances unfortunate accidents with whites, who they might contact en route, were bound to occur, and the Joncaire's hoped that the situation might swiftly degenerate into an English–Iroquois war. Yet, the Iroquois Council considered the Chabert's double-tongued and not to be trusted, and the Iroquois–Catawba conflict was avoided.

Daniel Chabert, reporting to the French authorities in 1751, wrote, "Though we seem to be holding our own, or even gaining, in the immediate Iroquois country, such is not the case on the Ohio. Because of pressure we have brought to bear, the Delawares have now moved away from our immediate reach and deep into the Ohio country, close to their brother tribes, the Shawnee and Miami. Almost all of the Ohio Indians are showing strong affection for the English who sell them goods at low rates, make ample gifts and give them gunpowder for just asking."[34]

Old Belt, a powerful war chief of the Chenussio Seneca who had stirred his warriors against the English, regretted his former attitude in 1759 and blamed the influence of the Joncaire brothers for his pro-French sympathies when he became allied with the English. "I have wiped the French sand from my eyes and have said farewell to the brothers Joncaire, who were the ones who filled my eyes with sand and plugged my ears....Now the eyes are clear and see well and the ears are unplugged and hear everything."[35]

Mixed race men, such as Charles Langlade and the Joncaire brothers, maintained their status as clan members as they moved among the Native Americans speaking at their councils and leading their war parties. Among the Europeans they were often looked down upon as mere "half-breeds" who were useful in dealing with the Indians but unsuited for proper society. Ultimately, a number of mixed race persons from the Northeast woodlands would form a separate people, the Metis, who mediated between the French and the Algonquians in the 18th century and who would challenge the British government of Canada in the 19th century. Chief among these was Louis Reale, a member of the Canadian Parliament, who led a revolt of the Metis people in the 1830s.[36]

Notes

1. Quoted in Ronald Dale Karr, ed., *Indian New England, 1524–1674: A Compendium of Eyewitness Accounts of Native American Life* (Pepperell, MA: Branch Line Press, 1999), 62.

2. Allen W. Eckert, *Wilderness Empire* (Toronto: Bantam Books, 1980), 19.

3. Quoted in Karr, 64.

4. John Dunn Hunter, *Birth, Nursing, and Education of Infants: Education and Amusements of Youth* (London: Longman, Hurst, Rees, Orme, Brown, and Green, 1824), 267.

5. Henry Rowe Schoolcraft, *Algic Researcher, North American Indian Folktales and Legends* (Minneola: Dover Publications, 1999; reprint of the 1839 edition), xxxv–xxxvi.

6. For instance, Bonin had no first hand knowledge of the "painless" births experienced by Indian women. Men, especially white men, were not allowed to be present. He also fails to specifically detail the correction, or lack thereof, of male children leaving the reader to assume that male children went without correction of any sort.

7. Since Bonin's memoir was translated from French to English, the author has changed the term "cabin" to "dwelling" in an effort to maintain an authentic image of village life.

8. Andrew Gallup, ed., *Memoir of a French and Indian War Soldier, Jolicoeur Charles Bonin* (Bowie, MD: Heritage Books, Inc., 1993), 221–222.

9. Hunter, 264.

10. Louise S. Spindler, "Women in Menomini [sic] Culture," in *The North American Indians, A Sourcebook*, ed., Roger C. Owen (Toronto: Collier-Macmillan Limited, 1971), 598.

11. Spindler, 600.

12. Spindler, 601.

13. Quoted in Karr, 60.

14. Hunter, 266.

15. Hunter, 266.

16. See Robert E. Ritzenthaler and Pat Ritzenthaler, *The Woodland Indians of the Western Great Lakes* (Garden City, NY: The Natural History Press, 1970), 117–126.

17. Loomis Havemeyer, *Ethnography* (Boston: Ginn and Company, 1929), 298.

18. C. Keith Wilbur, *The Woodland Indians, An Illustrated Account of the Lifestyles of America's First Inhabitants* (Guilford, CT: The Globe Pequot Press, 1995), 65.

19. Gallup, ed., 220.

20. Richard White, *The Middle Ground, Indians, Empires, and Republics in the Great Lakes Region, 1650–1815* (New York: Cambridge University Press, 1991), 63.

21. Gallup, ed., 221–222.

22. Gallup, ed., 222.

23. Schoolcraft, xxi.

24. James E. Seaver, *A Narrative of the Life of Mrs. Mary Jemison* (Syracuse, NY: Syracuse University Press, 1990), 30–34. Mary Jemison's narrative was given verbatim to Seaver in 1823 and first published by him in 1824.

25. Gallup, ed., 219.

26. Gallup, ed., 219.

27. Gallup, ed., 220.

28. White, 68.

29. White, 69.

30. White, 63–64.

31. See George Devereux, "Homosexuality Among the Mohave," in Owen, ed., 409.

32. White, 215.

33. Eckert, 139.

34. Eckert, 196–197.

35. Eckert, 642.

36. Eckert, 123.

5

A World Wrought from Nature

A well-integrated culture is one in which the various parts fit neatly together and serve to reinforce one another.[1]

—Philip K. Bock, anthropologist

Material Culture

Although they spoke different languages, the woodland environment in which the Indians of the Northeast lived caused their material cultures to be quite similar. While local conditions varied, the resources on a regional level were generally comparable. Stone, bone, bark, reeds, and animal hides were used as utilitarian materials, and similar sets of foods, dyes, and medicines were extracted from plants, roots, and barks. It was the teaching among many tribes that every tree, bush, or plant had a use, but not every Indian nation possessed the same repository of knowledge concerning these materials. Available resources greatly effected the local material culture. Some tribes, for instance, were destitute of birch bark for making light-weight canoes and resorted to heavier tree barks, such as red elm or bitternut hickory. Others fashioned dug-out vessels that were stable and strong from whole logs. Many tribes lived within convenient traveling distance of the ocean or salt-water bays where whales, clams, oysters, and other marine life were basic foods, while others relied on fresh water aquatic species from marshes and lakes. Geography, the season of the year, and chance greatly affected the daily menu.

Native American knowledge of herbal medicines was remarkable, but not all Indians had equally accessible or identical woodland pharmacopoeias. Indian remedies were largely individual, rather than universal, and they were learned one or two at a time from the observation of their interactions in the environment. In addition to vegetable substances believed to have an effect when taken internally or when applied externally, it was widely believed that a large number of substances had their effect simply by their presence nearby or their appearance, even in the absence of actual contact.[2]

Tools
Throughout the region, Indian weapons and tools were essentially the same: the knife, axe, and adz of stone; the hoe, awl, and needle of bone; the fire whorl (or flint and steel); the grinding stone; the bow and arrow; the spear; the war club; and the tomahawk. Although some native copper and meteoric iron were available, the Indians were essentially a stone-age people until metal objects were introduced from Europe. This should not be seen as a major disadvantage to the development of their culture, however.

Glassy stones (lithics) composed of igneous materials such as chert, rhyolite, obsidian (volcanic glass), and flint leave a razor sharp edge when fractured by a sharp blow. A properly fractured stone can be surgically sharp. Moreover, the stone blanks produced thereby can be further shaped or sharpened by applying pressure to the edges, usually with a deer antler or other hard organic tool. The process is one that can be carried out with remarkable precision to form cutting edges, scrapers, knives, axe and adze heads, and projectile points for use on spears and arrows. The Iroquoian name for flint *(tawiskaron)* has the same root as the word for "winter ice," which could be fractured in a similar manner. Oddly, the Mohawk, known as the People of the Flint, lived in an area of New York where sources of flint were scarce, and the name may suggest a different geographical origin for the tribe.

Although limited quantities of appropriate geological materials might be found almost anywhere, significant deposits—left behind by the scraping action of the great ice sheets of 25,000 and 50,000 years ago, respectively—were widely dispersed throughout the Northeast woodlands region. The consequences of these ice sheets can be seen in topographical examples, such as New York's twin-tailed Long Island and Massachusetts' Cape Cod. Often, appropriate stones were found in the outwash of rivers and streams or along the seashores very far from their original place of deposition. A major geological formation rich in chert existed along the Niagara escarpment that ran south of Lakes Ontario and Erie through western New York and Pennsylvania. This passed through the territory of the Seneca, the Erie, and the Attiwandaronk (Neutrals). Another source of chert and flint ran from Gettysburg, Pennsylvania to South Mountain in Maryland through Susquehannock and Delaware lands.

Certain tribes exchanged lithic (stone) materials through broad-based trade networks focused on sources as far away as Michigan and Minnesota. Archeological evidence of trade items brought into New England included mica and quartz crystals from the Carolinas, galena from Missouri, flint from Illinois, obsidian from the Rockies, and copper from the Great Lakes. The woodland nations resident in Kentucky, Tennessee, and the Ohio Valley also seem to have participated in these exchanges. The volume of the trade items found suggests a wide-spread and vigorous intertribal trading system. The exchange of ideas that paralleled this trade also provided a valuable mechanism for cultural development with the pattern of daily existence trending toward a more sedentary life and a more extensive agriculture. Reciprocal trade was a mechanism by which a culture with its common language, artifacts, and rituals might be spread throughout the Northeast woodlands in the absence of warfare.

It is obvious from available evidence that there was a major economic flow of lithic material from the western interior of the Great Lakes to the Atlantic coastal plain. Moreover, dozens of obsidian projectile points from the coastal mountains of the Pacific Northwest have been found as far east as New York and as far south as Florida. The extensive distribution of exotic lithic materials foreign to the place of their origin attests to the existence of such networks.

On the French River north of Lake Huron was a stretch of rapids and falls known as the Sault de Calumets where the Indians looked for stones that could be made into tobacco pipe bowls. Red stones were considered the most sacred of all those available for making the calumet. These materials were traded by both the Potawatomi (People of the Sacred Fire) and the Mascouten (People of the Fire) who were noted for dealing in these materials. The red pipestone—a soft, reddish, iron-rich form of a mineral known as Catlinite—was eroded from underground sources in Minnesota, but it could also be found in Tennessee. Bluestone (blue-green Catlinite) generally came from the Appalachian mountains. A salmon alabaster pipestone shaded from pink to white could be found in quarries in southern Manitoba. Black pipestone, actually a marbled white on black, came from South Dakota and was widely used by Plains Tribes for ceremonial pipes.

Task-specific groups of collectors among the Indian tribes might periodically range beyond their home territories in search of a supply of appropriate lithic materials. Once found, the raw materials were shaped into rough blanks at the quarry site and taken to camps where the flint knappers probably stayed while the quarrying took place. This step eliminated the need to carry a heavy weight of waste stone from the region. It also seems certain that a significant number of blanks, unfinished blades, and projectile points were cached in pits for future use both near the site of the deposit and in home territories so that they would not interfere with the casual mobility of the tribe.

Indians quickly learned to transfer some of their bow and arrow technology to other purposes. One of the advanced uses of small bows was as a fire whorl or as a reciprocating drill. When used as a fire whorl, a bow string of thick leather was wrapped once around a fire stick that was drilled into a wooden base made of hard wood. The friction quickly produced smoke and coals for making fire. Bow drills used hard, quartz points on similar shafts to bore out even the hardest materials. Bows could also be made into saws when strung with wet rawhide encrusted with quartz sand. These tools allowed soft stones to be cut into slabs and shapes in preparation for boring. Polishing could be done with an abrasive grit, and a wet animal hide, or raw hide, could be wrapped around a stick and used with crushed white quartz to make grooves in stone celts or to shape wooden handles. Fine grits of sand progressively brought the surface to a fine smoothness and a rubbing with animal fat or grease gave the item a polished finished. The efficiency of these methods, as attested to by finely crafted calumet pipes and effigy figures, was remarkable.

Shelter   Although the form of Iroquoian housing was significantly different from that of their Algonquian neighbors, the forest materials used in their construction were essentially the same. Because the trunks of trees from virgin forests were too large to handle with stone age tools, the Indians harvested their structural materials from second growth forests, such as clearings where the older trees had been girdled or killed by fire. Here, small diameter trees grew in bunches with tall straight trunks that were more easily cut into convenient lengths. Those used for longhouses by the Iroquois were somewhat more substantial than the supple saplings used by the Algonquians to build their wigwams *(we-gi-was)*. The single-family Algonquian structures were made of bark supported on a framework of saplings and small tree trunks sunk into the ground and bent over into a dome with a door opening and a smoke hole. The bark coverings could be stripped and carried to the next seasonal campground.

Woodlands Indians eschewed the use of animal skin abodes, such as the Buffalo-skin tepees of the Great Plains or the seal-skin homes of the sub-arctic tribes. Both Algonquians and Iroquoians preferred the more efficient bark, branch, or reed mat coverings. Trees whose bark could be peeled into large sheets were preferred because big sheets made the job easier, but these needed to be harvested in the spring when the bark was easily peeled away. The sheets were either flattened or held to shape by weights that kept them from curling uncontrollably while they dried. When it was available the Iroquois favored elm bark for sheathing their longhouses because it dried very hard and flat much like a piece of modern plywood. They usually lashed the sheets to the framework with their natural furrows running horizontally using twisted or braided cords made from water-soaked strips of basswood or hickory bark, which shrink and become tighter as it dried.

This illustration from an antique textbook shows a cutaway of the structure of a wigwam, or *we-gi-was*. These were often circular or oval in floor plan with a domed roof of bark or reed mats supported by a skeleton of saplings lashed together with plant fiber or vines.

A contemporary observer, Jesuit Father Jean de Brebeuf, noted of longhouses, "I cannot better express the fashion of [these] dwellings than to compare them to bowers or garden arbors—some of which, in place of branches and vegetation, are covered with cedar bark, some other with ash, elm, fir, or spruce bark; and although the cedar bark is best, according to common opinion and usage, there is, nevertheless, this inconvenience, that they are most susceptible to fire as matches." Longhouses were approximately 20-feet wide and 20-feet high regardless of their length, which ranged between 30 and 300 feet. Each had a center aisle 10-feet wide with family compartments or cubicles on either side. The aisle was a common space used for cooking. The roof was rounded rather than peaked, and smoke holes were left open along the ridge-line. The ends were left either slightly rounded or flat, and they could be added to if the clan grew.[3]

William Bradford has left the following description of the Algonquian wigwam:

The homes were made with long young sapling trees, bended and both ends stuck into the ground. They were made round, like unto an arbor, and covered down to the ground with thick and well wrought mats, and the door was not over a yard high, made of a mat to open. The chimney was a wide open hole in the top, for which they had a mat to cover it closed when they pleased. One might stand and

The conic Algonquian teepee (right) was only one of many forms of temporary family shelters. In 1788, Thomas Davies painted this picture of an Indian family encamped opposite the city of Quebec that also shows light-weight bark canoes and adult and children's clothing.

go upright in them. In the midst of them were four little trenches knocked into the ground, and small sticks laid over, on which they hung their pots, and what they had to seethe. Round about the fire they lay on mats, which are their beds. The house were double matted, for as they were matted without, so were they within, with newer and fairer mats.[4]

The Big House Among the more sedentary Algonquians, and the Delaware especially, was found a permanent village structure, similar to the Iroquois longhouse, that was used as a council house. Unlike the common longhouse, the structure always had a center post. Called the Big House in Algonquian, the structure varied in size, but 30 feet by 50 feet was considered an average size. Here the elders met to discuss policy and make decisions concerning village or tribal matters.

Among the Delaware, the Big House also reflected a deeper significance because the structure itself was said to reflect the universe. In the late 19th century, Chief Joseph Montour left an Indian impression of the traditions embodied in the Big House. "The Big House stands for the Universe; its floor, the earth; its four walls, the four quarters [directions or winds]; its vault, the sky dome, atop which resides the Creator in his indefinable supremacy." The center post that represented "the staff of the Great Spirit with its foot upon the earth, its pinnacle reaching to the hand of the Supreme Deity." The Delaware recognized three clans or totems: Turtle, Turkey, and Wolf. These were assigned appropriate places on the floor. The Big House had two doorways, the eastern door pointing to the sunrise and the western door to the sunset. The north and south walls represent the horizon, and the roof represents the visible sky. The center post had two faces carved on it, one facing east and the other west. These represented the creator. Twelve additional faces were carved on the posts supporting the north and south walls. In addition there were four posts framing the east and west doorways.[5]

A Big House Ceremony was held annually among the Delaware. During the 12-day ceremony the people gathered periodically, the women on the north and the men on the south. Absolute celibacy was practiced during this period because the participants were supposed to keep a clear frame of mind. The primary purposes of the celebration were to thank the creator and his principal agents and to remind the people that the spirit powers were realities.

The Sweat Lodge Every village had a structure known as a sweat lodge. This was a squat structure built somewhat like a wigwam. The skeleton was made of 12 sapling uprights bent over and tied in the center. These were covered with sheets of bark that were themselves often covered over with an outer layer of blankets or skins when in use. A fire was built at the entrance and stones were heated therein. The hot stones were brought into the lodge, and water was thrown on them. The steam produced was thought to purify all those who entered and stayed for the duration of the sweat lodge ritual. During the ceremony, the participants sang and prayed. An entire buckskin, complete with head and antlers, was hung on a pole outside while the lodge was being used.

There were always two sweat lodges placed at opposite ends of the village—one for the males and one for the females. These were usually near a stream or other source of clean water. Well or ill, most Indians bathed daily and visited the sweat lodge once or twice a week. They also used a visit to the lodge as a cure for various diseases and as a general preparation for some great undertaking or conference. The use of the lodge was a community matter, and a village crier went about announcing when all was ready. Nonetheless, it was unusual for more than a dozen people to be in a sweat lodge at one time. Some participants brought their own herbs and potions to place on the hot rocks as a personal cure.[6]

Fire In the metaphorical speech of the Indians, to establish a fire at a site was to identify it as one's own, and to let a fire go out or to put it out was to extinguish that claim. An annual ceremonial rekindling of a fire at the winter solstice reasserted the claim of ownership. This was a common concept shared by many pre-industrial peoples. From a practical point of view, however, the Indians had neither the manpower nor the tool technology, as did Europeans, to put up hundreds of cubic feet of firewood just to maintain a blasting fire. Indians generally collected available deadfall for use as firewood and stacked the branches in or near their shelters. Europeans sometimes called this fuel *squaw wood* because Indian women could be seen coming in from the edges of the forests with bundles of sticks on their backs supported by the ubiquitous tumpline. When the deadfall and available underbrush were used up, the village or camp was moved to an area with better resources.

The Iroquois built many small fires in their longhouses rather than one great raging furnace in order to conserve this resource, and the Algonquians rarely had more than one fire burning in their wigwams, even in the severe cold of winter. Both the wigwam and the teepee were relatively easy to heat. Firewood was often arranged like the spokes of a wagon wheel with one end of each stick in the burning center of the fire. Obtaining fuel and tending the fire was women's work, and it was not unusual for an elderly woman to sit beside the fire throughout the night feeding the sticks into the embers alternately inch-by-inch while the rest of the family slept.

The introduction of metal hatchets and axes relieved the shortage of deadfall firewood somewhat, but it created a task—chopping firewood—that was not a normal part of the Native American work regimen. Moreover, prior to the introduction of flint and steel to create a spark, fires were commonly started by the friction of a fire whorl. One generally flat stick was placed upon the ground and another—round and long like a dowel—was drilled into it under downward pressure with the back and forth motion of a bow-like instrument, the leather cord of which was wrapped about the dowel. The effect of the friction was the almost instantaneous production of masses of smoke. If appropriate hardwoods were used, a small pile of red hot embers could be produced. When added to properly prepared kindling, a flame might be coaxed from these tiny points of light. The Indians were practical people, and fires were most often rekindled by borrowing embers from a neighbor.

Sparks could also be struck by banging two stones together. John Brereton, sailing the coast of New England in 1602, noticed that many Indians carried "a purse of tanned leather, a mineral stone and a flat emery stone, tied fast to the end of a little stick. Gently he striketh upon the mineral stone, and within a strike or two, a spark falleth upon a piece of touchwood, and with the least spark, he maketh the fire." The identity of the stones used by these Indians is uncertain, but the "mineral" and "emery" stones may have been forms of quartz, iron pyrite, or meteoric iron, which were used in such a manner in Europe in place of flint and steel. A good number of meteoric iron objects have been uncovered in the sub-arctic regions of Canada. Pyrite struck on pyrite could also give a spark, and it was seemingly used by the Beothuk of Newfoundland to produce sparks that would ignite a small pile of bird down. Five Beothuk burials uncovered in the 1990s had pyrite among the grave goods, and fragments of pyrite have been found in a number of house pits at archeological sites in Canada. Such pits were used for storage of grain, dried gourds, projectile points, and other items. Captain Le Jeune described the use of pyrites among the Montagnais in 1634, suggesting that the sparks were caught in the down of the underside of an eagle's thigh. Pyrites were available in abundance in Illinois, Tennessee, and Missouri. The twin metallic crystals were believed to have some magical powers when used with the proper incantations, and their brassy yellow color (Fool's Gold) and usefulness as fire starters may have supported a trade in the material among the tribes.[7]

Hunter-Gatherer At the time of contact, all Indian groups in the Northeast woodlands relied to a large extent on hunting, fishing, and gathering for their food. The Algonquians, in particular, followed a common *transhumant* (seasonal) pattern of land occupation moving between summer and winter residences. Many hunter-gatherer bands lived seasonally within a variety of ecosystems, or traveled to geographically specialized locations to harvest riverine salmon and shad, or to tap the coastal shellfish beds. Throughout the year, they generally harvested available small game from the margins of the woodlands, but they relied on large game animals from the depths of the forests during hunting seasons specified by the clan. Nonetheless, no Indian hunter would bypass a fair shot at a game animal at any time of the year, if it presented itself, unless he was trying to escape detection in enemy territory.

Animal skins provided both furs for trade and the material for clothing. Yet, they needed to be processed chemically if they were not to be consumed by decomposition in a short time. Europeans called the process tanning, and, among whites, the trade of the tanner was men's work. Among the Indians, much of the task of leather-making fell to the women. The men would commonly bring home the eviscerated carcass of the animal, having consumed the tastier internal organs, such as the heart or liver, on the trail. This left the skinning, butchering, and tanning to the women. When the animal was skinned, the long cut that began at the belly was extended down the shoulders, haunches, and legs to provide panels at the corners that could be used to make sleeves with a minimum of sewing. If the skins were meant for the fur trade, all the meat would be scraped from the inner surface, rubbed with deer brains to help fix the leather, and dried on oval hoops. These skins would be bundled for transportation and trade. If meant for use as leather, the skins were scraped and soaked in an alkali combination of water and hard wood ashes, which helped to dissolve the hair on the skin. The skins would be scraped to smoothness and then soaked in a water and oak bark solution. The bark contained a high concentration of the natural chemical tannin, which fixed the leather. Rubbing with deer brains, rinsing with water, and smoothing with bone implements or "soft" stones made the leather pliable and appropriate for clothing. Properly processed deer and elk skin was durable, comfortable, and as soft as velvet.

Animals such as deer, elk, or moose provided skins from which clothing could be fashioned, but other parts of their bodies were useful also.

Deer sinew could be dried and twisted into an extremely strong and resil-
ient thread. For needles, pins, and awls the tiny bones of fish, bear, raccoon, mink, sable, or otter were harvested. Some of these were provided
with natural eyelets for pulling thread, and others naturally formed good
fishhooks. Ribs were used for scrapers and shoulder blades for digging.
The teeth of beaver, designed by nature for cutting, could be mounted in a
wooden handle to form an efficient hand tool for smoothing wood and
hollowing bowls. Antlers were particularly important because they were
dense and hard. Held tightly in the hand of a flint knapper, the tough
antler brought pressure to bear on the chipped edge of flint to form arrowheads, spear points, chisels, and knives. Hafted on a long handle, the antler made an efficient and useful pickax. Harpoons were often pointed with
deer or moose antler.

                   Indian women spent a good deal of time weaving and plait-
Basketry   ing natural materials into useful forms and articles. As early
                  as the 1640s, European observers noted that the Indians used
baskets to store all kinds of food and household supplies. The native peoples of the Northeast woodlands made their baskets of dyed or naturally
colored ash and oak splints, and they sometimes incorporated braided
sweet grasses or dyed porcupine quills into their designs as a means of
decoration. Birch bark and cedar bark containers were also common. The
women plaited small baskets that were hung from their waists to hold
seeds or berries during gathering and large baskets to hold maize or beans
brought in from the fields. "Certain baskets were fine enough, yet loose
enough, to sift flour; others when wet would seal tight as a drum." The
Indians also produced a large hamper that could be used much like a
backpack. The tumpline, or forehead brace, for carrying back-pack loads
was often woven and plaited from animal hair or shredded cedar bark.
Among the Indians this ubiquitous helpmate was used almost exclusively
by women, but the French coureurs de bois and engages adopted them
when packing out large bundles of furs or skins.[8]

The native peoples of New England were known for their beautiful
splint-wood baskets. Yet, there is some evidence that they did not begin
making splint-wood baskets until they learned how to prepare the splints
from Swedish colonists around the Delaware Bay in the 1600s. If this is
true, the new technology moved rapidly among the tribes of the woodlands. In this regard, it may have been the introduction of metal tools that
made the production of thin pliable splints practical. Prior to this infusion
of technology, the natives seem to have made their baskets of coils of plant
fibers or thin vines plaited and sewn together. For this purpose they commonly bundled together willow twigs, sweet grass, or pine needles into
long rolls, but they could also use many other plant materials, including
sumac, cattails, sedges, and corn husks.

While oak splints were valued for their strength and durability, those of
ash lent a silky appearance to a finished basket that was highly desirable.

Indian craft objects were always neat and carefully wrought, and they were often delicately decorated. Geometric designs and careful illustrations of birds, beasts, flowers, and fishes were often incorporated into the structure. Craft materials could be stained with natural dyes. Porcupine quills were a favorite choice for application to footwear and garments. Green stains came from pond scum or the corrosion on native copper, brown from walnut hulls, blues and purples from crushed berries, yellows from clay, black from charred wood, and red from ochre.

The best ash trees for basket making were those that grew most vigorously in the summer months leaving dense growth rings that could be more easily separated from the pithy winter layers. After an appropriate tree was chosen, it was cut down and submerged in a pond or bog for at least one year. Once thoroughly soaked the tree was debarked, scored lengthwise with the grain, and pounded with a wooden mallet along its length to pulverize the porous layers and separate out the splints. If the splints were too thick,they could be split further or drawn down to a uniform thickness using a hatchet or knife blade. Finished splints were used directly or rolled into coils for future use. These were always soaked before weaving, and they could be stained at this point. A star-shaped foundation of crossed splints was laid down, and one-half of one of these was split lengthwise to provide an odd number for weaving in and out. The foundation splints were usually folded over to finish the top of the basket.

The Indians of Connecticut were well-known for the quality of their basket work, which included rectangular, round, and oval containers with and without lids, as well as flat mats and bowls. Nipmuc, Mohegan, Pequot, Niantic, and Wampanoag nations produced a regional form of basket splint with a squared edge in the eastern region of the state, while the Indians of the western region were noted for the beveled edges on their splints. The Abenaki, Micmac, Penobscot, Passamaquoddy, and Iroquois nations all made quality baskets, and they contributed to a commercial basket-making industry that began in the 1800s. Since a well-made splint basket can last a very long time if kept dry and properly used, it is almost impossible to distinguish native basketry from the traditional and commercial periods of production without resorting to destructive testing.

Indian women wove skirts and capes from grasses, reeds, and the fibrous parts of tree bark. Mats for the floors, sides, or roofs of shelters were also woven or plaited from plant materials. The Indians kept no livestock that might have provide wool, but they did collect the hair of the animals they used for food. These could be twisted into thread or woven into cords. The horsehair girdle was an item of some importance to women because they believe it brought about human fertility.

Pottery   The Indians of the Northeast woodlands used unglazed burnt clay pottery for dry storage, for carrying liquids, and for cooking. The technology of making pots seems to have come into use about the same time as the introduction of maize agriculture to the region. Prior to this innovation pots were laboriously carved from a soft mineral known as soapstone (steatite), which appeared in large quantities in outcroppings throughout New England. These could withstand direct heat without splitting. Alternatively, a skin- or clay-lined hole in the ground or a carefully crafted bark container was used for boiling or stewing foods. In these cases, hot rocks were added to the liquid to heat it. Once Indian women acquired the ability to make pots that would withstand fire the older methods were generally abandoned. Likewise, brass and cast iron pots and kettles tended to displace the clay pot as a cooking utensil, but the clay pot continued to be used for dry storage.

Potting seems to have been regarded as women's work. Both Algonquian and Iroquoian pots were graceful, unpretentious, and utilitarian having little in the way of decoration accept along the lip or upper collar of the pot. Although they varied in quality from region to region due to the quality of the clay, Indian pots were remarkably thin and strong. Algonquian pots were slightly taller and more egg-shaped than Iroquoian ones, which were rounder. Gray clay would be gathered from a stream bank and ground shell or sand worked into it until all the lumps were gone and the potter was satisfied with its texture. Woodland Indians did not use a potter's wheel or kiln. The potter gained the height desired by mingling wet clay with grit, powdered rock, or shell, rolling the mixture into strips with her hands, and adding one strip above another, rounding and shaping the vessel as she worked. Continuous patting with a stick wrapped with wet fabric made the pot solid. The pots were often rounded or pointed at the bottom rather than flattened so that they could be set into the fireplace coals. The crafted pot was allowed to dry

A typical camp that might have been occupied by a nuclear family. Please note the brush shelter and the skins drying in the background as well as the baskets, wooden platters, and the pottery jars around or in the fire. This pre-contact re-creation was meant to reflect Indian life in northeastern New Jersey.

for several days, and then placed in the fireplace among the hot coals until it turned red and hardened.

Utensils Although potting and basket making were clearly women's work, the production of wooden dishes and bowls was left to the men. The bowl maker used the natural diameter of the log to determine the size of his dishes, chopping out a section with a stone axe and producing the concave and convex surfaces using fire to char the wood and scraping away the unwanted material with a flint tool or a clam or oyster shell. By alternately wetting and heating the inside and outside surfaces of the wood, bowls and dishes of remarkable thinness could be achieved by this method. Among the woods preferred for bowl making were hornbeam, elm, white oak, basswood, and rock maple. Burls and knots in the wood were especially valued for bowl making. The hard roots of the mountain laurel were often carved into spoons, ladles, and stirrers. Deer antler could be split and polished to make a spoon or a narrow tool for removing the marrow from bones.

While meat could be eaten raw or thrown on or roasted over the fire, most vegetable foods required a good deal of preparation before cooking. Every Indian family had either a mortar and pestle or a set of grindstones for preparing meal from corn kernels or for pounding nuts and acorns into a usable pulp. A mortar could be fashioned from a hollow stump or log, and any hard branch could be fashioned into a pestle. Grinding plates and rolling-pin shaped grinders were usually of sandstone. The women could be seen on most days standing by their mortars pounding nuts or leaning over the grinding plate on their knees and working the grains of corn back and forth in a rocking motion.

The Bow and Arrow   With the possible exception of the tomahawk, no article of their material culture has come to be more closely associated with the Indian than the bow and arrow. Nonetheless, Indians of the Northeast woodlands generally used bows of an unsophisticated and inefficient design. The overall performance of Indian bows was adequate, but it was a good deal less efficient than that of European and Asian types. Bow construction techniques included a single stave of wood (self-bow), a wood stave with sinew reinforcement (backed bow), and a combination of wood, horn, or antler with sinew backing (composite bow). Hide glue could be used to attach the backing or hold the laminate layers together. Native American bows ranged from three to six feet in length, and the native bowyers used a variety of materials to make the bow stave. They relied on natural materials that met certain requirements dictated by the intended use, most important of which was flexibility without breaking.

Several species of plant and animal materials met these requirements. Ash, hickory, locust, cedar, juniper, oak, walnut, birch, choke cherry, serviceberry, and mulberry woods were used for the basic body of the bow or for arrows. Bow strings most frequently were made of sinew (animal back or leg tendon), rawhide, or gut. However, plant fiber strings from the inner bark of basswood, slippery elm, or cherry trees could be made, but they were generally much more labor intensive than animal fiber strings.

The height and strength of the archer determined the ideal draw weight of the bow. A combination of the length of draw and the draw weight of the bow determines the cast (propelling force) of the bow. Adjusting either or both of these features allows the arrowhead to be made larger or smaller as needed. The draw weight of the bow also determined the ideal weight and diameter of the arrow shaft. Even a bow with a high draw weight can only throw an arrow so far. If the arrow is too heavy, it will not fly far or fast enough to be very useful. A shaft that is too thick or too thin will also lead to problems. It must compress enough to bend around the bow stave as it is launched by the string. If it does not bend, the arrow flies wide of the target. If it bends too much it may shatter, or it will wobble in flight—a high speed vibration that dissipates energy and reduces the striking force. The length of the draw, also determined by the body of the archer, determined the length of the arrow and the bowstring.

The maximum cast of the bow determined the ideal weight of the point. This is how it is known that certain "arrowheads" can not really have been used on an arrow, at least not to any good effect. A general rule of thumb is that a stone arrowhead will be less than 1 1/2 by 3/4 inch in dimensions and will generally weigh less than one ounce. Larger projectile points probably would have been set in the shaft of a spear, a lance, or as a knife tip fasten in a wooden or antler handle.

Arrow shafts were made out of shoots, such as dogwood, wild rose, ash, birch, chokecherry, and black locust. Reeds from common reed-grass were also used with some frequency throughout North America, with the exception of the Great Plains. Arrowheads attached to short pieces of wood (foreshaft) and knocks of antler glued to the feathered wooden ends (endshafts) were often inserted in the hollow ends of reeds so that they could be reused if the reed broke. These lightweight arrows were particularly good for shooting birds and small animals at close range where a simple hit incapacitated the target. The foreshaft would often remain in the animal after the reed broke away. Blunts—looking like pencil-thin baseball bats with a bulge in place of the arrowhead—were also used on small animals and waterfowl where impact alone would disable or kill the prey. Moreover, if used over water, the blunts and reed arrows floated and could be easily retrieved via dugout or canoe.

Fletchings of bird feathers were sewn to or inserted in the shaft. Feathers of wild turkey were preferred, but many other birds, including eagle, crow, goose, hawk, and turkey, were often used. Sinew was generally used to attach the fletching by first stripping some of the feathers from the front and back of the vane and then tying the vane to the shaft in front of and behind the remaining feathers. Sometimes plant twine was used to sew through the quill. Hide glue was often used with the sinew ties. Animal products, such as sinew, have the advantage of tightening as they dry. The fletchings balanced the weight of the arrowhead to prevent the arrow from tumbling end-over-end in flight. When properly fletched with the vanes at a slight angle to the shaft, an arrow will spin in flight producing a gyroscopic effect that helps it maintain an ideal trajectory. A similar effectiveness is gained by a football quarterback when he makes the football spin during a long pass. In fact, until the invention of rifled guns, bows generally proved to be more accurate and could shoot arrows further than powder-thrown missiles fired from smoothbore muskets. They were also quicker to reload.

The wood for the bow was obtained by splitting out a likely piece from the limb of a tree and using the outer layers, including the sap wood. Scraping and rubbing with edged stone tools and sanders formed the basic shape of the bow, which might by elliptical or ovid in cross-section. Recurves on the ends of the limbs of the bow were created by bending the wood backward over a hot rock and holding the shape until it cooled and set. Once shaped, the bow was set aside in a dark dry place to season. Here it might remain for months or years depending on need.

If the bow were to be backed, the Indian artisan would first make a glue by boiling salmon skin or the hoofs of deer. This he applied to the back of the bow (the part facing away from the archer). As the glue boiled, the maker would prepare long strips of sinew by chewing and separating the fibers from the hind leg of a deer until they were soft and pliable. These would be glued in overlapping layers to the back of the bow being dried, then smoothed and rubbed between the application of individual layers. The wood of the bow was excellent in resisting the compression of being drawn on the inside (facing the archer), but the outside was placed in tension by the same motion. This tension threatened to break and splinter the wood as in the breaking of a green stick. The sinew backing helped the bow resist this tension and made it more elastic.

If correctly made, a bow formed a perfect circular arc when drawn. This was slightly flattened at the handle. The height, strength, and personal preferences of the archer determined the length of the bow and the ideal draw weight. Although they were not calculated by the Indians, it seems that draw weighs of 45 to 50 pounds were considered best for hunting. A combination of the length of draw and the draw weight of the bow determined the propelling force of the bow. The Indian archer determined the ideal draw weight by feel. Adjusting the length or draw weight (or both of these features) allowed the arrowhead to be made larger or smaller as needed. Most Indians owned several bows of various weights dedicated to a myriad of purposes.

Indian bows were practical and precise, but they did not compare favorably with the best of European or Asian examples with regard to effective range or complexity of form. Advanced bow and arrow technology proved to be complex, and it was governed by a number of seemingly counterintuitive principles involving the compression and elasticity of wood. The elastic balance of the bow, the resilience of the bowstring, and the aerodynamic balance and appropriate weight of the arrow were all important to success. Nonetheless, when properly fashioned from available materials, the Indian was able to make the bow and arrow an effective personal weapons system and hunting tool.

According to traditions shared by archers from many cultures, a bow left strung or standing in an upright position when not in use got tired and lost its shape. It should be stored unstrung, lying down, or at least in a horizontal position. Bow strings made of natural materials lost some resiliency in damp or rainy weather, but they did not become so ineffective as to prevent hunting or battle. Indian archers accepted many of these ideas suggesting that there is some truth therein, but they added a couple of concepts and taboos of their own. These included that no person should step over a bow lest it be disturbed in its rest; no child should handle it lest its strength be sapped; and no woman should touch it lest it be defiled. Violating any of these taboos was thought to make the bow shoot crooked.

Wampum   Regardless of their linguistic stock, the Indian nations highly valued wampum as a decoration, as a medium of exchange, and as a device for recording traditions and agreements.

Sewan (loose beads) were made in flat disks of clam or oyster shell and as cylindrical beads, in either white or dark blue (sometimes called black), taken from the conch (welck) or the quahaug clam, respectively. When strung together the sewan were called *wampum*, which term came from the Algonquian Indian word *wamp-umpe-ag* for white string of shells (*wamp*–white, *umpe*–shell string, *ag*–representing the plural). It seems certain that in the pre-contact period wampum was not considered money or currency of any sort among the Indians. Rather, it was regarded as a highly appreciated gift or token that represented a significant demonstration of good faith and friendship. When a conference resulted in a treaty or agreement, a string of beads was presented as a physical embodiment of the understanding, and when given as part of a condolence ceremony, it represented the heart-felt sympathy of the giver. In a culture that relied on oral memories rather than writing these beads were very important as symbols.

The flat-disk sewan seem to have been the earliest form of wampum, and they were highly valued as decoration. They were a convenient form for use on dresses and shirts, or for incorporation as decorations in the hair. The long cylindrical wampum beads were more difficult to produce, but they were more easily adapted to use in necklaces or when stitched together. In the form of belts, wampum were exchanged upon the occasion of ceremonies or tribal conferences. It was possible to vary the pattern of dark and light beads on the belts to form a pictograph as a memorial of events or agreements, but the idea that they could be read like hieroglyphs is generally incorrect.

The tribes that resided on the Northeast Atlantic coast seem to have had a monopoly on the raw materials needed to make sewan, but its use and production did not extend to the tribes of the southern Atlantic coastal regions until whites put a currency value on it in the 17th century. For a long period, which extended up to the time of the American Revolution in some places, this was set at three black beads or six white beads to the English penny. Although the size of the bead was set at 60 to the English foot, the most common unit of exchange for strings of wampum found in period documents was the fathom (six feet). Using these values, the English considered the Indians of Narragansett Bay and Block Island to be rich.

While both the flat white and dark sewan disks could be fashioned from almost any shell material, the conch and quahaug were exclusively used to produce the highly valued cylindrical beads. The conch—actually the Knobbed Atlantic Whelk—has a spiral core or column around which the shell grows. When the thin shell wall is broken out, the column can be drilled down its length and made into cylindrical white beads that can be shaped and ground smooth with a stone. Archeologists have found these conch in various stages of development at Indian camp sites, especially in the area of Oyster Bay on the north shore of Long Island. The Algonquian-speaking

Indians on Long Island called the place *Meht-anaw-ach* (or earshell country) for the availability of conch shells and giant quahaug clams. Only white beads could be made from the conch. The more rare and more valuable blue beads, known as purple or black, can be made only from the thick blue portions of the quahaug that occurs near the hinge of the shell. Quahaug were available in almost any season, but Adriean Van der Donck, an early Dutch visitor to the area, was under the impression that the conch was "cast ashore from the sea" only twice a year.[9]

The Indian tribes that inhabited the coastal regions surrounding the sheltered waters of Long Island Sound were particularly blessed with vast quantities of the raw materials for making sewan in the form of unbroken shells. The Dutch recorded the Indian name of Long Island as *Sewanhacky* (or Land of Shells). The shores of Shelter Island, Gardiner's Bay, and Oyster Bay were littered with archeological evidence of widespread sewan manufacture, and it seems certain that the Indians that lived there traded the beads and disks that they made to other nations in the interior as a commodity. By gift, trade, or barter wampum produced on the Northeast Atlantic coastline found its way as far west as Wisconsin and the Dakotas, and as far south as Virginia and the Carolinas.

The Rockaway and Canarsee tribes of the western end of Long Island (present-day Brooklyn, New York) doubtlessly traded the finished beads, sewan, and strings of wampum with other tribes, and examples from that area have been found as far west as the western-most Great Lakes and as

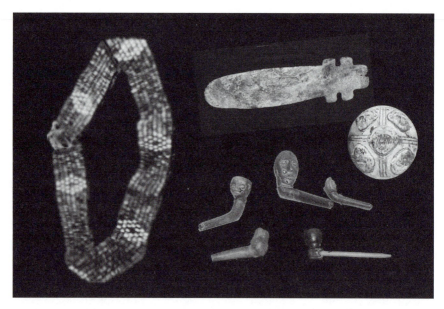

A sampling of Native American decorative arts including (clockwise) a copper pendant, an amulet of the Four Winds, a group of effigy pipes, and a belt of wampum.

far north as Hudson's Bay. Thousands of beads have been unearthed in Iroquoian villages in central and western New York, which may indicate their use as part of the tribute paid to them by the coastal tribes.

Decorative Arts Early observers noted the ingenious methods used by the Indians to decorate their clothing and personal items with quills, sewan, beads, and ribbons. "The women manifest much ingenuity and taste in the work which they execute with porcupine quills. The colour of these quills is various, beautiful and durable, and the art of dyeing them is practiced only by females." Indian women often formed societies of quillworkers and bead-decorators akin to the medicine and warrior societies found among men, and an accomplished quillworker or bead-decorator might be accorded the same social status as that of a noted warrior or hunter. As with most Indian societies, there were initiations, rules, and taboos to be followed. "It is said that quillworkers go blind if they ever throw a porcupine quill into the fire, or if they do quillwork at night. It is also said that a quillworker will prick her finger a lot with quills if she sews any moccasins in her home. She is not supposed to eat certain foods, such as porcupine meat, nor should she allow anyone to pass in front of her while she is quilling."[10]

Young girls learned their decorating technique through the auspices of these societies. Their eagerness to learn reflected tribal custom, and their skill enhanced their standing in the community and their eligibility for marriage. "A girl who helped the grown-ups, who could tan and bead and quill well, was much honored," noted one native woman. "The men kept track of their brave deeds and us women used to keep a record of our kind of deeds." Young Indian girls applied themselves industriously to the mastery of this decorative work by working on the clothing of their dolls. A Fox Indian woman recalled how her mother introduced her to such work, "When I was twelve years old, I was told, 'Come, try to make these.' They were my own moccasins. 'You may start to make them for yourself...for you already know how to make them for your dolls'...She only cut them out for me."[11]

Quality quillwork required great patience and dexterity. Careful workers took great pride in not carrying the stitch through the underside of the hide or fabric, thereby assuring a clean backing. Using bone awls and needles—or later, metal ones—sinew or thread, and a bone or wooden quill flattener, Indian women created intricate patterns on both skins and broadcloth that featured largely geometric patterns derived from earlier traditional woven work. Not until the 19th century did curvilinear and floral designs appear in the eastern woodlands and the Great Lakes region. Nonetheless, the Indians of these regions came to be known for the tremendous diversity of their techniques and the bright coloration of their designs. "Every women...had patterns cut from stiff birch bark which she laid on the material to be decorated...Patterns were pricked with a stiff fishbone around the outline and then cut."[12]

In the early days before the introduction of European dyes, porcupine and bird quills were used in their natural state or colored with root or vegetal dyes. "To dye red or yellow" the Indians chose certain roots and mosses "which they find on a species of fir tree." These they put into a pot of water made acidic by boiling currants or gooseberries in it. "The vessel is then covered tight, and the liquid is made to simmer over the fire for three or four hours." Into this dye the quills were immersed for several minutes or until they took their color. One observer noted that "these colours never fade." The quills, which were carefully sorted by color and size, were carried or stored in the dried bladders or intestines of large animals that served as pouches. It was not uncommon for quillworkers to become ill from soaking the quills in their mouths to soften them.[13]

The increased availability of glass trade beads eventually caused the disappearance of the quillwork societies and their replacement with beading societies. Colorful beads were much easier to use than the dyed quills, and they did not require hours of preparation. Indian women quickly adapted their quillwork patterns to beading with both outlines and whole areas being covered in beads. The trade in glass beads went back to the earliest days of European discovery, and quantities of colored glass beads were carried by explorers in the 16th and 17th centuries. Manufactured beads were much more versatile than handmade sewan. Fur traders introduced large quantities of the Italian beads into the Northeast woodlands by the third quarter of the 17th century, and their use spread west into the plains regions by 1800.

These beads—approximately the size of a match head and virtually indestructible—were known as pony beads, and they were gradually replaced by the much smaller seed beads. A six-foot strand of small, single glass beads commanded the price of one beaver skin in 1760, but as the beads became more plentiful the price fell. In 1807, two pounds of beads could be had for the same skin. The earlier pony beads from Italy—made in Venetian factories and sold to exporters throughout Europe—were usually available only in white, red, black, or blue, and they varied in size and texture somewhat. Ironically, this lent a soft and subtle character to the finished work. Due to their larger size and general rarity, they were often used sparingly as trim around quillwork. The smaller seed beads were generally made in eastern European factories, and they came in a wide spectrum of very bright colors and very even shapes. The difference between the two types can easily be discerned even from a distance. Yet, Indian items cannot be dated through this method because both beads were used simultaneously over a great span of time, and they were often recycled from one project to the next.

As colorful cloths and ribbons became available Indian women incorporated them into their work as appliqués and borders. The ribbons commonly came in dyed cotton and wool with some silk being available. When actual ribbon was not available, the Indians would make long strips from blankets that were appliquéd in stripes, geometric patterns, and other designs found in quillwork, beadwork, and animal hair embroidery. Ribbon borders decorated a variety of garments, including blankets, shawls, moccasins, breech clouts, belts, and shirts. Jesuit fathers sometimes encouraged such decorative work for church vestments and altar cloths. In 1762, a missionary described the burial costume of a Delaware matron as having leggings lined with ribbons. "It was not uncommon for a 12-inch border to consist of as many as twelve ribbons, each cut, sewn, and appliquéd so as to form overlapping patterns."[14]

The Great Lakes tribes, in particular, had a long heritage of making and decorating colorful bags (parfleche) made from vegetable and animal fibers such as hemp, nettles, plant stalks, moose, buffalo, or horse hair. By the middle of the 18th century, cotton thread and woolen yarn had replaced local fibers. The Indians employed a variety of finger weaving techniques to create the bags. Typically, they colored the yarns and then wove them into geometric or animal patterns. Among these were the mythological Thunderbird and Panther figures as well as symbolic designs representing the wind and the four directions.

Canoes   Without the native watercraft know as the canoe, or the larger bateaux, most travel in North America would have been impractical. Pierre Esprit Radisson reported that the Indians could paddle 50 miles in a day making one stroke every second. The stroke itself was short with one hand pushing forward on the top of the handle while the other pulled back passed the hip. The back and shoulder were put into every stroke. Only such effort and coordination could drive canoes upriver against the flow of the water.

Radisson, who saw scores of canoes being made during his time in the forests, noted that canoes came in many sizes and were designed for many purposes.

In those days travel meant canoes: gay canoes, slender and graceful, with painted prows and flashing paddles, able to travel on a heavy dew; tired canoes, loaded to their gunwales with meat or corn or peltries, pushing through the sluggish waters; steady canoes, moving tirelessly over the placid lakes; daring canoes, diving down the glass-green rapids, skillfully dodging the rocks as if they had eyes in the bow; quiet canoes, creeping noiselessly through the mist of morning or under the stars; fat canoes, no bigger than a bathtub, barely able to float one man and his duffle; great war canoes, carrying a dozen men or more to do battle with their enemies; canoes for racing, for family travel, for heavy cargoes; canoes of elm or birch bark—silver white, banded with black gum … The canoe is an independent creature. There is nothing one can do for it except to keep it in repair.[15]

Jolicoeur Charles Bonin, a French soldier serving in New France during the French and Indian Wars, has left a detailed description of a canoe of the period.

Canoes are the most frequently used water transport in upper Canada because
they are light enough to make the necessary portages around the frequent rapids. They are made of light wooden strips as thick as a strong lath, bent half double, then curved in a half circle. They are placed four or five inches apart with the
ends attached to a slender pole bound with wooden straps like barrel hoops. Five
crossbars are placed along the inside of the canoe which is from twelve to twenty
feet in length or more. These crossbars hold the canoe open...across the widest
part and narrows toward both ends. The framework is covered on the outside with
birch bark sewed together with wooden withes. The seams are then covered with
gum or resin to keep them watertight. These boats are very light. Loaded, they are
easily managed by two men, one at each end.[16]

Radisson reported that a team of eight men and women could complete
a canoe in a day or two depending on the availability of appropriate
materials. Four men and at least one women worked from each end.
Ideally, the waterproof skin of the canoe was made from a single sheet
of bark that was harvested in spring when the sap was flowing and fashioned by summer so that it remained pliable, but if a canoe was needed
at other times of the year hot water was used to allow the bark to fit the
shape of the framework without splitting. Any seams in the waterproof
skin were overlapped and sewn (by the women) with pine roots through
holes made with a bone or metal awl. The seams were then covered with
strips of plant fiber or cloth and coated with gum or pitch. This gum was
commonly mixed with ground charcoal and softened over a fire. It was
applied with a wooden paddle. Where birch was not available, elm or
spruce bark might be used, and there is some evidence that moose skin
(leather) could serve as a substitute. The availability of appropriate trees
often dictated the type and size of the canoes used by individual tribes.
Birch bark canoes were common among the Ojibwa of the Great Lakes, the
Iroquois of western New York, the Algonquians of western New England,
and among the Micmac, Penobscot, and Abenaki of Maine.[17]

In the Great Lakes forests there was a wealth of birch bark that could
be fashioned into lightweight vessels. Some Iroquoian canoes were made
of the heavier barks available in central New York, and they tended to
be less agile, but still effective, watercraft. However, closer to the ocean
shore or where there was a scarcity of appropriate bark, dugout canoes
predominated.

Dugout canoes were usually made during the winter. Roger Williams
of Rhode Island included separate Algonquian terms for dugout canoes
made of pine, oak, and chestnut. Such discrimination of language was not
uncommon in Algonquian. Only three dugout canoes of Native American
manufacture in the 17th century have been found in New England, and
each has been found submerged in the water of a pond held down by a
load of stones. These may have been placed under water for winter storage.
Another example has been found submerged in the Mohawk River and is
on display at the Johnson Homestead in central New York. This suggests

Theodore De Bray's often referenced engraving of the dugout crafting process from 1590. Historians consider his engraving essentially correct in its depiction of the scorch and strip techniques used in crafting a dugout canoe.

that the Iroquois were not unfamiliar with the type. The dugout canoe was heavy in comparison to its bark-covered cousin. Certainly a single man could not carry it, yet it was remarkably stable and durable. There are credible reports of dugout canoes capable of carrying almost two dozen persons being used to hunt whales among the ocean waves of the Atlantic.[18]

The first step in building a dugout was to find a tree of appropriate length. It was important to find a length of wood that was straight, but any slight curvature in the log was made to face the bottom of the craft. In the absence of metal tools the Indians were forced to burn down the tree chosen for their project. They accomplished this by placing a wide band of wet clay around the base of the tree about a meter from the ground and building a fire around the unprotected part. By alternately burning and scraping the tree was finally felled. The unwanted branches and tops were removed in a similar fashion. Champlain described a process by which the entire log was surrounded by controlled fires that were used to quickly give the project its approximate shape in terms of its length and width. The log was usually floated to find its most natural orientation in the water. This noted, it was then removed from the water, the bottom flattened, the ends shaped, and the entire outside smoothed with flint tools and clam or oyster shells serving as cutters and scrapers, respectively. The log was then placed on its flattened bottom for hollowing of its interior by alternate burning and scraping. The bottom of the craft was purposely left thick to act as a natural ballast, and the sides were made thin to diminish the overall weight, but not so thin as to be flimsy. A properly constructed dugout would continue to float even if filled with water.

The Appearance of the Woodland Indians

The tribes that occupied the northeastern quadrant of North America were not all that different in appearance from one another, making it unnecessary and even redundant to describe each nation separately. Many of the items of clothing worn by these nations, before the effects of white contact had taken root, were generic in nature and designed around the same set of available materials. These were chosen largely for their practicality and included furs, skins, brain-tanned and oak-tanned leather, grasses, feathers, bone, and other items found in the natural environment. Individual and tribal differences in dress and accessories were largely rooted in the decoration of these items.

Louis Antoine de Bougainville, who spent many years among various native tribes, noted, "I see no difference in the dress, ornaments, dances and songs of these different nations. They are naked save for a breechclout, and painted in black, red, and blue, etc. Their heads are shaved and feathers ornament them. In their lengthened ear lobes are rings of brass wire. They have beaver skins for covering, and carry lances, arrows, and quivers made of buffalo skin."[19]

C. Keith Wilbur, an expert in historical Native American dress, notes, "As elsewhere in the woodlands the usual dress of the day was a breechclout and moccasins. Any travel through the brush and brambles called for protective leggings and shirts. Cooler weather could be met with the insulation provided by a feather or fur cloak. The air pocketed fur was worn against the skin. Women might also wear skirts of soft deerskin or woven grass or the pliable inner bark of trees."[20]

There is a particularly incomplete picture of the appearance of the Atlantic coastal tribes of Maine and Massachusetts, and many of the contemporary European accounts and illustrations that are available have proven to be untrustworthy. Yet, it seems certain that there were more similarities in their dress than there were differences with other tribes. Early 17th-century explorers described the men of the Canadian Maritimes as being clothed in furs of bear, otter, beaver, and fox and the tanned skins of elk and deer with the hair removed. In summer they made a girdle around their waist on which they attached a skin that went between their legs and was attached again at the rear. Their feet were covered year round in buckskin moccasins with the leather drawn together into plaits or puckers in front as did the Chippewa of the Great Lakes. In winter, or when traveling in tall grass or brush, long leather stockings were attached to this girdle also, and the men wore a loose cape of skins around their necks usually

A period drawing of Algonquian women and their typical cool weather dress made of tanned animal hides. Note the knee-high footwear (or leggings), the decorations and fringe, and the cradle board on the woman's back on the right. The figure at the left may be a man carrying a bow and arrow and wearing a hood.

with the right arm exposed in the style of a Roman toga. Early descriptions also tell of painted decorations as well as brass and copper ornaments sewn on to these deerskin robes.

It would probably be an error, however, to assume that Native American costume made of deer or other animal skins was uniformly of their natural color. The soft leather skins were often stained—in part, in patterns, or in whole—with black soot or charcoal, red ochre, ground blue azurite, yellow and white clay, green verdigris, or other natural colors. Early explorers reported that the skins used in Native American clothing were well dyed in vibrant colors even in the 16th century before dyestuffs were available from European traders. "The color being given to them that is wished and in such perfection that when of vermilion they look like very fine red broadcloth and when black...they are of the purest."[21]

The Effect of European Contact The surviving clothing artifacts that serve as examples of Native American clothing have remarkable refinements in cut and exhibit such sophistication in assembly that it is uncertain that they were not affected by European contact. Although the basic garments were of native construction, the native style may have been considerably looser and less tailored then a rudimentary inspection might suppose. The long period of contact between the woodlands nations of the Atlantic coast and whites resulted in "a gradual Europeanization of their art and technology." Furthermore, the multi-tribal reorganizations and amalgamations that followed the native dispersions during the 17th century may explain the hybridized appearance of many native objects now in Native American museums and collections.[22]

The 17th-century woodland Indians had no cloth of their own manufacture, whatsoever. Once the tribes came into contact with Europeans and began selling them furs for trade items, they gladly adopted cloth shirts made of coarse linen, and blankets, loincloths, and leggings made of wool dyed in many vibrant colors. "The men of every nation differ in their dress

This period illustration is of the Mohawk war leader Tiyanoga, known to the English as King Hendrick. He wears a combination of native and European articles. The metal pipe tomahawk, metal gorget, cloth ruffled shirt, and woolen blanket are all accommodations of native dress taken from the whites.

very little from each other, except those who trade with the Europeans," wrote Bougainville.[23] A great number of the male Indians began to dress in European-style jackets and vests mixed with loincloths, Indian leggings, and native footwear. The women were not so quick to give up their traditional clothing styles, but they readily replaced skins and woven grass with colorful skirts and wraps of wool broadcloth.[24] Lieutenant Henry Timberlake, a British officer, noted of the Indians, "They have now learnt to sew, and the men as well as women, excepting shirts, make all their own cloths.... [in] their favorite colors of blue and red."[25]

Hair Styles The women generally wore their straight, black hair long with beads, wampum, or feathers for decoration, "so long that it generally reaches to the middle of their legs and sometimes to the ground." They sometimes wore a small cap or coronet of brass or copper on their heads.[26] With regard to their hair, Jolicoeur Charles Bonin, a French soldier, noted, "They keep it long, full and shiny; taking care to rub it frequently with bear grease which thickens it, and covering it with powder made of rotten wood. They make it as large as one's fist, then wrap it with eel or snake skin. This pigtail is flattened on the back, and rounds a little higher up. As their hair very often grows long, they turn it up halfway down, making the pigtail thicker, and as large at the bottom as it is at the top."[27]

A center hair roach was most common on the head of male Indians, but some tribes allowed the hair to grow to great length. Male Indians had no patience for facial hair, plucking it out by the root with clam-shell twisters, and they did the same process to create their hairstyles. William Bartram reported that the men shaved their heads leaving only a narrow crest or comb beginning at the crown of the head, where it is about two inches broad and about the same height. The hair was "frizzed upright." The term "Ottawa" was a colloquialism for these people that referred to this curious scalplock dressed in a ridge or roach down the middle of the head. Although the Iroquois also wore their hair in this manner, the term was almost uniquely applied by the French to these people with whom they were most familiar.[28]

Other nations removed the hair from the front of the head, and as the style moved further to the back of the head, the hair gradually widened to cover the "hinder part of the head and back of the neck" in a lank of hair terminating in a tail or tassel, the length of which was ornamented in various ways. Also reported were hairstyles in which the right half of the head was shaved leaving the left side long so that the hair would not interfere with the operation of the bow.[29]

The scalplock was the objective of the widely misrepresented process of scalping. The taking of a scalp or hairlock as a trophy or proof of having killed an enemy in warfare was an ancient Native American custom. The Europeans, who traditionally took whole heads for this purpose, did not introduce scalping to the Indians. They did formulate and foster a scheme for the payment of bounties based on the presentation of scalps, or whole heads. The frontier population of Europeans seems to have been particularly terrorized by reports of scalpings.

Headdresses   The war bonnet composed of a trailing double-line of feathers—familiar to school children as a symbol of Native American dress—was an item used by the Plains Indians, not by those of the woodlands. Nonetheless, there is strong evidence that woodland Indians adorned their heads in some fashion. James Adair, who studied several woodland tribes from 1735 to 1744, described the men as fastening several sorts of beautiful feathers to a lock of hair on the crown of their heads, "frequently in tufts; or the wing of a red bird, or the skin of a small hawk. And every Indian nation when at war trim [decorate] their hair after a different manner through contempt of each other. Thus we can distinguish an enemy in the woods so far off as we can see him."[30]

As to headdresses among the Algonquian, naturalist William Bartram found a "very curious diadem or band, about four inches broad...encircling their temples." This was decorated with stones, beads, wampum, porcupine quills, and a large plume or feather "of crane or heron" set in the front peak.[31] Similar caps were worn by many Iroquoian peoples. On the other hand Peter Kalm, who traveled among the Huron, found that they wore no hats or caps whatever, and when among the Abenaki, he reported women who had "funnel-shaped caps."[32] Colonel James Smith, who spent some time in western Pennsylvania with the Caughnawagas,

In this detail of a Benjamin West painting, the variety of headdresses and hairstyles among the Delaware of Pennsylvania is clearly portrayed.

noted the use of red handkerchiefs in place of hats.[33] Finally, John Knox, who traveled among the Micmac tribe of northeastern Canada, noted the use of a turban-like headgear by both males and females.[34]

After returning from a long time on the warpath, Radisson noted that his Mohawk foster sisters "cleaned him up, dressed his hair...put feathers on his head, and tied up his hair with beads." He also noted that the "typical Iroquois headdress" consisted of "a cap with an upright silver band, like a crown. This was adorned on the top with a cluster of white feathers, and a single eagle plume tilted backward from the forehead. The feather was so fastened in a tube that it would revolve and turn in the wind."[35]

Outer Clothes Both genders wrapped a large animal skin or piece of blanket-cloth (about six-feet square) around themselves by way of outerwear.[36] Wearing fur of black otter or black bear was generally considered a symbol of gladness and welcome. The Hurons were described as using "a shaggy piece of cloth, which is either blue or white, with a blue or red stripe below. This they always carry over their shoulders, or let it hang down, in which case they wrap it around their middle."[37] In inclement weather, the Indians "fasten their blanket below with their belts, and make them pass over the head like a monk's hood, arranging them so well that they expose only their nose and hands."[38] Otherwise the men threw their blanket loosely over one shoulder, and, even in the hottest weather, they might be seen strutting about their villages like Roman senators in a Shakespearean tragedy.[39] In 1766, Jonathan Carver noted that Indian men threw their blanket loosely over one shoulder "holding the upper side of it by two corners, with a knife in one hand, and a tobacco-pouch, pipe &c. in the other. Thus accoutered they walked about their villages or camps."[40]

It was noted that the blankets supplied to the Indians by the French were "made in Normandy of very fine wool," but they were expensive in terms of the number of furs demanded. It was thought that the blankets supplied by the English were "coarser" but of better value because the English traders would accept both skins and furs in exchange.[41] Late in the period, Radisson's Hudson's Bay Company established a "point" system that valued blankets as to their quality or size. The higher points were of greater value. Men and women reportedly used blankets of 2 or 3 points for outer garments, while the children were provided with slightly smaller ones down to 1 point. It should be noted that the point system was not universally used by all traders, and it was often imitated by unscrupulous persons to cheat the Indians.[42]

Basic Men's Garments Most Indian men could not be persuaded to use trousers, "for they thought these were a great hindrance in walking."[43] Jean-Bernard Bossu reported that the male war leaders even in winter went "naked, like the other warriors, and the scars on their bodies distinguished them from their men and take the place of military commissions."[44] This report seems extreme, but the men certainly had a great aversion to the wearing of breeches, "for to that custom, they affix the idea of helplessness and effeminacy."[45] They wore instead a slip of cloth or dressed skin known as a breechclout (loincloth) that was about a half meter wide and a meter and a half long.[46] This they passed between their legs and under a conveniently broad belt or cord tied around their waists. A French soldier noted, "The two ends of the loincloth are folded over in front and in back, with the end in front longer than the one in the back."[47] Another observer noted that the breech-clout was "like a short apron or skirt."[48]

Both men and women seem to have favored the European style of shirts, but they were reported to have left the collars and cuffs open as it "would be a most insufferable confinement" to fasten them.[49] "The young people are dandies, and the women are fond of wearing ruffles bordered with lace. They never take [the shirts] off, except to sleep, until they are used up for time, and finally they become black from use."[50] Peter Williamson, a captive in Pennsylvania in 1754 noted, "The better sort have shirts of the finest linen they can get...but these they never put on till they have painted them of various colours...and they never pull them off to wash, but wear them till they fall apart."[51]

The consumption of shirts among Indians was very great. A plain men's shirt could be bought for a good sized beaver pelt or deerskin. The price doubled if the shirt had ruffles, and for children a smaller pelt or skin was charged. Shirts were sometimes decorated with vermilion (red) or verdi-gris (green) mixed with animal grease.[52]

The Ottawas were reported to have developed, instead of shirts, "a kind of waistcoat of blue or red cloth, cut in pieces, so that with four or six cords they can cover half the body and the arms."[53] Richard Smith, who toured the great river valleys of the Hudson, Mohawk, Susquehanna, and Delaware near the end of the French and Indian War, noted of the natives that he saw even at that late date, "Clothing they use but little, sometimes a shirt or shift with a blanket or coat, and sometimes the latter only, without linen."[54]

Basic Women's Garments
There is no evidence that women wore loincloths. Instead, they wore a skirt of deerskin or cloth. They took a square piece of cloth similar to that used as an outer wrap that they placed around their waists as a "sort of loose petticoat" reaching only to the middle of the leg. Elizabeth Hicks, a captive, made such a petticoat or skirt for herself describing it as "formed by doubling the cloth so far as to have one fold a quarter of a yard below the other; this is wrapped round the waist, and reaches a little below the knee." The skirts were reportedly covered with "brass runners and buck-les" by way of ornamentation, and the edge was sometimes bordered with red or other colored strips of material.[55]

An observer noted of women's fashion in body garments, "Those who trade with the Europeans wear a linen garment [shirt] the same as that used by the men; the flaps of which hang over the petticoat. Such as dress after their ancient manner, make a kind of shift with leather, which covers the body but not the arms."[56] The leather used to make the basic native shift was reportedly deerskin, buffalo, or elk. "The arms, to the shoulders, are left naked, or are provided with sleeves which are sometimes put on, and sometimes suffered to hang vacant from the shoulders." The design of the shift among north country nations fell from the shoulders to below the knee in one piece. This garment covered the shoulders and the bosom and was fastened by a strap passing over the shoulders and gathered about the waist by a belt.[57]

Waist belts seem to have been made of leather, twisted bark fiber, a wide strip of broadcloth, or plaited from yarn. They were used with either shirts or shifts to bring in the garment about the waist. One observer also noted that "the Indian females continually wear a beaded string round their legs [hips], made of buffalo-hair...[that] they reckon a great ornament as well as a preservative against miscarriages, hard labor, and other evils."[58] In general, each woman had one basic body garment that was worn as long as it would last and was then thrown away "without any attempt at cleanliness" being made in the interim.[59]

Children's Garments Until they were four or five, children went entirely naked in good weather, and they were provided with a little blanket in which to wrap themselves when the weather was bad. Thereafter, children seem to have worn the same styles and designs as their parents with the exception of size. Girls were noted to wear shifts much shorter than the matrons. The Reverend Reuben Weiser recounted the details of native children's clothing made by a young, captive German girl named Regina after her rescue in 1744.

They had a kind of sack, made of deer-skin, just large enough to go over the body, and extending from the hip-bones almost down to the knees. This curious bag-shaped garment was either kept up by being tied around the waist with a bark string, or supported by suspenders over the shoulders, also made of bark. The arms, legs, and all the upper part of the body were naked and exposed to the cold; still, in very cold weather, Regina had also a small, dirty, thin blanket and moccasins and leggings.[60]

Leggings Both males and females wore leg coverings. Called by many names, such as leggings, leather stockings, mitasses, or Indian gaiters, all were essentially the same item of clothing. They were worn for protection against thorns or brush, and may have helped in avoiding snake bites of which the Indians had great apprehension. "The legs are preserved from many fatal accidents that may happen by briars, stumps of trees, or under-wood, &c. in marching through close, woody country."[61] Nicholas Cresswell, who traveled widely through the back-country, considered leggings an essential item. "These are pieces of coarse woolen cloth wrapped round the leg and tied below the knee with a string to prevent the snakes biting you."[62]

Leggings were usually made of leather or coarse cloth—scarlet blanket wool was reported to have been a favorite among the Great Lakes tribes. Pierre Pouchot, commandant of Fort Niagara, described women's leggings as stockings "made of flannel cloth fringed with red, white, or blue. This gaiter is sewed up following the shape of the leg, with four finger breadth of stuff outside the seam. This strip is bordered with ribbons of different colors, mingled with designs of glass beads, which forms a very pleasing effect...Besides this they wear garters of beads, or porcupine quills, bordered four fingers wide, which are tied on the legs."[63] Another observer reported that the leather stockings "hung full of the hoofs of the roe deer in the form of bells, in so much as to make a sound exactly like castagnettes."[64]

John Knox, a contemporary journalist, gave a very full account of the construction and use of leggings and described the adoption of these useful and necessary items by whites.

They should be at least three quarters of a yard in length [and] three quarters wide, then double it, and sew it together from end to end, within four, five, or six inches of the outside selvages, fitting this long narrow bag to the shape of the leg; the flaps on the outside, which serve to wrap over the shin, or fore-part of the leg, tied round under the knee, and above the ankle, with garters of the same color...For my part, I think them clumsy, and not at all military; yet I confess they are highly necessary in North America.[65]

Woolen and leather leggings of Native American style were adopted by most white frontiersmen and rangers. Many French and English troops serving on the frontiers would appear in uniform coat, waistcoat, and shirt only to be clothed from the waist down in moccasins and breeches topped with Indian leggings or leather stockings. Central New York is presently called the Leather Stocking Region by the state.

Almost every school child knows that Indians wore leather **Footwear** moccasins on their feet. Several styles of moccasin construction have been identified as being that of Algonquian, Iroquoian, or other tribal type. A one-piece construction, "an ancient form," seems to have been favored by the tribes of the Southeast.[66] One observer noted that the skin was "gathered at the toe and are sewn above and behind with a raised flap on either side. This is turned down over the cord below the ankle which ties on the shoe." The front seam and side flaps were often covered with an appliqué of woven porcupine quills or decorated woolen cloth.[67] In the eastern areas of Canada, a separate top, or vamp, covered the instep and was sewn to the body of the shoe with a thick puckered seam. In the Great Lakes region, both styles seem to have been used. A more complicated design, requiring three pieces and often attributed to the Iroquoian peoples, had a separate sole of tough leather to which the sides of the moccasin were stitched with deer sinew. There was a seam along the top of the foot and at the heel. This style also had flaps that turned down over the ankle.[68] The folded edges, as well as the fronts and backs, could be decorated with ribbons, dyed porcupine quills, glass beads, or tiny copper bells.[69]

The women made the footwear for the men as well as themselves using deer sinew or a thread made from the bark of a linden tree, which the French called *bois blanc*. The bark was taken from the inside nearest the wood, boiled in water for a time, and pounded with a wooden club until it became soft and fibrous. The women then sat twisting the fibers into a thread by rolling it on their thighs with the palms of their hand. The bark thread so manufactured was the equal of "a fine hemp cord," according to contemporary observers.[70]

The leather skins used for moccasins were sometimes dressed in the European manner and at other times left with the fur on them.[71] A British observer noted, "They make their shoes for common use out of skins of the bear and elk, well dressed and smoked, to prevent hardening; and those for ornament out of deer-skin, done in the like manner."[72] It was also noted that the natives frequently went without moccasins but usually wore their leggings even when bare-footed.

The Indians also had shoes for winter wear "formed like laced boots."[73] Reported to be quite efficient, these boots were very warm and relatively dry. "They wrap their feet with pieces of blanket, and the sides of the shoe form a half boot which prevents the snow from getting in, while their feet would freeze in European shoes as many have unhappily proved."[74] Some northern tribes formed a one-piece, footed trouser of buckskin that was tied at the ankles and the knees, and worn with a mid-thigh length shirt of the same material.

John Josselyn reported the use of snowshoes by Indians. "In the winter when the snow will bear them, they fasten to their feet snow shoes which are made like a large Racket we play at Tennis with, lacing them with Deer-guts and the like."[75] By distributing a person's weight over a broad area, snowshoes supported the Indian on the surface of the snow pack and eliminated the need to break through the crust with each step. For native peoples snow shoeing was not a recreational sport. Making and using snowshoes was an essential survival skill that allowed them to move and hunt in winter. Although snowshoes were used throughout the region, there were a number of local variations of style. Among these were the bear paw, beavertail, swallowtail, and elbow shoe—each selected for specific snow types and terrain. Long narrow forms with an upturned toe were used for travel in open country, while oval shoes with or without short tails were best suited to hilly terrain or the brush and scrub of the forests. Each form was held open by one or more crossbars. During a single winter season several types may have been used. The bear paw and elbow style were simple tail-less ovals made of a single, wooden stave

A warrior, regaled for a midwinter raid, went to war nearly naked but heavily armed. It was said that the Indian's skin became "all face" because they refused to cover themselves except in the harshest of weather conditions. Note the snowshoes, moccasins, and leggings.

bent around while the beavertail and swallowtail forms had short trailing tails. The Cree and Ojibwa were noted for a long narrow form made of two staves secured at both the toe and tail.

It was a man's work to fashion the snowshoe frames, and he usually used ash or birch to do so. By carving the stave and whittling areas of weakness, the stave could be steamed and bent around to the desired shape. One or two short crossbars—or spreaders—were mortised into the frame, and the tail ends of the stave were tied together. Once the frame was completed, the Indian women did the rawhide infilling work with interwoven lacing made from untanned moose, elk, or deer hide. Winter shoes often had additional rawhide lacing wrapped around the central portion of the frame to increase traction on icy surfaces. The shoes were often decorated with tufts of wool, lengths of yarn, strips of trade cloth, or braids of animal hair. These decorations also muffled the sound of the shoes crunching on the snow as hunters tracked their game. Spring shoes—meant for wet snow—were usually made without cloth so that they would not soak up moisture. During the European trade period paint, stain, or varnish was sometimes used to accent the lacing or the frame.

Body Paint   Peter Kalm noted the use of body paint among the Hurons of Lorette in French Canada.

Many of them have the face painted all over with cinnabar [red vermilion]; others have only strokes of it on the forehead and near the ears; and some paint their hair with the same material. Red is the color they chiefly use in painting themselves, but I have also seen some who had daubed their face with black [denoting death or war]...They formerly made use of a reddish earth, which is to be found in this country, but as the Europeans brought them vermilion, they thought nothing was comparable to it in color...Verdigris [is used] to paint their faces green. For the black color they make use of the soot off the bottom of their kettles, and daub the whole face with it.[76]

A French soldier serving in the middle of the 18th century noted that the natives painted themselves by dipping their fingers in the color with which they wanted to paint their faces and dragging them across and down the face forming stripes. "Many...tribes...are satisfied with painting the face and body in different colours, first rubbing themselves with bear grease, and then daubing on black, red, blue, and green. This is an ordinary decoration for them. Often, when they are at war, they use it, they say, to frighten or intimidate their enemies...They also paint prisoners black when they intend to kill them, as well as painting themselves black when they return from war after losing some of their men." [77]

Tattoos   The Indians tattooed various designs on their bodies that remained as long as they lived. On their faces they impressed figures of snakes, scrolls, lines of tears, and other symbols of importance to them. John M'Cullough, a captive among the Delaware, believed that these "hieroglyphics...always denote[d] valor."[78] Jean-Bernard Bossu noted, "If anyone should take it into his head to have himself tattooed without having distinguished himself in battle, he...might have the design torn off him, skin and all."[79]

The color most used in tattooing was black. Peter Kalm did not recall ever seeing any other. However, he noted, "The men who accompanied me told me that they also use red paint and that black and red are the only colors used."[80] Other contemporary observers described tattoos in red, black, blue, and green—"all bright colors." The blue and green could be made from verdigris, a copper acetate compound, which varies from blue, to blue-green, to green depending on its various chemical structures. Verdigris was a particularly poisonous compound if taken in quantity internally, but seems to have had no ill effect when applied to the skin mixed in grease. The red dye came from cinnabar, which the French and English traders called "vermilion." The black was made by taking a piece of alder wood, burning it completely and allowing the charcoal to cool. Gunpowder, being black, was also used on occasion to color tattoos.[81]

The chosen pigment was pulverized, usually by rubbing it between the hands. This powder was put into a vessel of water and allowed to stand until it was well saturated. When they wished to paint some figures on the body, they first drew the design on the skin with a piece of charcoal. When a man wanted to have his entire body tattooed, he stretched out on a board, and the tattooer marked out as much of the design that they desired to have inscribed as could be done in one sitting. The persons being tattooed, both men and women, would rather die than flinch during the process. The women bore the pain "with the same courage as the men in order to please them and to appear more beautiful to them." Nonetheless, the operation was bloody and dangerous as infection could easily set in and cause the subjects to lose their lives or suffer a serious illness.[82]

A contemporary journalist noted that to make the image the Indian artists used a needle, "made somewhat like a fleam," used by physicians to let blood, or an instrument said to have several needles fastened together between two pieces of wood.

[They] dip it into the prepared dye and with it prick or puncture the skin along the lines of the design previously made with the charcoal. They dip the needle into the dye between every puncture; thus the color is left between the skin and the flesh. When the wound has healed, the color remains and can never be obliterated. The men told me that in the beginning when the skin is pricked and punctured, it is rather painful, but the smart gradually diminishes and at the expiration of a day the smart and pain has almost ceased.[83]

No form of antiseptic seems to have been used, and a brief infection seems to have been an expected part of the process. Another observer noted, "the blood must flow from the part thus cut by the tattooer's stroke, a swelling follows, forming a scab which falls off after a few days. Then the wound is healed and the tattooing or pattern stands out clearly. The healing takes a shorter or longer time depending on the amount of tattooing done. It is very curious to see a man tattooed in this way, especially when the entire body is tattooed in colors."[84] One observer noted that in the later part of the colonial period the custom of tattooing was dying out among the Indians.[85]

Jewelry and Ornaments

Native Americans were fond of wearing finger-rings and ear-rings even before their contact with Europeans. Naturally occurring copper and gold were in use by the Indians for generations. Both men and women used naturally occurring coarse diamonds, garnets, amethyst crystals, and other smooth or polished stones in their jewelry. Soapstone, a soft mineral of gray to green color, was often fashioned into pendants, ornaments, and other geometric shapes by rubbing them with damp deerskin or sawgrass dipped in fine sand. Of course, any stone or bit of metal with an interesting shape could be worked into a piece of decoration. Holes could be bored in soapstone with a pointed stick dipped in sand with relative ease. Bear and elk teeth were commonly worked up into necklaces or attached to dresses, and shark's teeth and shell (mother of pearl) were sometimes imported from coastal regions for the same purposes. The claws of many animals were used in a similar manner, and the toes of deer and elk, when hollowed and strung, made a pleasant sound as the Indians moved.

After European contact, natives quickly acquired brass and silver rings; Christian crosses; medals representative of Catholic saints; large and small bells; pendants cast in the shapes of turtles, bears, and birds; and brass and silver wire. The double beam cross of Lorraine was particularly popular among the French allied Indians. A warrior of the Delaware nation was noted to have had "a large triangular piece of silver hanging below his nose that covered almost the whole of his upper lip."[86] The European traders also supplied items of brass, silver, and tin such as arm-plates, wrist-plates, ear-bobs, and gorgets. "Both sexes...commonly load the parts [of the body] with each sort in proportion to their ability of purchasing them." They were especially fond of these items if they were received as gifts and "would never part with them for the sake of the giver."[87]

Ear Loops The native women bored small holes in their ear lobes through which they passed ear-rings and pendants much as women do today. However, the women generally avoided the custom of some young men who distinguished themselves by creating giant loops in their ear lobes. Women seemingly never followed this practice, and the young men could not extend their ears in this manner unless they had been tested as warriors. The ear-loops were reported to have reached a diameter of four inches.[88] "The young heroes cut a hole round almost the extremity of both their ears, which till healed, they stretch out with a large tuft of buffalo wool mixt with bear's oil. They then twist as much small wire round as will keep them extended in that hideous form."[89]

The following description of the Indians at a native wedding feast survives from the 1740s. It is useful in giving an overall picture of the Indians in what could be considered their finest dress.

The squaws were covered with a blanket and round their wrists, arms, necks, and ankles were several strings of wampum. Some of them had on their heads a cap of coarse cloth as wool, others a sort of a coronet of party colored feathers. The men and boys were likewise covered with a blanket without any embellishments except some of them had a hole in the thick or lower part of their ear big enough for me to put my finger through, and in this hole was put sundry strips of fine cloth of several colours which cloth hung down their shoulders like a fore horse's top knot. Some of them had their pipe run through their ear and hung by the

Descriptive Classifications for Common Lithic Artifacts

Term	Observable Characteristics
Core	Any mass of stone from which one or more flakes have been struck that exhibits no evidence of edges having been prepared on it for use as a tool.
Hammerstone	Usually a fist-sized, roughly spherical or oblong cobble with or without artificial shaping, having evident wear on it indicative of battering.
Stone Axe	A large, thick tool formed by flaking or pecking followed by grinding and/or polishing. In outline the artifact may look like a triangle, a rectangle without grooves (a celt), or an oblong with a full or partial groove used for attaching a handle (hafting).
Grindstone	A stone artifact with a flattened, slightly concave surface closely associated with a cylindrical (rolling pin) or oval shaped grinder.
Blank	A chipped stone artifact in uncompleted form with a length-to-width proportion generally that of a completed item like a projectile point or knife.
Point	A class of bifacial chipped stone tools having some artificial modification for attachment to a shaft or handle, sharp symmetrical edges and pointed tips. This class includes arrow and spear heads, knives, and drills.
Scraper	A uni-facial or bi-facial chipped stone artifact with steep working edges generally greater than 40 degrees.
Weights	Small stone artifacts formed by grinding for attachment to fishing weirs and nets as sinkers or to aid in casting. Grooves were often incised by using sawgrass and sand.

bole. One Indian I observed had a hole bored through the bridge of his nose and through it was put a ring of brass from which hung a pendant stone of a pearl colour and about the shape and size of a Thrush's egg.[90]

Notes

1. Harold F. McGee, ed., *The Native Peoples of Atlantic Canada, A History of Indian-European Relations* (Ottawa: Carleton University Press, 1983), 154.

2. Frances Densmore, *How Indians Use Wild Plants for Food, Medicine and Crafts* (New York: Dover Publications, 1974; reprint of the 1928 edition), 326–327.

3. Reuben Gold Thwaites, ed., *The Jesuit Relations and Allied Documents* (Cleveland: Burrows Brothers, 1898), vol. 8, 105.

4. William Bradford in Dwight B. Heath, ed., *Mourtis Relation* (Cambridge: Applewood Books, 1986), 24.

5. Paul A. W. Wallace, *Indians in Pennsylvania* (Harrisburg: The Pennsylvania Historical and Museum Commission, 1986), 72.

6. Wallace, 30.

7. Ingeborg Marshall, *A History and Ethnography of the Beothuk* (Montreal: McGill-Queen's University Press, 1996), 302.

8. Howard S. Russell, *Indian New England Before the Mayflower* (Hanover, NH: University Press of New England, 1980), 60.

9. Reginald Pelham Bolton, *Indian Life of Long Ago in the City of New York* (New York: Harmony Books, 1934), 101.

10. Judith Reiter Weissman and Wendy Lavitt, *Labors of Love, America's Textiles and Needlework, 1650–1930* (New York: Wing Books, 1987), 237.

11. Weissman and Lavitt, 239.

12. Weissman and Lavitt, 243.

13. Weissman and Lavitt, 238–239.

14. Weissman and Lavitt, 250.

15. Stanley Vestal, *King of the Fur Traders, The Deeds and Deviltry of Pierre Esprit Radisson* (Boston: Houghton Mifflin, 1940), 98–99.

16. Andrew Gallup, ed., *Memoir of a French and Indian War Soldier, Jolicoeur Charles Bonin* (Bowie, MD: Heritage Books, Inc., 1993), 38–39n.

17. Russell, 195.

18. Russell, 198.

19. Louis Antoine de Bougainville, *Adventures in the Wilderness. The American Journals of Louis Antoine de Bougainville* (Norman: University of Oklahoma Press, 1964), 118.

20. C. Keith Wilbur, *The Woodland Indians, An Illustrated Account of the Lifestyles of America's First Inhabitants* (Guilford, CT: The Globe Pequot Press, 1995), 54.

21. Wilbur, 54.

22. Michael G. Johnson, *American Woodland Indians* (London: Osprey Publishing, 2000), 41.

23. James F. O'Neil, ed., *Their Bearing Is Noble and Proud: A Collection of Narratives Regarding the Appearance of Native Americans from 1740–1815* (Dayton, Ohio: J.T.G.S. Publishing, 1995), 38.

24. Peter Kalm, *Peter Kalm's Travels in North America* (New York: Dover Publications, 1964), 560.

25. Henry Timberlake, *Lieutenant Henry Timberlakes's Memoirs* (Marietta, GA: Continental Book Co., 1948), 150.

26. Timberlake, 76–77.

27. O'Neil, ed., 29. See also Andrew Gallup, ed., *Memoir of a French and Indian War Soldier, Jolicoeur Charles Bonin* (Bowie, MD: Heritage Books, Inc. 1993), 215.

28. O'Neil, ed., 77–78. Quoting William Bartrum.

29. O'Neil, ed., 77–78. Quoting William Bartrum.

30. O'Neil, ed., 2. Quoting James Adair.

31. O'Neil, ed., 77–78. Quoting William Bartrum.

32. Kalm, 563.

33. O'Neil, ed., 16. Quoting Col. James Smith.

34. O'Neil, ed., 19. Quoting John Knox.

35. Vestal, 20–21.

36. O'Neil, ed., 2–3. Quoting James Adair.

37. Kalm, 471–472.

38. Pierre Pouchot, *Memoir Upon the Late War in North America Between the French and English, 1775–1760* (Roxbury, MA: E. Elliot Woodward, 1866), vol. II, 187–193.

39. Jonathan Carver, *Travels Through the Interior Parts of North America in the Years 1766, 1767, and 1768* (Minneapolis: Ross & Hanes, 1956), 222–231.

40. Carver, 222–231.

41. Pouchot, 187–193.

42. Pouchot, 215.

43. Kalm, 560.

44. O'Neil, ed., 31. Quoting Jean-Bernard Bossu.

45. O'Neil, ed., 2–3. Quoting James Adair.

46. Having the hair or fur removed by scrapping after soaking in a vat of oak bark, the leather was softened by rubbing in the brains of deer mixed with rotten wood crushed into a powder.

47. O'Neil, ed., 29. Quoting Jolicoeur Charles Bonin.

48. Kalm, 556.

49. Carver, 222–231.

50. Pouchot, 187–193.

51. O'Neil, ed., 14. Quoting Peter Williamson.

52. O'Neil, ed., 33. Quoting Alexander Henry.

53. Pouchot, 187–193.

54. Richard Smith, *A Tour of Four Great Rivers. The Hudson, Mohawk, Susquehanna and Delaware in 1769* (New York: Charles Scribner's Sons, 1906), 83–84.

55. O'Neil, ed., 45. Quoting Elizabeth Hicks, a captive in Ohio.

56. Carver, 222–231.

57. O'Neil, ed., 2–3. Quoting James Adair.

58. O'Neil, ed., 2–3. Quoting James Adair.

59. O'Neil, ed., 44–45. Quoting Alexander Henry, Esquire. The issue of "cleanliness" was reported by Elizabeth Hicks.

60. Reuben Weiser, *Regina, the German Captive* (Baltimore: T.N. Kurtz, 1860), 132–133.

61. O'Neil, ed., 19. Quoting John Knox.

62. Nicholas Cresswell, *The Journal of Nicholas Cresswell, 1774–1777* (New York: Dial Press, 1928), 61.

63. Pouchot, 187–193.

64. O'Neil, ed., 43; Bernard Romans, *A Concise Natural History of East and West Florida* (Gainesville: University of Florida Press, 1962); first published in 1775.

65. O'Neil, ed., 19. Quoting John Knox.

66. Johnson, 42.

67. O'Neil, ed., 29. Quoting Jolicoeur Charles Bonin.

68. The one piece, knee high "Apache" boot, which combined a moccasin with leggings, was not used in the eastern woodlands.

69. O'Neil, ed., 29. Quoting Jolicoeur Charles Bonin.

70. Kalm, 564.

71. Carver, 222–231.

72. O'Neil, ed., 2. Quoting James Adair.

73. Pouchot, 187–193.

74. Pouchot, 215.

75. John Josselyn, *An Account of Two Voyages to New England* (London: G. Widdows, 1673; reprint, Boston: William Veazie, 1865), 100.

76. Kalm, 471–472.

77. O'Neil, ed., 28. Quoting Jolicoeur Charles Bonin.

78. Archibald Loudon, *A Selection of Some of the Most Interesting Narratives of Outrages Committed by the Indians in Their Wars with the White People* (London: S. Hooper and A. Morley, 1808), 292.

79. O'Neil, ed., 30–31. Quoting Jean-Bernard Bossu.

80. Kalm, 577.

81. O'Neil, ed., 28. Quoting Jolicoeur Charles Bonin.

82. O'Neil, ed., 31. Quoting Jean-Bernard Bossu.

83. Kalm, 577–578.

84. O'Neil, ed., 28. Quoting Jolicoeur Charles Bonin.

85. Loudon, 292.

86. Loudon, 258.

87. O'Neil, ed., 4–5. Quoting James Adair.

88. O'Neil, ed., 16. As reported by Col. James Smith.

89. O'Neil, ed., 4. Quoting James Adair.

90. Isabel M. Calder, *Colonial Captives, March, and Journeys* (Port Washington, NY: Kennikat Press, 1935), 16.

6

The Bountiful Earth Mother

On every side, far away beyond all knowing, stretched a vast labyrinth of woods and water, an endless wilderness rich in countless furs, a hunter's paradise.

—Stanley Vestal, Historian

Food and Farming

Before the advent of white immigration to North America, no draft animals had been harnessed to pull at loads; no plow had ever cut into the soil; and no wheel had turned upon its trails or across its plains. Although lacking these innovations, Native Americans were able to cultivate the soil and provide sufficient harvests of agricultural produce to address their immediate needs and add to their store of natural provisions. As far as researchers know, the entire provision of Native American food, housing, clothing, and utensils was accomplished by human labor with the assistance of only the simplest hand tools and fire.

Clever and painstaking methods were utilized throughout the Northeast woodlands to accomplish this feat. Loads, for instance, were carried on the backs of both men and women with the help of a tumpline—a wide band placed across the forehead that helped to steady the backpack and relieve some of the load on the back and shoulders. Stocks of food and seed for the next season were buried in pottery jars in large pits that were covered in reed mats and earth so that the Indian family could move from their summer homes to their winter residences. The homes, themselves, were made from natural materials, collected locally, and combined in a creative manner to provide protection from both the elements and enemies.

The soil of the Northeast was not all rich, dark, and fertile. Filled with rocks, trees, and tangled undergrowth, the soils of New England were particularly deficient for large-scale farming in European agricultural terms. Only a small portion of the open areas could be deemed fertile loam, and far more was considered only fair for raising extensive crops. Heavy soils rich in plant nutrients would have been too labor intensive for farmers working with stone-age agricultural devices and without the aid of draft animals. Therefore, native farmers purposely chose sandy loams and gravel-filled alluvial deposits in which to farm. Many of these were located in places free from unexpected frosts, near bodies of fresh water, or on hillsides with good drainage. The earliest Europeans found it necessary to add lime and manure to such earth to increase its fertility, and the Indians resorted to ground shell and chopped fish as fertilizer and to a periodic regimen of burning over wide areas of land. Unfortunately, the burning of leaf cover seriously retarded the formation of natural compost, and it did not help the balance of acidity in the soil. After a few years of intensive agriculture, yields fell to levels unworthy of their labor, and they abandoned the fields and allowed them to remain fallow for several seasons so that they might reclaim their natural fertility.

As to the size of their enterprise, Indian agriculture was either extensive or rudimentary. Large fields with corn hills in the tens of thousands often covered more than 30 acres—the spaces between the mounds averaging a little more than a yard apart. The mounds were created and kept clear of weeds by the application of simple hand tools alone. Almost no cultivation was necessary after the corn plants had gained some height because they outstripped the growth of the weeds. Moreover, the ears could hang for a long time and could be picked at leisure. Unlike the grains favored by the whites, corn also required no threshing or winnowing.

Early accounts of the extent of Indian agriculture noted adjoining fields numbering in the hundreds of acres interspersed with orchards, berry banks, rows of sunflowers, and vines right up to the edge of the forests. On the other hand, many natives kept small garden plots from a few tens of meters square to the size of an acre or two. John Smith noted that the Indians planted in May and June while subsisting on acorns, walnuts, and fish. Differences in the extent of farming were normally attributed to the diversity of tribal customs or the overall availability of arable soil in the region.

Captain John Smith in Virginia noted that each stalk of corn produced an average of two ears, and that each ear produced between 200 and 500 kernels. Modern hybrid varieties are designed to produce only one ear of high quality corn per stalk when planted in rows, but the actual number in unhybridized plants depended greatly on the plant density in the field. Native corn hill planting may actually have increased the yield in terms of the number of ears produced if not their quality by modern standards. Nonetheless, with aboriginal farming techniques alone, sandy loam and alluvial soils will yield approximately 60 bushels of shelled corn per acre throughout most of the region. Based on a village of 120 persons working 30 acres, researchers estimate that Indian corn fields could produce an average of 15 bushels of shelled corn per person annually. Under these circumstances, about 50 percent or slightly more of the total subsistence needs of the community may have been met.[1]

Dug open by archeologists, many abandoned corn hills have revealed gravel and fist-sized stones that may have helped to keep the soil texture loose and to moderate the internal temperatures against the effects of unseasonable frosts. Once established, such corn hills could be used for decades with the application of simple fertilizers, and the collapsing domes of earth could be easily scraped back into shape after a hard winter or a heavy season of rain.

Although schoolbooks often suggest that Indian men hunted and Indian women farmed, this division of labor is over simplified. Men actually did much of the heavy work preparing the fields for cultivation before they departed on extensive hunting trips or raids. Among these tasks was the girdling of trees with stone axes and fire in order to remove the dense canopy of leaves that prevented the sunlight from reaching the ground. "Between these trees," wrote John Smith, "they plant their corn, whose

This diorama in the state museum in New York shows both men and women working in the cornfields. Indian women often brought their children into the fields with them, and the older ones served to scare off crows and deer with a bag of throwing stones from their perch above the corn stalks.

great bodies do defend it from extreme gusts [of wind], and the heat of the Sun; whereas that [corn grown] in the plains, where the trees by time they have consumed, is subject to both; and this is the most easy way to have pasture and corn fields, which is much more fertile than the other." Once dead, the trees could be cut down or left standing. By leaving some trees standing, and by not removing any stumps, erosion was retarded somewhat, and the roots and stumps decaying in the soil provided for a reserve of nutrients that might be released over time. It may have taken generations to completely clear large fields without draft animals, and the stumps that dotted most open areas labeled them as once having been Indian fields.[2]

Once cleared of heavy brush and saplings by the men, the light soils and sandy loams of Indian fields were easily made into mounds and cultivated by the hands of women. The most extensive fields were owned by the community of clan women, as were the village dwellings, orchards, and vines. Early-contact illustrations suggest that the Indians may also have cultivated crops in long rows in some areas. These drawings, however, seem to fly in the face of eyewitness testimony to the contrary. In either case, the soil between the mounds or rows was left relatively hard and packed, and it supported little unwanted vegetation such as grass, vines, and weeds.

In light soils, the food producing plants did well without deep plowing as long as there was not an extended drought. In such a case, water was brought to the plants in gourds and calabashes from nearby sources. Nonetheless, it has been determined that periods of deficient rainfall in summer and fall occur in the region about once every three years, but they seldom last long enough to affect all the crops grown in a particular season. Only several dry years in succession would have resulted in a significant loss. The Indians seem to have been able to adapt to these agriculturally limiting environment conditions, yet there is scant evidence of native irrigation ditches or canals in the Northeast region.[3]

Many parts of the Northeast quadrant experienced too short a growing season for large scale agriculture to be successful, yet, most Indians were able to maintain small garden plots, vines, berry patches, and orchards to complement a diet of game and fish. They used naturally occurring and cultivated fruits of every kind available in the region, and they took simple steps to ensure their growth and continued abundance. They ate berries, grapes, pears, and apples freshly picked, and they dried any surplus to diversify their winter diet. They encouraged the growth of raspberries, blackberries, strawberries, mulberries, and low-bush blueberries in open places by removing unwanted vegetation and shade trees. Blueberries—natural ones, not those plump ones developed during the 19th century—grew particularly well in burned-over areas, and they attracted deer and other game animals for the hunters.

Grapevines abound in the northeastern forests with plants taking root in any open space and vines growing up into the forest canopy. The "Wolf" grape variety grew spontaneously in the forests and along the edge of clearings, but its fruit was seedy and tart and had a thick skin. Nonetheless, the natives so cherished the fruit that they cut away competing branches and may have cleared land and transplanted vines to favorable locations. Bunches of grapes could be left on the vines in the sun to form natural raisins. Indian currants are referred to by many European observers, but the actual identity of this fruit remains unclear.

Indian agriculturists actively supported orchards of fruit trees, especially apples and pears, and great care was given to highly valued and productive acorn and nut trees. These included the common acorns of white and red oak, beechnuts, chestnuts, butternuts, hickory, and many others. Because the trees produced more abundantly when their branches were open to the sun, Indians took care that other trees did not interfere with the best of their nut producers. Indian women and children collected thousands of nuts from the ground each fall and often spread mats or blankets under trees to help in the collection. Nuts could be roasted or boiled, and the meat of the nut was pounded into a paste or powder that could be used like a coarse flour after the shells had been sifted out. Hand-sized acorn cakes were often baked under coals or on hot flat stones with fresh or dried fruit mixed in with the otherwise tasteless paste. Dried fruit and nuts were also mixed with pounded dried meat and animal fat to

A very early engraving showing some of the natural bounty that Indian families were free to access for subsistence.

form a preserved high-calorie foodstuff called pemmican. This was stored in a parfleche (a leather storage bag) for future consumption.

The greatest difference between Native American and European style agricultural practices was that surrounding animal husbandry. It can be said that the greatest visible differences between Indian agriculture and colonial farming were hogs and hay. The Indians had no need for hay fields or for pasture because they kept no livestock; but as a consequence their fields, when left fallow to recover from decades of farming, quickly became overgrown with grasses, weeds, and brush. It was partly for this reason that whites considered them abandoned and took possession of them.

On the other hand, the natives of the Northeast woodlands had no general concept of the breeding or ownership of animals. Even the dogs that resided in the villages did so of their own volition. The deer, beaver, bear, elk, and moose of the frontier were not owned until they were killed during the hunt. Colonials claimed year-round ownership during the entire life of their animals. Hogs were of great value to the colonials because they reproduced themselves in large numbers and fed themselves in the brushwood. The practice of releasing hogs into the underbrush to fend for themselves caused no end of problems with Indian hunters, who freely killed the beasts without recognizing the ownership rights of whites.

By the 1670s, the expansion of white farms and plantations into the interior had created increased friction with the natives. The spark that raised the conflict known as Bacon's Rebellion took place in the Potomac Valley in the summer of 1675, when the local militia from Virginia crossed into Maryland and slaughtered almost two dozen Doeg and Susquehannock Indians in a feud over some missing hogs. The Indians retaliated, and the whites demanded further retribution. Back and forth along the frontier, raid and counter-raid followed. Thirty-six whites living along the Rappahannock River were killed during the attacks.

Ultimately, the situation turned white against white as Nathaniel Bacon and the royal governor, William Berkeley, came to loggerheads over how to deal with the Indians. Bacon and his followers called for 1,000 volunteers to raid the Indian settlements, but he refused to disband his army calling for sweeping changes in the colonial government. Even the colony's women played a roll, and they were among the rebellion's most active zealots. Bacon's death, unrelated to the crisis, ended the rebellion, and Berkeley brought in troops to chastise the rebels.[4]

The Corn Culture To the extent that the tribes of the Great Plains can be described as being part of a buffalo or horse culture, or those of the Desert Southwest can be described as a pueblo culture, the natives of the Northeast woodlands seem to have lived in a corn culture. The growth and use of corn was the overriding characteristic connecting the various Indian tribes of the region.

A native myth suggests that corn was one of the primal ingredients in human creation. The Creator initially made men of three different types, but each proved to be unworthy so he drowned them in a great lake. The Creator then made a fourth type, whom he found to his liking, and provided him with a sister (Woman) to ease his solitude. The man had a vision in a dream of five men coming from the forests to ask for his sister's hand in marriage. Where and when these men were created is not addressed by the story. Being a good brother, the man allowed his sister to choose among the suitors based upon how they presented themselves.

The first came as Tobacco, but Woman rejected him. He then drooped and died back into the ground. Other suitors appeared as Bean, Pumpkin, and Melon in turn, and each, while attractive, was rejected and withered away like the first. Finally, the fifth suitor appeared as Corn (maize), and he was immediately accepted. Woman and Corn married and all future generations of human beings proceeded from their union. Woman, nonetheless, did not forget her rejected suitors, and as plants and vines sprang from the ground she named them in remembrance of each, and thereby ensured their continued growth, cultivation, and use.

An alternative tradition suggests that the seeds of Corn, Beans, and Squash (or pumpkin) were brought to Woman by a crow, or blackbird, from the garden of the Creator himself. For this reason, many native tribes refused to kill crows although they raided their fields for seeds. The seeds are also attributed to the manitou, Kantantowit who lived in the Southwest. Many native traditions suggest the southwestern region of the continent as the origin of the corn culture with its "three sisters" of agriculture: maize, beans, and squash.

Various stories addressed the source of tobacco, which was highly venerated and useful in ceremonies, but useless as a source of nutrition. One such tale has the plant springing from the grave of a venerated clan matron; another that it was given to humans in the remote past in return for the sacrifice of their virgin daughters during a period of great famine; and another that it was stolen from the grasshopper by an Indian hero. The Indians chewed tobacco as a cure for toothache, but they also used it as a general pain killer, topical antiseptic, and as a drawing medium for snakebite. The burning or smoking of tobacco was part of many rituals and political discussions.

Regardless of their origin, the seeds of corn, beans, and squash (or pumpkin) were considered by all the peoples of the Northeast quadrant as great gifts. Corn, or maize, seems to have been developed at least 7,000 years ago from a wild grass that grows and reseeds itself naturally in Central America. It seems certain that native farmers selectively planted types that grew in larger ears with more succulent kernels that could ripen in a shorter growing season. This allowed the maize culture to move northward into the Great Lakes region. The corn observed by Europeans was probably introduced in the Northeast around A.D. 800 to 1000 and it was well established as a primary food crop by the time of first contact. These dates overlap with a dry period from A.D. 1000 to 1200 that was characterized by intermittent drought, brush fires, and warming temperature. It was about this time, or shortly before, that maize, beans, and squash seem to have become part of the subsistence base.[5]

"The hilling of Maize plants with hoes is a North American technique, not an introduction from Mexico, as were the plants themselves. With corn and hoes apparently came triangular arrow points and ceramic vessel shapes that were rounder than the earlier ones and that had thinner walls." The archeological evidence of these sudden changes in lifeways suggests a migration of people from elsewhere either as a whole or as an influential agent of change. "At this time unquestionably... came the corn ceremonies and the calendrical lore that regulated the timing of gardening activities and mobilized the labor necessary to clear the land, keep down the weeds, and plant and harvest the crops."[6]

Natives utilized four major varieties of corn including a short-seasoned type grown in the Canadian Maritimes and Maine as far north as the Penobscot and Kennebec River valleys. This produced a small ear no longer than the width of a hand. Above these latitudes the growing season was too short to support corn agriculture. The hard variety known as flint corn was best suited to drying and storage. Other species produced large ears and plump kernels. Indian corn came in white, yellow, blue, red, and multicolored varieties. Indian hunters and warriors often carried some parched corn in their leather girdles, so that no matter how bad the chase or how separated a man became from his companions he always had some nourishment with him. At home the dried kernels were pounded into a flour, made into a wet paste, and baked under the coals of the fire. Bogaert described a cake of corn flour formed into "a small loaf of bread baked with beans" that seems to have been a traveling staple of the Indian diet.[7]

There is a Penobscot tradition regarding the development of Indian corn varieties. Corn is a grass, and like all grasses it grows up in sections sometimes as high as 18 feet. The ears spring from the joints in these sections. According to the Penobscot, the native farmers noticed that the ears in the joints closest to the ground ripened earlier than those in the upper sections. There was as much as seven days growth difference between successive joints, and five weeks from bottom to top. The Indians supposedly chose only the ears from the lowest joints for seed corn, thereby producing a plant that ripened in only three months from the time of planting. This explanation, while not botanically correct, suggests that Indians attempted to pick and choose among the available varieties of natural foods in their environment. Unfortunately, the new plants seem to have lost their ability to self-propagate, requiring the Indian farmers to prepare the ground by hoeing, to implant the seeds manually in the mound, and provide fertilizer.

Beans Indians used beans as an iron ration to ward off winter starvation and as a source of non-animal protein year round. They often grew beans among the mounds of corn plants using the corn stalk as a natural trellis and planting squash or pumpkins among the spaces between the corn hills. The Indians of Maine are reported to have built a tepee-like structure of long poles in a circle some 10 feet in circumference planting the beans around the base and letting the vines find their own way to the top. Indian women supposedly put four maize kernels and two beans in each planting hole, and the two growing together somewhat alleviated the nitrogen depletion caused by growing continuous crops of corn alone.

Beans are a type of legume that tends to fix nitrogen in the soil or even increase it. The variety of beans planted was enormous, and white, red, yellow, green, and speckled types have been identified. Some of the bean vines at least seem to have been of the low bush variety. The Indians ate certain types fresh from the fields, pods and all, or used it as a bean paste or as a thickener for soups. Many beans were sun-dried in the pod by hanging them on a cord in the sun or over a slow fire, or by spreading the individual beans on pieces of bark to dry. Dried beans were stored in baskets or earthenware pots and could be preserved for long periods.

Squash, or Pumpkin Samuel de Champlain, Roger Williams, and John Carver, among others, all reported that the Indians grew melons, pumpkins, cucumbers, and squashes. These may have served as a carbohydrate substitute for bread. The observers mention many types of squashes: round, crane-necked, oblong, small, and flat. The small variety seem to have been eaten directly while the crane-necked type were hung from poles under cover of the weather for future use. It seems that the Indians took some defenses against putting the different types too close together in order to prevent cross-pollination. It is unlikely that they understood this mechanism, but they may have been operating under the restrictions of a taboo or simply following what they learned by observation. Calabashes and gourds were also grown, not for their food value but for their convenience as storage containers, water bottles, and utensils. Vine crops attracted hedgehogs and rabbits, and the Indians depended on their dogs and the young boys of the village to root out these pests and add a little meat to the cook pot.

Roots While less romantic in their origins, roots and tubers were of particular importance to the Indian diet. Although the "Irish" potato had its origins in the New World, there is scant evidence that native farmers in the Northeast purposely cultivated it. Root plants similar to the sweet potato or yam were more common. Among those tubers that occurred naturally was the Tuckahoe, an edible wild tuber gathered in marshlands in the summer. The Indians also commonly dug the Jerusalem Artichoke and the groundnut. The Jerusalem Artichoke has a root that produced a good deal of plant sugar even in poor soil, and the plants were particularly prolific in good soils. The tubers had an excellent chance of surviving in a hard freeze. The groundnut was often called the "rosary" by Jesuit observers because the pear-shaped, rusty, or dark-colored tubers were strung along the root system much like beads. Groundnuts were rich in starch and, if dried and ground, produced a coarse flour that compared favorably to wheat flour.

Closely related to these naturally occurring tuberous plants was the sunflower, which was valued for the abundance of seeds that were produced in its flower. The plants were easily grown and the seeds easily harvested. The latter could be eaten directly, pressed for oil, or dried in the sun for future use. Sunflowers were purposely planted along the margins of the cultivated fields in order to provide maximum sunlight. Indian children were stationed in the fields while the seeds developed to keep away thieving birds.

Harvesting the Marshland

Indians inhibited many areas that included extensive marshlands that might be exploited for their wealth of natural resources. Marshes rank among the most productive ecosystems on earth. In an Indian grant of land to the Dutch made in Flushing (Queens County, New York), the Sachem reserved the right of "cutting the bullrushes forever" along the shore and among the meadows. When another Long Island tribe conveyed ownership of the Shinnecock Hills to whites, they were allowed "to plow and plant and cut timber for fences and fuel, and also to cut flags and bullrushes and such grasses as they usually make their houses of and to dig ground nuts."[8]

There are many ways to categorize these marshes. Among them are landlocked *pocket marshes* (either spring or rain fed), *fringing marshes* found along the edge of salt-water sounds and bays, and *creek marshes* with their constant inflow of freshwater. These three types support three unique plant communities (smooth cordgrass marshes, big cordgrass marshes, and the cattail marshes). The types tend to transition one from the other according to the topography of a particular region. Low lying marshes flood with salt water twice a day while upland marshes flood only during storms or unusually high tides (spring tides). The animals and plants that live in these marshes are specialized as to how well they can withstand the drier conditions of the upland marshes or the wet condition of regular flooding with salt water.

The smooth cordgrass plant dominates the regularly flooded saltmarsh because it has special glands that excrete excess salt that enable it to live where other plants could not. Few animals eat this plant, but it serves as the habitat for a multitude of animals, such as muskrats, box turtles, fiddler crabs, marsh mussels, and nesting birds. Marshes provide food and resting areas for migrating waterfowl, herons, and egrets and are associated with fish spawning and nursery areas for small fish, shrimp, and blue crabs. Contrary to popular belief, few reptiles live in salt marshes, but they were commonly infested with hundreds of species of annoying insects on which other animals fed.

Salt marshes are transition zones between land and water that occur along the inter-tidal zone along the shores of estuaries, creeks, and sounds where salinity varies from ocean strength to that of fresh water lakes in upland rivers. These marshes are subject to rapid changes in both depth and salinity twice a day because of the 12-hour cycle of high and low tides. The mud flats that border saltmarshes are excellent breeding grounds for the highly prized oysters and clams. The entire North Atlantic coastline of America can be characterized as an estuary zone. Estuaries are ancient river valleys that have sunken below sea level through the various mechanisms of geology so that they become affected by the ocean tide cycles some distance inland. The Hudson River valley of New York is a classical example of an estuary with tides of various strength and salt to brackish waters as far inland as the falls near Troy, New York.

While cordgrass is generally inedible, the cattail plant provided one of the most important of marshland foods. Easily recognized by its white, dense, furry, and cigar-shaped seed head that stands atop a long stalk, cattails grow from a dense maze of rhizomes (tuber-like roots) in the mud of marshes, swamps, lakes, and ponds in both brackish and fresh water. The 9-foot-tall cattail is sometimes confused with a common 12-foot-tall reed that tolerates more salt in the water but cannot grow in shallow water like the cattail. Both types produce edible young shoots in early spring.

The spring cattail shoot has an odorless, tender, white inner core that tastes sweet and pleasant. It is very easy to harvest and is highly nutritious, just peel and eat. The proportion of food to waste varies, but just a few large, late spring stalks can provide a meal. The shoots contain a number of B vitamins, potassium, phosphorous, and the all important vitamin C. The shoots also secrete a sticky, mucilaginous jelly that can be used to thicken soups. The male flower head is edible and somewhat like corn without the central core. These flowers also produce large quantities of edible pollen just before the summer solstice that can be harvested and used like a fine flour. The rhizomes (or roots) contain a great deal of starch that can be pounded out of the fibers, once they have been dried, and used as an additive to thicken stews and soups.

The Indians also used cattails as a non-food resource material. They used the jelly as a salve on wounds, sores, and boils and as a cure for toothache. The inedible parts of the plant, such as the dried leaves, were twisted into dolls and toy animals for children, woven into baskets, or incorporated into mats. The leaves were also used as thatch for roofing, and archeologists have found in protected caves woven cattail mats that are more than 10,000 years old. The white seed puffs, collected in late summer, were used like absorbent cotton, and Indians put them into moccasins and cradleboards as insulation. Finally, the brown, dried husk of the flower head supported a smoky and slow-burning flame that was used to drive away insects.

The cattail plant grows worldwide and is so primitive that it dates back to the time of the dinosaurs. It is self-propagating with the bursting seed heads easily establishing new colonies of rhizomes, and the Indians found such vast areas of plants growing naturally that they did not bother to cultivate it. Whites seemingly ignored the plant as a food source. Like the smooth cordgrass plant, the cattail tends to improve water quality and lower salinity wherever it grows.

Wild Rice Rice was one of the food staples found in fringing environments, and it was particularly important among the populous Great Lakes tribes, such as the Ojibwa (Chippewa, Ottawa, etc.). The most common form was a wild rice (*Zizania palustris*) that grew in shallow lakes and streams of the Great Lakes region and ripened in late August and early September. An alternative species (*Zizania aquatica*), also an annual, grew in the St. Lawrence River valley and the coastal areas of the eastern and southeastern states. A third type (*Zizania texana*) grew in small areas of Texas.

Rice was so important to the Menominee of the Great Lakes region that they were known as the Wild Rice people, and they made annual sacrifices of tobacco to the manitous to assure a good harvest. Persons in the first year of bereavement and menstruating women were banned from the rice fields, which were important enough to the subsistence agriculture to be guarded by outposts setup for the purpose of monitoring the crop.

Each family or clan had its own rice fields. Sometimes they harvested fields in several locations. Native Americans were known to have attempted the propagation of new rice fields by mixing rice grains into balls of clay and dropping the seed balls into likely stands of water. This resulted in some, but not significant, increases in natural stands of rice. Wild rice seeds of the Great Lakes variety require immersion in near freezing or freezing water for at least three months to germinate. Rice is self-pollinating, and two weeks after pollination the seeds appear. About four weeks later, depending on proper environmental conditions, it is ready for harvesting. However, the seeds on any tiller will mature at different times, and on secondary tillers they mature later than on main tillers. Harvesting the entire yield, therefore, required careful timing and repeated trips to various stands.

When the rice in a particular location was deemed ready for harvest, the leaders of the clan declared to the people that the time had come to gather it in. In the morning, the Indians set out in twos and threes in canoes with a woman or older child in the bow facing the rear. The canoe was usually propelled by a pole, and the steersman stood in the rear ready to brace the vessel as the woman pulled the tall stalks of the rice plant over the side and knocked the grains from the plant into the bottom of the canoe. When the vessel was filled to capacity it returned to the shore, and the rice was put into bark or pottery containers to be carried back to camp.

In the camp, the rice would be relieved of twigs and pieces of stalk and spread out in the sun to dry. The dry rice was then put into a dry kettle to be parched to loosen the husks and to improve its chances of long-term storage. The work was hot and tiresome because the grain needed to be turned constantly with a wooden paddle to keep it from scorching. The Indians removed the husks by walking on the parched rice in a pit lined with a deerskin, and they winnowed the grain from the chaff by throwing the grain up into the wind in large finely woven trays. Many canoe loads might be harvested in a single day, and the families might stay in the area harvesting and preparing the rice for storage for several weeks.

The rice grain has a high protein and carbohydrate content and is low in fat. It surpasses or is equal to many other cereal grains in this respect. The nutritional quality of wild rice is a little higher than that of oat groats, which are one of the better cereals for human consumption. The mineral content of wild rice, which is high in potassium and phosphorus, compares well with corn, wheat, and oats, and it is an excellent source of many B vitamins. Unfortunately, the rice contains two fatty acids that are easily oxidized to form rancid odors.

Parched rice, like popcorn, could be eaten as it was without further cooking, but the Indians favored it boiled with corn, beans, squash, or meat added to it. Sometimes plain rice had a little animal grease or maple sugar added to it for flavor. Like beans and dry corn, rice could be cached in any dry container for future use, and there is evidence of an entire dug-out canoe filled with rice being buried on a sunny hillside so that the family could return to it later in the year.[9]

Fowling   Indian hunters, men and boys, also harvested a wide variety of birds and bird's eggs including ducks, geese, turkeys, partridge, woodcock, pigeons, pheasants, and quail. So immense were the seasonal flocks that populated the North American lake regions that a hunter might chance a valuable arrow that could knocked down a bird even on the wing. He might bring one to ground with a well-thrown club, or hunt them with a spear in their roosts at night with the aid of a flaming torch. Throwing sticks about two feet long (the diameter half the size of the butt and tapered from the handle to the butt) were used in an overhand-sideways manner that made them spin when tossed through the air. This action was very effective in disabling the birds. These same weapons were used on small game, such as rabbits and squirrels. An average hunter could bring in 8 or 10 birds a day in season. It was laughingly said that they ate every part of the bird except the feathers and the beak, often roasting them whole on a stick over the fire.

Hunting

Indian men seemingly spent half the year hunting and the other half preparing to do so. Game animals were an important food asset, and also a source of skins (leather), fur (for warmth or trade), implements, and cordage. A mature deer or elk could dress out to 100 pounds of fresh meat, a black bear 300, a moose almost twice that, and a buffalo bull (where available) close to the better part of a ton. Yet, the idea that these large game animals roamed everywhere in the Northeast quadrant of North America is misleading.

Deer and elk were generally available everywhere, but they required open areas for grazing in order to thrive. There may be more deer in the forest regions of North America today than there were in the 17th and 18th centuries. Bear and moose were solitary animals that inhabited inconvenient places, such as marshes, swamps, islands, or the deep woods; and buffalo, more prevalent in the plains state, could be found roaming in many places not normally associated with them, such as New York, Pennsylvania, Kentucky, Ohio, Indiana, or Illinois. Yet, these buffalo were not found in the overwhelmingly large herds common to the Great Plains of the 19th-century West.

Although deer and elk were more numerous, moose were probably the most important game animals for those Indians living in the colder northern regions, but unlike buffalo that roamed in herds, moose were solitary animals that had to be hunted individually. Indian hunters developed techniques for dealing with this circumstance particularly the use of mating calls made of bark to attract the animals and of snowshoes that allowed the hunter to quickly approach moose bogged down in belly deep snow. Moose were also hunted from canoes if they were found swimming in ponds or lakes. It was not unknown for hunters to set overhead snap

Indians were practical hunters. Large game animals, such as moose, elk, and deer, were most easily taken when in the water or when slowed by deep snows.

snares for large animals, such as moose, elk, or deer that were actuated by the weight of the animal, but they always risked the possibility of the animal breaking free or damaging their tackle.

As a source of game, every tribe maintained a hunting ground and jealously protected it from incursions by other native hunters. They kept these hunting grounds open and attractive to game by periodically burning off the underbrush. These ground fires kept the woods free of undergrowth and encouraged the growth of young, tender vegetation and berries that the animals found attractive in summer and fall. The Indians were careful, moreover, to locate their hunting grounds some distance from their villages, orchards, and agricultural fields because these animals could devastate young corn plants and eat an entire season's output of apples or berries in a single night. Closer to home, individual hunters set up traps, snares, and deadfalls to secure smaller game and fur-bearing animals. The latter became increasingly important as the 17th century wore on and the local source of fur became exhausted through over harvesting. Thereafter, Indian men spent more and more time securing furs for trade away from home.

To some extent, the game animals favored by Indians as a source of food in times of plenty depended on their core religious beliefs. It was thought that the characteristics of the animal were underscored in the eater of its flesh. Fleetness of foot, for instance, might come from eating venison (generally considered deer meat), and great strength might come from consuming bear. Yet, most Indians would not let their scruples interfere with a nice piece of roasted polecat (skunk), muskrat, or dog, if the need arose. Many smaller animals were used for food: rabbit, squirrel, panther, wildcat, badger, beaver, raccoon, turkey, duck, goose, partridge, pigeon, fox, wolf, and dog to name a few. When food was scarce snakes, lizards, mice, rats, and small birds might make an individual meal. Young boys often sought out small game near the village using bows with blunt arrows, rocks, throwing sticks, clubs, spears, nets, or traps.

Harmen van der Bogaert reported in 1634 that the Iroquois kept bear cubs, whose mothers had been killed, in enclosures to be fattened for use as food at a feast or celebration. He saw two tame bears in as many villages. "[The bear] had been in there almost three years and was so tame that it ate everything given it." Bogaert wrote that he "wanted to buy the bear, but they would not part with it." The structures in which the bears were kept were small log houses or pens made by driving stakes into the ground. These enclosures were inside the village stockade. The bear was an important animal to the Iroquois, not only as a source of food, but as a religious and clan symbol. The Bear Clan (one of three major divisions among Iroquois families), the Bear Society (an important medicine society), and the Bear Dance (held at the Midwinter Ceremony) were all integral to the Iroquois way of life.[10]

Hunting parties were serious assemblages of adult men led by experienced elders. They were often formed in late fall and again in late winter, and large groups of hunters traveled to the hunting grounds in order to maximize the expectation of success for the entire tribe. The village was the center of the social and cultural life of its inhabitants from late summer until late autumn when it broke up to establish temporary quarters in the hunting grounds if they were more than a few days journey away. The old men with some women and children were generally left behind to care for the village.

Small groups composed of a handful of men and older boys might be out hunting at any time of the year, but several hundred persons might participate in the seasonal hunts. The main encampment many have been emptied of most persons at these times. Captain John Smith left a brief description of the hunting camp. "Their hunting houses are not so labored, substantial, nor artificial as their other, but are like our soldiers cabins. The frames set up in two or three hours, cast overhead with mats, which the women bear after them (the men), as they carry likewise corn, acorns, mortars, and all the bag and baggage to use."[11]

LaSalle suggested among his observations that the Indians hunted in clans. To embark on a winter hunt was to leave their stock of stored food behind, and if the hunt failed to live up to expectations for any reason, the hunters and those of their families that accompanied them faced famine if they could not get back to their caches. Jacques Marquette reported a near starvation of the Miami, Mascouten, and Kickapoo in 1673 because their tribal hunts failed to harvest enough game. In the winter of 1675–1676, more than 60 Mississauga starved to death north of Lake Erie because sufficient game could not be found, and the weather prohibited their returning to their village bases.[12]

Nonetheless, large quantities of meat could be preserved by smoking and drying in these temporary camps and carried by the women back to the main village to be guarded by the older boys from predators. Archeological evidence suggests that these group hunting camps were quite some distance outside the main village area, usually in the interior uplands. Bogaert saw some longhouses among the Mohawk with "at least 40 or 50 quarters of venison, cut and dried" hanging in the rafters. This was in January of 1634, immediately after the late fall hunt, and it is evidence of the stockpile of food laid in by Indians before entering the depth of winter.[13]

The hunters exhibited several techniques for harvesting game including small band and large group hunting. Using the equivalent of bush beaters to drive the animals from the forests along a prepared path, the Indians funneled the game toward positions held by the best shots with bow and arrow or with a spear. Sometimes the animals were driven over a cliff or other precipice to be bludgeoned to death by waiting huntsmen at the bottom. Being herd animals that were easily stampeded, scores of buffalo met their fate in this manner. Fire surrounds were also used to drive the herds of game.

There was an annual seasonal hunt with the emphasis placed on securing deer both for meat and for hides. Nonetheless, a regular regime of hunting by individuals might take place at any time of the year. Solitary hunting was probably considered risky and inefficient, and most hunters went in pairs or in small groups of friends or relatives. The Indians engaged in hunting to secure food and hides for clothing and other uses, but it should be remembered that it served as recreation and sport for men as well. A series of hunter's cabins was encountered by Dutch trader Harmen van der Bogaert in 1634 that were evidently maintained with water and preserved foodstuffs at intervals along the trails throughout Iroquoia. These structures were somewhat like public hospices and were frequently erected by an Indian in response to a dream or vision.[14]

Short hunting trips were made during lulls in the farming, fishing, or warfare cycles. The hunters took elaborate precautions to conceal their presence in a tree stand or blind with their weapons. They blew deer and moose calls and sometimes wore animal skins with the heads attached over their own heads and shoulders, yet, they could stay silently

The Indian hunter, or warrior, could blend into the background of his environment with remarkable efficiency. Individuals might remain virtually motionless for hours, and groups might go undetected in an area for several days.

at their posts or thread their way through the woods all day without sighting a single game animal. Hunting the fleet-footed deer with bow and arrow was something else again, but the Indians often employed special techniques there as well, some involving a high degree of skill and cunning.

Inevitably, they developed a number of tricks to attract game. Decoys were used, open-end pens were constructed, noose snares were set on deer trails, and baits and scents were placed out to attract deer and elk. "These savages," Thomas Harriot noted, "being secretly hidden among high reeds, where oftentimes they find the deer asleep, and kill them." Deer were also hunted at night with torches, especially from canoes. The light momentarily dazed and froze the deer as they drank at the water-side. Native bows were relatively weak when compared to their European counterparts, and hunters needed to get close to their quarry if they wished to be successful. In order to enhance their opportunities, Indians learned to simulate bird calls and animal sounds, especially those of waterfowl and baby deer (fawns), and they took care to mask their odor and disguise the scent of their bodies.[15]

Native Americans hunted by spear, lance, or bow and arrow. Spearheads constructed from sharp rocks and shaped into a point became a deadly force. A flint knapper could produce a large number of small projectile points from a single piece of flint, obsidian, or chert. These stones left a razor sharp fracture when struck a sharp blow. Most collections of Indian arrowheads are actually assemblies of spear points. These stone projectiles were fastened to a semi-flexible pole ranging in length from five to six feet that was made from young sapling trees stripped of the bark. One end of the pole was notched, and the point inserted. A string-like substance called sinew was used to bind the arrowhead to the shaft. Lightweight lances, really javelins, could be thrown remarkable distances in the open field, but the spear was a thrusting weapon better suited to the bush and brambles of the woodlands.

American Indians did not always have the bow and arrow. It was not until about A.D. 500 that the bow and arrow was adopted in Iowa, some 11,500 years after the first people came to that region, and it seems to have moved east and northeast thereafter. Primary benefits of the bow and arrow over the spear were more rapid missile velocity, a higher degree of accuracy, and a greater mobility. Arrowheads also required substantially less raw materials than spearheads. Even with the gun's many advantages in the historic era, bows and arrows are much quieter than guns, allowing the hunter more chances to strike at the prey. For smaller animals, a herding system of nets served for quick catches. Once subdued, the netted animals were dispatched with spears or clubs. Indian hunting techniques were neither quick nor painless for the prey. Nets could be created from sinew, vines, or the inner lining of tree bark, or they could be made of braided hair from buffalo, horses, or other large animals.

The main time for trapping and hunting was mid-winter when small family groups retired from the main village to their special places inland. The snow allowed animals to be tracked more easily, and it slowed their progress and limited their range perceptibly. Wounded animals left a clear trail of footprints and blood in the snow. When snow was on the ground the hunter usually pulled the carcass home on a toboggan. Otherwise, he trussed it up and carried it on his back or more likely that of his wife.

A 17th-century observer, Thomas Harriot made special mention of the hunting of black bears, which he said were "good meat," adding that "the inhabitants in time of winter do use to take and eat many. They are taken commonly ... in some islands or places where they are, being hunted for as soon as they have seen of man, they presently run away, and then being chased, they climb and get up the next tree they can. From whence with arrows they are shot down stark dead, or with those wounds that they may after easily be killed." Bear hunting was often considered a way in which a young man could prove his bravery, especially if he ventured into a cave with a spear and fought a hand-to-hand battle with a drowsing burin.[16]

Fishing

The most dependable source of food was often fish or shellfish. The fisheries tended to be more reliable than agriculture, and many Algonquian tribes living on the Great Lakes or along the Atlantic coastline abandoned the concept of extensive agriculture in favor of fishing. Nonetheless, most fishing people continued to keep small family garden plots. Certainly fishing and gathering seafood were important lessons that a young person would learn early in life. Almost without exception native villages were located near the water: an inlet, a river, a seashore, or a lakeshore. If not directly on the water, the site was usually no more than a few days' journey away, and the whole tribe, save a few old people and children who were left to protect the fields, usually traveled to the tribes favorite fishing places.

The Atlantic seashore was the obvious choice for eastern tribes, and huge heaps of clam, quahaug (large round clam), and oyster shells have been identified along the shores of Chesapeake Bay, Delaware Bay, the coastline of New England and the Canadian Maritimes, New York's Long Island Sound, and even in areas of what are today modern mega-cities, such as New York, particularly in the Bronx and Brooklyn. Dozens of giant clam banks (heaps of waste shell) have been identified on Cape Cod (MA), in Warwick (RI), and in Milford (CT). Many of these clam banks are several feet deep and may cover 10 to 20 acres in total area, testifying to their long use as extractive shellfish harvesting sites rather than as villages. Lobsters and crabs were also harvested. The excess meat from these types of shellfish could be dried and preserved over smoky wood fires right on the beach. Evidence of animal bones taken from food and trash pits suggests that while the Indians harvested the bounty of the shoreline, they also supplemented their stock of foods by hunting along the margins of the local woodlands.

There is also evidence of the harvesting of freshwater clams and crayfish along inland waterways and lakes. The Ojibwa groups around Chequamegon, Keweenaw, Green bay, and Sault Ste. Marie relied on the wealth of fish available in local waters to the point that they did not plant extensive crops. When the fish were abundant, these fishing peoples preferred to remain in their villages taking only local game and avoiding the prolonged winter hunts. However, when their garden patches failed or the fish were not as numerous as expected, they faced the particular horror of famine. Under these circumstances, they were forced to hunt and gather or die. Nonetheless, the combination of marginal agriculture, expedient hunting, and reliable fishing usually met their needs. Father Claude-Jean Allouez noted that the Potawatomi strove to fill their lodges to overflowing with a stock of smoked herring and whitefish in the fall and anxiously awaited the run of sturgeon in the spring to fill their stomachs.[17]

The explorer Henry Hudson attested to the abundant food supply available in the waters surrounding present-day New York City. He said that the Indians caught all kinds of fish with seines including young salmon and sturgeon, and Harmen van der Bogaert noted that "there are six or seven or even 800 salmon caught in one day. I saw houses with 60, 70, and more dried salmon."[18] Archeological evidence of sturgeon scales taken from food pits excavated on the island of Manhattan in the 1920s suggests that the rivers swarmed with fish. In the shallows along the shores of the East River were oysters, clams, and scallops in incredible numbers that grew to immense proportions.

More than two dozen native camping and fishing sites were identified in Bronx County, New York alone. On Zerega's Point, for instance, evidence was found of a Native American fishing station with a small fresh water spring nearby. Mixed in with the shell mound were some small fragments of pottery and other Indian objects. There was also an extensive settlement along the beach on Throg's Neck reached by an ancient Indian pathway. "Many food-pits, several fireplaces, some human burials and much broken pottery and stone artifacts" among the shell mounds point to a long occupancy probably by the Siwanoy or the Weckquaesgeek. The latter tribe sold the land to Jonas Bronck in a treaty dated 1642.[19]

The rhythm of Native American life was often dictated by the annual runs of shad, salmon, and other anadromus fish. These were types that lived in salt water but spawned in fresh. The Indians were accustomed to travel to their favorite fishing spots in April and May in order to take advantage of these runs. Near the shore, from March to September, they could net mackerel and herring that ran in huge schools right up along the shore from their heavy dugout canoes. They could also take to the water in groups to harpoon porpoise, seals, or whales.

The treaties made by coastal tribes with the English and the Dutch often showed a great concern that the Indians be permitted to continue their fishing along the seashore even though they may have transferred ownership of the land to the whites. Indian fishermen often specifically reserved any "great fish" washed up or beached upon the shore as their own, suggesting that the beaching of porpoises, dolphins, and whales that we see today also took place 300 years ago. They also harvested the nearby salts marshes.

Inland tribes gathered in the spring at the falls of rivers to spear salmon or shad returning upstream to spawn. They also preyed on bass, sturgeon, ells, and cod. They harvested the freshwater lakes and ponds of pike, pickerel, trout, turtles, frogs, and other tasty pan fish. Whites reported observing Indian women in the water of lakes standing waist deep while fishing. Taking as many fish as possible with spears, nets, and traps, the Indians would split and dry the fish over slow fires or in the sun in order to preserve them for future use. Inland tribes would often trade their surplus of dried meat with coastal or lake tribes for smoked seafood in order to vary their diet.

Native Americans traditionally fished with hand-made spears and a system of temporary fences used for herding the run of fish into one part of the stream. For the most part, the Indians caught their fish in net-like obstructions called weirs, which they placed across streams or channels. The weirs were made of reeds woven or tied together and anchored to the bottom by poles stuck into the sand. With their tops extending above the surface of the water the weirs looked very much like fences and were arranged in varied patterns designed to catch the fish and then impound them. Fishing spears were crafted from a forked sapling pole around 5 to 6 feet tall. The forked ends would be sharpened and then notched and tried to create a pinch and hold mechanism for plucking fish from the stream. Gates and dams allowed fish to swim into a trapping area, and this process could be repeated until enough fish were caught to feed all the hungry families. The Nipissings were so successful in taking whitefish that they traded it to other nations as a commodity.

At the mouth of a river, the Indians drove stakes into the bottom, which held them firmly in place. But up the river, where the current was much stronger, the stakes would not stand up for long. To overcome this difficulty, the Indians built stone walls out from shore, extending down into the river for almost 30 to 40 feet. The walls were built at an angle of about 75 degrees and heading upstream. Some of the stones were quite large. After these walls were built, the stakes were driven between the rocks, and in that way the river could not undermine them. There is no doubt that, in the early times, these fish weirs were numerous for miles along the river, as far as the shad and other fish went to their spawning grounds. The fish once went up the river by the tens of thousands.

A 17th-century observer, Thomas Harriot, described the Indian's weir-fishing technique as the setting of reeds or twigs in the water, which they planted next to each other, so that their space grew still narrower, and narrower, thus preventing the fish, once imprisoned, from swimming out again. Harriot added that yet another fishing technique "which is more strange, is with poles made sharp at one end, by shooting them into the fish after the manner as Irishmen cast darts, either as they are rowing in their boats or else as they are wading in the shallows for the purpose." These spears or harpoons were sometimes fitted with sharp points made from the hollow tail of a sea crab, possibly a Horseshoe crab.[20]

It was also reported that the Indians caught a wide variety of fish, including "trout, porpoise, rays, oldwives (probably menhaden), mullets, plaise (flounder), and very many other sorts of excellent good fish, which we have taken and eaten, whose names I know not but in the country language...For four months of the year, February, March, April and May, there are plenty of sturgeons. And also in the same months of herrings, some of the ordinary bigness of ours in England, but for the most part far greater, of eighteen, twenty inches, and some two feet in length."[21]

A 19th-century researcher noted the following odd bit of anecdotal information concerning the various methods used in Indian cooking. The descriptions are as interesting as they may be apocryphal.

All Indians were trained to be observant. They can easily tell by examining an encampment what nation of Indians the party were of who occupied it. For instance in a Shauwanoa [Shawnee] encampment the kettle is suspended from a horizontal beam which rests upon two forked sticks placed in the ground vertically at the opposite ends of the beam. The Ottawas spread their kettle from a single stick which is placed in the earth and extends across the fire. The Wyandots also use the beam, but they always encamp between two trees, against which they lean two poles which support the beam. The Chippewa use two sticks, which are run into the ground and crossed at the opposite ends.[22]

Condiments

It has been suggested that the Indians had a depleted sense of taste because they eschewed the use on their foods of salt and strong sauces so popular with Europeans. Yet, the great variety of vegetables, fishes, and meats that they enjoyed suggests rather that they had delicate and discriminating palates. Dried and fresh berries, ground nuts and seeds, and the leaves of certain plants, such as wintergreen and mint, were used to add flavor to an otherwise bland diet.

Without question, the favored condiment of the Indians was maple sugar. In spring the sap of the tree was collected in pots and jars, and the water was boiled off by adding heated rocks to the liquid. Maple sugar was kept as a syrup, as a crystal, and as a crushed sugar. Dried squash was often crushed into maple syrup and made into a bread. The thickened sap was sometimes used directly as an ingredient mixed with corn meal or on meat, and the crystallized form was given to children as a treat. Honey was collected and used in much the same way. Children also sucked on cornstalks using them much in the same way that other cultures used raw sugar cane.

Notes

1. Stephen R. Potter, *Commoners, Tribute, and Chiefs, The Development of Algonquian Culture in the Potomac Valley* (Charlottesville: University Press of Virginia, 1993), 46.

2. Potter, 33.

3. Potter, 38.

4. See Selma R. Williams, *Demeter's Daughters, The Women Who Founded America: 1587–1787* (New York: Athenaeum, 1976), 162–163.

5. Potter, 101.

6. Dena F. Dincauze, "Prehistory of Southern New England," in *The Pequots in Southern New England, The Fall and Rise of an American Indian Nation,* ed. Laurence M. Hauptman and James D. Wherry (Norman: University of Oklahoma Press, 1990), 29–30.

7. Charles T. Gehring and William A. Starna, eds., *A Journey into Mohawk and Oneida Country, 1634–1635: The Journal of Harmen Meyndertz van der Bogaert* (Syracuse, NY: Syracuse University Press, 1988), 3.

8. Jacqueline Overton, *Indian Life on Long Island* (Port Washington: Ira J. Friedman, Inc., 1963), 123.

9. See Robert E. Ritzenthaler and Pat Ritzenthaler, *The Woodland Indians of the Western Great Lakes* (Garden City, NY: The Natural History Press, 1970), 25–26.

10. Gehring and Starna, eds., 9.

11. Quoted in Potter, 41.

12. Richard White, *The Middle Ground, Indians, Empires, and Republics in the Great Lakes Region, 1650–1815* (New York: Cambridge University Press, 1991), 46–47n.

13. Gehring and Starna, 21.

14. Gehring and Starna, 25.

15. Ritzenthaler and Ritzenthaler, 20.

16. Ritzenthaler and Ritzenthaler, 20.

17. White, 44.

18. Gehring and Starna, 13.

19. Reginald Pelham Bolton, *Indian Life of Long Ago in the City of New York* (New York: Crown Publishers, Limited, 1972; reprint of the original 1934 edition), 137–138.

20. Ritzenthaler and Ritzenthaler, 17.

21. Ritzenthaler and Ritzenthaler, 18.

22. Paul A. W. Wallace, *Indians of Pennsylvania* (Harrisburg: The Pennsylvania Historical and Museum Commission, 1986), 125.

III

THE INDIAN FAMILY AND THE SPIRITUAL WORLD

7

Native American Ceremonies and Rituals

When a person has suffered a great loss caused by death, his throat is stopped and he can not speak. With these words, I remove the obstruction from your throat so that you may speak and breath freely.
—The Third Wampum String of the Condolence Ceremony

Traditional Religions

The Indians had no strict creed and enforced no orthodoxy of belief. There was, therefore, a great latitude in the details of their religions. An exhaustive study of the many beliefs, diverse rituals, and complicated ceremonies of all the woodlands nations is beyond the scope of this work, but certain characteristic elements can be highlighted.

Indian religions were remarkably durable, withstanding physical persecution from the Spanish, ceaseless badgering from the French, and the benign neglect of the English. Kakowatchiky, a respected elder chief of the Shawnee, explained to the Moravian missionaries of Pennsylvania that Indians "believed in God, who had created both the Indian and the white man. But...after what he had seen of white men on the frontier, he preferred Indian ways and beliefs; for...the white man prayed with words while the Indian prayed in his heart."[1]

The Native American conception of the spirit world generally reflected the things that they saw about them. The flat earth was the realm of wind and clouds populated with humans, animals, and spirits. The sun, moon, and stars had their course in the great circle of the sky that was the roof of the human world and the floor of the skyland—the abode of the Great Spirit (also known as the Creator, or Master of Life). It was from this heaven that the man-beings, or the Powers Above, descended to create the visible and tangible environment on earth. The earth was the floor of the universe for humans, and under this was the realm of the Powers Below, who sent upward the spring waters and forces of life that animated the plant world and supported that of animals. Both the realm above and that below could be inhabited by the souls of departed humans, who in death only changed their dwelling place. The birds were thought to act as messengers between the earth and skyland, while serpents and the creatures of the water were intermediaries with the world below.

The Delaware believed that spirits controlled the world of nature for human benefit, and they recognized three orders of supernatural beings: certain spirit forces (manitou) on earth; 11 appointed spirits who acted from the heavens; and a Great Spirit, or Creator, who dwelled in the twelfth and highest heaven. The creator had existed from time immemorial and had created all of heaven and earth. The appointed spirits—Sun, Moon, Earth, Fire, Water, House, Corn, and the Four cardinal directions (East, West, North, and South)—were thought to have brought the Indian all the gifts of nature. The Shawnee were unique among Native American nations in that they believed the creator spirit to be a female. However, their world view, or cosmology, was similar to that of most other native tribes. The world was thought to be an island on the back of a great turtle who swam slowly through the oceans supported at its corners by four enormous animal spirits, such as snakes.[2]

The Iroquois believed in a creator who embodied the health and creativity of nature, but their creator rarely interfered in human endeavors. Instead, he used his *orenda* (magical power) to oversee a dualistic spiritual world that existed for the Indians on a practical and personal level. Good and evil forces constantly interacted with humans. The most active of these spirits, known as manitou, were thought to meddle in human activities at every opportunity in an amusing way, but other spirits were neither malicious nor helpful. They simply existed. The ceremonial spirits of maize, beans, and squash—the "Three Sisters" of Indian agriculture—were examples of how the Indians assigned spiritual personality, or manitou, to all the material things around them.

Four was a sacred number among Indians almost everywhere, and the roots of this idea may be found in the four cardinal points of the world from which the wind blows. These winds were often given the personification of spirits. The Jesuits recorded a Potawatomi (Algonquian) tradition concerning these directions. The north wind brought ice and snow; the south wind the warmth that brought maize, beans, pumpkins, and melons; the west wind the life-giving rain; and the east wind the morning light and the daily passage of the sun. The Iroquois ascribed the cause of the wind to a Wind Giant known as Ga-oh who lived in a great cave. The entrance to his abode was guarded by four animals: Bear, Panther; Moose, and Fawn.

When Bear was prowling, the north wind was strong; when Panther was roaming, the west wind was violent; when Moose spread his breath on the land, the east wind was rainy and chilled; and when Fawn returned to its mother, the south wind blew gentle and warm.

Snakes and serpents figured prominently in the Indian pantheon of spirit creatures. Among these mythical spirits of the Indian underworld were certain serpents endowed with powerful magic, or *orenda*. These serpents were generally inimical to humans, and they were deemed the cause of infected or noxious bodies of water in which they lived. Such infected water was thought to destroy all that might come in contact with it.

Chief among the comic manitou were Bear, Rabbit, Raven, and Fox, who came to represent the four seasons in some mythologies. These four generally made life miserable for Inchworm, a trickster-like protagonist of many native folktales who uses his cunning to outsmart his bigger foes. Bear, in particular, was constantly chasing Inchworm and trying to kill him. Inchworm was ultimately killed, but not before he impaled, but did not kill, Bear on a flint pike set out before the entrance to his lodge for his protection. Rabbit was almost an amusing figure—playing jokes and getting himself into trouble. Rabbit's jokes were often obscene and filled with sexual innuendo. Raven, the most serious of these four, was revered as the bringer of seeds, and Fox was noted for his cunning, stealth, and love of dancing and singing. Fox also had a dark side as a subtle flatterer and master of disguise.

Ritual

In the deeply religious world of the woodland Indians there were supernatural beings, the spirits of animals, plants, sun, sky, and earth from whom the natives sought guidance through the application of ritual. In semi-agricultural, hunter-gatherer societies like these, native groups put great store in ceremonies surrounding the ripening of the crop, the success of the hunt, the harvest at the fisheries, or the annual quantity of berries or nuts produced by the forests. Although they gathered in groups for festivals and ceremonies, Indians devoted a larger portion of their religious life to secret worship, private rituals, and individual spiritual preparation. The most private and individual rituals where those practiced in preparation of one's death.[3]

The objective of many Indian rituals was to please the friendly spirits and to mollify the unfriendly ones that populated the world. The smoking of tobacco, for instance, was viewed as a sign to the spirits that the Indians had faith in their benevolence. On the other hand, Native American religious beliefs were populated by a number of prohibitions, each taken quite seriously. For example, the remains of slain animals had to be treated with respect, and no waste was to be tolerated. Moreover, menstruating women were not allowed to handle the meat taken from game or sleep in the lodges of their husbands because their alleged uncleanliness would offend the spirits. Dietary and gender-based religious elements such as these were not unique to Native American thought. Similar rules could be found in Islam, Hinduism, Judaism, and even Christianity, where females, until recent times, were prohibited from handling the Eucharist, administering most sacraments, and entering the altar area.

As the Indians became further and further removed from the pre-contact era, however, they tended to lose many of the discrete meanings behind some of their rituals and ceremonies. Moreover, as the contacts between whites and Indians became more common, their interactions on a religious plane became more complicated. By 1750, for example, many Mahican Indians were referring to the Great Spirit as Orenda, or as a manitou, when speaking to English missionaries. Whether this was evidence of a fundamental change in their beliefs or an awkward attempt at explaining the magical power *(orenda)* of spirits for the edification of the white missionaries is uncertain. Christian missionaries continued to express inaccurately the Indian concept of manitou as a purely malicious spirit (not quite the equivalent of the Christian Devil) and to emphasize the Great Spirit as a single embodiment equivalent to the white man's monotheistic God throughout the period because it fit the traditional Judeo-Christian paradigm. However, the native concept of the Creator generally rejected the idea that a single, all-powerful, and otherwise benevolent spirit could also cause death and suffering, or allow them to exist in the world. This was the same logical conundrum posed by the Satan–Deity dualism of the 17th-century protestant faith. Nonetheless, by the Revolutionary period many eastern tribes seem to have lost much of their traditional understanding of the distinctions between good and malicious spirits due largely to continued exposure to Christian doctrine.

Late in the 18th century, a Shawnee elder related an updated Indian version of Creation to a white journalist in this manner.

The Master of Life...who was himself an Indian, made the Shawnees before any other human race; and they sprang from his brain: he gave them all the knowledge he himself possessed, and placed them upon a great island, and all the other red [Indian] people were descended from the Shawnees. After he made the Shawnees, he made the French and the English out of his breast, the Dutch out of his feet, and the long-knives (Americans) out of his hands. All these inferior races of men he made white and placed them beyond the stinking sea (the Atlantic Ocean).[4]

Harmony and Discord

According to many Indian legends, humans, animals, and plants once lived together in peace and harmony. However, humans invented weapons and began to kill animals for food without observing the proper rituals and ceremonies that the animals themselves required. Many hunters carefully set aside the bones of animals with as great care as they did those of their own relations. Others kept the heads and skins away from dogs and other scavengers by placing them in trees or on scaffolds and honored them with prayer and the smoke of tobacco. These rituals assured that the animal spirit could return to its clan so that it had never really died. Nonetheless, human hunters often failed to follow through on the proper rituals, and the animals decided to punish these evil-doers.

At a great council, the animal spirits decided on a powerful punishment for those who did not follow the appropriate rituals. Each animal clan chose a physical punishment with which to afflict miscreant humans. The deer clan, for instance, chose to inflict humans with rheumatism, and other animals' clans chose fevers, arthritis, neuralgia, headaches, and other ailments common to people who lived out-of-doors. The plant clans thought that the animals were too severe, but they could not convince them to temper their punishments. Therefore, in sympathy with humans, each variety of herb, plant, or tree volunteered to provide a remedy for some portion of those afflictions that the animal clans had visited upon the Indians in order to maintain the balance of the world.

Myths like these mirrored the reality that faced the Indian every day. Although Native Americans were generally healthy in their pre-contact environment, their world was not disease-free. Evidence suggests a list of possible ailments that needs a medical degree to decipher. It includes New World diseases, such as tuberculosis and syphilis, that were unknown in Europe; but also bacillary and amoebic dysentery; viral influenza and pneumonia; various forms of arthritis; problems, such as rickets or scurvy, that were brought on by vitamin deficiencies; various viral fevers; parasitic infestations, such as round worms; bacterial pathogens, such as streptococcus and staphylococcus; dysentery, cholera, and malaria; and salmonella and other food poisoning agents. Add to this a wide spectrum of possible annoyances, such as fleas, ticks, mosquitoes, and bees; snake and animal bites; common colds, fevers, diarrhea, and stomach aches; environmentally induced coronary and respiratory ailments brought on by eating fats and breathing smoke-filled air; and any number of ailments brought on by unresolved dental problems.[5]

Worship

The Indians generally treated their environment with a respect that matched their lack of an advanced technology, but not with the adoration that is sometimes ascribed to them. They also practiced their religion out-of-doors eschewing sanctuaries and the interior of permanent ritual structures to worship in the wind, under the sky, or at the water's edge. They made long prayers in these open places, the same ones used by their fathers and grandfathers before them and learned their supplications word-for-word from their tribal elders as children. This aspect of their religion led some of the Jesuit fathers to misinterpret Indian religious practices as the worship of animals, rocks, and trees—a concept at odds with those ideals actual held by most Native Americans.

The daily routine of hunting, chopping, and burning practiced by Indians mitigates against any deification of the environment. Indians hunted and fished until the game or catch was so depleted that it would no longer support those activities. They stripped the bark from trees and girdled them, purposely burned the forest underbrush to open the woods for hunting, and farmed the land until it refused to yield—sometimes beyond exhaustion. They then moved on without attempting to revitalize the area. Decades of abandonment were sometimes required to bring the forests and farmlands back into production. They rarely felled trees or cleared forest tracts because it was difficult to do so with stone tools, but they quickly took to doing so when supplied with saws and metal axes. Moreover, the pressures of the fur trade and the desire for manufactured items diminished the old reverence for the animal spirits to the point that it brought criticism from the traditionalists among the Native American. In some cases, disputes erupted that literally split the tribe.

Ritual Cannibalism

Cannibalism was one of the most striking aspects of Native American life, but human flesh was not considered a food source. The ritual eating of an enemy was an attempt to assimilate the power of the victim in the same way that the consumption of a deer or bear was thought to provide fleetness of foot or great strength. Nonetheless, some Indians practiced a more brutal form of cannibalism in which pieces of the prisoners flesh were cut away while they still lived, and roasted and eaten before their faces. This type of cannibalism provided a form of psychological torture. Robert Cavelier, Sieur de La Salle, witnessed a "prisoner tied to a stake and tortured for six hours with diabolical ingenuity while the crowd danced and yelled with delight, and the chiefs and elders sat in a row smoking their pipes and watching the contortions of the victim with an air of serene enjoyment."[6]

This particular form of torture seems to have been favored among the Seneca, Miami, Potawatomi, Chippewa, and other Great Lakes nations. Moreover, the traditional name for the Mohawks among the Algonquian nations meant "man-eaters," and both the Mohawk and the Delaware were recorded to have torn the heart from a defeated enemy and to have eaten it raw. The practice of cannibalism among the woodlands nations does not seem to have died out until late in the 18th century.[7]

Good and Evil

Long before humans walked the earth—before the creation of the earth itself—there was, according to Huron tradition, a race of man-beings who lived in a land above the sky in peace and harmony under the rule of Earth Holder (Dehaohwendjiwakho). In the progress of time, Earth Holder took a wife, who was named Ataentsic according to the Jesuits who recorded the story. The union produced a pregnancy, but Earth Holder became jealous believing that Ataentsic had been unfaithful to him. Earth Holder, at the suggestion of Aurora Borealis, cast Ataentsic out of heaven. He uprooted the Tree of Life that grew in the center of skyland and threw his wife down the hole it created in the sky and into the mortal realm. Here, she came to rest on the back of the Great Turtle that moved through the blackness of the heavens. A small bit of dirt from the bottom of the ocean came to rest on the turtle's back and grew to be the earth that humans came to inhabit. The daughter of Ataentsic, called Breath of Life, gave birth to the twins Iouskeha and Tawiskaron, who served the purposes of humans as the spirits of good and evil on earth.

Similar stories of the birth of good and evil are told in many tribal cultures. Among these are the generic Algonquian pair Manabozho and Rabbit; the Micmac pair Glooscap and Marten; the Montagnais brothers Messou and Lynx; and the Menominee twins Manabush (also Fire) and Wolf. It was common for the secondary brother in each of these myths to take the form of an animal. Often they are killed by the elder twin or brother and resurrected in some fashion through the interposition of some other supernatural power.

The earth itself was a potent spiritual power, usually given a female persona. Algonquians gave her the name Nokomis (Grandmother), but the Iroquois addressed her as Eithinoha (Our Mother). To the Indians the earth was a living entity, and all plants received their subsistence from it. Through the plants the earth fed humans in the form of corn, beans, squash, and other foods of their kind. Earth's daughter, according to the Iroquois, was Onatah, the corn spirit; but, among the Ojibwa, the corn spirit was a male youth named Mondamin, who was killed and sprang forth from his grave as maize. Chakekenpok, the man of flint, was thought to have been a child of Nokomis. He was killed by one of his brothers, his body scattered about in large rocks, and his entrails, scattered in small bits about the landscape. The flakes and fragments of flint and chert were supposed to represent the evidence of these internecine battles.

Iroquoian mythology posed as opposites Hiawatha and Athatotarho (an Onondaga chief sometimes known as Tadoaho). Hiawatha was good, wanted peace and unity, and was logical and clear in his thinking. Athatotarho was evil, had a twisted mind and warped sense of justice, and took extravagant pleasure in creating conflict and disharmony. According to Iroquois tradition, Hiawatha's efforts to unite the people were opposed by Athatotarho, whom he eventually defeated. However, it was Athatotarho who had killed Hiawatha's daughters. Most Onondaga were afraid of Athatotarho because he was thought to have magical powers and was reputed to be an insatiable cannibal. His hair was said to be formed of snakes, and his arms and legs were gnarled and deformed.

The mythological battle between Hiawatha and Athatotarho was very similar to the New Testament biblical battles between Jesus and the Devil. In Iroquois tradition, the battle was joined at the instigation of Deganawida, a Huron holyman known as the "Peacemaker." Deganawida—who favorably paralleled the role of John the Baptist in Jesuit teaching—brought a message of brotherly peace that won the support of Hiawatha. The birth story of Deganawida also paralleled both the Old Testament Mosaic tradition and the New Testament Messianic one. A woman and a child escape the dangers of war by going into the wilderness to live. Here, in a dream, the mother was told that her daughter would give birth to a child through divine intercession. This child would have a special mission to promote peace among humans. Moreover, the story of Deganawida included his rescue as a baby from the waters of a great lake much like that of Moses being plucked from the Nile. The child, Deganawida, grew up in the forest wilderness and went forth to announce to the people a three part message: good news, power, and peace. These three concepts were meant to unify the separate nations of the Iroquois. Hiawatha's only defect as a mythological hero was that he stuttered in his speech, a characteristic said to afflict Moses when he had great things to say.

The Condolence Ceremony

The Ceremony of the Dead, or the condolence ritual, was widespread among the tribes of the Northeast woodlands. Iroquois tradition has it that Hiawatha was given the five basic rituals of the Condolence Ceremony by Deganawida. These rituals were followed by most common people, and each required the giving and exchanging of strings of wampum between the mourners and the consolers. These exchanges happened throughout the rituals, but in the last two, the progression was completed as all the strings were returned to the consolers by the mourners. This signified what we would call closure. Other rituals included a number of spoken parts acknowledging the founding ancestors of the tribe or clan and reminding the listeners of the structure of the Iroquois League, retelling the way the members were related as participants, and stressing the value of cooperation.

Hiawatha expanded the condolence ritual to include 14 burdens, or acts that needed to be followed for the healing of those who were in mourning. These expanded principles became the Condolence Council Ceremony that was used for the death of a chief or the loss of another important person. A Condolence Council was convened after the death of a tribal leader, and when the mourning rituals were completed, it was followed by the installation of a new leader. Besides relieving grief, the Condolence Ceremony was thought to strengthen the bonds within the confederated tribes and revitalize the concepts of good news, power, and peace.

Condolence rituals of some type were common to all Indian societies in the region because they cleansed those who were in despair of their grief

It was a widespread custom among the tribes of the woodlands to take the remains of their ancestors with them as they moved from one village to another. One year after a death, amid renewed lamentations and rituals, the corpse would be disinterred and the bones sorted and laced into bundles that could be carried on the march.

and helped to refocus the attention of the living on the needs of the survivors. The replacement of a dead family member with a captive or adoptee was not only an attempt to maintain the size of the tribe, but it was also a means of raising up a successor to fill an important position in clan life. Moreover, a great reverence was given to the bones of the dead, and, when a village was moved, the bones of those who had died in the interim were taken to the new village site with great ceremony.

Some tribes used a coffin-like container for the remains of the dead, while others allowed the corpse to decay on a scaffold wrapped with finely woven mats. The most common burial was in the ground. The Mohawk made a large hole in the earth and placed the body in a squatting posture wrapped in an animal robe or blanket. The body was often accompanied by ornaments and other property of value but not of a bulky nature. Utensils and weapons were often broken before being included in a burial to prevent desecration of the site. The grave was then covered with timber and earth. Harmen van der Bogaert described the Iroquois graves that he saw in 1634. "We saw three graves in the manner of our graves: long and high. Otherwise their graves are round. These graves were surrounded with palisades that they had split from trees, and were so neatly made that it was a wonder. They were painted red, white, and black. Only the chief's grave had an entrance, above which stood a large wooden bird surrounded by paintings of dogs, deer, snakes, and other animals."[8]

Ghosts

Besides animal and plant spirits; elemental spirits of air, earth, and water; and the many manitou, there were human ghosts that populated the unseen Indian world. The concept of a human spirit or soul that lived on after death varied in its details throughout the Northeast. Some tribes believed in single souls, while others thought that each person had several souls. The loss of one caused sickness or near death. The loss of all or of the principal one caused death. These souls were often associated with different body parts, the vital organs, the blood, and the breadth. The soul was not discernible to the average human, but shamans and priests might see it as a shadow or an unsubstantial image.

Most tribes held a belief that ghosts were a temporary part of their material world. The ghost (or the soul) of a human did not immediately transfer to a higher plain, but reached there only after a long journey. Ghosts were invisible on earth, but they revealed their presences in the form of voices, such as those of children playing in far away fields, or in the form of unexplained noises in the lodge. Ghosts were frequently thought to inhabit abandoned corn fields, old villages, and the site of graves. Ghosts could not cross water, but they could cross ice and snow in winter. Some tribes thought that frost was a sure sign of the nearby passing of a ghost.

Anecdotal evidence suggests that most Indians considered ghosts unfriendly or potentially harmful. This was especially true of the spirits of murder victims, suicides, sorcerers, or persons who died a particularly unusual or horrible death. Moreover, they had a great fear of the ghosts of any enemy warriors they killed in battle. This may be why some Indian societies required their warriors to go through a period of purification before returning to the community from battle. The ghosts of lost hunters were thought to endanger Indians when they were far from the village, but the existence of the ghosts of captives tortured to death in the village does not seem to have caused great concern because of the steps taken to ward them off. Children were known to blow the ashes into the air from the site of a torture to prevent the ghost of the victim from remaining in the vicinity. La Salle observed and reported that after a captive had been killed and eaten "in the evening the entire population occupied themselves in scaring away the angry ghost by beating with sticks against the bark sides of the lodges."[9]

Among those who died a normal death, the very young and the very old were thought most likely to have their ghosts linger in and around the village. As in life, they were thought too weak to make an arduous journey to the higher plain. Some tribes placed the spirit world 10 days away, others several months, and still others believed an entire year had to pass before a ghost found its way there. The ghost of the very young and infants were thought incapable of the trip and were sometimes thought to come back as a newly born child. Grave goods and donatives of food were thought to serve as provisions for the journey to the spirit world, which was usually thought to exist in the Western sky. This has often been misrepresented as a "Happy Hunting Ground," but it was much more. The higher plain was a place where the spirits of the dead lived a life very much like that on earth—hunting, playing, and even making love and war.

Among the Mohicans, there was a death tradition in which the constellation of the great bear figured prominently. It was believed that the spirits of the dead went to a joyous meeting in the west with all the others of the tribe who were deceased. The dead greeted the new spirit while wearing the fur of black otter or black bear, which was a sign of gladness and welcome. The hunters among the dead followed an annual cycle know as the Celestial Bear Chase, which began in spring and lasted throughout the summer. In the fall, the hunters wounded the bear whose blood turned the color of the leaves. In winter, the hunters killed the bear, and its fat was the snow that fell upon the ground. As spring approached, the fat melted and turned into the sap rising in the trees, which the living harvested as maple sugar.

Gaasyendiet'ta, the Comet

Gaasyendiet'ta, also known as Deh-on-niot, was closely associated with death and the appearance of comets or meteors. Which of these two celestial phenomena was more closely related to him in the Iroquoian pantheon is open to question. Nonetheless, Gaasyendiet'ta was the most powerful of man-beings, greater even than Hino, the Thunderer, and second only to Iouskeha and Tawiskaron (the twins of good and evil, respectively.) He was often described as Death itself, or the servant of death (an angel of death). Gaasyendiet'ta had the face of a wolf, the wings of a vulture, the body of a panther, and the claws of a hawk. He needed all these physical characteristics to gather souls.

In the form of a comet—his most common and accepted outward guise—Gaasyendiet'ta's appearance was a sign of dire calamity and imminent death. Gaasyendiet'ta wandered the pathways of the spirits and came to earth to gather souls when he deemed it timely. The sick feared him, and the dying were said to hear him clawing at the door, where he whined like a cat if the spirit were departing or barked like a wolf if it were not yet ready to travel. He was sky colored and could sit among the tops of the trees where no one could see him. To hear his voice was an ill omen, and to see him caused the observer's death to soon follow.

The infrequent appearance of comets caused them to be associated with portents in many cultures. However, common meteors (or shooting stars), which can be seen streaking overhead on most clear nights, do not tend to instill the same levels of anxiety as the more unusual appearance of a comet. Nonetheless, the appearance of shooting stars flaming through the sky was associated with death and was sometimes thought to be souls pushed from the tail of Gaasyendiet'ta and falling back to earth in one last fiery show for all to see. In other cases and among other peoples, meteors were thought to be firedragons, a horned reptile-like supernatural being, forced by the Creator to live in the deepest portions of lakes and rivers so that they would not set the world afire. Yet, they were permitted to fly from one deep body of water to another at night as shooting stars. The firedragons were reputed to have the power to assume the human form, and they were often the antagonists in many weird tales and stories, which were told around the fires of the lodge during the long winter nights. Like the serpents that they resembled, firedragons hibernated during the winter months and could not overhear the stories that the elders told about them at the winter campfires.[10]

Woodland Lore

Indians recognized a long-standing relationship between humans and the world of spirits around them. According to Henry Rowe Schoolcraft, a 19th-century observer of American Indians and their traditions, "Manitoes [sic] constitute the great power and absorbing topic of Indian lore. Their agency is at once the ground work of their mythology and demonology. They supply the machinery of their poetic inventions, and the belief in their multitudinous existence exerts a powerful influence upon the lives and character of individuals." Manitou were of many kinds, grades, and powers. They could be benign, fun-loving, teasing, malicious, or violent, and Indians needed to create heroes in their mythology with physical, magical, or spiritual powers strong enough to baffle the most malicious among them, overcome the most fearsome, and outwit the most cunning.[11]

Although his work is not without error, Schoolcraft's excellent and exhaustive remarks on the character of Native American folktales bear repeating.

[Though] they appear to be of a homogeneous and vernacular origin, there are distinctive tribal traits, but the general features coincide. The ideas and incidents do not seem to be borrowed or unnatural. The situations and circumstances are such as are common to the people. The language and phraseology are of the most simple kind. Few adjectives are used, and few comparisons resorted to. The style of narration, the cast of invention, the theory of thinking, are eminently peculiar to a people who wander about in the woods and plains, who encounter wild beasts, believe in demons, and are subject to the vicissitudes of the seasons. The tales refer themselves to a people who are polytheists...[and] the machinery of spirits and necromancy...supplies the framework of these fictitious creations.[12]

Hino, the Thunderer

Hino was the Iroquois personification of thunder and lightning, and as such he was appropriately pictured as carrying a huge bow and flaming arrows. His wife was Rainbow, and he had many attendant spirits who were active participants in his adventures. Known as the Thunderer, Hino was thought to be the guardian of the heavens and a generally benign spirit who was the eternal enemy of evil and a hater and destroyer of all things noxious. He was credited with killing a particularly dangerous great serpent that was about to swallow all of mankind. Among his attendants was Gunnodyah, a youthful hero who was once mortal but had joined Hino in his battle against the serpent. Another was Dew Eagle, or Oshadagea, whose lodge was in the western sky and who brought the dew of the lakes in the hollow of his back.

Besides Hino, who was an Iroquoian personification, there was a wider recognition among Algonquian peoples of the Thunderbird, an invisible spirit with flashing eyes (lightning) and great flapping wings (thunder). The Thunderbird was a widely accepted spiritual figure among native peoples, and it was surrounded by many assistants chiefly hawks and eagles. Among these the Golden Eagle was most significant. If it were not for the Thunderbird, it was thought that the earth would become parched and the grasses and crops would wither and die.

Mythical Monsters

Among the evils to which Indians were exposed were a number of mythological beings including giants made of stone, flying heads that appeared in the sky, sea and lake monsters, fire breathing dragons and serpents, and giant rattlesnakes. These were not very different from the monsters that appeared in European mythology. The water monsters, in the form of a horned water snake or giant fish, were thought to devour persons lost in lakes, on rivers, or on the sea. These were much like the mythical sea serpents feared by European mariners. Among the other supernatural beings who inhabited the land of the Indian were the "little people" who lived deep in the forests and possessed extraordinary powers, much like the leprechauns of Ireland; the one-eyed giants, such as Polythemus, who was outwitted by the Greek hero, Odysseus; and the man-eating ogres, such as Grendel, who was destroyed by the hero Beowulf, King of the Geats.

Among Iroquoian-speaking nations, tiny woodland beings fit into a number of distinct categories. Dwarfs, or gnomes (Gahongas), from two- to three-feet tall could rip whole trees from the ground despite their small size. These dwarfs were supposedly armed with rock throwing slings rather than bows and arrows, and they lived underground in caves or under great rock formations. The Gandayah were a second group of tiny beings believed to be the guardians of, and in league with, the game animals. It was they that released animals from traps and caused fish to escape the weirs or nets when fishermen became too rapacious. A third group of small people (Ohdowas) were thought to be two-thirds the size of an adult human. They were associated with bow hunting and often befriended human children lost in the woods. A lack of game in the forests was often attributed to their presence. Finally, there were the All Face People who, as the name suggests, consisted mostly of a great head. These last were considered a great danger to humans, and contact with them was almost always fatal. They often found their way into tales of terror as the antagonists.

There was an Indian folktale concerning these dwarfs involving Nihancan, the spider, who was traveling in the forests in search of a berry patch. While eating, Nihancan heard the sound of wood cutting coming from across a stream. Here, he found a dwarf making an arrow out of an immense tree, and he marveled that such a small person could accomplish such a feat, much less use such a huge arrow. The dwarf took up the challenge and dared the spider to be a target. Nihancan, thinking to fool the dwarf, went to stand on a hillside further away than a shout could carry and taunted the dwarf to hit him. The dwarf took aim and fired the arrow; and Nihancan took great fright as the huge missile bore down upon him. The spider ran back and forth, but the arrow followed him every which way he turned. Finally, it came down upon him driving him into the earth with only his head left above ground. The dwarf came to retrieve his arrow, and he helped to extricate Nihancan and cared for his bruises. The spider never visited that part of the forest again.

Giants (called Chenoo among the Micmac and Abenaki) also inhabited the forests of Indian imagination. One of these, unnamed in native folklore, was responsible for the Indian receiving the dog. Two Ojibwa Indians were traveling in a canoe on one of the Great Lakes when they were blown so far across the lake that they could not paddle back. Exhausted from fighting the wind and waves, they were glad when their damaged canoe was blown ashore. Yet, their initial joy was extinguished when they saw the footprints of a giant along the shore. Growing fearful they attempted to hide, but a huge arrow thudded into the ground near them. A giant emerged from the woods who was so immense that he carried a dead moose carcass from his belt like it was a rabbit.

The giant proved friendly, however, and having been informed of the Indians' predicament, he invited the men to his home where he fed and cared for them. Drawn to the giant's home by the smell of the humans within, a windigo—a mythical monster of the Northeast woodlands noted for eating human flesh—demanded that the giant hand over the two men to him. The giant refused. Taking a tree that he used like a stick, the giant turned over a large bowl by the fire, and a great animal that looked like a wolf emerged. The Indians had never seen such an animal, which the giant called a dog. At the giant's command the dog sprang at the monster, chasing him and snapping at his heels until he had fled far away. Then the dog returned to his place by the fire and sat quiet and friendly.

The two Indians were very grateful to the giant and much impressed by the dog. The giant was pleased, but he was surprised that the Indians were not familiar with the dog, which he said he would give them. He then ordered the dog to take the men to their home. This, the Ojibwa said, they could not do because their canoe was too greatly damaged, but the giant also possessed magical powers. He made the dog grow to immense size, and placed the Indians on his back. The dog then leapt into the water and swam across the great lake with the Indians hanging on tightly. Once ashore in their own country the dog returned to normal size, and the Indian people kept dogs as companions and guardians, thereafter.

Beyond this legend, the historical and archeological record shows that most Indians kept tame, medium-sized dogs, which they called by the name *mekane* in Algonquian. Early theories suggested that young wolf pups were stolen from their mothers and made into pets, but this simplistic idea denies the physical differences between the dog and the wolf. Indians were openly afraid of packs of wild wolves and drove them off or killed them whenever they appeared. Modern theories suggest that dogs and men naturally came together in prehistoric times in a symbiotic relationship that benefited both, and it should be considered that the Indian and his dog had a long relationship that covered many generations. Although dogs were known to have been eaten under certain circumstances (and pups were considered a delicacy), it is certain that individual canines were held in high esteem. Archeologists have found the remains of dogs, carefully buried and accompanied by grave gifts, that left no doubt that the dogs were regarded as pets. Nonetheless, dogs earned their keep by watching over the village and in the corn fields, driving off prowling beasts of prey, and aiding the hunters in driving deer. The Indians kept no domestic cats, and dogs may also have helped to keep rodents and other pests around the lodges under control.

The Windigo

One of the most feared and savage supernatural creatures to inhabit the forests was the windigo. The legend of this evil spirit's existence and its interaction with humans is well known among the Algonquian-speaking tribes from the Canadian Maritimes to the western-most Great Lakes. The term *windigo* has many alternate spellings (wendigo, windego, wetiko, windikouk, etc.), but it seems to derive from the Algonquian root words *witiku* or *weendigo*, which generally translate as monster. Its ancient use seems to have embraced giants and other voracious beasts, but by the time of European contact it had been firmly linked to beings that practiced cannibalism.

The common windigos were evil spirits that inhabited the bodies of lost hunters or people who had been in a state of famine for too long and who had turned to cannibalism as a last resource for survival. They were often considered ice-monsters because they related to the starving time of mid to late winter. In a werewolf-like manner, the host human became violent and antisocial and often tried to fight off the craving for human flesh even after it had returned to civilization. Many Indians thought to be suffering from a windigo spirit were known to have gone into isolation in the deep forests in order to save their families from themselves.

A person could become a windigo by simply confronting the evil spirit in the forests or by being bitten by its human host. The spirit could also enter a person through a spell cast by an evil sorcerer. Most windigos initially looked like a human, but they became more ogre-like and ugly with time. As they ate additional victims, they seem to have gained in supernatural power. Most tales say that the windigo rode on the winter wind while howling inhuman screams and preying on any flesh (including humans) that it happens upon. In the absence of human food, it was also thought to eat rotten wood, swamp mosses, and certain forest mushrooms inedible to normal people.

The windigo was not immortal and could be fought off with the good magic, protective charms, and the help of dogs. One Ojibwa tale records the success of a shaman named Missabah, who fought and killed a windigo with the help of the Great Spirit by turning himself into a giant. He thereby relieved his people of a long period of anxiety and distress. Another tale has a little girl and her dog defeating a windigo, and a third has a woman pouring a kettle of hot tallow over the monster to kill it. Once dead, the windigo's evil spirit could be destroyed only by completely burning the body of the host human, so that not even a bone remained, and scattering the ashes to the four winds.

Mythical Heroes

One of the most enduring and popular of Algonquian heroes was Manabozho. Son of the West Wind and an unwilling Indian maiden, Manabozho was accorded a Herculean record of mythical accomplishments. He was orphaned at birth, waged war with his father, destroyed monsters and evil spirits, performed extraordinary and heroic feats, survived being swallowed by a great fish and a great deluge, and overcame a giant pair of fire-breathing serpents. There was "scarcely a prominent lake, mountain, precipice, or stream in the northern part of America which is not hallowed in Indian story by his fabled deeds." Yet, the stories of Manabozho were not a single saga or compendium, but rather they showed up in fragments and detached episodes in native lore. He was often the central figure who, through invention, alteration, or transposition, become the hero of many of the stories told around the campfires during the long winter nights.[13]

Nonetheless, Manabozho was a paradox in terms of his own humanity. He was mortal, driven to low and common expedients, and often exercised the same powers as the magicians or demons that he conquered. Interwoven among these traits were tales of personal achievements, privation, exhaustion, endurance, miracle working, and tricks of every sort. Manabozho was placed in every scene within the range of Indian imagination from the competitor on the Indian playground, to hunter, to giant-killer, to all-knowing wiseman. How long he lived on earth was not related in these tales, but there was general agreement that he ultimately went to reside with his brother the north wind. He was regarded everywhere as a benefactor who was admired for his personification of superhuman strength, creative innovation, and sage wisdom.

Unlike Hiawatha, who may have been an actual historical person, Manabozho was never considered to have been real. He was always portrayed as a mythological construct. Scarcely any two persons relating the same tale regarding him agreed in all the minor circumstances of the story. The storyteller embellished the tale as he saw fit. It was also not unusual for Native American stories to come to an abrupt halt, without a finished literary ending. The tale-teller would simply say that the story went no further or that he had heard the tale from his own parents or grandparents in exactly the same way. This was to be expected in a culture that relied on orally transmitted traditions and folklore, and the Indians themselves seemed to have accepted this open-ended format.

Another common character of Indian folklore was Wenebojo, a rather foolish fellow whose name among the Ojibwa (Chippewa) meant "giant rabbit." Wenebojo was a mortal being whose moral behavior often left something to be desired. The tales told about him were filled with foolish pranks, obscenities, and the Indian equivalent of bathroom humor that never failed to bring joy and laughter to the audience. Wenebojo had no compunction about killing other Indians or animals if it furthered the plot of the story, but he was also able to use magic to bring them back to life. Nonetheless, it was Wenebojo's human characteristics, foibles, and common failings that made him popular among Indian audiences.

Although Wenebojo was generally a comic figure, tale-tellers often gave him credit for introducing the Indians to important aspects of their culture. He was credited with introducing agriculture, hunting, and the knowledge of medicinal plants to the Indian. He brought them the ritual use of tobacco. It was also he who supposedly set forth the ritual of the Mid'ewinwin, or Medicine Dance.[14]

The Calumet or Peace Pipe

The importance of the calumet ceremony among all Indian rituals cannot be overstated. Incorrectly known as "smoking the peace pipe," the use of the calumet formed an important part of the ceremonies surrounding many forms of negotiations. Besides peace, the pipe was used to ratify alliances, exchanges, blood feuds, war, truces, and trading agreements. An analogy might be made between the Indian use of the calumet with its tobacco smoke and the Christian use of the cross or holy water as a consecrating device. Nonetheless, it was the significance behind the ceremony, and not the pipe or tobacco, that sanctioned an agreement and made it binding. It was thought that violation of a compact formed by the parties partaking in the calumet was an unforgivable sin and an unpardonable breech of protocol, so contemptible as to warrant death for the violator.

Jesuit Father Jacques Gravier noted, somewhat naively, that the calumet was for the Indian "the God of peace and of war, the arbiter of life and death. It suffices for one to carry and show it [the calumet] to walk in safety in the midst of enemies who in the hottest fight lay down their weapons when it is displayed." Father Louis Hennepin suggested that the pipe was rather more like a safe conduct or pass honored among allies, but it could be produced to signal a desire for a truce and the beginning of negotiations with an enemy. During discussions, the pipe was passed by hand from participant to participant. Protocol suggested that the pipe be passed stem-first to the left, and each person who took part in smoking the pipe was made responsible for enforcing any agreement made during the discussion. If a person did not agreed with the decision being made, he did not smoke and immediately left the assembly.[15]

The calumet pipe itself was described by Father Hennepin in 1679 as "a large Tobacco-pipe made of red, black, or white marble; the head is finely polished, and the quill [pipe stem] ... is commonly two foot and a half long [and] made of pretty strong reed or cane." Hennepin ventured several opinions concerning the meaning of the decorations on the calumet, but ultimately determined that "every nation adorns the calumet as they think fit according to their own genius." The calumet was always made in two pieces—a stem and a bowl—that supposedly represented the union of a man and a woman.[16]

Evidence suggests that the calumet ceremony originated on the Great Plains—possibly among the Pawnee, who according to a tribal myth had received it from the sun. The calumet reportedly spread east to the Sioux and the Illinois in the 17th century, and then to the Algonquian speaking peoples of the Great Lakes region. De la Salle reported that the calumet ceremony was the most common method used to end intertribal wars in all of the Illinois country. It is from his report that the idea of the calumet as a peace pipe may originate. According to the French, who adopted the ceremony as a negotiating protocol, the Siouan-speaking nations of the prairies apparently honored the calumet far more than any other Indian group. The Iroquois were among the last of the woodlands nations to adopt the practice, and they may have done so through a mechanism suggested by the French.

The calumet ceremony and other rituals were not mere "decorative coverings for agreements." They were the "sinews" that helped to bind together the methods under which social and ethical problems, even killings, could be handled in a specific way without threatening otherwise favorable alliances. Rituals and ceremonies were used "to secure the approval of the manitou," and they were shared and performed jointly by the tribes or by Europeans when dealing with the Indians. As inexact and artificial as they may have appeared to the European observers, these methods were based on cultural parallels recognized by the Indian peoples themselves. Many of the solutions reached through the calumet ceremony may have been "elaborate cultural fictions" filled with "theatrical images," or simplifications of extremely tangled and sometimes tenuous sets of understandings. Yet, for the participants, the calumet ceremonies and the rituals that surrounded them were also transformational events that could be remarkably influential in allowing a wide spectrum of social, political, and economic relations and exchanges to take place among otherwise competing tribes and antagonistic personalities.[17]

The Sacred Bundle

"The power of clans usually derived from an ancestral vision, and that power was actualized in a ritual bundle consisting of objects that symbolized the original vision."[18] An okama of great seniority, or a clan leader of high reputation, was often given responsibility for the ritual or sacred bundle among Algonquian-speaking peoples. In some cultures, the sacred bundle was owned by the tribal women and passed down through the female line, yet, in many cases it could only be used by men. To open the bundle without the proper ritual and ceremony was thought to invite disaster for the individual and the tribe. The collection of objects in the bundle represented songs, stories, dances, prayers, and ceremonies—large and small. Its purpose was to provide reminders of the oral traditions and ideas of an otherwise non-literate society. All of the many details and meanings behind the objects in the bundle were passed down from keeper to keeper and clan to clan over the generations.

Some of the objects in the bundle may have been thousands of years old; some only recently added. Included among these researchers have found calumet pipes, arrow fragments, animal bones, stuffed birds, an unusually perfect ear of corn, counting sticks, hawk bells, glass beads, and small European and American flags. Fetishes were often included. A fetish was an object that was regarded as possessing consciousness, volition, immortal life, and magical power that enabled it to accomplish abnormal results in a mysterious manner. Such an object was thought indispensable to the person or group that possessed it. Yet, its power demanded a price in the form of prayer, sacrifice, feasts, and protection. The inclusions of fetishes in the sacred bundle was one way of ensuring their proper treatment and continued efficacy. Nonetheless, a fetish could lose its power and degenerate with time into a sacred or lucky object, such as a charm, amulet, or talisman, with its original meaning lost.

Like the calumet, the adoption of a sacred bundle among the woodland tribes seems to have had its origins in the prairie west. Both the Pawnee and the Sioux (Lakota) of the Great plains held age-old mythologies concerning the origin of the sacred bundle. The most long-lived of these seems to be of White Buffalo Calf Woman, who supposedly introduced the sacred bundle more than 2,000 years ago to the people of the plains.

Two warriors were out hunting buffalo when White Buffalo Calf Woman appeared to them, first as a white buffalo calf and later as a beautiful Indian maiden. One of the warriors was found to have evil thoughts in his mind, and a great black cloud covered him and instantly removed all the flesh from his bones. The second warrior, a good man, was very much afraid and knelt down to sing his death song. However, White Buffalo Calf Woman admonished him and told him that she would return in four days. Meanwhile, he was to gather the people, the elders, and the leaders of his tribe at that spot. This he did.

On the fourth day, White Buffalo Calf Woman descended from a cloud in the sky in the form of a white buffalo calf, and as she rolled about on the ground (as buffalo are wont to do) she arose once again as a maiden. This time she carried the first great sacred bundle in her hand. She entered the circle of the village with the bundle singing a sacred song. For four days she stayed among the people teaching them about the bundle and its meaning.

There were seven sacred ceremonies that White Buffalo Calf Woman introduced to the people. One of them was the sweat lodge, or purification ceremony. Another was the naming ceremony for children. Among the remaining ceremonies were those for healing, adoption, marriage, and the vision quest. The seventh and most important ceremony was the sun dance, or people's ceremony that took place during the summer solstice or longest day. She also taught the people all the songs and rituals that went with these ceremonies and instructed the keepers of the sacred bundle to be caretakers and guardians of the sacred land. When she left the circle of the village, she promised to return one day to retrieve the sacred bundle. In this way, it was made clear that the keepers of the bundle were its custodians and not its owners. As she left she made several prophesies. One of these involved the appearance of a white buffalo calf, which would signal that her return was near. At that time White Buffalo Calf Woman would initiate an everlasting period of harmony, balance, and spiritually.

The parallels among the seven sacred ceremonies of White Buffalo Calf Woman and the seven sacramental of the Christian Church are remarkable. It is quite probable that these parallels helped the Jesuit fathers spread Catholicism among the Indians. In this regard, the Blessed Virgin Mary of the Roman church was used as a parallel to the religious feminine often found in Native American theology.

The Deer Sacrifice

The Mahican believed that the sacrifice of freshly killed game had been learned from a great hero—a shaman and prophet who had come down from heaven to marry a Mahican girl. The deer sacrifice was one that hoped to assure the continued success of the hunter. A newly killed deer was hung in the lodge from a ceiling pole until the meat was ready to eat. The hunter who had killed the deer took it down and skinned and quartered the animal very carefully. The butchered deer was then reassembled on an altar in a lodge prepared for the ceremony in such a fashion that the animal might seem whole to the watchful eyes of Wauntheet Manitou, sometimes known as the Great Spirit.

Two or more old men presided over the deer ceremony. One of these, acting the part of the shaman, prayed out loud to the manitou asking that he grant all the hunters present success in finding food. The man who had given the deer then gave a string of wampum to the men who had presided over the prayers, and the animal was cut into small pieces to be boiled in a large pot. When cooked, the meat was distributed to all that were present except the original hunter, who took nothing as part of his sacrifice. The deer skin and the inner organs were given to a needy widow in the camp. The ceremony ended with the old men calling aloud to the Great Spirit to take note of what they had done.[19]

Magic and Shamanism

Observers from the Old World of Europe generally believed in witchcraft, and they sometimes misunderstood Indian religious or care-giving practices and categorized them under the headings of magic or necromancy. This belief generally came from the mistaken contemporary observation that Indians had "in all their tribes, and every band of them, a class of Magi, who affected to exert the arts of magic, offered sacrifices to idolatrous things, and were consulted as oracles in peace and war." Certainly all tribes recognized some person in their midst (generally called a shaman) who represented a connection with the spirit world or who possessed a unique knowledge conducive to bringing the good will of the manitou to the people. With rare exceptions, most of these persons were male. Their power was obtained during a vision quest, but their ability was essentially a self-proclaimed one. There was usually no outward sign of visionary power or separation from the others. Hunters and warriors would consult the shaman because they had many spirit helpers and had shown wisdom in the past. For this reason, most shaman did not actually begin to practice their arts or claim their position until middle age gave them the benefits of the respect granted to all elders. True shaman were venerated for their good counsel and not for their magical or medical powers.[20]

Nonetheless, many types of magicians, conjurers, and sorcerers were loosely associated with shamanism. The English called these persons Powwows; the French called them Jongleurs; and they were known among themselves and among other Indians by terms such as *djasakid* or *webano*. This class of shaman also served to find missing persons and lost articles or to discover the source of disease or ill-fortune. They were often consulted for the purpose of supplying hunting and war talismans, love charms, or healing potions.

Certainly, there were persons among the tribes who used trickery and deception to uphold their positions, and they were generally feared rather than respected. Often these men exhibited a physical defect, blemish, or bodily imperfection that was used to support their claim to unusual power. For instance, the Shawnee shaman Tenskwatawa, known as the Prophet, had a blind eye and scarred eye socket acquired in his youth through an accident that leant an air of authority to his message.

There were many persons whose primary concern leaned toward the darker side of the art of shamanism. The *wabeno* (literally, Morning Star Man) openly claimed the power to practice evil. He usually put his abilities to nefarious purposes such as revenge, sorcery, or the overturning of the plans of an enemy through the dark use of magic. The *webano* excelled at trickery, slight-of-hand, and misdirection. He could plunge his hands into boiling water or hot coals to retrieve objects or even small animals apparently with no outward discomfort, and he could often affect an appearance or disappearance in a ball of fire or plume of smoke. It may be too strong to suggest that *webanos* were mere charlatans taking advantage of their less sophisticated neighbors. Indian shamans often employed the principles of sympathetic magic (the idea that like produces like), obvious pantomimes, and open stagecraft to effect their objectives.

Some *webanos* were house-shakers who used confederates to disturb the structure from the outside to mimic the entrance or departure of spirits. They may also have been experts in ventriloquism or the use of distinctive voices. Most relied on more than a passing knowledge of the physiological and psychological effects of plants, herbs, and poisons on humans. *Webanos* often claimed the ability to change their shape and to assume the guise of a bear, a fox, an eagle, or other animal, and may have done so in pantomime to effect a cure or psychological effect. If a novice *wabeno* began his practice too early in life, or with too little skill and artistry, he might forfeit his claim to power and, if unsuccessful in producing tangible results from his magic, might even forfeit his life.

The Great Medicine Society

The shaman played a significant role in all festivals and other religious matters that affected the Indian community. However, they were not priests, ministers, or doctors in the European sense of the word. Among the Ojibwa (Chippewa) of the western Great Lakes there was an actual priesthood known as the Mid´ewiwin, or Great Medicine Society, the study of which has come to characterize an entire class of persons practicing shamanism. The *mid´e* priests, or sucking doctors, claimed powers of healing and clairvoyance that generally benefited the health of the community, and they were found among many Algonquian-speaking tribes. The formation of an organized body of *mid´e* priests may have been in response to a great fear of the pantheon of evil spirits who were in conflict with the supreme spirit known as Mid´emanido.[21]

An analogous position to that of the *mid´e* priest among Iroquoian tribes was the Sunachkoo (exorcist) or Koutsinacha (devil hunter). These persons were clearly different from the Atsinnachen (magician) or the Agotsinnachen (a prophet or soothsayer). All were part-time religious/ magical specialists who interacted with the supernatural in both private and public rituals where cures or divinations were to be affected.[22]

A single *mid´e* priest, or *mid'e,* was considered as powerful as a *webano* and was often called upon to undo *webano* spells and potions. As a group, they may have had several members in a single band or village who formed a Medicine Society with the primary purpose of dealing with questions of individual rather than community health. The *mid´e* priests were responsible for holding certain annual and semi-annual ceremonies, especially the Mid´ewinwin, or annual Medicine Dance.

A long semi-circular lodge was often built of boughs for the purposes of the Medicine Society, and it was from this structure that the Medicine Lodge Society received its name. It consisted of a pole framework left open to the sky except for cedar or pine boughs placed along the sides up to a level of two or three feet. Although the bases for *mid´e* rituals were primarily supernatural, practical techniques were not neglected, and to gain entrance to the Medicine Lodge Society as a *mid´e* priest, a candidate had to show some ability to actually affect a cure beyond the desire to join due to having a dream or a vision. An initiation fee composed of goods, skins, or trade items was expected of the candidate.

Disease was thought to originate from sorcery, spirit possession, disease-object intrusion, breach of taboo, or a loss of soul. Only through communication with the spirit world could a healer find the absolute cause of the illness and apply the appropriate remedy, if there was one. The *mid´e* priests possessed various degrees of competency, which required training

The *mid´e* priest used bones, charms, skins, rattles, masks, unusual stones and minerals, and
some herbs in the curing ritual. Human bones
and tobacco were considered particularly powerful. Spitting, dancing, vomiting, singing, and the
clapping of hands were often used to drive out
evil spirits.

and initiation. Each individual *mid´e* carried a large array of medicines in
his bag. Some of these he learned from others, but many were the product of his own dreams, observations, and insights. He did not try to treat
all ailments because he could not reasonably expect to find all remedies
through his dreams; nor could he invent his own remedies because only
those that came freely from the manitou had power. *Mid´e* priests often
specialized in certain areas, and it was not unusual for one *mid´e* to call in
another to provide specific cures, even if they came from distant villages.

With regard to their woodland pharmacopoeias, the medicines used by
the *mid´e* were individual prescriptions, but some general principles were
followed. The *mid´e* seems to have placed great significance in the physical
appearance of certain medicinal plants and roots. With the stalk and small

root hairs gone, the life and essence of the plant were thought to reside in the bulk of the tap root itself. A class of double roots were highly regarded because they resembled the legs of a human. This suggested that it was useful for curing people. The *mid´e* harvested his remedies locally, but as the seasons changed it was not usual for the *mid´e* to travel to other locations to gather plants and roots that grew in a variety of environments and soils. It was an unfailing custom that he place a little tobacco in the hole in the ground from which he harvested the plants. This was to reward the manitou for making the plant available for the benefit of man and to ask the plant that it do its best when used.

The stalks, leaves, and flowers of plants were usually dried by hanging. Roots were cleaned of earth and left to dry. Bark was gathered when the sap was in the tree. This was the time when it was most easily pried away from the tree. After drying these materials, the *mid´e* divided and placed them in small packets in his pouch ready for immediate use. All these items could be pounded into a coarse powder for use. If several substances were thought effective in combination, they were commonly pounded together. Certain roots were cut into small pieces and some barks were shredded so that they could be chewed. It was not uncommon for the *mid´e* to carry a "Bear Claw Necklace" that was made, not of bear claws, but of thumb-sized pieces of various medicinal roots strung together for the convenience of transportation.

Liquid medicine was usually made by steeping in hot water as with a tea, but the liquid was not measured out in any way. A large swallow constituted an average dose, but a cupful was occasionally taken. Sipping seems to have been out of favor among most *mid´e*. Medicines were also administered externally by application as a dry dust, as a cream mixed with tallow or fat, or as a poultice. The *mid´e* often chewed a root or piece of bark before applying it topically to his patient. Some medicines were pricked into the skin or wound with a set of bone needles selected for that purpose. Dried herbs and powder were often boiled and the steam taken in by the patient, or they were sprinkled on hot stones and the smoke inhaled. This was often done in an enclosed space, such as a small hut or sweat lodge. Many dried herbs were smoked in a pipe, and these were sometimes mixed with tobacco. Finally, certain remedies were administered as an enema through the use of an apparatus made from a hollowed stick and a deer bladder.[23]

Some of the methods used as cures may seem disgusting to us, but the sophistication and discretion of the *mid´e* was remarkable. Moreover, he was not adverse to practicing a bit of basic surgery. Recent archeology suggests that some of these procedures may have been remarkably modern in their objectives, including efforts to operate on the skull to remove foreign objects or relieve otherwise unremitting pressure. Less spectacular, but more common perhaps, were the splints made for immobilizing the fractured arms and legs of the injured and the supports that were fashioned to strengthen the weak limbs and joints of the elderly or deformed. These were often assembled from wood or bone using wet rawhide as a binding agent, which tightened and hardened as it dried.

Common blood letting was a procedure frequently used with a number of small incisions or gashes taken at the forearm, ankle, or near the source of the pain with a sharp flint knife. This procedure—very much in favor in Europe for hundreds of years—was commonly used for sprains, swellings, snakebite, or any other inflammation. Blood was often sucked from these incisions through a tube made of horn. Afterward, a healing medicine was applied to the scarified surface either as a cream or as a powder. An instrument very like that used for tattooing was used in applying medicines beneath the skin for the treatment of headaches, dizziness, neuralgia, and rheumatism.

A simple knife—either of flint or metal—was used for amputations, which were dangerous, painful, and frequently lethal. These procedures were usually restricted to cutting below the elbow or below the knee. Nevertheless, if the patient survived the shock of surgery, the wound was tied off, and the bloody stump was dressed in a dry pounded bark that was renewed as often as it became damp. Several contemporary observers noted that nothing else was used, and that the wound often healed perfectly. It should be remembered that a well-formed flint edge can be as sharp as surgical steel. The knife was also used to open boils, sores, and eruptions and to cut away warts. It was used to open gangrenous wounds and loosen the infected flesh, which was not cut away but was washed out by the application of a liquid medicine. Wet wood pulp or a bark mash was often applied thereafter to hinder further infection.

Also among the *mid´e* priests were those who practiced a crude form of dentistry. Splinters from trees struck by lightning were collected for use as lancets in many applications, especially for ailments of the gums. If a patient suffered from a toothache, the gum was cut with these splinters until the blood ran freely. If a tooth were hollow or decayed, an awl (usually of native copper) or other metal instrument was made red hot and seared into the tooth. If it was thought necessary to remove the tooth, it was struck forcibly to loosen it and pulled out by tying a sinew to the root and giving a quick jerk.

Bogaert witnessed several attempts to cure persons of sickness, but his observations must be read with care as they were influenced by his own European understanding of both the cause of illness and its cure.

Two men came to me and said that I should come and see how they would drive out the devil...There were twelve men here who were to drive him out...When we arrived, the floor of the house was completely covered with tree bark over which the devil-hunters were to walk. They were mostly old men who were all colored or painted with red paint on their faces because they were to perform something strange. Three of them had garlands around their heads upon which were five white crosses. These garlands were made of deer's hair which they dyed with the roots of herbs. In the middle of this house was a very sick person who had been languishing for a long time, and there sat an old woman who had an empty turtle shell in her hands, in which were beads that rattled while she sang. Here they intended to catch the devil and trampled him to death, for they stomped all the bark in the house to pieces, so that none remained whole. Wherever they saw a little dust on the corn, they beat it with great excitement, and then they blew the dust toward one another and were so afraid that each did his best to flee as if he had seen the devil. After much stomping and running, one of them went to the sick person and took an otter [skinned with the head attached] from his hand, and for a long time sucked on the sick man's neck and back. Then he spit in the otter and threw it on the ground, running away with great excitement. Other men then ran to the otter and performed such antics that it is a wonder to see; indeed, they threw around hot ashes and embers in such a way that I ran out of the house.[24]

Bogaert failed to record the effect all this had on the patient, but it seems certain that the men he saw were members of a medicine society and that at least one was a sucking doctor. In another case, Bogaert witnessed two men entering the house of a sick person to cure him. Once again no report of a cure was forthcoming from the observer.

As soon as they arrived, they began to sing, and kindled a large fire, sealing the house all around so that no draft could enter. Then both of them put a snakeskin around their heads and washed their hands and faces. They then took the sick person and laid him before a large fire. Taking a bucket of water in which they had put some medicine, they washed a stick in it 1/2 an ell long [about 15 inches]. They stuck it down their throats so that the end could not be seen, and vomited on the patient's head and all over his body. Then they performed many farces with shouting and rapid clapping of hands, as is their custom, so that sweat rolled off them everywhere.[25]

In the 18th century, an English missionary named Timothy Woodbridge went among the Mahican on the upper Housatonic River in order to spread Christianity. Here he was warmly received by a chief named Umpachenee, who gave him leave to instruct members of the tribe in the white religion and provided a feast for him. Obviously, there were some among the villagers who were upset concerning the threat this implied for their traditional beliefs. Subsequent to the feast, several members of Umpachenee's family fell seriously ill, probably, Woodbridge thought, from poisoning of some sort.

The victims lay sick with fever and stomach pains for several days. Woodbridge prayed for them, but Indian healers were called in to treat them, nonetheless. According to Woodbridge, the healers put all the sick in a wigwam and built up a great fire. They then danced and danced around the fire until they were wet with sweat and nearly exhausted.

They would then go outside, strip naked, and stand in the cold air or roll in the snow to cool off before returning to dance some more. They would repeat this process up to half a dozen times in a single night. The "treatment" was only partially effective as two of the affected died.

It was obvious that murder had been committed, and a group of shaman (powwows according to Woodbridge who witnessed the event) were assembled to discover the culprit. About 40 Indians sat around a fire in the wigwam shoulder-to-shoulder each holding two painted sticks about 18 inches long. The eldest shaman began the ceremony by lifting his eyes to heaven and asking that the Great Spirit provide an answer as to the identity of the culprit. All in attendance then began to sing while rapping their sticks together. This continued for the better part of an hour with the elder continuing his incantations throughout. Finally, one of the shaman stood up, striped down to his breechclout, and began to dance about the fire. When he became exhausted, another man took his place, and he was replaced by a third and a fourth in order. This dancing, rapping, and singing were interrupted only for a smoking of the pipe and further incantations. The ceremony produced no result in finding the murderer. Yet, the Indians saw no harm in the attempt, and the failure seemingly did not disenchant them with the process. Moreover, it was quite possible, according to Woodbridge, that the murderer or his accomplices were part of the investigating assemblage. Nonetheless, the attempt at civil behavior and justice impressed the Englishman because the Indians seemed to be undergoing a genuine spiritual experience.[26]

False Faces

Mask societies were another notable element of woodland religion. The False Faces were a "medicine" society, not in terms of "magic" but rather in terms of health care. When worn, a carved wooden mask, usually of grotesque portions and details, helped the wearer to represent the mythological being asked to aid mankind in the elimination of disease. Society members might blow tobacco smoke through the mouth of the masks upon the sick to heal them. Another mask society was the Corn Husk Faces whose members wore masks made, as the name suggests, from corn husks during the midwinter rituals connected with farming. Almost all of the woodlands nations gathered annually for the greencorn, midwinter, and harvest rituals where the activities of the mask societies were prominently displayed.

Among the Shawnee, Creek, Choctaw, Chickasaw, and other tribes of the Southeast, the Green Corn celebration was of immense importance. It lasted from four to eight days, and was an occasion for amnesty, forgiveness, and absolution from guilt. The ceremony involved purging oneself to cleanse the body and the lighting of new fires in the hearth to cleanse every home.

Notes

1. Paul A. W. Wallace, *Indians in Pennsylvania* (Harrisburg: Pennsylvania Historical and Museum Commission, 1986), 127.

2. Michael G. Johnson, *American Woodland Indians* (London: Osprey Publishing, 2000), vol., 228, 37.

3. Johnson, 37.

4. Wallace, 120.

5. William A. Starna, "The Pequots in the Early Seventeenth Century," in *The Pequots in Southern New England, The Fall and Rise of an American Indian Nation*, ed. Laurence M. Hauptman and James D. Wherry (Norman: University Press of Oklahoma, 1990), 44.

6. Francis Parkman, *La Salle and the Discovery of the Great West* (New York: The New American Library of World Literature, 1962), 42.

7. Johnson, 33; Wallace, 123.

8. Charles T. Gehring and William A. Starna, eds., *A Journey into Mohawk and Oneida Country, 1634–1635: The Journal of Harmen Meyndertz van der Bogaert* (Syracuse, NY: Syracuse University Press, 1988), 12.

9. Parkman, 42.

10. See Harriet Maxwell Converse, *Myths and Legends of New York State Iroquois* (Albany: University of the State of New York, 1974).

11. Henry Rowe Schoolcraft, *Algic Researcher, North American Indian Folktales and Legends* (Minneola: Dover Publications, 1999; reprint of the 1839 edition), 52.

12. Schoolcraft, xxxii.

13. Schoolcraft, 72.

14. Robert E. Ritzenthaler and Pat Ritzenthaler, *The Woodland Indians of the Western Great Lakes* (Garden City, NY: The Natural History Press, 1970), 137–138.

15. Quoted in Richard White, *The Middle Ground, Indians, Empires, and Republics in the Great Lakes Region, 1650–1815* (New York: Cambridge University Press, 1991), 21.

16. Quoted in White, 21.

17. White, 93–94.

18. White, 38.

19. Patrick Frazier, *The Mohicans of Stockbridge* (Lincoln: University of Nebraska Press, 1992), 22.

20. Schoolcraft, xxi.

21. Johnson, 36.

22. Gehring and Starna, 40–41n.

23. Frances Densmore, *How Indians Use Wild Plants for Food, Medicine and Crafts* (New York: Dover Publications, 1974), 330.

24. Gehring and Starna, 17–18.

25. Gehring and Starna, 10.

26. Frazier, 31.

8

The Tomahawk and the Cross

In the 17th and 18th centuries…gifts were not merely bribes or wages; allies were not simply mercenaries; women were not merely prostitutes; missionaries did not just buy their converts; murderers did not kill simply for gain and then buy off those who would avenge their victims. Life was not a business, and such simplifications only distort the past.
—Richard White, historian

Religion in Early America

The part played by religion in early America cannot be overstated. Five of the English colonies were established by Puritans for religious ends: Plymouth (1620), Massachusetts Bay (1630), New Haven (1638), Connecticut (1639), and Rhode Island (1644). The two others were the Catholic colony of Maryland (1633) and the Quaker colony of Pennsylvania (1682). French, Portuguese, and Spanish colonies, though not free of religious turmoil, closely coordinated the economic and social objectives of their governments with the purposes and goals of the Roman Catholic Church even if they did not directly coordinate in their efforts with the Papacy. The French came to the New World specifically to convert the Indians and pack out furs. While they aligned the purposes of their explorations with their religion, the financial benefits of the fur trade generally escaped the church fathers in France. Nonetheless, a great deal of wealth in other forms was bestowed upon the French missionary orders, particularly the blackrobed Jesuits.

Spanish explorers and colonial administrators in Central and South America were conspicuously attended by the Franciscan fathers of the Roman Catholic faith. A mendicant (begging) order, the friars eschewed all temporal wealth, but sought power in the spiritual sense.[1] In like manner, French Jesuits accepted their mission to convert the Indians of North America and to help rid the woodland forests of heathenism and heresy. The same fervent spirit moved many Anglo-Protestants, but many factors caused religious life on the English frontier to be difficult. Uncompromising bigotry was only one of these. Influential clergymen, both Catholic and Protestant, encouraged the raising of armed forces among the Indians and instructed their faithful converts among the natives that to bear arms one against the other was to do God's work.[2]

New Spain

The Spanish set the first foothold in North America early in the 16th century, and they established a temporary mission to the Indians in Virginia in 1526, 80 years before the founding of the first permanent English settlements in nearby Jamestown. The Spaniards promised certain destruction for any Protestants entering the region; however, the local natives drove them out killing all the clergy and sparing only a young boy among the acolytes to tell the tale. In 1565, the Franciscans established the settlement of St. Augustine on Florida's east coast, and within three years there were missions on the south and west coasts of Florida and in Georgia and South Carolina.[3] Pedro Menendez de Aviles, appointed adelantado of Florida, wrote to the Spanish king that Protestants and American Indians held similar beliefs, rooted in Satanism. "It seemed to me that to chastise them...would serve God Our Lord, as well as your Majesty, and that we should thus be left free from this wicked sect."[4] Philip II wrote back, "Cast them out by the best means possible."[5]

The Spanish viewed the Native American populations of Mexico and Central America as lost in a wilderness of paganism, and the Franciscans had as their goal the establishment of their own values among the Indians. While the Franciscan missions generally preserved the Indians who resided in them from physical destruction, the friars made no attempt to preserve their native culture. Quite the reverse. The worst precepts of an intolerant religious inquisition in Spain seemingly crossed the Atlantic with the good fathers. A Spanish missionary wrote, "Once idolatry is known, one must not rest until it is altogether eliminated....Conversion must be total: no individual, no fraction of the individual, no practice, however trivial it may seem, must escape." Armed with such a powerful bias, the Spanish justified their barbaric and appalling treatment of the Indians and the virtual elimination of their native way of life wherever their rule extended.[6]

Spain ruled vast areas of the Americas for 200 years before the struggle between France and England for an empire in North America began in earnest. Yet, as a consequence of the English victory over the Armada in 1588, Spain lost its position as a great naval power and had its influence further reduced by its inability to subdue the Dutch "heretics" in the Spanish Netherlands. This failure worked to English purposes throughout the reign of Elizabeth Tudor. Consequently, by the opening of the 17th century, only Holland, France, or England had a feasible chance of wresting control of North America. The French army was in ascendancy on the continent of Europe, and the English and Dutch fleets vied for control of the commercial sealanes. The struggle for economic, political, and military supremacy in Europe quickly spilled over into the American wilderness involving the Native Americans of the region in a series of wars on their own lands marked by commercial ruthlessness, religious intolerance, secular bigotry, and appalling inhumanity.

The English Frontier

The earliest permanent English settlement in North America, located in Virgina, dates from 1607. By 1620, another settlement had taken root at Plymouth in far away Massachusetts. Both centers expanded and multiplied. Yet, at the end of the 17th century, the English colonies were still confined to the Atlantic coast and coastal plain by the Appalachian Mountains. On the south at the Ogeechee River they bordered the Spanish settlements in Florida, and in the north at the Penobscot River they faced an uncertain and changing border with the French that ran through the forest wilderness of Maine. The frontier remained an ambiguous boundary shifting through the forest with every European treaty. The Indians did not always understand the implications of the boundary decisions made between these warring Europeans.[7]

The outstanding exception to English Protestantism in the colonies was the Catholic colony of Maryland. These Catholics were served by a small group of Jesuits under Father Andrew White until 1645. The work of these Jesuits was hampered by protestant malcontents who were allowed access to the colony, and also by the hostility of the Susquehanna Indians who lived at the head of Chesapeake Bay. Many Catholics remained in the colony of Maryland after Protestantism had been established there by law during the English Civil Wars (1640–1649). However, their churches and missions were plundered, and the priests that did not escape were sent to England for trial. The Piscataway (Conoy) Indians of Maryland, almost completely Christianized by the Jesuit fathers, sought refuge from the new protestant government with the Delaware or with the Iroquois of the north. Here they quickly lost all distinction as a unique people.[8]

New France

French explorers had entered the St. Lawrence River in the 1530s and 1540s, but it was not until 1608 that a settlement was established by Champlain. Within two decades, the French had explored into the Great Lakes, but little settlement had taken place. In 1633, a group of entrepreneurs known as the Company of One Hundred Associates were given a large grant of land in New France. In return for the right to trade for furs and appoint a governor in New France, the Hundred Associates promised to settle 4,000 colonists within 10 years, protect them, and support the Catholic missions to the native population.

Initially, the sole spiritual ministers of the colony were to be Jesuits, and crown policy insured that the settlers were wholly Roman Catholic. No one whose devotion to the church was suspect was allowed to emigrate to New France. If there was any doubt concerning their devotion to the faith, French emigrants were required to renew their baptismal and confirmation vows before the church fathers in Quebec. Two forces governed the lives of these settlers. One was their church and their religion, and the other was the specter of death haunting them from the fringe of the woods in the form of the Iroquois.[9]

Francis Parkman described how he believed the Catholic faith manifested itself in New France in the 17th century.

Over every cluster of small white houses glittered the sacred emblem of the cross. The church, the convent, and the roadside shrine were seen at every turn; and in the towns and villages, one met each moment the black robe of the Jesuit, the gray grab of the Recollet, the formal habit of the Ursuline nun. The names of saints, St. Joseph, St. Ignatius, St. Francis, were perpetuated in the capes, rivers, and islands, the forts and villages of the land; and with every day, crowds of simple worshipers knelt in adoration before the countless altars of the Roman faith.

Yet, Parkman's descriptions were based on his visit to Quebec in the last half of the 19th century, and while historians laud his exhaustive research and the meticulous preparation of his manuscripts, the facts present a slightly different picture of religious life in New France in the 17th century from those that he gleaned 200 years later.[10]

It is quite certain that both the French colonists and the Native American converts to Catholicism were wholly dependent for their religious survival on just a few priests. A census of the clergy in Quebec in 1686 shows that they made up a much smaller number than their ultimate influence on events in New France would suggest. There were 44 secular priests, 43 Jesuits, 12 Recollets, 12 seminary students, 28 Ursuline nuns, 13 sisters of Notre Dame, 26 Hospital nuns of the Mercy of Jesus, and 16 Hospital nuns of St. John. The first church in New France was built in Quebec in 1633, but it was destroyed by fire and its stone replacement, Notre Dame (1657), stood in sharp contrast to the churches of the other districts of

New France that were mostly crudely built wooden structures without adornment. Rather than the "countless altars" described by Parkman, it was more common to have no church at all.

The Jesuits controlled all the missions to the Indians in New France, including 1 in Illinois (established in 1690), 18 in the Georgian Bay area, and 3 large conclaves in the St. Lawrence Valley. The Recollet fathers served only in Cape Breton, Acadia, the Seminary of Quebec, and at a mission at Tamarois (1690) on the west bank of the Mississippi River.[11]

While the Indian missions were usually staffed with at least one full-time Jesuit priest, for most Catholic settlements there was no resident clergy. The number of Frenchmen in New France was so small, possibly no more than 3,000, that it was impossible to assign a priest to each of the scattered settlements and farmsteads. Consequently, the available clergy were assigned to parishes comprising many hundreds of square miles of wilderness territory. A parish might reach for 50 miles along a river and a days walking into the interior, for it was largely by canoe that the priest made his spiritual visits to his flock. Practically every house and important native village in New France stood in sight of some body of water within reach of this functional native craft. With a servant to help paddle a canoe in the rivers and streams, or pull a sledge along their frozen surfaces in winter, the solitary priest commonly carried a portable altar, a communion set, a bottle of holy oil, and a few supplies into the forests. Under these conditions, he managed to minister to his entire flock three or four times a year.

Jesuits

The Jesuit fathers stand out in the history of New France. It is quite clear that much of the early history of New France revolves around the struggles of the Jesuit missionaries to hold their own against the aggressively anti-Christian factions among the Iroquois. Parkman devoted one of the seven volumes that comprised his monumental study of this period solely to the Jesuit order in New France. As a religious order, the Jesuits had no distinctive habit, but they were noted for the simple black cassocks that they wore. The black robed Jesuits ultimately dominated all the other groups of clergy in New France.[12]

The Bishop of Quebec

Until 1656, the church in Canada was presided over by the Father Superior of the Jesuits in Quebec rather than a bishop. Since the time of Champlain, the governors of Canada had ruled the civil government in cooperation with the Council of Quebec, a group made up of representatives from three municipal districts (Quebec, Trois Riviers, and Montreal), the administrator of Montreal, and the Father Superior of the Jesuit order in

Almost all of the influence gained by the French over the
Indians in the 17th and 18th centuries came through the
efforts of Jesuit missionaries who went out into the wilderness, lived among them, and cared for their corporal
and religious needs. *The Jesuit Relations* are the records
of their experiences, and they serve as a primary source
for the history of the period and the ethnography of the
native people.

Canada. In 1657, however, Francois de Laval, a Jesuit, was appointed the
Pope's Apostolic Vicar in Canada and given a vacant bishopric in Arabia
to lend him ecclesiastical stature.

The immediate result of Laval's arrival in Canada in 1660 was a hostile
encounter between the Jesuit leader and the Governor-General of the colony, Pierre d'Argenson. Argenson was the fifth man to hold the post of
governor, and he had shown his willingness to defend Canada against
the incursions of the Iroquois, personally leading a group of volunteers
into the forest in pursuit of an Onondaga raiding party. However, he
was no match for the Jesuit bishop who systematically took every opportunity to belittle his position and authority. In almost every encounter

with Argenson, Laval chipped away some of his power as governor and claimed it for his order. Argenson found himself perplexed and increasingly frustrated. At length, in 1661, he asked to be replaced. In fairness to Argenson, his replacement was no more successful than he in stemming Laval's quest for power.

Many colonial officials in French America discreetly questioned the motives of the Jesuits, who seemed to consider New France their own private domain established ostensibly for the conversion of Indian souls, but lucrative in a layman's economic sense, nonetheless. This attitude was openly expressed in a report to the colonial ministry in Quebec by Antoine de la Mothe, Sieur de Cadillac, founder of the French trading post at Detroit. "The missionaries should act in good faith, and...though these Reverend Fathers come here only for the glory of God...nobody can deny that the priests own three-quarters of Canada. From St. Paul's Bay to Quebec...the greater part belongs to the Jesuits or other ecclesiastics."[13]

Like many of the government officials in New France, Cadillac was "not an especially religious man." As an undoubted critic of the Jesuit fathers, his attitude antagonized some of the resident priests, especially Father Superior Carheil of the Indian mission at Michilimakinac with whom he almost came to blows. "I do what I can to make them my friends," he wrote, "but, impiety apart, one had better sin against God than against them...for the offense is never forgiven in this world, and perhaps never would be in the other."[14]

Radisson felt that the Jesuits were as interested in the beaver trade as they were in saving Indian souls. There was no doubt that the order was constantly trying to find a way to get the Cree, the Montagnais, and other tribes of Hudson's Bay to bring furs down the Saguenay River. If the Jesuits could make inroads among these northern tribes, they thought they could make themselves masters of the trade and gain influence over the government. Their purpose was both temporal and spiritual. If they could develop an economic hegemony among the traders, they believed they could establish a theocracy of Christian Indians in the wilderness. The Jesuits had laid numerous schemes to control the fur trade that had indirectly frustrated Radisson's own plans for developing commerce with Hudson's Bay. Nonetheless, in his narratives, he placed no blame in their direction and indeed praised them for their charity and their kindnesses in interceding for him with the governor on several occasions.[15]

Although there was friction between the Jesuits and the civil authorities, the order seems to have had a genuine desire to convert the native population to Catholicism and to establish firm foundations for the continued growth of the Church among the Native Americans. In the end the Jesuits were able to confound their detractors by the "single-hearted devotion of their missionary work among the Indians." Their self-sacrifice, the hardships they endured, and their triumphs or martyrdom were all set down in meticulous detail in the *Jesuit Relations*, but there is little recorded about the parish priests who came to serve the scattered flock of inhabitants.[16] The system for governing New France was finally overhauled by the crown in 1664. Thereafter, the governor was appointed directly by the King. The council was made larger, ultimately expanding to 12 persons and weakening the power of the Jesuit representative.[17]

From the historic record, it seems certain that Bishop Laval's actions were not aimed at personal aggrandizement. The church, his order, and the conversion of the Indians to Christianity seem to have been the absorbing forces in his life. "Winning the savage souls that roamed [Canada] to the Cross stirred his blood...He shared the Jesuit dream of some day converting all the wilderness area into a kind of Peaceable Kingdom." Laval fought the alcohol trade to the Indians, and served until 1688 when he resigned and returned to France. During his residence there, he fought to maintain the prerogatives of the clergy over the civil government that he had created. He returned to Quebec as Bishop of Quebec from 1694 to 1705. Having battled with six governors and seven civil administrations, he spent the last three years of his life in quiet retirement.

The Indian Missions

Through the establishment of a number of Indian missions in the Northeast woodlands, Bishop Laval led the most successful effort at Christian conversion in the history of the Jesuit order. He did not hesitate to send his black-robed fathers to establish missions in the wilderness if he thought there was the slightest chance of winning Indian souls to the Catholic Church. These undertakings, often made by lone priests, entailed incredible hardships. "A missionary destined for this great work must make up his mind to lead a very strange kind of life, and endure unimaginable destitution of all things; to suffer every inclemency of weather, without mitigation; to bear a thousand impertinence, a thousand taunts, and often, indeed, blows from the Infidel Savages, who are at times instigated by demons—and all this without human consolation."[18]

Nonetheless, Jesuits brought energy and dedication to the task of converting the Native Americans. Unlike the Spanish fathers, however, the Jesuits seem to have tolerated, if not accepted, much of the native lifestyle and culture as long as it did not affect their Catholicism. Father Jacques Bigot, like many other missionary fathers, considered himself an essential bridge for the Indians between their traditional ways and the changes thrust upon them by European contact. Father Sabastien Rasles (sometimes spelled Rale') spent more of his life living among the Abenaki than he did in European society. He learned their language and was so trusted by the Indians that he was allowed to speak at their most solemn councils. Moreover, Father Isaac Jogues returned two times to his missionary duties even though he had been horribly tortured and mutilated by the traditionalists among the

Iroquois. He was finally killed by Iroquois warriors on his third attempt to bring Catholicism to the natives.

Excavations of archeological sites known to have been Jesuit missions in New York and New England have turned up brass rings and silver or brass crucifixes that were handed out by the missionaries among the Indians. Father Jean Enjalran requested additional crosses, rings, and rosaries, reporting that he had stripped himself of almost everything in giving such gifts as rewards to the Indian children for reciting the catechism or being baptized. Although the Jesuits felt that these items helped them win converts, it is quite certain that many Native Americans wore these tokens as mere decorations not knowing their religious meaning and regarding them as any other amulet or charm. Similarly, the Indians often expressed the belief that the priests by "throwing water upon [their] heads" subjected them to the will of the governor of Canada and exercised a special magical power over them.[19]

It should be noted that the missions did not attract Indian populations, nor could forts or trading posts sustain a concentration of natives for any long period in the absence of outside pressures. No matter how dedicated to their Catholicism, no matter how much they desired European goods, the most pressing needs of the mission Indians were for security and food. Hunting beaver and undertaking long and arduous journeys to complete their exchange for trade goods could only be justified in times of plenty when the Indian family was free of the threat of attack. It was only through the turmoil and insecurity created by the Great Dispersal that the Jesuits were able to make their gains among the Indians of the Great Lakes Region.

Throughout the dispersal, the Jesuits took on some of the aspects of an intertribal glue as remnants and fragments of tribes and clans, driven west by the Iroquois, merged and coalesced around the missions for protection. The Jesuit fathers at St. Ignace were a prime target of Iroquois vengeance during the dispersal, and many refugees starved when they refused to leave the overcrowded confines of the mission island at St. Joseph. The strength of the missions and the breadth of their influence only became apparent after the end of the refugee period. The process was not as obvious everywhere as it was at Sault Sainte Marie, where the Jesuits preceded the Indians anticipating their return to an old village site whose primary attraction was the local fisheries. A new cadre of Jesuits followed in the footsteps of the refugees. They did not come to unite the tribes or in search of their earlier converts. They came to look for new souls to save.[20]

The French civil authorities viewed the missions as the equivalent of outposts guarding the main avenues of attack into New France. In fact, most of the missions in the east were situated just far enough from the border of English and Dutch settlement to make it difficult for a determined attack to surprise them. Once the Dutch had been removed from the colonial scene by a series of Anglo-Dutch naval wars in Europe, the French fur traders and government officials came in the wake of the missionaries to arm and recruit the Indians for war against the English settlements. The traders, thereby, obtained their furs, the officials their Indian allies, and the Jesuits their converts.[21]

The English were as devoted to religion as any Frenchman, but they generally dismissed the French missionary activity as a mere subversion of native allegiance. They displayed little understanding of the dedication of the Jesuits to the conversion of souls. It was widely believed by the English settlers—and not without supporting evidence—that the Jesuits were actively inciting the Catholic Indians against the Protestant English settlements. The Jesuits were accused of bringing presents of powder, ball, and guns to the tribes and of announcing the support of the French government for their raids. By the end of the 17th century, there were a number of the mission villages well located to serve this purpose.

The earliest French Catholic mission in what was to become New England was founded in 1613 on Desert Mountain Island, Maine. This was almost immediately destroyed by Englishmen, and the priests were carried off to Virginia to stand trial. Two important Abenaki missions were located at Penobscot (1633) on the Maine coast and Norridgewock (1646) on the Kennebec River. Both missions supported large villages under the influence of Jesuit fathers. Penobscot was one of the farthest outposts of the French influence at the end of the 17th century. Abenaki villages were also located at Trois Riviers, and on the St. Francis River. St Francis was a particularly active jumping off point for Abenaki war-parties planning attacks on the English settlements as the river opened a practical route by canoe to the New England border.[22]

Many of the Abenaki of Maine removed themselves to the St. Francis mission of Father Jacques Bigot as early as 1683. The mission housed, besides the Abenaki, a large number of related Algonquin Indians who were refugees from King Philip's War (1675) in New England and a smaller population of Caughnawaga Indians of Iroquoian lineage making it one of the most successful strongholds of Catholic Indians in New France. Although the Caughnawaga remained aloof, a great deal of intermarriage took place among the Algonquin refugees and the Abenaki. The inhabitants of St. Francis soon acquired among the English a reputation as devout Catholics and unshakable allies of the French.

The Caughnawagas were often counted as Mohawks. Originally from Ossernenon near Auriesville, New York (where Isaac Jogues met his martyrdom), the Caughnawagas had separated from their Iroquois relatives in the historical period mainly due to their adoption of Catholicism, but they maintained a kinship bond with the more English-leaning Mohawks. Compelling evidence indicates that the French colonial ministry actually gave explicit instructions to Abbe' Francois Piquet, a Sulpician priest of Montreal, to establish a separate mission 100 miles up the St. Lawrence River from Montreal (called La Prairie) for the purpose of winning over the Caughnawaga Iroquois of that region to the French alliance.[23]

The Jesuits may have converted more than 4,000 Iroquois in the decade of the 1670s, and the list of converts included several prominent Mohawk leaders. Twenty percent of the Mohawk population alone may have taken Baptism, but it has been estimated that half this number were death-bed conversions. While the Jesuits thereby divided the Five Nations somewhat between Christian and traditionalist factions, few of the converts failed to remove themselves to the French missions. Driven out by an informal form of social segregation, some 600 Caughnawaga Christians moved to La Praire, and 160 more moved to the Lac des Deux Montagnes mission near Oka on the Ottawa river. A few dozen more joined their Catholic Huron cousins at Lorette.

These migrations were often led by women converts among the Iroquois who drew their kin with them and "spread family connections in ways that would affect trade and war for generations." Ironically, because the pro-French elements departed, those Iroquois remaining in central New York became increasingly anti-French in their sentiments. Traditionalist Iroquois, some of whom were actively pro-British, gradually gained political dominance over Iroquoia and drove the interests of the Five Nations toward Albany and away from Quebec.[24]

The use of Christianized Indians for the purpose of carrying war to the English frontier settlements was a matter of French crown policy. It was understood among the officials at Versailles that "in most cases the movements of war-parties upon the frontiers were generally first ordered or sanctioned or suggested by Louis [XIV] himself." A French official wrote, "If Abbe' Piquet succeeds in his mission, we can easily persuade these savages to destroy Oswego." Another official suggested that, as the French and English were ostensibly at peace, "The only means that can be used for such an operation in times of peace are those of the [Caughnawaga] Iroquois." The French were hard pressed, however, to convince the Caughnawagas to attack their Mohawk kin, and the English could not convince the Mohawks of the faithlessness of their brethren.[25]

The war party that attacked Pemaquid, Maine in 1689 was known to have been composed of warriors from the missions at Penobscot and Norridgewock who set out in their canoes and gained the advantage of speed by traveling to the point of their attack on the Kennebec River. These same missions, predominantly populated by the Abenaki, were thought to have served as a rallying point for the attack on the English at York, Maine in 1693. The Indians were supposed to have been incited to make war by their priests, particularly fathers Jacques Bigot, Sabastien Rasles, and Louis Thury, who seem to have had great influence among them.[26] These observations were based on the reports, narratives, and journals of English captives taken by the raiders, and they must be viewed with some skepticism.[27]

The hatred toward Catholics, and toward Jesuits in particular, was deep-seated and engendered among the English from an early age. John Giles, a young English boy captured by Indians in a 1689 raid on Fort Penobscot, Maine and carried off to Canada, noted,

[A] Jesuit of the place had a mind to buy [ransom] me…He gave me a biscuit, which I put in my pocket, and not daring to eat it, I buried it under a log, fearing he had put something in it to make me love him. When my mother [who had also been captured] heard talk of my being sold to a Jesuit, she said to me, "Oh, my dear child, if it were God's will, I had rather follow you to your grave, or never-more see you in this world, than you should be sold to a Jesuit; for a Jesuit will ruin you body and soul."

The theme of anti-Catholicism and anti-Protestantism should not be underestimated when studying the events that took place on the frontiers in this era.[28]

The almost continuous warfare between the French and English colonies after 1690 exposed the Indian missions to attack and made the missionaries marked men. In the *Jesuit Relations* it was observed that Father Rasles, in particular, had become "odious to the English" as they were convinced that his endeavors to confirm the Abenaki in the Catholic faith constituted the greatest obstacle to their plan of settling the interior of New England. "[T]hey put a price on his head; and more than once they had attempted to abduct him, or take his life." Finally, a large force of English and allied Indians was raised in 1724 to attack the mission at Norridgewock. The attack completely surprised the inhabitants who, having few warriors among them, fled from the English to the other side of the river. "Father Rasles, warned by the clamor and the tumult…promptly left his house and fearlessly appeared before the enemy. He expected by his presence either to stop their first efforts, or at least to draw their attention to himself alone…As soon as they perceived the missionary, a general shout was raised which was followed by a storm of musket-shots that was poured upon him. He dropped dead at the foot of a large cross that he had erected in the midst of the village."[29]

Huron Conversion The Huron were initially the power base of the French–Native American alliance. Jesuits who came to Huronia in the first part of the 17th century were among the first whites to come among them, and they were very successful in converting them to Catholicism. Increasing Jesuit linguistic competence, expanding trade, and French diplomacy closely tied the Hurons to the French. After 1640, Catholic Hurons were supplied with guns, and more than half their population was considered Christianized. Unfortunately for the French, the Huron and the Iroquois were openly hostile to one another. Minor blood feuds, raids of outlying villages, and attacks on hunting parties characterized the relations between these powerful nations. In 1642, the raids escalated into war as the Mohawks cut off the Ottawa River fur trade route, and the Seneca completely destroyed a frontier Huron village.

The Mohawk and Seneca virtually exterminated the Hurons during 1649. From 30 villages, more than 7,000 refugee Hurons fled to all points of the compass. The Jesuit priests living in Huronia were either killed, or they made their way in terror to Quebec. The dispersal of the Hurons and their associated cantons was a cultural catastrophe with widespread consequences for both the Indians and the French.[30]

Iroquois Conversion

A large part of New York and Pennsylvania served as the home of the Iroquois Confederation. Through an unfortunate circumstance, Champlain had gained for the French an enmity with the Iroquois by siding with their Montagnais, Algonquin, and Huron enemies in the early days of French colonization (1609). Though the Iroquois were involved with the Dutch at the beginning of the historic period, they were largely self-serving in their dealings with the English in the 17th century. However, they remained bitterly anti-French for more than a century. For these reasons, no permanent Catholic mission to the Iroquois was established within the limits of their confederacy during the colonial period.

It was hoped that the Iroquois could be attracted to the French if they shared their religion. Many attempts were made to draw off the Iroquois from English influence by this means. The best known among these were the journeys of Father Isaac Jogues through the Mohawk Valley. In 1642, Jogues, possibly the best known Jesuit missionary in colonial history, was captured by a party of Iroquois and taken to a Mohawk village near Auriesville, New York. Jogues and his companions (among whom were several Hurons) were cruelly treated. The Hurons were burned at the stake. Jogues had his nails torn from his fingers, two fingers crushed, and a thumb sawn off. Of the two lay brothers who accompanied him, one was killed and the other was adopted into the tribe. Jogues was ransomed by the Dutch 15 months after his initial capture and returned to France. In 1646, he set out again to establish a mission among the Iroquois. He was again captured in the company of a Huron, brought to the village at Auriesville and tortured. This time he was killed, and his head was placed on the palisades that surrounded the village. The site of his martyrdom is now a Jesuit memorial.

In 1653, Father Joseph Poncet was captured by Mohawks near Montreal. He was also tortured but was released to carry overtures of peace to Quebec. As a consequence, although the peace feelers were thought to be insincere, the Jesuit mission of Ste. Marie was established near the capital of Iroquoia at Lake Onondaga in 1655. A party of 50 French colonists and a half dozen Jesuit priests built a palisade enclosure, a wooden chapel, and several barracks on the shores of Lake Onondaga. Other mission stations were established, thereafter, with each of the five Iroquois nations; the Onondaga, Cayuga, and Oneida were seemingly most open to the Jesuit influence, but the Mohawk and Seneca were less so.

However, many Iroquois accepted the tenets of Christianity selectively without total acceptance or rejection of the new beliefs. "The Indians seem more often to have sought to add to [their] spiritual arsenals than to fill spiritual vacuums...to have taken on Christianity as another weapon for assuring their well-being, without abandoning traditional ways of life." As the missionaries attempted to extract a total acceptance of Catholicism and an abandonment of traditional practices, the more skeptical traditionalists among the Iroquois became increasingly influential. For this reason, the Jesuits had favored bringing their converts into mission settlements where they could be supervised. Nonetheless, a little more than a year after Ste. Marie had been built, hostilities broke out near Montreal, and by 1658, it was thought prudent to close the mission and all its outposts. During the next three decades only sporadic attempts were made to Christianize the Iroquois nations.[31]

In 1666, the French decided to chastise the Mohawks. The first attempt misfired, but in 1667, a force of 1,100 men under the Marquis de Tracy descended into the Mohawk Valley burning one village after another. As the attack came late in the season, the Mohawks lost much of their crops for the winter and faced starvation. They, therefore, joined with those tribes of the Confederacy more inclined toward the French and sued for peace. The peace treaty entered into in 1667 left New France in relative peace for 20 years. However, as renewed war in Europe approached in the last decade of the 17th century, the Catholics among the Iroquois increasingly withdrew from the Mohawk Valley toward the Catholic missions in Canada. By 1694, a great schism had taken hold between the traditional and Christianized Iroquois.

English Missions to the Indians The zeal and influence of the French Jesuits has rightly given them a disproportionate place in the history of colonial America. However, their missions were not the only efforts put forth to Christianize the natives. The largely abortive efforts of the English to bring Protestantism to the native peoples of New England came too late and were prosecuted with too little vigor to tie the Indians to them through the instrument of religion. Moreover, the Protestant faith seems to have lacked much of the mysticism and ceremony that drew the natives to Catholicism.

Thomas Mayhew, Jr. began preaching the Protestant faith to the Wampanoag Indians on the island of Martha's Vineyard in 1640, and after epidemics in 1643 and 1645, a large number of the survivors made the Protestant religion their own by blending the new faith with their own traditions. This form of conversion was unacceptable to most of the Puritan ministers. In 1641, John Elliot translated the Bible into the native dialects of Massachusetts and set about teaching the Native Americans to read it. Between 1642 and 1667, Elliot established 14 "praying towns" in which the natives were expected to assume European manners and dress. Puritan authorities, innately rigid in their concepts of propriety and good form, tried to force the Indians in the "praying towns" to abandon their customary wardrobe, ornaments, and language, which were looked upon with scorn. They insisted that all ties to native culture be eradicated. In 1645, Emmanuel Downing, an English Puritan, wrote in a letter, "I doubt whether it be a sin in us, having power in our hands, to suffer them [the Indians] to maintain their worship of the devil."[32] However, during King Phillip's War in 1675, the colonists rounded up nearly all the "praying Indians," imprisoned them, or hunted them down. After the crisis, the praying towns were reopened, but they were now viewed less as missions and more as Indian reservations in the worst sense of the term.[33]

In 1717, in an effort to attract the Abenaki, the Reverend Joseph Baxter attempted to establish a mission on the Kennebec River of Maine. The Reverend Cotton Mather unrealistically hoped that this mission would attract a "considerable number of our eastern savages...from the popish to

During the Pequot War of 1637 and King Phillip's War of 1675, the colonists rounded up Indians, imprisoned them, or hunted them down. The English attacked their villages, burned their crops, and enslaved many of those who survived. These wars, unfortunately, set an inhumane and drastic precedent for how white America would deal with the Indians for the next two centuries.

the Protestant religion." In 1735, the Massachusetts government appropriated money to place a minister among the natives at Fort Drummer on the Connecticut River. Neither mission was considered wholly successful.[34] Even among the English-leaning Iroquois, the French were viewed to have been more accepting of Indian ways.[35] "Brother," said an Onondaga diplomat to the English, "you must learn from the French [priests] if you would understand, and know how to treat Indians. They don't speak roughly; nor do they for every little mistake take up a club and flog them."[36]

An Indian college was opened at Harvard in 1654 so that when Elliot died he left a number of native born preachers among his flock. After the French and Indian War, in 1769, Reverend Eleazar Wheelock opened a school in Hanover, New Hampshire for natives recruited from St. Francis and elsewhere. This is commonly considered the founding of Dartmouth College. Nonetheless, the Iroquois clearly rejected Wheelock's request to educate their youth. Mary Jemison, who lived among the Iroquois for 60 years, noted, "I have seen...the effects of education upon some of our Indians, who were taken when young from their families, and placed at school before they had had an opportunity to contract many Indians habits, and there kept till they arrive to manhood; but I have never seen one of those but what was an Indian in every respect after he returned."[37]

Only the English Quakers and German Moravians seem to have made any significant inroads among the natives in terms of the Protestant religion. Nonetheless, a visitor to a Moravian mission in Seneca country in western Pennsylvania reported, "The wandering life [of the men] is not fit to receive the benefits of our religion which requires a sedentary life; they forget in the woods the precepts they have learnt, and often return as ignorant as ever. Their women who are most constantly at home appeared on the contrary tractable, docile; they attended prayers in their chapel with great modesty and attention."[38]

Many of the Indians who converted to the Protestant faith seem to have taken every opportunity to revert to their traditional religion in much greater numbers than did those who undertook to become Catholics. This may be due to the fact that the Catholic missionaries went to the native villages to build their churches and chapels, lived among them, and decorated them with all the religious paraphernalia that had been abandoned by Protestantism. The Jesuits, in particular, became totally immersed in the Indian culture and way of life.[39]

Yet, it would be an oversimplification to credit such concepts as the sole cause of the failure of Protestantism among the Native Americans. Growing interests in trade and mercantilism, and the increasing acceptance among the colonists of many Protestant sects, finally seem to have blunted the nascent English programs of native conversion more than the use of corporal punishment or the absence of religious trinkets. The once unified ranks of English Protestantism, disordered by sectarian wrangling and doctrinal bickering, utterly failed to pry the Catholic Indians from the

French because of their own lack of organization and common purpose. In this way, the more dogmatic and focused Catholic missionaries among the French had a distinct advantage. Ultimately, however, economic inducements and geopolitical factors appear to have been more persuasive than the influence of religion in the battle for control of the North American continent.

The Blending of Beliefs

It has been said that Indian religious beliefs were remarkably durable and that many natives accepted the tenets of Christianity selectively blending them into their traditional ceremonies and rituals. Many Christian saints, for instance, exhibited the better characteristics of traditional Indian manitous. They could talk to animals like St. Columba or silently withstand the pain of stigmata and other wounds like St. Francis Assisi or St. Stephen. The figure of Jesus crucified suggested similar scenes of trial by torture that were highly regarded by the Indians. Such Judeo-Christian legends blended well with Indian beliefs.

Jesuit teaching among the Algonquians stressed devotion to the Virgin Mary, a powerful female religious and spiritual figure that drew many Indian women to the Catholic Church. It was often at the behest of the clan mothers that whole bands or villages removed to the Catholic missions. Yet, in an effort to stem the predisposition of native women toward a perceived sexual promiscuity, the Jesuits tended to emphasize that Mary was powerful due to her virginity and chastity. This attracted large numbers of young women and older girls to their congregations, but when Indian women became Christians they often exchanged sexual inhibition for sexual abstinence forming, in the Indian way, a ritual society of virgins and celibates.

This was almost unheard of among native peoples, going well beyond the Algonquian sense of a woman's prerogative with respect to sex. Such measures outraged both the young men, who found their sexual opportunities diminished, and the elders (male and female), who felt that their traditions were being challenged. In one case, the tribal council, feeling that these celibate females were acting in defiance of their authority, dispatched a group of warriors armed with clubs to disrupt the services carried out by a Jesuit for an audience composed mostly of celibate Indian women.[40]

While the Iroquois generally rejected the Jesuit message of Roman Catholicism, many Algonquian tribes were open to it. Nonetheless, there was always the potential danger to the missionaries posed by those who felt that Algonquian traditions were being subverted by Christianity. The adversaries of Christianity among the natives based their attacks partially on the argument that prayer was ineffective and that baptism brought death. The latter idea being supported by the many death-bed baptisms of infants and the elderly performed by overzealous Jesuits. A chief of the Illinois asked, "Has this man [the priest] who has come from afar better medicines than we have, to make us adopt his customs?" An Illinois elder warned, "Leave their myths to the people who come from afar, and let us cling to our own traditions."[41] In 1706, Father Gravier so offended the cultural status quo among the Peoria Indians that a group attacked and grievously wounded him. Although the Christian women present cared for him, the priest never fully recovered and ultimately died of complications to the wounds that he had received.[42]

In their diatribes against Christian conversion, many Indians made reference to the idea that baptism "tamed" the convert, making them like livestock that could be slaughtered at will. To restore themselves to their previous status, an unnamed woman visionary identified the keeping of livestock (tame animals) with the loss of the Indians' free nature. To restore their free will, she suggested that the Indians had to break their connections with the tame. To restore wild deer to the forests, tame cattle and hogs had to be slaughtered. In the Great Lakes region among the Ottawa, Ojibwa, and Cree, dogs were kept as aids to hunters, and among the tribes further west, horses had also become integral to the hunt. Algonquian traditionalists among the tribes actually mandated the killing of dogs and horses because as the only domesticated animals kept by Indians, they made natives "too white." Needless to say there was great resistance to these decrees.[43]

Notes

1. G. J. Marcus, *The Formative Centuries, A Naval History of England* (Boston: Little, Brown, & Co., 1961), 86; Alfred Thayer Mahan, *The Influence of Sea Power Upon History, 1660–1783* (New York: Dover, 1987), 50–53.

2. Paul A. W. Wallace, *Conrad Weiser, Friend of Colonist and Mohawk: 1696–1760* (Lewisburg, PA: Wennawoods Publishing, 1996), 51.

3. David J. Weber, *The Spanish Frontier in North America* (New Haven: Yale University Press, 1992), 94–96. In 1769, with much of the continent lost to the English, the driving force behind continued Franciscan mission building would be in the person of Father Junipero Serra of California.

4. Weber, 60–64.

5. Weber, 120–121.

6. Tzvetan Todorov, *The Conquest of America* (New York: Harper Perennial, 1987), 204; Wallace, 57.

7. Ralph Bennett, ed., *Settlements in the Americas: Cross-Cultural Perspectives* (Newark: University of Delaware Press, 1993), 147.

8. Daniel J. Boorstin, *The Americans: The Colonial Experience* (New York: Vintage Books, 1958), 7.

9. Walter D. Edmonds, *The Musket and the Cross, the Struggle of France and England for North America* (Boston: Little, Brown and Company, 1968), 79.

10. As quoted by Francis Parkman in John H. McCallum, ed., *The Seven Years War: A Narrative taken from Montcalm and Wolfe, The Conspiracy of Pontiac, and A Half-Century of Conflict* (New York: Harper Torchbooks, 1968), 17.

11. Edmonds, 79–82.

12. Edmonds, 43–44.

13. Allan W. Eckert, *Wilderness Empire* (Toronto: Bantam Books, 1980), 5–6.

14. Eckert, 4.

15. Stanley Vestal, *King of the Fur Traders, The Deeds and Deviltry of Pierre Esprit Radisson* (Boston: Houghton Mifflin Company, 1940), 140.

16. Wallace, 117; Edmonds, 82. Full translations of *The Jesuit Relations* can be found in most college libraries and online on the Internet.

17. The One Hundred Associates appointed governors for three decades (1633–1663). There were six in all. Champlain (1633–1636) was the first. Montmagny (1636–1648) was second and served the longest of the six. The third and fourth were D'Ailleboust (1648–1651) and de Lauson (1651–1658). The fifth was d'Argenson (1658–1661), and the last was D'Avaugour (1661–1663). Thereafter, the governor was chosen by government ministers in France and appointed by the King. Louis de Buade, Comte de Frontenac et Pelluau, known simply as Frontenac, was twice appointed Royal Governor.

18. Edmonds, 97–98.

19. Colin G. Calloway, *The Western Abenakis of Vermont, 1660–1800: War, Migration, and the Survival of an Indian People* (Norman: University of Oklahoma Press, 1990), 46–49.

20. Richard White, *The Middle Ground, Indians, Empires, and Republics in the Great Lakes Region, 1650–1815* (New York: Cambridge University Press, 1991), 19.

21. White, 23.

22. Samuel Adams Drake, *The Border Wars of New England, Commonly Called King Williams's and Queen Anne's Wars* (Williamstown, MA: Corner House Publishers, 1973), 150n.

23. The present site of Ogdensburg, New York.

24. Ian K. Steele, *Warpaths, Invasions of North America* (New York; Oxford University Press, 1994), 121–122.

25. Drake, 11, 146; Eckert, 126–127.

26. Colin G. Calloway, *Dawnland Encounters: Indians and Europeans in Northern New England* (Hanover, NH: University Press of New England, 1991), 86.

27. Drake, 76, 154.

28. Drake, 33.

29. Calloway, *Dawnland Encounters,* 81–82.

30. Steele, 70–71.

31. Calloway, *The Western Abenaki,* 51.

32. Louis B. Wright, *The Atlantic Frontier: Colonial American Civilization, 1607–1763* (New York: Alfred A. Knopf, 1951), 124.

33. Colin G. Calloway, *New Worlds For All: Indians, Europeans, and the Remaking of Early America* (Baltimore: The Johns Hopkins University Press, 1997), 74–75.

34. Calloway, *New Worlds,* 171.

35. Calloway, *Dawnland Encounters,* 59–60.

36. Calloway, *New Worlds,* 171.

37. James E. Seaver, *A Narrative of the Life of Mrs. Mary Jemison* (Syracuse: NY: Syracuse University Press, 1990), 32. Mary Jemison's narrative was give to Dr. Seaver in 1823 and first published by him in 1824.

38. Albert E. Stone, ed., *Letter from an American Farmer and Sketches of Eighteenth-Century America by J. Hector St. John de Crevecoeur* (New York: Penguin Classics, 1986), 377–378.

39. Calloway, *Dawnland Encounters*, 60.
40. White, 73.
41. Quoted in White, 59.
42. White, 74–75.
43. White, 507–508.

IV
THE INDIAN FAMILY IN CONFLICT

9

Wilderness Warfare

The manner in which these tribes make war renders a handful of their
warriors more formidable than a body of 2 or 3,000 European soldiers.
                                                —*The Jesuit Relations*, 1667[1]

The Character of Indian Warfare

Warfare was accorded considerable importance in the woodlands
culture, but the Indian nations did not enter into it promiscuously. The
objectives of any military undertaking were to enforce the political domination of one tribe over another and to provide for a solid chastisement
of unruly neighbors through the mechanism of a good bloodletting.
In the pre-contact and early contact periods there seems to have been a
good deal of this intertribal violence. Fighting in the forests among small
groups was infrequent and sporadic, and usually consisted of guerilla tactics, skirmishes, lightning raids, and ambushes along solitary trails.[2] This
type of warfare was known to the French as *petti guerre*, or the small war.

In the days of intertribal warfare, although hundreds of warrior might
take the field, there was little loss of life. Native weapons were more
conducive to wounding than to killing. Warfare was seemingly played
at—like a cat and mouse game; and there was a remarkable contrast
between the imposed order and hierarchy of European armies and the
self-discipline and individualism of Indian war parties. Each conflict was
an opportunity for individual participants to gain recognition and honor.

Wars of long duration and complete mobilization were almost unheard of in pre-contact America, yet, the woodlands were rarely at peace. The threat of war had taken its toll in the region. Many tribes placed their villages on hilltops surrounded by strong defensive works composed of palisades of long poles interlocked at the top by a fighting platform. The Abenaki of New England made it a standard practice in a time of conflict to abandon the potential war zone, or any disputed area, in order to be free to fight without endangering their families. This was not unusual. Many native communities withdrew to safer areas in order to avoid the domination of rival tribes.

Even before the advent of white intrusion, the Lake Champlain region along the New York–Vermont border had become uninhabited except for a few villages at Swanton (Missisquoi) on the Vermont side. The upper Connecticut Valley, except for a Sokoki village near Vernon and a Cowassuck village at Newbury, was deserted except as a hunting ground; and the populous Pocumtuck tribe continued to live near Deerfield in Massachusetts only under a tenuous agreement with the Mohawk. With respect to warfare on a tribal scale, the Mohawk, as the most warlike nation in the region, had the largest number of enemies, most of whom were Algonquians.

In the aftermath of white arrival, 10 of the Algonquian bands inhabiting the lower Connecticut Valley as far south as Wethersfield openly invited the English at Boston and Plymouth to settle among them as a stop to Mohawk aggression. In similar fashion, the Indians of Massachusetts Bay welcomed the English settlers at Salem and Cape Ann as a buffer to the Canadian Abenaki who were likely to invade their villages by sea. Moreover, when the English went to war with the overbearing Pequot of Connecticut, the neighboring Mohegan served as guides and scouts for the whites, and the Nipmuck and Niantic cheered on the whites as they pursued the Pequot to virtual extinction.

War provided an opportunity for men—particularly the young men—to gain individual war honors through feats of personal bravery and good leadership. A successful warrior was assured respect and prestige among the members of his clan and tribe, and if he were particularly successful, his reputation could, and did, extend beyond his own nation. At certain public events or during certain ceremonies, warriors were given the privilege of relating their heroic feats to all assembled without fear of being thought braggarts. The Ottawa/Chippewa warrior Pontiac, or the Mohawk leader Joseph Brant might serve as examples of men whose prestige exceeded the bounds of their own people. Yet, one was the enemy of the British and the other their ally.

Pontiac has been described as proud and arrogant, and as a leader he was said to be domineering and somewhat dictatorial. He had a mercurial temper and a vindictive disposition, but even as a young man the warriors of his own age followed him and looked to him for leadership and counsel because he was clever and fearless. He rarely missed a meeting of the Ottawa council at Detroit, and he freely expressed his opinions to the elders assembled there. Although he considered himself Ottawa, he also took an active part in the councils of his mother's people, the Chippewa. It was obvious from his involvement in tribal politics that he was preparing himself for chieftainship, but his desire did not automatically make him a war chief.

In 1746, Pontiac was part of a party of two dozen warriors led by the war chief, Winniwok, who was also the head man of his village. The Ottawa had gone south to raid in Cherokee territory in Georgia, a trip that took five months to complete. In the subsequent raids on Cherokee villages, 11 of the Ottawa had died including Winniwok, who had fallen beneath the war club of a Cherokee defender. Nonetheless, 37 scalps had been brought back to the Ottawa village near Detroit, and Pontiac laid claim to 7 of them. This was a great accomplishment. The death of Winniwok left two vacancies in the hierarchy of Pontiac's village. The old chief was mourned and replaced as head man by another elder. Meanwhile, the council chose Pontiac to fill Winniwok's secondary position as war chief. By 1760, Pontiac had ingratiated himself with the French and had become an intertribal leader of some importance among the Huron (Wyandots) and Potawatomi as well as among the Ottawa and Chippewa with whom he was related. He used his reputation to initiate an unsuccessful general uprising among the Midwestern tribes against the British in 1764.[3]

Joseph Brant (Thayendanegea), even at age 32, was initially thought of as an upstart among his own Mohawk relations with great pretensions and little experience in warfare, but he quickly came to be viewed as the foremost war leader among the Iroquois during the American Revolution. Because he could speak the dialects of all six Iroquois nations, he was able to establish a group of young volunteers to fight against the American patriots on the side of the British Crown. He attracted most of his recruits from among the Mohawks, his mother's people; but he generally failed to influence the Oneida and Tuscarora warriors who sided with the Americans due to the influence of protestant missionaries who had come among them in the 1750s. Moreover, he became easily embroiled in disputes with the leaders of other Iroquois nations, particularly the elder Seneca leaders Cornplanter and Old Smoke with whom he did not always enjoy a warm, working relationship.

Brant distinguished himself throughout the Revolution by leading numerous raids on patriot settlements and keeping the frontier regions in constant turmoil. He was so active in pursuing the war in the New York and Pennsylvania border regions that he was identified by eyewitnesses as simultaneously leading raids that were hundreds of miles apart—a physical impossibility given currency among the white settlers only because of his reputation. Brant was seen by his Indian contemporaries as a man of exceptional ability, high character, and strong convictions—all important qualities for a native war leader. However, he was generally criticized for taking up the hatchet against his fellow Iroquois among the Oneida and Tuscarora, burning their villages and scattering their people. Brant may be the best-known Mohawk warrior, but he is also considered the man who broke the Covenant Chain that had joined the Iroquois together since the days of Hiawatha and Deganawida, the Peacemaker.[4]

The Iroquois Warrior

The Iroquois had a long history of warfare. They were particularly proud of their military prowess, and they were greatly feared by their neighbors because of the savagery and martial ability that they brought to the field of battle. In the 17th century alone, it has been calculated that the Iroquois attacked 51 different enemies or combinations of enemies, and were attacked by at least 20 different Indian nations acting separately or in consort. In the same 100-year period, they were involved in 465 hostile encounters of which they initiated 354. It should be noted that many of these encounters took place during the Great Dispersal—an uncharacteristically prolonged period of active warfare. In less than a decade (1643–1653), the Iroquois had considerably reduced the absolute number of their enemies (including men, women, and children) and their ability to wage retaliatory war against them. One Iroquois chief, speaking at the turn of the 18th century, noted no more than a half dozen remaining tribes that regularly made war upon his people.[5]

Father Gabriel Druillettes noted in 1651,

It is certain that all the nations of savages which are in New England hate the Iroquois, and fear lest...he [the Iroquois] will exterminate them. Indeed, he has broken the heads of many of their men, finding them hunting beaver, without making any satisfaction. Moreover, it is certain that the Sokoki [Abenaki of western Massachusetts] have been allied to the Algonquians, and are very glad to deliver themselves from the annual tribute of porcelain [wampum beads] which the Iroquois exact—nay, even, to revenge themselves for the death of many of their fellow-countrymen, killed by the Iroquois. Besides that, they hope for the beaver hunt about Quebec, after the destruction of the Iroquois.[6]

The Mohawk nation, in particular, levied tribute in the form of wampum from many tribes in the region stretching from the borders of present-day Canada, to New England, to Long Island, New Jersey, and parts of Pennsylvania. As late as 1669, the Algonquian-speaking tribes of New England launched a multi-tribal, full-scale attack on Iroquoia (known as the Ouragie War for one of its prominent leaders), and they were delivered a heavy defeat at the hands of the Mohawk who rallied to the defense. Thereafter, many New England tribes left the Berkshires and White Mountains region and migrated to the St. Lawrence River valley where the French welcomed them with food, clothing, trade goods, and firearms.

In some areas, the tribes found subservience to the Iroquois superior to resistance, and many Indian leaders found accommodation and outward submission the best strategies for dealing with the warlike and easily angered Mohawk. Among these were many bands among the Delaware, the Canarsie, and the Wappinger of southern New York.

It can be said with some authority that the French and the Iroquois were in turmoil almost without interruption throughout the 17th and 18th centuries. The French formed a long-standing enmity with the Iroquois in 1609 when Samuel de Champlain, in the company of friendly Montagnais and other Algonquians, met a large party of Mohawk at Crown Point (New York). The Indians and their traditional enemies engaged in a series of long-range insults and lined up for a battle that probably would have resulted in a few minimal casualties, but the French intervened with their muskets causing the death of several important Iroquois warriors and thereby changing forever the face of Indian warfare in the Northeast.

Champlain noted that he had loaded several balls into his weapon. "The Iroquois were much astonished that two men should have been killed so quickly, although they were provided with shields made of cotton [sic] thread woven together and wood, which were proof against their arrows...Of our Indians fifteen of sixteen were wounded with arrows, but these were quickly healed...Having feasted, danced, and sung, we three hours later set off for home with the prisoners."[7]

Harmen van der Brogaert noted that the Iroquois were so warlike as to practice at war. While visiting a Mohawk village in the winter of 1634, he reported:

An [Indian] man came shouting and screaming through some of the houses here. However, we did not know what it was supposed to mean. After a while...they said it was nothing against me. [They were] going to play with one another. There were four with clubs, and some with axes and sticks so that there were 20 men under arms; 9 on one side and 11 on the other. Then they went at each other, fighting and striking. Some wore armor and helmets which they made themselves from thin reeds and cord woven together so that no arrow or axe could penetrate to cause serious injury. After they had skirmished in this manner for a long time, the adversaries ran at one another; and the one dragged the other by the hair as they would do with conquered enemies.[8]

The Abenaki Warrior

Certainly the English found their Abenaki foes equal to, if not superior to, the Iroquois, who were English allies during the mid-18th century. The Abenaki, however, were not a single people, nor did they form as unified a confederacy as the Iroquois. This allowed the English to take advantage of divisions between the associated Abenaki bands, who each tended to follow their own strategy for survival among the whites rather than pursuing a single policy. Yet, the general acceptance of Catholicism by the Abenaki and the presence of Jesuit missionaries living among them helped to erect a territorial barrier of ranging warriors between New France and New England. This was a virtual "Wall of China" manned and maintained by Abenaki raiding parties that restricted Anglo-colonial expansion to the immediate coastlines of Connecticut, Massachusetts, New Hampshire, and Maine.[9]

Abenaki villages on the St. Francis River were particularly active jumping off points for war-parties planning attacks on the English settlements because the river connections opened a practical route by canoe to the New England borders. In 1745, the French, supported by 200 Abenaki and 20 Caughnawaga from St. Francis, attacked the towns of Saratoga and Balston just north of Albany, killing or capturing more than 100 individuals, burning almost all the substantial buildings, and taking away the towns' possessions. The destruction was so complete that the survivors burned their own fort and retreated to Albany.

Later that autumn, Abenaki warriors from the same mission harassed the New England border regions and attacked down the Merrimack Valley. An Anglo-American scouting party of eight men was ambushed. Only one Englishman survived. It was found that five of the party had been killed outright, scalped, systematically chopped up, and their hearts, genitals, and entrails had been removed. The last two men had disappeared, and their fate remains unknown. Because of horrors like these, the flourishing mission at St. Francis was attacked in 1759 by a force of Anglo-American rangers and Stockbridge Mahicans under the command of Colonel Robert Rogers. The mission was completely destroyed in what can only be called a revenge attack. Its church, all its records, and the crude native shelters were burned. An estimated 200 French–Indian warriors were killed, and their families were scattered into the woods without food or possessions. Finally, scores of scalps, both new and old, were retrieved and returned to Portsmouth, New Hampshire.[10]

Blood Revenge

For both white colonials and Indians, violence was a disproportionately large fact of life, and many persons, Indian and white, were killed either through accident or on purpose. For whites used to European style concepts of justice, it was an important legal requirement that the exact person who committed a crime be found out and punished, usually through an execution carried out by the state. "The blood of France is usually repaid among us only in blood," stated Pierre de Vandreuil, Governor of Quebec. For the Indians, however, identifying the individual murderer was not as important as discovering the group to which he belonged, for it was the group that was held responsible for the crime, and justice might be exacted on anyone in the group by the relatives of the victim. The difference between these two interpretations of justice caused no end of trouble between whites and Indians.[11]

Revenge raids were often initiated at the request of the clan matrons, who kept a careful account of people killed on all occasions and kept their memory alive until the loss was satisfied. This obligation fell on the children of the men of the aggrieved clan, who—due to the exogamous nature of Native American marriage—lived with their mothers in another clan. "Thus the obligation to avenge the death of a person belonged to another clan, and prisoners who were brought back for adoption were given by the warriors to their fathers' households, and not the one in which the [captors] lived. This aspect of revenge warfare served as a means to reinforce ties among the clans." In fact, the decision to adopt, torture, or kill a captive lay with the aggrieved clan mothers rather than with the members of the war party. The three outcomes (adoption, torture, or death) were not mutually exclusive. A captive might be tortured to near death before his adoption, and a long and painful torture almost always preceded an execution.[12]

The clan matrons could also put an end to a revenge raid by declaring against it, but blood feuding was such a strong cultural factor that the raids were not easily put aside even by the women. The clan mothers often proved more blood thirsty than their men. This aspect of Indian culture frustrated the Europeans who tried to prevent warfare among the tribes by dealing solely with the male representatives of the tribal councils as they would with whites. Yet, these men were often powerless to enforce their wills on the clan matrons if the women were not willing to ignore the obligation to replace loved ones lost in war.[13]

Much of the intertribal raiding and counter-raiding among Native Americans was fueled by this need for blood revenge. Small groups of related warriors would slip off into the wilderness to seek out and kill the members of other tribes with whom they had a grudge. The usual basis for a raid was the death or mistreatment of one of their own clan members. In this regard Bonin noted, "When…injured, [the Indian] is capable of going [six hundred miles] or more to surprise his enemy and satisfy his revenge with blood." Blood revenge caused intertribal hostilities to drag on for long periods. Moreover, if a white colony or government executed a murderer who was an Indian, his relatives might take revenge on other whites who were otherwise completely disassociated from either act. To the whites this was a gross injustice and a cause for retaliation upon the Indians.[14]

As a clan member, an Indian man was under some obligation to support his relatives and take revenge should one or more of them be killed by an enemy. However, internecine squabbles, accidents, and murder were not uncommon, and they were often mediated by the payment of goods, slaves, or wampum. According to Mahican tribal records, mothers would warn their children never to commit murder not only because their own lives would be endangered but also because they would endanger their beloved relatives.

It was the custom...when any murder was committed in the nation, to have the murders executed by a relation of the murdered person. If the murderer repented of his crime, had been useful to his friends and relations, and was beloved by them, in such case they collected a quantity of wampum and gave a ransom for his life. Or, if this was not done, the murderer, to save his life, might go a great way till he should find some enemy of his tribe from whom, if he could bring a prisoner to die for him or a scalp with wampum. Either was received as Nanptanteon, or a ransom of his own death.[15]

Captives

The Mohawks had adopted so many prisoners during the intertribal wars of the 17th century that pure-blooded Mohawks were a minority of the population in many of their own villages. The taking of Indian captives was less common among the Algonquians who went to war easily enough but generally eschewed torture as a form of entertainment. The Abenaki, who reveled in taking English women and children as prisoners for ransom, were generally an exception to this rule because they found a market for white captives among the French at Quebec who would ransom them.

The clan structure allowed for a certain amount of ease with which male captives might be adopted as clan members and thereby "raise up the dead" by providing a person in the victim's place. This feature of clan-based Indian society figured prominently among the coureurs de bois, woodsmen, and fur traders who married native women and had children with them. All of the progeny of adopted males were considered full clan members because questions of legitimacy flowed through the females. Often the men choosing to go on a revenge raid would announce their intention of taking up a raiding party for the purpose of finding appropriate victims for adoption from within an offending clan or tribe. The dead might also "be covered up" by presenting goods to the dead man's relatives as an equivalent. To refuse an appropriate compensation between aggrieved parties of the same tribe was equivalent to a great insult, and between tribes it demanded a declaration of war.

According to the native way of thinking, all murderers were considered madmen, but the madness was usually temporary and could go away. Therefore, executing a person for murder was unjust because it did not allow him to return from his altered state. The cultural logic of the Indians in these matters was difficult for whites to accept. Yet, European standards in this regard simply could not be applied with any practicality, and royal governors of both the French and English colonies constantly tried to find some transcultural fiction that could be agreed upon to insure justice without creating a spiral of continuous blood-letting. For example, in 1706, Cadillac required that an Ottawa chief accused of murdering a Frenchman appear before him so that he would have the native "in his power, to grant him life or put him to death," thereby effectively placing the chief temporarily in the position of a slave or a captive where his fate could be decided. This was more comprehensible to the Indians than a European-style trial, sentencing, and execution. These legal protocols were unprecedented in their culture.[16]

The War Party

War parties rarely exceeded 30 warriors or about 10 percent of the eligible men in a village because the absence of more men would have left their own families vulnerable to attack. Nonetheless, small parties of less than a dozen young warriors were commonly on the prod at almost any time of the year.

The reasons for undertaking a raid were taken seriously and usually fell into one of two categories. Either they were a part of an economic or military strategy undertaken by the whole tribe, or the consequence of blood revenge carried out by a small group of warriors. The latter was particularly prevalent among small groups of warriors who would go to war specifically to take Indian captives for torture or adoption when members of their own clans were killed.[17]

When whole tribes went to war, hundreds of warriors could be deployed. A Jesuit observer, Father Sebastian Rales, noted of the Abenaki in 1723,

As soon as they have entered the enemy's country, they divide into separate companies—one of thirty warrior, another of forty, and so on…Afterward the signal is given to strike all together, and at the same time in different places. Our two hundred and fifty warriors spread themselves more than twenty leagues [about 40 miles] of country, where there were villages, hamlets, and houses; and on the appointed day made simultaneous attacks, very early in the morning…[carrying] desolation into all the country.

It was reported that the Abenaki who took part in this particular operation killed more than 200 persons, captured more than 250 women and children, and returned with their canoes filled with booty, while only a few warriors were wounded on their side.[18]

Individuals wishing to become war leaders first needed to organize and successfully lead a series of small raids. Some 19th-century historians treated this process like it was a civil service examination with specific requirements. "To become an accepted War Chief it is necessary that a man should have led at least 4 war parties…at each time take one or more scalps and that he should return his followers unhurt to their villages" after which he could demand his appointment as a right. This was a somewhat naive and romanticized view of the process that brought a man to recognition as a war leader.[19]

An individual organized his war party by sending word of his intentions to the members of his clan by a messenger who explained the purpose of the raid and its justification to the assembled warriors and young men. These messengers sometimes carried a stick or hatchet painted red as a symbol of their purpose. The messenger often drove the stick into the ground or struck the hatchet into a tree to announce his purpose. Beneath this symbol he might sit with a calumet and entertain interested warriors. Those warriors who wished to join in the raid took the proffered calumet from the messenger and smoked it. At an appointed time, the volunteers met with the raid sponsor for a feast during which they were given a more complete outline of the proposed raid. It was generally easy for a noted and successful warrior to recruit young men to war because they had yet to establish their own martial reputations.

The leader often related the series of dreams, omens, or visions that had brought him to call for the enterprise, and each warrior was asked to pledge himself to the undertaking. The men thereafter painted themselves with totemic symbols and marks of their past military deeds. The Marquis de Montcalm noted in a letter to his wife written in 1756, "The Indians are villains...even when fresh from their toilet, at which they pass their lives. You would not believe it, but the men always carry to war, along with their tomahawk and gun, a mirror to daub their faces with colors, and arrange feathers on their heads, and rings in their ears and noses."[20]

The sponsor of the raid usually led it, and he carried a sacred war bundle as a symbol of his position and authority. In the bundle, there may have been a number of traditional clan and tribal objects, or items dictated by the vision or dream of the sponsor. The leader would open the bundle, speak of the significance of the objects, and relate his former deeds and heroics to his companions, who would smoke tobacco, make a sacrifice to the manitou, and eat a feast (usually of young dog or wolf).

The war party would then send out advanced scouts and make its own way stealthily into the country of the target enemy. This could be a long trip with the file of warriors maintaining a distance consuming dog-trot for many hours each day. Some raiding parties traveled hundreds of miles through the forests to make a raid that would only last for minutes. Once near the enemy village, the war party would make a fireless camp, open the sacred bundle, and sing songs associated with warfare or pray for the aid of the manitou. The contents of the sacred bundle would then be distributed among the members of the party, each item representing some skill of war, or conferring on the receiver good luck or some form of magic. The warriors then moved into the position in the night in quiet apprehension of what was to come.

If the war party intended an ambush, no one hunted and the warriors lived off the food they had brought with them from their own country. More commonly, however, the warriors would rush upon the enemy position or village just before dawn with clubs, tomahawks, spears, or bows and arrows. Those who killed an opposing warrior were credited with the greatest honor, and the man who drew first blood from the enemy was often awarded a belt of wampum after the raid was completed. War honors were also awarded for touching an enemy. This was called counting coup among the plains tribes, but it was not as highly considered among woodland Indians. Touching a living enemy warrior was given greater credit than touching the fallen.

War parties would sometimes build a temporary fortification some distance from their intended target to serve as a staging area or a fall-back refuge in case of a sustained pursuit. Regardless of victory or defeat Indians made every effort to remove their dead and wounded from the battlefield. They might also leave messages and taunts for their victims on the trees near these camps. With the bark stripped away, symbols and totems would be painted on the bare wood with moistened powders of vermilion, verdigris, and charcoal daring their enemies to follow them and promising that they would be cut from the face of the earth if they attempted to do so.

Pierre Radisson reported that, as a young man who had been adopted into the Mohawk nation, he accompanied a war party into the territory of the Erie. Beaching their canoes and hiding them some distance from the Erie "fort," the party spent a worrisome night in the forest while two men scouted the area. Before daybreak the party had moved down the shore to the edge of a lake on which there was a "shelter made of rushes." Nearby they spied a fishing party of Erie—five men and four women— who they surrounded and massacred. The booty of the unlucky fishermen was only some deer skins, "hair girdles," and dried fish. Further on they found another shelter occupied by an old woman and two children. These unfortunates they dispatched and threw into the water because they could not keep up on the retreat should the war party be discovered. Radisson reported that every person in the party now had a scalp and one man had two, making the strength of the war party six or seven depending on whether the hair of the children was taken.

The Mohawk now positioned themselves for an attack on the larger village by lying in wait for another night. This was not unusual. Such was the dispersed nature of Indian living in the security of their own territory that an enemy war party might stay concealed in an area for several days, killing individuals singly or in small groups without detection. On the next day, the Mohawk saw a group of 20 men and women working in the fields outside the village, but they remained concealed. Nonetheless, toward evening they were discovered by four men and three women who came along to gather firewood. Two of the Erie men and all three women were captured. One additional man was killed, and the last escaped. Knowing that the alarm would quickly spread, the war party began a running retreat with its captives. By dawn, the Erie women were falling behind, so the Mohawk killed them and threw their bodies in the water. By midday, the Mohawks had retrieved their canoes and made good their escape with the two male captives.

The war party later came upon another small band of Erie. Radisson claimed that there were nine Erie warriors and their families in this group. Into these the Mohawks sprang from ambush. "Hampered by their families the Erie men fought and defended themselves lustily, covering the escape of their women." When the women were out of sight, the surviving men fled. Five Erie were felled by Mohawk arrows. One of the Mohawk was mortally wounded by two arrows to the bowels, and he had been cracked in the head by a war club. Seeing that their comrade was dying and could not continue on, his friends "put an end to him" so that he might not "languish." The war party delayed their flight long enough to provide a pyre for the slain Mohawk. "We burned him with all speed, that he might not...put ourselves in jeopardy." Radisson noted that both groups in this fight were armed with at least some muskets, the firing of which caused some fright among the women; but he also noted that a man could let fly a dozen arrows in the time that it took to reload one shot from a firearm.[21]

On the return trip, which was reported to take up to two weeks, the warriors recaptured some women who had escaped an Iroquois village. In one of these, Radisson was given a share. The raiders then spent some time fishing and hunting. Apparently the party passed Niagara Falls, which Radisson described as "precipices with horrible falling waters." All the way home through Iroquoia to the country of the Mohawk, the party was greeted by fellow Iroquois and entertained and feasted in the villages in which they stopped. The total booty of the trip was 22 scalps, 5 captives, and several score of beaver pelts. Once home, Radisson gave two scalps to his foster sisters and presented a captive women to his Mohawk mother as a slave. He saw that the male captives were made to run the gauntlet, after which they were soundly beaten and tortured. Having served with honor, Radisson was loaded with wampum by his admirers, pampered by his mother, and dressed with decoration in his hair by his sisters.[22]

Scalping

Scalping was a common practice among Indians that seems to have replaced the taking of whole heads as practiced in an archaic period. The idea that whites introduced scalping to the Indians is not supported by reliable evidence, and the practices and rituals surrounding scalping were intertwined in Indian culture before Europeans arrived.[23] Montcalm noted of the Indians, "They make war with astounding cruelty, sparing neither men, women, nor children, and take off your scalp very neatly—an operations which generally kills you."[24] It should be noted that it was the whites, and not the Indians, that placed a monetary value on scalps presented as proof of the death of an enemy.

It is clear that Indians were taking scalps long before the intrusion of whites. It is probable that more Indians than whites were scalped by other Indians as it was among their martial protocol and not that of Europeans that scalps were taken.

Scalps were the "medals" and "ribbons" of Indian warfare. A roughly circular portion of the victim's scalp was cut from the crown of his head, stretched upon a hoop, and displayed on a stick or pole in the warrior's camp. A Scalp Dance was often part of the triumph accorded successful warriors on their return. If the raid had been one of blood revenge, the scalp might be given to the widow, mother, or sister of the slain man whose death had prompted the raid. Occasionally scalps were added to the contents of the sacred war bundle. A successful warrior, at his death, often had his scalp stick or pole displayed at his graveside to attest to his prominence in war.

Weapons

For centuries, Native Americans had fought among themselves in a conservative, if seemingly inhumane, manner using knives, clubs, and tomahawks made of wood and stone. The weapons available to all the woodland tribes were essentially the same (the bow and arrow, the spear, the lance, the tomahawk), and their way of making war was remarkably similar.

Depending on availability, a number of different woods were used to manufacture these weapons. Witch hazel, hickory, ash, beech, and maple were all used for bows, clubs, hatchet handles, and spear shafts. Cedar, alder, and ash were crafted into arrows. The bows were generally between three- and six-feet long and notched at the ends to take the bowstring. Shorter bows were used for hunting and longer ones for war. The bow-strings were often made from twisted sinew. War arrows—two- to three-feet long—were made from the dried young sprouts of alder, or they were split from the heartwood of cedar or ash. They were fixed with three to five half-feathers split lengthwise and attached with a hide glue supported by a thin spiral of sinew. War arrows were fitted with triangular heads of flint, quartz, bone, or copper metal. Iron and steel arrowheads were rare because muskets had generally replaced bows by the time such materials arrived. A warrior carried 40 or 50 arrows in a leather or woven-rush quiver. The range of war bows with this type of arrow depended on many factors, but most experts agree that it was effective to between 100 and 120 yards. This was not much outside the effective range of a smoothbore musket of the period.[25]

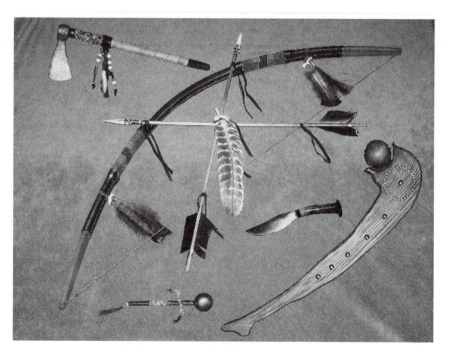

A sampling of authentic woodland weapons.

The original native tomahawk was a very different instrument from that commonly known today. Iron- and steel-edged weapons were a European innovation. The native version was about 30 inches long, and a large knob of wood or stone did its lethal work by smashing the body of the enemy. The head of the weapon might actually be the solid root ball of a small tree pulled from the ground, trimmed of its roots, and left with a portion of the trunk cut and thinned to an appropriate length and thickness to act as a handle. The whole weapon was usually scraped smooth and carved with simple decorations. A chipped stone was sometimes embedded in the root ball to make an effective puncture weapon. Clubs were also made from stone triangles and rectangles without grooves (a celt) that were tied or jammed into a handle, or from an oblong stone with a full or partial groove pecked or ground around it that was used for firmly attaching a handle (hafting). The gunstock tomahawk—so named from its resemblance to that part of a musket—was made of wood with flint projections and probably developed independent of Indian exposure to the white man's weapon.

William Wood, a settler from Plymouth Plantation, has left a description of fighting Mohawk warriors published in 1634. They come "running, and fiercely crying out...not fearing the feathered shafts of strong-armed bow-men.... [T]heir right hand Tamahaukes be staves of two foote and a halfe long, and a knob at one end as round and bigge as a [17th century] football.... [O]ne blow or thrust with these strange weapons, will not need a second to hasten death."[26]

The Way of War

Native American warriors employed tactics against Europeans that were simple and effective. They generally struck first without a formal declaration of war, using the basic offensive tactic of surprise. They commonly attacked isolated cabins and remote settlements, often at dawn. They often attacked solitary farmers working in their fields after mid-day, and more than once fell upon farm carts driven by women or children. It was not unusual for an abandoned cart or riderless horse to serve as the first sign of a larger problem. Most attacks, however, took the form of ambushes made in forested regions. From Dollard's defense of Long Sault in 1660 to the defeat of Braddock on the Monongahela almost a century later, the Indian offensive generally prevailed except where their own tactics were used against them. These were especially effective against non-military targets, such as small parties of settlers or fur traders. A surviving description from the early colonial period notes, "The place where they fought was of great advantage to the savages, by means of the thick trees, behind which the savages through their nimbleness, defended themselves, and so offended our men with their arrows."[27]

The Indians' tactics evolved with time and with contact with Europeans. They abandoned their traditional practice of not fighting through the winter months to launch crucial forays in the snow against such targets as Deerfield, Massachusetts and Schenectady, New York. Ironically, as the tactics used against the whites by the Indians became increasingly influenced by European ideas, the defensive tactics employed by the whites became more Indian-like because the settlers realized their innate effectiveness. In this regard, almost all the colonies employed experienced woodsmen called rangers. Only Pennsylvania and New York seem to have neglected the establishment of a formal corps of these paid frontiersmen to watch their outlying borders. The southern colonies of Virginia and the Carolinas raised more than 1,000 border rangers. The rangers patrolled the frontiers, held down depredations, and tried to keep abreast of the temper of the natives.

The best known group of rangers were those raised by Robert Rogers from among the tough woodsmen of the New Hampshire frontier. Rogers' Rangers could rival any Indian war party in ambush, murder, and scalpings. Like chameleons, they combined Indian moccasins and leggings with uniform coats that were sober green in spring and faded to an almost perfectly camouflaged green-yellow by fall. They were seemingly impervious to weather, bivouacking in the snow, silently flashing past enemy outposts in winter on ice skates, and penetrating their lines on snowshoes.

Nonetheless, hundreds of miles of ever-shifting frontier settlements were not readily defensible against Indian raids. Since the Indians rarely chose

Colonial militias periodically organized punitive expeditions into the frontier regions, an effective strategy so brutal as to deter further incursions.

to stand and fight with their families in peril, colonials learned to threaten and burn the natives' crops and villages. The Indians were thereby forced into an active defense that could be broken by trained soldiers. Recurrent hostilities and the need for repeated colonial forays into the border regions, with all of their political and economic consequences, posed a dilemma for colonial officials that they could never resolve. Nonetheless, a series of overwhelming victories by militia forces in the 17th century caused colonials to exaggerate their abilities in this regard.

As a result, they tended to look down upon the regular British troops brought to the colonies to fight the French Army in the second half of the 18th century. However, British Col. Henry Bouquet exhibited an exemplary understanding of Indian offensive tactics during the French and Indian War, which was confirmed by his signal victory at Bushy Run in 1764 during Pontiac's War. He wrote, "[T]here were three basic principles in the Indians' method of fighting: first, fight scattered; second, try to surround; and third, give ground when hard pressed and return when the pressure eased."[28]

Firearms among the Indians

Europeans generally hoped to avoid spreading firearms technology among the Indians. For example, Jesuit Father Pierre Biard warned as early as 1612, "Clearly...if firearms [are] once placed into the hands of [these] undisciplined men, the masters [the French] have much to fear and suffer."[29] In New England, William Bradford regretted the opening of trade in firearms to the Indians "which may turn to ye ruin of many [colonists]."[30] The Indians shifted from traditional weapons to firearms as quickly as they became available, but it has been pointed out that the Indians "never really mastered the white man's weapon."[31] The native war practices in terms of tactics, prisoners, and personal behavior on the field of battle changed little even with the introduction of firearms. Nonetheless, martial strategy among the tribes shifted from the use of petty skirmishes to the waging of major battles, and from a generally defensive to an offensive posture.[32]

Oddly, the introduction of firearms among the Indians, while significant, was less effective in changing their life style than one would think. The introduction of metal tools, such as knives, hatchets, and cooking pots and kettles, had a greater effect in changing the daily life of some Indians than did guns. Moreover, the trade in muskets was never very large, and the Indians seem to have had great difficulty in incorporating them effectively into their methods of woodland warfare. More often than not the Indians fired their weapons into the air using them to instill fear and terror. Nonetheless, colonists and settlers expressed great fear that the Indians would become armed with technologically advanced weapons.

By 1676, almost all the tribes of New England had converted to firearms, and many of the western tribes were armed with gunpowder weapons to a lesser extent, which reflected their distance from the source of supply. This was accomplished through a combination of economic and political pressures that pitted the Europeans against each other in a contest for native alliances. Yet, the Indians generally failed to develop a technological support for their firearms comparable to that available to the colonists. The adoption of firearms, therefore, made the Indian largely dependent on Europeans for powder and lead ball as well as for repairs.

As late as 1659, some of the western tribes had to be convinced to adopt firearms. Radisson found that he had to appeal to the almost universal fear of the Iroquois, who were well supplied with muskets by the Dutch, to get some western Indians to take up the whites man's weapon. In a harangue of the assembled warrior of one village he said, "It is arms that kill, not beaver skins. What will your enemies [the Iroquois] say when you die without defense? You know the French way. We fight with arms, not skins…Do you image that the French will come up here [to trade] after most of you have been killed through your own weakness. Will they come to baptize your dead?" Radisson was delighted when his plea was accepted and the elders sent out the criers through the village saying, "Women, get your husbands' bundles. They go to get the wherewithal to defend themselves and keep you alive."[33]

Muskets of the period were wildly inaccurate, and native hunting techniques were well established and remarkably efficient, even if prosecuted with archaic weaponry. Trade muskets, where available, were not as fine as the weapons used by whites. Even when possessed of firearms the Indians often found themselves with unserviceable weapons for lack of powder or repairs. Those Frenchmen charged with the development and expansion of trade with the native population generally understood this dependence and used gunsmithing services as a means of binding the Indians to them. Yet, the French always demanded that the Indians bring their weapons into the trading towns for repair. English traders, on the other hand, understood their role as providers of powder and shot but avoided dealing in repairs, choosing instead to supply an entirely new weapon to their customers in the field albeit at an exaggerated cost in terms of furs to the individual Indian.

Early in the 17th century, the governor of Maryland blamed the Swedes for arming the Indians in his colony. This the Swedes did openly, supplying not only long arms but also small wall cannons to the Susquehannocks to defend their villages against the attacks of the Seneca. Yet, the French were the first to acquire an unsavory reputation among other Europeans for supplying firearms to the Indians for use against whites. The French responded by condemning the English traders for the same practice, and the English blamed the Dutch, who in turn looked again to the French. The French sold guns to the Indian residents of their missions, and they were often accused of using the offer of firearms as a tool of conversion.

It seems, however, that it was the Dutch who were the major source of firearms in the earliest period of their proliferation among the Indians— that is before they lost their colonies to the English in 1672. Evidence suggests that more than 30,000 beaver pelts were traded to the Dutch for muskets, powder, and lead during this period. While dealing in firearms with the Indians was initially made a capital offense in New Netherlands, of 700 Mohawk warriors appearing for a council at Trois Riviers in 1641, the Jesuit Barthelemy Vimont reported that almost 400 had firearms acquired from the Dutch post at Fort Orange (Albany). By 1652, the Dutch West Indies Company had decided to supply firearms to the Mohawks "as sparingly and secretly as possible" so that the Indians might better protect Dutch interests in and around the Hudson-Mohawk region. Making mercenaries of the Mohawk was a purposeful decision taken by the Burghers at Albany as part of their security plans.[34]

The geographical position of the Iroquois in central New York with major French, Dutch, and English trading posts surrounding their territory seems to have given them an advantage over their native enemies with regard to munitions and firearms. Although the Indians of the French– Algonquian alliance also seem to have been well-supplied with firearms, one historian notes that "it seems fair to conclude that the Iroquois were better armed." Yet, only the Mohawks among the five Iroquois tribes had open access to Dutch traders at this time, and they jealously guarded their unique relationship with them even from their close relations in the Iroquois Confederacy.[35]

The Indians quickly recognized the value of firearms as a weapon in warfare, yet, they never really became proficient in their use in a military sense. In order to conserve gunpowder, they tended to underload the powder charge, and they often fired indiscriminately in battle failing entirely to mass the power of their weapons in volleys as did the Europeans. Their fire was sporadic and promiscuous, and contemporary observers noted that many shots were fired high into the air. Those unfamiliar with firearms, even among white recruits to the militia, were constantly admonished to aim low as the natural tendency of the marksman is to underestimate the flatness of a bullet's trajectory and overestimate the distance to the target. Training was also needed to compensate for shooting up or down a slope. There is no evidence that the Indians were made aware of these details of shooting.

Muskets, as opposed to the more precise rifles carried by mid-to-late 18th-century colonial frontiersmen, were wildly inaccurate in any case. Even in the hands of trained militia, they were ineffective at ranges greater than 75 yards. In the dense forests of the Northeast woodlands, the unimpeded line of sight was so short as to place a target equally within the lethal range of a musketball or an arrow. Finally, the Indians utterly failed to maintain their gunpowder weapons or clean them regularly, and the constant demands they made for gunsmiths to repair their weapons suggests that not all the muskets in their possession at any given time were serviceable.

Historians report that matchlock muskets (arquebuses) predominated over flintlock (snaphance) muskets in America before 1645. By the beginning of the 18th century, however, almost all of the firearms used in America were based upon the same standard smooth-bore, flintlock technology then common to the armies of Europe. Most firearms, including pistols, fired a generally large lead ball between .63 and .75 caliber, but more than half a dozen different calibers were commonly used during the period. The visually intimidating pistols were actually wildly inaccurate and useful only at very close quarters. The more accurate and longer-range rifle did not become a major factor in military warfare until the American Revolution.

French and Dutch firearms were generally of superior quality when compared to English military arms of the period. The steel-mounted French weapons were somewhat lighter and more precise than the brass-mounted weapons of the English, but the English weapons were more sturdy and could withstand greater abuse without failing. The Tulle Fusille de Chase (hunting musket of .63 caliber) was a favorite with the Canadiens and the Indians because it was shorter (42 inches) and lighter in weight than standard military weapons. The Dutch offered a dependable trade gun with both iron and brass furniture that was well-liked by the Indians. The standard English long arm was the Tower Musket of .75 caliber. This was lovingly known as the Brown Bess, and it changed very little through a number of long land (46 inch) and short land (44 inch) patterns. The English also introduced an Indian trade gun that came to be known as the "Northwest Gun" because of its prominence as a trade item in the lakes region after 1763.

All European nations of the 18th century produced standard military muskets for their line troops that supported a socket bayonet, but the Indians universally disdained their use relying instead on tomahawks and knives. Indian trade muskets, being shorter and often stocked to the muzzle, usually had no place to fix a bayonet in any case. The Indians often cut down standard weapons if they came into their possession by taking 10 to 12 inches from the barrel to make the musket more convenient to use in the brush and undergrowth. They also favored smaller caliber weapons because they yielded more balls per pound of lead and required less powder per load. There is some evidence that the French, at least, tried to initiate the use of prepared paper cartridges among the tribes of the Algonquian alliance in order to conserve their powder resources and speed loading, as was the case among white troops. Nonetheless, most contemporary illustrations of Indians with firearms in their possession include the ubiquitous powder horn made famous by the American frontiersmen of a later date.[36]

Notes

1. Quoted in Colin G. Calloway, *Dawnland Encounters, Indians and Europeans in Northern New England* (Hanover, NH: University Press of New England, 1991), 154.

2. The term *guerilla* was not in common use until the 1800s when Spanish freedom fighters opposed the armies of Napoleon.

3. Allen W. Eckert, *Wilderness Empire* (New York: Little, Brown and Company, 1969), 68.

4. Barbara Graymont, *The Iroquois in the American Revolution* (Syracuse, NY: Syracuse University Press, 1972), 53.

5. José Antonio Brandao, *Your Fyre Shall Burn No More: Iroquois Policy Toward New France and Its Native Allies to 1701* (Lincoln: University of Nebraska Press, 1997), 31.

6. Quoted in Calloway, *Dawnland Encounters*, 142–143.

7. Quoted in Calloway, *Dawnland Encounters*, 139.

8. Charles T. Gehring and William A. Starna, eds., *A Journey into Mohawk and Oneida Country, 1634–1635: The Journal of Harmen Meyndertz van der Bogaert* (Syracuse, NY: Syracuse University Press, 1988), 10.

9. Samuel Adams Drake, *The Border Wars of New England, Commonly Called King Williams's and Queen Anne's Wars* (Williamstown, MA: Corner House Publishers, 1973), 150n.

10. Eckert, 83.

11. Richard White, *The Middle Ground, Indians, Empires, and Republics in the Great Lakes Region, 1650–1815* (New York: Cambridge University Press, 1991), 86.

12. Brandao, 37.

13. Brandao, 38.

14. Andrew Gallup, ed., *Memoir of a French and Indian War Soldier, Jolicoeur Charles Bonin* (Bowie, MD: Heritage Books, Inc., 1993), 216.

15. Quoted in Patrick Frazier, *The Mohicans of Stockbridge* (Lincoln: University of Nebraska Press, 1992), 49.

16. White, 87.

17. Ian K. Steele, *Warpaths, Invasions of North America* (New York: Oxford University Press, 1994), 118.

18. Calloway, *Dawnland Encounters*, 154.

19. Paul A. W. Wallace, *Indians in Pennsylvania* (Harrisburg: Pennsylvania Historical and Museum Commission, 1986), 121.

20. Quoted in Eckert, 431.

21. Reported in Stanley Vestal, *King of the Fur Traders, The Deeds and Deviltry of Pierre Espirit Radisson* (Boston: Houghton Mifflin, 1940), 56–57.

22. Vestal, 59.

23. Calloway, *Dawnland Encounters*, 167.

24. Quoted in Eckert, 431.

25. Howard S. Russell, *Indian New England Before the Mayflower* (Hanover, NH: University Press of New England, 1980), 191.

26. Quoted in William Brandon, *Indians* (Boston: Houghton Mifflin Company, 1987), 153.

27. Quoted in Brandon, 152.

28. John K. Mahon, "Anglo-American Methods of Indian Warfare, 1674–1794," *The Mississippi Valley Historical Review* 45 (1958): 260.

29. Harold F. McGee, *The Native Peoples of Atlantic Canada, A History of Indian-European Relations* (Ottawa: Carleton University Press, 1983), 29–30.

30. George T. Hunt, *The Wars of the Iroquois, A Study in Intertribal Trade Relations* (Madison: University of Wisconsin Press, 1972), 166–167.

31. Mahon, 255.

32. Steele, 118.

33. Vestal, 122–123.

34. Hunt, 166–167.

35. Hunt, 169.

36. It should be pointed out that this same flintlock technology remained in use with little change until after the conclusion of the Napoleonic Wars (1815).

10

The Fur Trade

The Indians spent the entire year in the act of trading or in preparing for it.

—Father Jean de Brebeuf, J.S.[1]

Dependence

The significance of the fur trade in New England, New Netherlands, and New France cannot be underestimated. Yet, it would be an error to assume that the introduction of European goods to the forests of North America created an instant dependence on them among the Indians. Father Pierre de Charlevoix observed that, as late as 1720, the wants of the Indians were "meager" and that they could have "easily dispensed with them." When the supply of powder and lead failed near the end of the French and Indian War in the 1760s, many nations resumed their hunting with bows and arrows. When the supply of cloth failed, they returned to garments made of skins.[2]

It is significant, however, that the tribes located furthest west returned to their native manufactures with the greatest enthusiasm while those in the east were most dramatically effected by scarcities of European goods. Given the limited capacity of the fur traders' canoes, the influx of European trade items in the west probably did not fundamentally change the basic native way of life even in the space of more than 100 years. Indian culture was conservative and generally resistant to the adoption of sweeping changes. Even in the east where cloth and metal items quickly displaced skins and implements made of flint, there is evidence that the native technologies most closely associated with basic subsistence and shelter persisted. This allowed the Indians to maintain a modicum of independence from the European traders while benefiting from their goods.[3]

There is significant evidence that the natives were first attracted to European goods for their symbolic value. "Northeast Indians, for example, equated glass beads with native crystal and valued mirrors highly because they reflected images and thus, like water, became tools of divination. Native copper, crystals, and shells already had rich ritual significance . . . and when given as gifts, created special bonds between societies." Gifts brought influence, prestige, and honor to both the giver and the receiver, and gifts of scare European goods were a cross-cultural necessity long before they became a material necessity.[4]

Often, the first piece of business in the trading process was to make presents and establish good-will with the entire tribe. Medard Chouart Des Groseillierss and Pierre-Esprit Radisson, who established the fur trade among the Cree and Chippewa of the north country, reported that they opened one negotiation with three sets of gifts—one for the men, one for the women, and the last for the children. The men received a kettle, two hatchets, six knives, and a sword blade. "The kettle, they explained, was to invite all friendly nations to the Feast Of the Dead, which they made once in seven years to renew friendships." The gift to the women was two dozen steel awls, four dozen needles, two tools for scraping skins, two ivory combs, two wooden combs, half a dozen tin mirrors, and some vermilion. Lastly the children were given small rings and trinkets "thrown into the air over their heads, causing a battle royal as they scrambled for the treasures." A feast and dancing followed during which Radisson took an old couple for his father and mother and called all those about him brother and sister—endowing them with a series of smaller gifts and establishing his kinship in native terms.[5]

Initially, there were faint rumblings of discontent among the native populations as the effects of the fur trade altered long-standing traditions and intertribal relations. One historian has noted, "It must never be forgotten, in studying the history of the American Indian, that in his mind intertribal affairs bulked large and solidly permanent, whereas the new and shifting relations with the white intruder seemed recent, shadowy, and evanescent by comparison." In one of the first speeches recorded during a Franco–Iroquois negotiation, the primary native spokesman began, "It is not trade that brings us here. Do you think that our beaver skins can pay us for all our toils and dangers? Keep them, if you like; or, if they fall into our hands, we shall use them only in your service. We seek not things that perish!"[6]

Yet, the Indians ultimately became more and more desirous of obtaining European trade goods. As they increased the volume of their hunting to satisfy the demands of the fur trade, many ritual observances that tied the hunters to the animal world were in danger of being disregarded or of being ignored entirely. This circumstance violated the sensibilities of the most conservative of native elders and shaman, who openly spoke of returning to traditional methods and values. The trading posts in particular were thought to be a destabilizing influence on the rhythm of intertribal commerce. They caused the natives to use unfamiliar and dangerous routes of travel and fomented territorial crises between neighboring Indian populations. Nonetheless, as the manufactured goods streamed into the wilderness, there were few natives who could not see their usefulness.[7]

Native Americans were sophisticated in their thinking and vastly pragmatic. It would be an error to suppose that trinkets, mirrors, and glass jewelry divested a simple people of their economic sense, or that the natives continued to use their archaic methods of tool-making and weaponry from the romantic perspective of centuries as we do. Knives and razors of steel and axes and kettles of iron were reliable and easy to use and maintain. Moreover, not all Indians were equally talented in the manufacture of projectile points, scrapers, and blades from stone, and the raw materials for their manufacture sometimes came from sources many hundreds of miles away. The trade goods freed the Indian family somewhat from reliance on their archaic sources by providing long-lasting items that did not need constant replacement. Woolen blankets and linen cloth were more comfortable and more colorful than animal skins, and the tedious process of preparing skins and weaving mats from marsh reeds and capes from grasses was gladly avoided. Vermilion (a bright red pigment) and verdigris (a blue to green pigment), which could be mixed with animal grease to form a body paint, were very popular because the colors were brilliant and not readily available from natural materials. Such pigments were highly valued even though they were not necessities. A contemporary observer noted, "Many persons told me that they had heard their fathers mention that the first Frenchmen who came over here got a heap of furs from the Indians for three times as much [vermilion] as would lie on the tip of a knife."[8]

Of all the possessions available to the Indians from the whites, the iron knife, closely followed by the axe or hatchet, seems to have been most in demand. Estimates of the trade goods that reached the western shores of the Great Lakes from Montreal in the 1690s include 28,000 knives and 2,500 hatchets.[9] In another list of the items bartered for the County of Westchester in New York, 300 knives headed the list followed by 185 axes and hatchets, 141 hoes, and 117 kettles and cooking pots. These iron implements resolved a number of difficult technological problems faced by the Indians every day and caused them to immediately cast aside the stone tools that they replaced. Brass and iron kettles allowed them great convenience in preparing their meats, maize, and roots in stews instead of roasting them over the fire or baking them in bark containers. As the dripping fats were no longer lost in the ashes, a great deal of caloric and nutritional value was saved. These lost calories were no small matter to a people who hunted and gathered for a living in a subsistence economy.

More importantly, European goods gave the natives abilities that they had not before possessed. Native Americans made many body paints and dyes from naturally occurring materials. Ground red ocher was the closest they came to the brilliant red of vermilion, and green could be made from tarnished native copper, which metal was available from the Great Lakes region. Nonetheless, European pigments were brighter and of better quality and consistency. Broken or cracked brass, copper, and iron kettles were also used to make projectile points, blades, and jewelry. Steel awls and needles were a boon to many forms of manufacture and decoration. Beads for wampum, cut from the shells of oyster, conch, and periwinkle and polished to size, could now be drilled with ease when compared to the laborious process required when using a bone awl. For centuries, the manufacture of wampum had been limited to coastal tribes who had access to the shells from which it was made. The importation of red, white, and blue porcelain beads, seemingly as highly valued by the natives as the natural product, greatly enhanced the stockpile of this culturally important item. The most dramatic impact of the fur trade, however, may be that it gave the Indians firearms. But this was not an immediate development, and up to 1640, the trade in firearms was very small.[10]

Native Middlemen

The Indians of the Maine coast were trading with Europeans in the 16th century, and a surprising abundance of manufactured goods was found among them by settlers in the 17th century. One observer noted "very good axes...and French shirts and coats and razors" among the Indians. In the trading process individual Indian trappers and traders often acted to their own advantage, but those bands who could act as middlemen occupied a "valuable strategic and economic position." Between 1607 and 1615, the Micmac and eastern Abenaki (both Algonquian speaking peoples) fought with the tribes of the interior for the position of middlemen in trading furs for manufactured goods available on the coasts of Maine and Nova Scotia. The western Abenaki and their relations among the Algonquians east of the Champlain Valley seem to have controlled the flow of trade goods and furs from the coast and throughout much of New England in the early 17th century.[11]

European and Native American fur traders differed considerably in the roles that they assumed in the trading process. The Europeans displayed a great division of labor among their traders. Some supplied the capital and political influence to secure a license, others operated the fixed trading posts, and finally some made the face to face negotiations with the Indians in the wilderness. Moreover, the colonial governments of every European nation represented in North America during the period acquired a corps of white negotiators whose prestige among the Indians enhanced their ability to bargain effectively. On the other hand, the Native Americans who dealt in the fur trade usually combined these many roles into a single person. The Indians that hunted and trapped were most often the same persons who did the trading. They transported the furs themselves and haggled over the bargain with varying degrees of success. A number of tribes attempted to control this aspect of the fur trade by installing themselves as middlemen. The 17th century Huron seemingly cherished the role. Some tribes welcomed their intervention; others decried it. Decades of bloody intertribal conflict, known as the Beaver Wars, were generated by the resulting commercial competition among the tribes for control of the middleman position.[12]

Trading Posts

European fur traders initially attempted to penetrate the interior of North America by utilizing the same trade routes that the native populations had used for centuries. The Frenchmen who penetrated the interior for the first time had trade as well as exploration on their mind. The two objectives of French enterprise in Canada were the colonization of the country and the development of the fur trade. The fur trade in New France was established in 1601 under a trading monopoly granted to Aymar de Chastes, an aged man who never saw Canada.

The vast distances involved in securing furs directly at their source caused the trading post to become the nexus between European and native cultures. The post at Tadoussac was near the mouth of the Saguenay River where it flowed into the St. Lawrence. Possibly the oldest such establishment in North America, it was begun by Pierre Chauvin de Tonnetuit in 1599, two years before the imposition of the fur trade monopoly. Tadoussac remained a disappointing enterprise, however, because too few furs came into it from the interior. Moreover, the French traders could not enforce their monopoly upon the Basque fishermen who traded in sight of the post with impunity.

In 1603, de Chaste died, and his monopoly was secured by Pierre du Guast de Monts. One of the first fur traders to act under de Monts patent was a Breton sea captain named Francois du Pontgrave who had come with Chauvin and Samuel de Champlain to New France in 1603. Pontgrave sailed in 1604 with a trading vessel loaded with metal tools, kitchen utensils, and useless trinkets such as bright buttons, caps, ribbons, and cheap jewelry. Their first attempt at creating a trading post was on the island of St. Croix in the Bay of Fundy, but this proved an unhealthy site for the Europeans. A second unproductive year was spent at Port Royal across the bay. The natives who visited these posts told of a bounty of furs from the lakes and rivers of the wilderness interior. The most valuable furs were those of beaver, taken in the winter when the coat was most heavy.

If the French wanted these at a reasonable price, they would have to travel inland to get them.

Acting on Champlain's desire to move into the interior, a base was opened at Quebec in 1608. Here was the great natural citadel that had been occupied and abandoned by the explorer Jacques Cartier decades before. Ironically, Quebec, 700 miles inland, had not been Champlain's initial choice for a trading post. Montreal, 500 miles further into the interior with its forested plains and with its connections to many navigable waterways, was his first choice, but it would have to wait for almost three decades to become the focus of the fur trade in New France. From these beginnings, the fur trade became the major commercial activity of the French colony with major trading posts and settlements lining the St. Lawrence River at Quebec, Trois Riviers, and Montreal.

One of the most advanced European trading posts in the early fur trade period was that of the Dutch. In 1614, a group of Dutch shipowners had the remarkable foresight to form the New Netherlands Company (Dutch West India Company), a fur trading monopoly. The small outpost of New Amsterdam was founded at the southern tip of Manhattan Island to support the main trading establishment near the head of navigation of the Hudson River at Fort Orange (Albany, New York). Henry Hudson had traded here with the natives in 1609 and found them cooperative and cordial. These Indians were probably Mahican. The New Netherlands colony soon proved immensely rich in terms of the trade in furs with the native population. There was an easy water route from the fur-rich interior of the continent down the Mohawk River or through the Lake Champlain corridor to Albany, from Albany by way of the Hudson River to Manhattan, and from Manhattan to the sea.

A Matter of Price

The price for most goods, but not all, was a matter of negotiation. Yet, in the 17th and 18th centuries, the idea of trade as a purely business enterprise had proceeded much further for Europeans than for the Indians. The Indian model for the structuring of price depended on several factors. Chief among these was need. Indians did not necessarily require that an exchange have an economic advantage or profit. Rather, they sought to satisfy as far as possible the needs that both parties brought to the exchange. Often these needs were social or cultural, and they applied to both the buyers and the sellers. The Indians placed great stress on the social relationship between the buyer and the seller. If the trader were a stranger, it was critical that a proper relationship be created. Friendship and mutual trust were essential. It was largely for this reason that frontier traders and coureurs de bois, who had married into native tribes or were adopted by them, were so successful. Through marriage, they were able to use their kinship relationship to accommodate their trade needs.

The Indians also brought to bear a uniquely modern foundational logic in terms of exchange that recognized that doing business together created a claim of the buyer on the seller and vice-versa. This was significantly different from the reigning European business model based on creating a native dependency on trade goods because it recognized that the trader was equally dependent on the Indian in any exchange. According to Indian cultural logic, European traders should act as if they were kinfolk fulfilling native needs or providing necessities—known in Algonquian as *besoin*—without regard to payment. "Once an appropriate social relationship had been established, an assertion of need for something could become a special claim on the thing needed." To be needy was to be deserving of aid, and the Indians often sought to portray themselves as weak, needy, and miserable in addressing Onontio, the Jesuits, or the traders for this reason. The emphasis on exchange as a way of satisfying their *besoins*, therefore, had a meaning quite different from that expressed in the European view of commerce.[13]

Finally, the Indians were often less concerned about the nature of the items being trading than one would expect. They often redistributed what they received among their kinsman and fellow villagers. This liberality was sometimes considered a form of personal vanity by which each hoped to increase his reputation and standing among his fellows. This kind of redistribution formed one extreme of the exchange process, while unfair practices, such as shoddy goods, cheating, and overpricing by whites, formed the other extreme.

With respect to this last facet of the Indian conception of trade, the English traders, who were less numerous than their French counterparts, seem to have created an advantage for themselves by lowering their prices, trading in deerskins (which the French uniformly refused to do), and providing better quality goods. Throughout the period, French trade with the Indians was controlled by strong monopolies, and the number of traders was regulated (to a greater or lesser extent) by the government. Beyond this, the value of pelts, be they beaver or other fur, was fixed with the advice of French governmental officials. The European market, therefore, was the ultimate determinant of the price that traders could pay for furs in the forest wilderness. This price fixing contained hidden perils. When there was a glut of furs on the market, the Indians continued to expect the same *bon marche'*, or best deal, that they had been given in previous years. When the French were unable to meet the native expectations, the economic and military alliances they had formed with the tribes shuddered. The low opinion Algonquians came to hold of venal French traders threatened not only their livelihood but their lives as well.[14]

The French officials at Quebec were certainly aware of this problem. In order to ensure a profit, French traders tended to charge more in terms of furs for their goods than English ones, but the government began attaching the giving of gifts to the exchange process with the expectation of specific services to be performed. In 1683, the "gift" of just two guns to the appropriate chiefs, a matter of little import in battle, assured the appearance in the field of 200 traditionally armed Algonquian warriors against the Iroquois. Ultimately, the need to provide such gifts became an annual occurrence. In order to assure native good will in the planned operations against the Iroquois in 1694, the French gave the In dians presents in 1693 valued at more than 10,000 livres, including approximately 160 trade muskets and 80 pistols. In just two decades this cost of "doing business" had risen considerably, and the French budgeted 20,000 livres per year for Indian presents. Thereafter, the gifts became a critical and continuing component of the French attempt to hold the loyalty of the Algonquian tribes and their Huron–Petun allies.[15]

The Upper Country

Organizing a fur trading expedition into the interior was a serious task. References to the *Pays d'en Haut*, or upper country, of New France usually encompassed the Great Lakes region centering on Michillimakinac and Mackinaw Bay more than 1,500 miles away. In order to reach the Upper Country early enough to make a return trip within the year, most fur traders were gone from the settlements from May to August when the rivers were clear of ice. They traded for furs brought from the west and north by Native American trappers for a few weeks and brought them down river to Montreal. Coureurs de bois often traveled an additional 500 miles to the immediate source of the beaver in the territories of the Miami, Illinois, Sioux, or Assinibione nations. These tribes welcomed the traders and the promise that their presence represented in terms of the prestige, wealth, and convenience that European goods might bring. The coureurs de bois often wintered over from one trading season to the next, living with their Indian wives and families and forming important relationships with the tribes. Nonetheless, when the French government withdrew these traders by law in 1690, the tribes were infuriated at the thought of having to deal with native middlemen or of being forced to travel to Montreal themselves to resume their trade.

The basic form of transportation for fur traders was the *canot du Nord*, or birchbark canoe. Canoes and bateaux (or bateau for one) would be loaded with trade goods for the outward journey and could hopefully hold many large bundles of furs on the return trip. These may have passed through many hands and have traveled many hundreds of miles from the interior. Only the strongest among the young engages would be recruited for such trips as they might have to paddle upward of 1,000 miles up river to complete their trading. They would then have to return to either Montreal or Quebec as quickly as possible to escape the winter ice.

Said to be valued at 300 livres each, the Indians often built one or two canoes annually to exchange with the traders for ornaments, vermilion, or beads. These functional watercraft were sometimes replaced by larger but similarly structured vessels known as *bateaux*.

Packing a canoe for these journeys required a good deal of skill. The fur trader required personal gear and supplies to ensure his own comfort and survival. As many as 30 separate articles were considered essential. Nonetheless, the fur trader could bargain for food items such as dried corn, peas, beans, smoked fish, and dried meats (either jerky or pemmican), as well as fresh fruits and vegetables. He could hunt for game in the forests and fish in the river, but these activities took precious time from his fundamental objective of traveling up country quickly and returning before the ice set in. Both in value and volume, therefore, trade goods accounted for the greatest part of the load. The major trade goods were broadcloth, woolen blankets, cotton and linen cloth, shirts, metal goods, fish hooks, spearheads, knives, hatchets, firearms, ammunition, and gunpowder. Tobacco, liquor, jewelry, trinkets, and other items that the native population might consider luxuries accounted for only a small fraction of the goods traded.

Clothing and cloth may have represented two-thirds of the trade goods brought into the interior. What was exactly meant by the English terms *broadcloth* or *strouds* is not clear from the surviving records of the fur companies, but they are generally considered to refer either to bolts of thick-weight wool cloth or finished woolen blankets. Blankets may have been white or gray-white with one or more wide red or blue bands woven into them. Traders also were known to carry a lighter weight red or blue fabric that the native women used for making skirts. The French gained access to red strouds (called *ecarlatines* in French documents) that never quite matched the English item in the opinion of the Indians. The difference in quality was so obvious that French traders often bought the English product in order to trade in Canada with Indians who showed, thereby, that they had become relatively sophisticated consumers. Finished clothing items, such as twilled coats, woolen capotes, bleached and unbleached shirts, and stockings, were highly regarded but probably came in a one-size-fits-all assortment of colors.

The French government generally frowned on trading guns with the Indians for furs, and those that appeared among the natives usually came as presents from the Crown. Muskets, and more rarely pistols, had no simple equivalent economic value by which the Indians could demand them in exchange for a quantity of furs. Firearms, shot, bar lead, bullet molds, and gunpowder were very important trade items, and many traders included them in their loads even if they were strictly forbidden to do so by law. Most natives highly prized powder and lead as a medium of secondary exchange even if they did not own a firearm. Weapons and ammunition often amounted to about one-eighth of the value of the trade goods. They were heavy but took up little room. As much as 600 pounds of each might be carried in a bateau paddled by 12 men with proportionately less being carried in the smaller canoes.

Highly prized metal tools and utensils made up about 10 percent of the total cargo of trade goods. Cauldrons and kettles of various dimensions accounted for about half of this category. They were usually made of copper and nested together to save space. Copper kettles were more highly regarded than iron ones by the natives who often broke them up to provide malleable metal for other purposes. The kettles were referred to as being of two, three, four, or more *fists,* an archaic measure equivalent to the volume of a clenched hand. The other half of the metal goods was comprised of knifes, hatchets, scissors, awls, sewing needles, brass and iron wire, chisels, scrapers, and a few metal arrow heads.

Liquor

Alcohol was considered a necessary part of the fur trade. Every canoe of trade goods sent into the interior had at least some liquor on board. The Jesuits detested the practice of trading alcohol to the Indians considering it the most potent weapon of the devil. Its introduction at the missions was thought to lead to the immediate physical and cultural degradation of the natives. The Indians were at first fascinated by alcohol's hallucinatory effect, which quickly brought about a state similar to that created by fasting for many days, but the novelty wore off to be replaced by an almost universal craving. "The introduction of alcohol into [their] hallucinatory world of dreams, demonology, and fractionalized emotions and spiritual beliefs could not have been anything but devastating. With a few drinks of brandy an Indian could release his soul from his body...as though they had been looking on from a point of vantage entirely outside themselves."[16]

Although many native peoples made a weak sort of beer from maple syrup or spruce buds, none of the western or northern tribes had discovered the purposeful process of simple fermentation, and no tribe practiced the distillation of liquor of any kind. They, therefore, had developed no tolerance for strong drink. Moreover, some historians hold that there was a physiological cause related to the sugar content of their blood that might explain the almost immediate addictive reaction that many Indians had when exposed to strong drink. Regardless of the cause, Native Americans exhibited an extraordinary susceptibility to the effects of alcohol consumption that most fur traders utilized and exploited to the detriment of the Indian population.[17]

Whether physiological, spiritual, or cultural, the effect of alcohol on Native American behavior was reported by contemporaries as pathological and devastating. "The liquor made them more than quarrelsome; it literally drove them mad." There seemed to be no limit to the senseless violence to which a drunken Indian might resort, and the women were equally effected. "Their habitual modesty evaporated," and they were capable of violent acts that they would not have considered in a sober state. Robert Juet, a sailor on the Dutch vessel *Half Moon,* noted in 1609 that, "there is scarcely a savage, small or great, even among the girls and women, who does not enjoy this intoxication, and who does not take these beverages when they can be had, purely and simply for the sake of being drunk." While the Indians quickly learned the negative effects brought on by alcohol consumption, they seemed powerless to resist it, and in many individuals it is certain that they experienced a physical addiction.[18]

The alcohol used in the fur trade was not rum or brandy, as such, but rather a watered down version of strong spirits known to the Canadian habitants as *whiskey blanc.* The least capable fur traders often resorted to dealing almost exclusively in this concoction because they could sell it profitably without any knowledge of Indian trading practices or even of native language. It was made in three strengths. The first and the weakest, 1 part spirits diluted in 36 parts of water, was meant for tribes new to alcohol. The intermediate strength for tribes familiar with liquor was cut with water by only one-sixth, and the strongest blend was cut by four. By adding a little river water, a barrel of brandy or rum, brought into the wilderness with a great expenditure of effort, could be made to provide many times its volume as a trade good. The sometimes lethal effects of even these diluted alcoholic beverages serves to emphasize the utter vulnerability of the Native Americans to the unscrupulous methods of many European fur traders.[19]

Coureurs de Bois

Some of the French who came to Canada found the Native American way of life attractive. These *coureurs de bois* (bush rangers) adapted themselves to Indian life and became skilled woodsmen. Some historians consider them quite picturesque and effective as woodland fighters, but their numbers were never significant in a military sense. They have been awarded a great deal of prominence in prosecuting French objectives against the Anglo-American rangers (as in Rogers' Rangers) in the 18th-century war for empire, yet, their true importance lay more in the cross-cultural kinship relations they formed among the Algonquians.

The coureurs de bois, driven largely by a disregard for the fur company's monopoly and by a desire to avoid the church's strict enforcement of religious duties, broke away from the boundaries of the colony of New France to live and trade among the native population. In the fur trade economy of the 17th century, they were generally considered outside the law, and a list of severe penalties was enacted against them as a deterrent to any more colonists joining their ranks. Yet, at one point as many as 25 percent of colonists in Canada chose the life of a coureurs de bois rather than remain in the settlements.

From time to time, certain traders among the French actually found it to their advantage to transfer their allegiance to the fur companies of other European nations. Groseillierss and Radisson were two of these. They initially opened the rich Hudson's Bay region to the French, but they believed that they were mistreated and cheated by the political administration in Montreal. They, therefore, joined the newly formed Hudson's Bay Company of the English, which drew almost all trade with the Cree nation away from the St. Lawrence to the north. In much the same way, Martin Chartier and Pierre Bisaillon helped to establish the foundations of the fur trade for the English colony of Pennsylvania.[20]

Certain persons among the French never ended their attempts to smuggle furs to the English at Albany and other places. In 1725, it was estimated that 80 percent of the beaver fur shipped from the colony of New York to Europe was obtained by French smugglers and coureurs de bois. Here, they could make a greater profit for themselves by denying it to the French Crown. Due to the need to compete with the smugglers, the coureurs de bois, and the aggressive English traders, the French Crown took a number of steps to influence the fur trade in their own favor. Among these, they raised the price paid for beaver, began to accept deerskins and other furs in trade, and increased the sale of brandy to the Indians. These concessions proved enough to satisfy the demands of the Algonquians into the late 1740s. Thereafter, the survival needs of a French colony at war with its English neighbors overcame the commercial needs of the fur trade, and the French Crown accepted the need to infuse money into the region in the form of gifts in order to maintain their alliances with the Indians.[21]

The English Fur Trade

It was not beaver, but deer and bear, that served as the staples of the fur trade in the Ohio Valley and lower Great Lakes. Here, subsistence and the hunt for furs remained closely linked into the 18th century. The goods the English brought by packhorse over the mountains to this region were much finer and less expensive than those of the French giving the English a trade advantage. They thereby attracted Indians from all over the Old Northwest, dwarfing even the trade of French Detroit.[22]

There were a number of English traders who, fearing that their native contacts in the New England fur trade would go north to the French or west to the Dutch at Albany, threw themselves into the wilderness in a fur-trading rivalry that would last through the 17th and 18th centuries. Having established the necessary logistics, the English trading posts "leapfrogged" into the interior following the Merrimack, Connecticut, and Hudson Rivers. In 1636, John Pychon opened a successful trading post at Agawam well up the Connecticut River near present day Springfield, Massachusetts, and Captain Richard Waldron established his post at Pennacock on the Merrimack River in 1668. The English also quietly displaced the Dutch at New Amsterdam in 1664 and took possession of their trading post at Albany in 1667. They gained the entire colony in 1672. Anglo-French violence along the frontiers, actually beginning with the French attacks on English settlements in 1690, continued almost without cessation through the reign of two English monarchs—William of Orange (King William's War, 1690–1697) and Anne Stuart (Queen Anne's War, 1702–1713).

The Treaty of Utrecht that ended Queen Anne's War in 1713 included a clause (Clause 15) that guaranteed equal French and English access to Indian trade. For almost a quarter century thereafter, Europe was at peace. When the childless Queen Anne died in 1714, the British throne passed to George I of Hanover. Over the next three decades, the embers of war smoldered in the American wilderness. The English built Fort Oswego on Lake Ontario at the mouth of the Oswego River in 1730, and it was reinforced in 1733. Abbe Francois Piquet, a French missionary, considered the post at Oswego "a great and evil menace...It not only spoils our trade, but puts the English into communication with a vast number of our Indians, far and near."[23]

From 1739 to 1742, England became involved in a meaningless conflict with Spain known as the "War of Jenkins' Ear." This was the first stage of two conflicts known in America as King George's War, named for George II. Following the Treaty of Aix-la-Chapelle, which ended King George's War in North America in 1748, English traders pushed as far west as the Miami River at Pickawillany. The English advances into the border areas west of Virginia and Pennsylvania were largely a product of commercial interests in the colonies that outweighed the statecraft that had ended the conflict in Europe. Within a year, the trading post at Pickawillany had taken on the look of a fort, and a dozen traders were working there to supply the needs of over 4,000 Indians.[24]

A contemporary observer noted the list of trade goods made available to Native American hunters and trappers by English by the middle of the 18th century.

The goods for Indian trade, are guns for hunting; lead, balls, powder; steel for striking fire, gun-flints, gun-screws; knives, hatchets, kettles, beads, men's shirts; cloths of blue and red for blankets and petticoats; vermilion and verdigris; red, yellow, green, and blue ribbons of English weaving; needles, thread, and awls; blue, white, and red rateen for making moccasins; woolen blankets, of three points and a half, three, two, and one and a half of Leon cloth; mirrors framed in wood; hats trimmed fine, and in imitation, with variegated plumes in red, yellow, blue and green; hoods for men and children of fringed rateen, galloons, real and imitation; brandy, tobacco, razors for the head, glass in beads made after the fashion of wampum; black wines, paints, & c.[25]

In 1751, John Fraser opened a trading post at the confluence of French Creek and the Allegheny River in western Pennsylvania at the village of Venango close to the Seneca, Cayuga, and the tribes of the lower Great Lakes. The violent response of the French to this post led to dire consequences. The town was completely destroyed and the natives scattered. The main chief, Unemakemi, also known as Old Britain for his allegiance to the English, was killed and eaten by French allied Indians. Although Fraser was fortunately absent at the time of the attack, two of his traders and all his goods were captured by the French. More importantly, the French began a program of fort building in the region that most historians of the period consider a direct cause of the French and Indian War.

King George's response to these reports was to order Robert Dinwiddie, governor of Virginia, to take drastic steps in 1754. "If you shall find that any number of persons shall presume to erect any fort or forts within the limits of the Province of Virginia [which then included the Ohio country], you are first to require of them to peaceably depart; and if they do still endeavor to carry out any such unlawful and unjustifiable designs, we do hereby strictly charge you...to drive them off by force." The young man chosen to carry this message to the French was George Washington. The ultimate result of the French and Indian War (the Seven Years War in Europe) was that Britain won a great empire in North America from which the French were largely excluded.[26]

Notes

1. Quoted in George T. Hunt, *The Wars of the Iroquois, A Study in Intertribal Trade Relations* (Madison: University of Wisconsin Press, 1972), 63.

2. Richard White, *The Middle Ground, Indians, Empires, and Republics in the Great Lakes Region, 1650–1815* (New York: Cambridge University Press, 1991), 131.

3. See the discussion in White, 139–141.

4. White, 99–100.

5. Stanley Vestal, *King of the Fur Traders, The Deeds and Deviltry of Pierre Espirit Radisson* (Boston: Houghton Mifflin Company, 1940), 162–163.

6. Reported by Father Pierre Chaumonot, S.J., and quoted in Vestal, 86.

7. Colin G. Calloway, *New Worlds for All: Indians, Europeans, and the Remaking of Early America* (Baltimore: The Johns Hopkins UP, 1997), 73.

8. James F. O'Neil, ed., *Their Bearing Is Noble and Proud: A Collection of Narratives Regarding the Appearance of Native Americans from 1740–1815* (Dayton, Ohio: J.T.G.S. Publishing, 1995), 10–11. Quoting Pierre Pouchot.

9. See White, 136.

10. Colin G. Calloway, *The Western Abenakis of Vermont, 1660–1800: War, Migration, and the Survival of an Indian People* (Norman: University of Oklahoma Press, 1990), 22.

11. Calloway, *The Western Abenaki*, 43; Hunt, 167.

12. Francis Jennings, *The Ambiguous Iroquois Empire, The Covenant Chain Confederation of Indian Tribes with English Colonies from its Beginnings to the Lancaster Treaty of 1744* (New York: W.W. Norton and Company, 1984), 62.

13. White, 129.

14. White, 110–111.

15. White, 104.

16. Walter D. Edmonds, *The Musket and the Cross, the Struggle of France and England for North America* (Boston: Little, Brown and Company, 1968), 48, 71.

17. Edmonds, 49.

18. Quoted in Edmonds, 48.

19. Edmonds, 48.

20. Jennings, 64.

21. White, 125.

22. Calloway, *The Western Abenaki*, 40.

23. Allen W. Eckert, *Wilderness Empire* (New York: Bantam Books, 1980), 184.

24. Calloway, *The Western Abenaki*, 40.

25. O'Neil, ed., 20. Quoting Pierre Pouchot.

26. Eckert, 240.

11

Intertribal Trade and Conflict

The great dispersal of Indian nations by the Iroquois was a cultural catastrophe with widespread consequences.[1]

—Ian K. Steele, historian

Cultural Perspective

One of the challenges of writing a history about the native peoples of America is that previous attempts at dealing with the subject fairly lacked both balance and restraint—being either too harsh with regard to the behavior of the Indians or too condemning of the effects of white contact on an aboriginal people. It has been pointed out that many of the vital interactions in the early history of Euro-Indian relations took place between and among the Indians themselves as they reacted to the changes wrought in their environment. Europeans sometimes played a role, but for 200 years, intertribal conflicts were often more fundamental to native life than were contacts with whites. This concept complicates the simple linear layering of Euro-Indian history and brings actors onto the stage who may not appear to have had an immediate effect on the overall outcome.[2]

Historians of the 19th century tended to see the Native Americans as a single "Indian enemy" with individual tribes engaged against the whites at discrete and separate intervals. These conflicts with whites have been compartmentalized into a series of "Wars," mostly for the convenience of historians: the Pequot War, King Philip's War, or the French and Indian War, for instance. Yet, intertribal conflicts can be found in many places and situations throughout early Native American history. Possibly, authors such as Francis Parkman and James Fenimore Cooper came closest to the reality of the situation by constructing an Algonquian–Iroquoian enmity as a framework for their work, but even they do not seem to have realized the true complexity of intertribal relations in this period. These relationships were often poorly understood or erroneously reported by the observers at hand. They swirled, spun, reversed themselves, and suddenly plunged forward again in a manner that was hard to follow while it was happening and difficult to chart from the distance of centuries. The effects on Indian families cannot justifiably be attributed to the negative influences of white intrusion alone.

Nonetheless, the politics, drama, and violence of intertribal jealousy and warfare emerge from the historical landscape in a definite pattern. It has been pointed out that "Indians warred, and Indians destroyed Indians." The complete terror that the Mohawk brought to the Northeast woodlands, for instance, had begun decades before the appearance of whites in the Hudson River, and it was a fact of everyday Algonquian life throughout much of the 17th century. There is no doubt that new patterns in daily life and society, based on the needs and desires engendered by the fur trade, led to increased friction among the tribes, to a greater sense of territoriality, and to an increase in internecine warfare. The Mohawk were the archetype of a tribe that turned intertribal aggression into a purposeful policy for establishing hegemony over their neighbors. As the easternmost member of the Five Nation Iroquois Confederacy, the Mohawk also held significant power over the lives and aspersions of whites, a power that many colonial governments were fearful to acknowledge. They proved to be the critical force—possibly the dominant force—affecting all the Northeast woodlands throughout the 17th and 18th centuries. In attempting to maneuver unscathed through the crises presented by the European powers vying for the North American continent, the Indian nations and the Mohawk, in particular, hardly proved helpless or clueless victims at the hands of a technically superior culture.[3]

The Mahican

The Algonquian-speaking Mahican, called Loups by the French, lived south of Lake Champlain at the headwaters of the Hudson River near present day Saratoga, New York.[4] According to tradition, their land rights stretched from the Housatonic River valley of Connecticut and Massachusetts to a point west of the Hudson River near Schoharie Creek where it enters the Mohawk River. Contemporary maps drawn by the Dutch show that the Mahican had a large number of villages near Albany and at least one village on an island in the mouth of the Mohawk River. They were among the first natives to trade with the Dutch in this region (1610), and they appear to have acted as middlemen in the diffusion of trade goods as far north as the St. Lawrence Valley during the first quarter of the 17th century. Indians traded for social and political reasons as well as economic ones, and it is very likely that many Mahican from the Housatonic Valley were attracted to the Hudson Valley solely in order to be in proximity to their kinsmen who were trading at Fort Orange near Albany.[5]

The Mahican jealously guarded their middleman status with the Dutch much to the consternation of the neighboring Mohawk, who had also made contact with Dutch traders. The Mohawk were just west of Albany with many of their important villages in the Mohawk River valley. By reason of their proximity, the Mohawk sought to exercise what they considered to be their natural prerogatives with regard to access to the Dutch. The Mahican resented the presence of the Mohawk in and around the trading post. They were buoyed by the support that was freely expressed by the Dutch, who were chafing under Mohawk interference with their trade coming from the "French Indians" living in the St. Lawrence Valley. Isaac de Rasiers, secretary to the Dutch governor, wrote to the directors of the New Netherlands Company, "I beg your Honors to authorize me to go with 50 or 60 men on an expedition to drive them [the Mohawk] off."[6]

For almost two decades, the Mohawk connived to gain some precedence in the existing Dutch trading system by peaceful means. They were particularly incensed by the tribute levied against them by the Mahicans when they came to trade with the Dutch in what was arguably their own backyard. The Mohawk expected to collect tribute from other tribes, not to pay it. Finally, in a concerted effort to disrupt the Mahican trading advantage and replace it with their own, the Mohawks opened a trade war with them in 1624. Although the initial clashes were unrecorded, it seems certain that the Mohawks were the aggressors in the ensuing conflict known as the Mohawk–Mahican War.

The Mohawk–Mahican War

In 1625, with the encouragement of the Dutch, the Mahican retaliated against the eastern-most village of the Mohawk, probably Schaunactada, which was situated near present-day Schenectady, New York. As both sides were still using traditional weapons, the attack and defense was little more than a skirmish by European standards. Yet, as territorial integrity and prestige ranked high in the process of Native American warfare, the Mahican gained in prestige by boldly invading what was unquestionably Mohawk territory. For some time thereafter, the war swung back and forth with the Mahican suffering almost as badly as the Mohawk. A contemporary Dutch observer noted of the conflict, "There have been cruel murders on both sides."[7]

Daniel van Krieckebeeck, commander of Fort Orange, probably thinking that his guns would help the Mahican to overpower the Mohawk, accompanied a group of Mahican with four or five soldiers on a subsequent raid in 1626. A few miles from the fort the party was set upon by the Mohawk who seem to have caught them in a storm of arrows from ambush. In the ensuing fight, the commander and at least three of his soldiers were killed along with upward of two dozen Mahican. One Dutchman escaped to report the details of the battle by jumping into a nearby body of water. The Dutch were horrified to learn later that the Mohawk had burned their captives alive and had eaten part of one Dutchmen. Isaac de Rasiers, rather disingenuously characterized the result as a "disaster caused by the reckless adventure of Krieckebeeck."[8]

The Mahican now appealed for support to the Algonquian-speaking Indians living near the French, but these demurred largely due to the continued intercession of the French governor, Samuel de Champlain, who wished to prevent the war from becoming a regional affair that would negatively impact the volume of furs coming to Quebec. Nonetheless, some of the Algonquians in New England, particularly the Abenaki, involved themselves on the side on the Mahican. These nations had been enemies of the Mohawk on other occasions, but the extent of their involvement seems to have been limited to the detachment of small raiding parties into the southern Berkshires and the Lake George region.

Little more can be known about the extent of the Mohawk–Mahican War because the Native American nations involved kept no written records and because there was no further involvement of Europeans. According to a detailed native tradition, however, the last major battle of the war was a decisive one. The Mohawk and Mahican forces were arrayed against one another on an island in the Hudson River. The island has not been definitely identified, but such set-piece gladiatorial encounters were not unusual in Native American warfare. Champlain had blundered into a similar affair between the Mohawk and a force of Montagnais at Crown Point in 1609.[9] According to the account, the Mahican were winning the contest until a group of Mohawk sprang from ambush, launching a furious flanking attack and killing many Mahican warriors. The Mahicans then sued for peace.[10]

The natural ferocity and military discipline of the Mohawk had finally beaten the Mahican and had effectively eliminated them as competitors for trading privileges with the Dutch. The surviving Mahican took refuge at Schagticoke on the Hoosic River in New York or moved into New England. Jonas Michaeleus, minister of the Dutch Reformed Church in New Amsterdam, wrote in 1628, "The Mahicans have fled and their lands are unoccupied." Nonetheless, the Mohawk continued to harass the Mahican refugees in their villages in southwestern Vermont and western Massachusetts for many years. Thereafter, the Mahican position became even more difficult due to the conflicting allegiances held by their Algonquian relations in New England and New France. The Dutch, whom the Mahican had valued as friends and trading partners, abandoned them and were soon allied with their former enemy, the Mohawk.[11]

Mohawk Monopoly

The immediate effect of the Mohawk–Mahican War was a rapid destabilization of the balance of power that had existed among the native tribes of the region. For their part, the French were disappointed at the increased power of the Mohawk who were their implacable enemy. The war also spoiled the trade in furs for the English traders far to the east in New England. The crafty and business-like Dutch immediately moved to acquire the vacant lands of the Mahican and seem to have avoided any long-lasting enmity among the Mohawk for having taken arms against them. In fact, a fur trading coalition was created between the victorious Mohawk and the Dutch that proved beneficial to both.

The Mohawk now held and strove to strengthen a virtual trading monopoly with the Dutch. They imposed onerous conditions upon all the tribes that wished to trade with Albany (Ft. Orange) extending even to the nations of their own confederation. In an attempt to underscore their new position, Mohawk war parties passed down Lake Champlain to raid the French settlements in the St. Lawrence Valley and to disrupt the fur trade to the north. They attacked and destroyed the Montagnais village at Trois Riviers, and during the next two decades, Mohawk war parties constantly filtered back and forth across the Lake Champlain and Connecticut River valleys from Agawam to Quebec. This almost ceaseless series of intertribal conflicts has been characterized as the "Beaver Wars."[12]

As a result of Mohawk aggression, many of the Algonquian-speaking peoples on the New England frontier were driven north to the French missions. Although they were much weakened by the losses that they sustained in these efforts, the Mohawk emerged from this period of upheaval as the dominant power in the Northeast, and most of the natives who remained in the region (with the notable exception of the Abenaki) went out of their way to avoid offending them.

Prior to the Mohawk–Mahican War, the Dutch had traded a little over 5,000 pelts with both Iroquoian- and Algonquian-speaking peoples. Afterward, the Dutch trade with their Mohawk middlemen alone increased in volume to over 7,000 pelts in its first year. In two years, almost 10, 000 skins of all kinds were being traded, and five years later this had increased to 30,000 skins. Although the Mohawk kept no formal record of the sources of their furs, it is almost certain from their subsequent actions that they were exhausting the beaver and other valuable fur-bearing species in all of Iroquoia and began acting as middlemen for furs trapped in the regions farther west. It was from this period that the position of the Iroquois Confederacy in the conduct of the fur trade assumed its unprecedented importance.[13]

Herein appears to lie both the genesis and the continued motivation behind the policies, alliances, and aggressive actions of the Iroquois in the mid-17th century. Propelled by circumstances set in motion by their

Mohawk brothers, the remaining members of the Iroquois Confederacy—particularly the Seneca in the west—followed a desperate course of striving to achieve total control of the fur trade in the Northeast by diverting all the skins coming from the interior into their own hands. No other tribes were to be allowed to trade directly with the Dutch in Albany, the French in Quebec, or the English in New England.

The Huron

West of Quebec, in a great triangular area now part of the province of Ontario, was the land of the Huron. This was a populous and rich region east of Lake Huron, bounded on the southeast by Lakes Erie and Ontario, and capped on the north by the Ottawa River. The heart of Huronia was the region surrounding Lake Simcoe (see Maps 2 and 3). The historian's knowledge of Huronia relies almost entirely on the reports of the French Jesuit fathers who served there. It seems certain that by the early 17th century the Huron had become almost exclusively a trading nation. Father Jean de Brebeuf reported that the region in summer was "stripped of men." Using their neighbors as sources of foodstuffs and other native trading materials, the Huron seemingly "spent the entire year in the act of trading or in preparing for it."[14]

The Huron were great friends and loyal allies to the French. They used their friendship to control all the trade in the north country and the Great Lakes in much the same way as the Iroquois hoped to control the trade with the Dutch that crossed New York. Yet, unlike their aggressive cousins for whom they held great enmity, the Huron seemingly lived at peace and at ease with their neighbors in their self-appointed role as master traders.

The economy of Huronia was almost purely agricultural with maize and fish being the principal articles of food. The Huron established firm alliances within their associated cantons (Petun, Attiwandaronk, and Erie) and with their Algonquian-speaking neighbors, on whom they relied for those things that they could not or would not produce for themselves. The easy conditions of life in Huronia with its many lakes, rivers, and fertile meadows made this arrangement relatively easy to maintain. So effective were the Huron at bringing out furs that no French traders penetrated Huronia or the Great Lakes before the middle of the 17th century.

The immediate neighbors of the Huron were related to them and included the Petun, the Attiwandaronk (Neutrals), and the Erie. While the Erie seem to have acted in total independence of the Hurons, the Petuns, who lived just to their west, were seemingly subjugated to them providing tobacco, beans, squash, and maize to Huron villages. The Attiwandaronk, or Neutral tribes, raised a great deal of tobacco, hemp, and meal in the area around the falls of the Niagara River. They were the source of much of the flint that was bartered among the tribes, but they did not trade very far from home. The Huron treated the production of the Petun and the

Neutrals as their own, using their corn, meal, and other materials as items of exchange in the fur trade with other Indians. In return they carefully guarded their relations against possible competitors.[15]

The Huron penchant for trade allowed them to establish a brisk commerce with the neighboring Nipissing, who themselves acted as middlemen in the great fur trading economy of the far north and west accumulating a large stock of beaver skins and buffalo robes. They also speared almost numberless whitefish in Lake Nipissing, which they dried and freely used as a trade commodity. Their pelts, robes, and dried fish were exchanged with the Huron in return for corn, meal, beans, and flint. The Allumette and Iroquet (who controlled the portages around the rapids in the Ottawa river), the Ottawas of the upper Great Lakes, and many other Algonquian tribes wintered near the Huron and had very cordial, if business-like, relations with them. The distant Montagnais of the Saguenay River region near Tadoussac produced great quantities of deer and moose skins, and even they allowed no other tribe than the Hurons to trade with them.[16]

Using means similar to those agreed upon with the Nipissing, the Huron annually gathered up and delivered to the French traders at Quebec the entire accumulation of furs gathered by the native peoples of an immense territory. "Such an economy would function very well so long as the complex and intimate tribal relationships upon which it depended were undisturbed." Not only the Huron, but each of the participating tribes, seem to have found an economic niche in this system of intertribal relations with each trying to maintain the middleman status with their immediate neighbors. Yet, only the Huron seem to have been able to take on the role of master traders acquiring furs from all the nations of the north country and funneling them into French warehouses in Montreal, Trois Riviers, or Quebec by way of the Ottawa River.[17]

Beaver, otter, buffalo, deer, moose, and even seal skins from Hudson's Bay were loaded in great bales by the Hurons onto a great fleet of canoes. Throughout the late summer and early fall "fur brigades" of 20, 40, and 60 canoes came down the Ottawa River at a time. At Allumette Island, the Ottawa River was obstructed by dangerous rapids, and the passage involved a considerable portage of canoes. It was the custom of the local Allumette and Iroquet nations to charge a considerable toll upon the value of the passing trade. Although they numbered only 400 warriors, they were respected by the more numerous Huron and greatly feared by the French.

Intertribal Negotiations

The Iroquois desire for hegemony extended in all directions from their central New York homeland in Iroquoia. They expected to control the drainage basin of the Great Lakes and Ohio River to the west, the valley of St. Lawrence to the northeast, the Lake George–Lake Champlain corridor to Canada as far east as the Connecticut River, and the southern flowing valleys of Hudson, Delaware, and Susquehanna Rivers to the Atlantic Ocean. All of these watershed areas originated in or touched on Iroquoia, and all were closely related geographically to a pattern of portages, trails, and waterways that extended throughout the Northeast woodlands. Iroquois aspirations were wildly optimistic because any of the many nations and bands that lived along these routes could claim control of them.

The Iroquois developed a dual military and diplomatic strategy aimed at controlling all these interlacing tributary systems that might provide transportation by canoe for any rival tribe carrying furs to the Europeans. It is remarkable that their strategy seems to have influenced events at critical times in the history of European colonization, thereby making decisive events of even simple diplomatic moves made in the wilderness forests.

As early as 1633, the Iroquois began seeking a trade alliance with the Huron in order to establish themselves as key players in the fur trade with French Canada. How this circumstance arose is somewhat obscure because of the lack of documentary evidence. Neither the Huron nor the Iroquois kept written records of their negotiations. However, it may have had something to do with the fact that Quebec was seized by Sir David Kirke, an English privateer, in 1629. There were no substantial records of intertribal activities and proposals kept by the English during their brief occupation of the trading post (1629–1632), but the instability caused by the eviction of the French seems to have been a signal for the Iroquois to act. Some historians have accused the Iroquois of insincerity in making trade overtures to the Huron, but they were certainly trying to find an accommodation with the recently returned French traders in 1633.

The *Jesuit Relations*, written contemporaneously with the events, reflect that the Mohawk managed to effect a friendly understanding with the Montagnais in 1635, and were trying to deal peacefully with the Huron as late as 1640. It should be remembered that, in the long run of intertribal relations, the Iroquois achieved their greatest successes through a judicious blend of carefully directed aggression and careful diplomacy. The French were greatly concerned that growing friendly relations between these disparate native groups might result in the Iroquois diverting Huron furs to the Dutch. Both the colonial officials and the priests became willing instruments in an effort to stop any diversion of trade away from Canada.[18]

The English colonies were no less aggressive in competing for the greatest advantage among the tribes. The colonies of New England, New York, Virginia, and Maryland seem to have been most involved in the process at the time, and they sometimes acted at cross-purposes. The Quaker-controlled legislature of Pennsylvania generally refused to participate in tempting the tribes to war on one another, and the Moravian missionaries who held unprecedented influence among the Indians, believed them to be both "tractable" and "docile."[19]

Amid the colonial wrangling, the Indians pursued their own interests as well as they could, but many tribes were forced into accommodations with their neighbors or with the colonies that they would not otherwise have considered. Consequently, all of the people living in the region, both white and native, became mixed together in an unavoidable network of strategies, counter-strategies, field tactics, and political gambits. The Mohawk, the least inclined of the Iroquois toward the French, had swallowed injury and insult to remain on good trading terms with the Dutch in 1629. They did so again toward the French in 1633, and would do so a third time when the English displaced the Dutch in 1664.[20]

Despite the occasional revenge raids made on the Huron by small bands of Seneca, there was little in the way of open warfare on the frontier between Huronia and Iroquoia. In response to the pleadings of their Jesuit priests, however, the Huron broke the general peace in 1639 by capturing a number of Seneca who were quietly fishing on Lake Ontario. Twelve of these were brought to Huron villages as captives and were burned to death. Shortly thereafter, a large body of Seneca who were rallying to the defense were defeated by Huron raiders, and many were taken to Huronia to be tortured and burned. Jesuit sources reported that the whole Iroquois Confederacy was in great fear of the Huron launching an attack on their villages at this time.[21]

The Iroquois again attempted trade negotiations with the Huron in 1640, but their proposals were largely disregarded and their ambassadors were treated in a surly and insulting manner. The Huron were openly "fearless and even contemptuous of them [the Iroquois]."[22] Throughout the year, the situation remained the same. The mass of the Iroquois generally stayed on watch in Iroquoia while an occasional skulking Huron was killed by war parties patrolling the tribal frontier. This circumstance placed the Iroquois in a difficult economic position. With their own sources of fur exhausted by more than a decade of over-trapping, their position of importance with the Dutch traders at Fort Orange was in jeopardy. In an attempt to strengthen their position, an Iroquois delegation made a petition of peace to the French at Trois Riviers. These overtures resulted in French assurances of friendship and cooperation "so vague as to give the Iroquois no privileges at all." There was, however, every reason for the Iroquois to consider the French untrustworthy and two-faced in these circumstances.[23]

Having been rebuffed by the French, the Iroquois quite consciously undertook a series of trade wars with the French Indian allies. They began by raiding the fur brigades on the Ottawa River, and they attacked a small outlying Huron village in 1642. Although the blockade of the Ottawa River was effective, the Hurons mounted a counter-offensive putting a force of 500 Iroquois warriors to flight. The Iroquois (principally the Mohawk) then extended the war to the Iroquets dispossessing them of their position of control on the lower Ottawa River. The Iroquets fled to winter under the protective eyes of the Huron, and the Iroquois closed the Ottawa River to the transportation of furs. By the summer of 1644, only one of four fur fleets reached Montreal. The Hurons attempted to bypass the Ottawa River route by detouring overland to the north to Quebec, but any Huron parties that passed to the south near Iroquoia were annihilated.

The French response to these circumstances was to give military aid to the Huron in the form of 20 soldiers armed with muskets. These traveled into the interior and wintered in the Huron villages. The soldiers returned as escorts with the fur fleet in the summer with almost 40,000 livres worth of skins. The Iroquois, "learning of the presence of French soldiers," abandoned any raids that had been planned and let it be known that they would entertain any messages of peace sent by the French. Both the Huron and the French were deeply worried by the effectiveness of the Mohawk blockade and were in the proper frame of mind to resume negotiations.[24]

The result of these peace feelers was a great conference with the Iroquois, which included the French governor, Charles de Montmagny, and Huron, Montagnais, Allumette, and other tribes. The French position with regard to an overall peace prior to this conference was that it must include all of their Algonquian-speaking allies. The Iroquois had shown a marked lack of enthusiasm for this particular proposal in the past, and their attitude was hardly diminished in the current circumstances. Nonetheless, the French were particularly eager to conclude a peace that would end the interruption of their trade. Consequently, they included in the treaty terms that essentially abandoned some of the lesser Algonquian nations to the whims of Iroquois aggression. The Allumette on the Ottawa River remained particularly apprehensive of Mohawk aggression and doubtful of their sincerity.

Nonetheless, this flawed peace held inviolate for some time. Even the Allumette lived in peace. In 1646, the greatest fur brigade in the history of the trade arrived at Montreal from Huronia. More than 80 canoes fully packed with prime furs worth more than 300,000 livres had traversed the Ottawa River without the slightest challenge from the Iroquois. So many bales of fur had been withheld during the Iroquois blockade that the traders had exhausted their annual supply of available trade goods. The arrival of this great fur brigade was a seminal event for the Iroquois.

The Five Nations had entered into a commercial treaty with the French and Huron with the hope of improving their own position, but they benefited not one iota from the renewal of trade. Their main reason for entertaining a treaty had been to increase trade and economic interaction for themselves, and it seemed that the terms of their agreement had not effectively improved their position. As long as the Hurons held the Georgian Bay–Lake Simcoe region, they controlled almost the entire fur trade of the Great Lakes and north country. There seemed to be no possibility of the Iroquois trading with other nations without violating the treaty. If the fur trade was to continue as it had in the past, with the Iroquois standing on the outside looking in, then they would repudiate the treaty.

The Huron had not been united in accepting the peace. Their policy toward the Iroquois had long been one of economic encirclement and isolation. When the Mohawk and Seneca heard that the Huron were negotiating an alliance against them with the Susquehannocks of Pennsylvania to their south and had tried to divide the Iroquois Confederacy by enticing the Onondaga into a separate agreement, they broke the treaty.

In 1648, having the support of the Seneca who had continued a separate series of revenge raids on the Huron in the interim, the Mohawks waylaid and killed a group of Huron ambassadors to the Onondaga. Meanwhile, the Seneca assumed a strategic position on the Huron frontier and cut off all communications between Huronia and the Susquehannocks. The Mohawk then attacked a Huron trading fleet within sight of Montreal, but they were repulsed. This fleet of 50 to 60 canoes manned by 250 warriors was worth a quarter of a million livres. However, this defeat for the Mohawk was somewhat offset by a successful Seneca attack on a frontier Huron village.

The type of systematic horror that the Iroquois would ultimately bring to Huronia was first attempted by the Attiwandaronk, or Neutrals, against one of their own neighbors. Sometime in the 1640s—tribal traditions collected many decades after the event being the only extant accounts—the Neutrals massed their warriors for an attack on an Algonquian village somewhere along the western shoreline of Lake Michigan. This stockaded village was most likely that of Fox or Mascouten (see Map 5). The villagers held out for 10 days. Ultimately, the Neutrals, many armed with iron weapons, overcame the traditionally armed defenders. More than 800 captives were taken and 70 warriors were burned to death. The old men had their eyes put out, and the women and children were taken as slaves or adopted to replace departed loved ones.

The Great Dispersal

The original strategy of Mohawk attacks in the St. Lawrence and of Seneca raids on the frontier of Huronia had not produced the desired results. Therefore, in March 1649, the Mohawk and Seneca launched the equivalent of an aboriginal blitzkrieg. This was no haphazard, spur of the moment attack. Rather than being unsophisticated, frenzied, and disorganized, the plan of war that they formed was shrewd, sober, and minutely organized. It was based on a series of sudden, unremitting, and massive assaults for which the Iroquois were to become notorious.

One thousand Seneca and Mohawk warriors quietly left Iroquoia in small groups in the autumn of 1648 and hunted in Ontario throughout the winter. In late winter, they assembled in the forests of Huronia and fell suddenly upon the Huron town at the French mission of St. Ignace (see Map 3). Attacking at dawn through the last of the melting snow, these warriors caught the Huron totally unaware, taking many captives and killing all but three Huron warriors. The attackers then immediately made a forced march to the village at the mission of St. Louis three miles away and completed another successful attack before nightfall. By dawn of the next day, they were on their way to the main Huron stronghold near Ste. Marie. Before they could mount a third attack in little more than 24 hours, the Huron, having been warned by the retreating survivors of St. Ignace, counter-attacked. Hampered by more than 100 captives and already carrying a heavy load of spoil, the Iroquois retreated with moderate losses. All the way back to Iroquoia they were hounded by 700 Petun allies of the Huron.[25]

The Huron had been totally unprepared for an attack of this magnitude and scope. The Iroquois had attacked the very center of Huronia with a singleness of purpose and organization that was daunting. No army of native warriors of such a size had ever before been seen in North America. So well guarded had been their plan that they had entered Huronia, concentrated their force, and swiftly moved to the attack without the least warning being raised by the Huron or their allies. Nonetheless, the Huron had driven them off with the loss of perhaps 200 warriors compared to about 300 Huron lost in defending the villages. The Petun who responded to the needs of their ally seemingly suffered no recorded losses during their pursuit.

With these facts in mind, there seems to be no convincing explanation for the abject terror that now seized the entire Huron nation. Fear seems to have divested them of both common sense and strategic judgment in this crisis as "they incontinently fled in all directions."[26] By May 1649, 15 Huron villages had been abandoned, and between 6,000 and 8,000 refugees had crowded on to St. Joseph Island in Georgian Bay where the Jesuits had a mission. Nothing seems to have been able to move them from their chosen refuge, not even hunger and death. When the French suggested that they return to their own villages on the mainland, the Indians refused saying that "they were not unnatural enough to abandon their wives and children...they would be devoid of sense to leave...and expose themselves to be tomahawked."[27]

Game remained abundant in the lands conquered by the Iroquois, but the Huron refugees and their hosts, confined by fear of their enemy to a small area, quickly depleted the available stock of animals. Father Claude-Jean Allouez attributed the famine on the island to over hunting, which left no breeding stock in the forests as the Indians were usually careful to do. Without extensive fields of their own, the Huron faced disaster when the local fisheries gave out. Even before the next winter set in, they were starving. Allouez observed that the women grubbed for roots among the partially frozen marshlands. Thousands died, and the remnants survived on a diet of roasted acorn paste and rock tripe—a species of lichen, which, when boiled, resolved itself into a black mess that was nauseating to eat but not without nutrition. The survivors of the tribe, about 500 persons out of several thousand, retreated to Quebec the next spring to take up residence at the mission at Lorette. Other refugees ran to the Petun, the Neutrals, or the Erie where they quickly lost their individual tribal identity.[28]

The Petun, Neutrals, and Erie were completely astonished at the consequences of the Iroquois attacks but did not immediately become apprehensive about their own safety. Then, in December 1649, they received news from friends and allies that the Mohawk and Seneca were again concentrating their warriors in the field. The Petun bravely went in search of the invaders, but could not find them. Two days later the Petun village at St. Jean, south of Nottawassaga Bay, was attacked in the absence of its warriors. Little was reported of the details of this attack as the Europeans at the village were all killed. Good sense and prudence born of experience now overtook Petun courage. The tribe dispersed with the same speed, but without the wild disorder of the Huron. Some of the Petuns went to the St. Joseph River, but most sought the protection of the Ottawa, which proved a wiser course. Subsequently, both the Petun and the Ottawa then fled before the Iroquois menace to Green Bay in Wisconsin. The inter-lake region centered on Green Bay, called the *pays d'en haut* by the French, thereafter became the focus of refugees from all over the region.

After the Huron dispersal, the Neutrals had abandoned their impartial stance in favor of the Iroquois, and they had taken the Huron refugees as slaves and captives. Unfortunately, the Neutrals had played host to the negotiations that the Mohawk and Seneca had considered a Susquehannock–Huron conspiracy. This branded them an imminent threat to the Iroquois. The Mohawk and Seneca decided that it was better to reduce the Neutrals immediately before they could engage in another such conspiracy.

In 1651, almost 600 Iroquois stormed a Neutral town killing the old and the young and dispersing almost 1,600 persons. The Neutrals then attempted a counter-attack, taking a Seneca town on the frontier of Iroquoia and scalping 200 Seneca warriors as a warning. Notwithstanding this bravado, for the third time in as many years, the willingness of an Indian nation to continue a confrontation with the Iroquois suddenly evaporated as the Neutrals scattered. Many fled to the neighboring Erie to the south. Others went directly to Green Bay. Most of the Neutral territory, noted for its fertility and easy living, remained virtually uninhabited for many years thereafter and served as a hunting ground for the Seneca.[29]

The Erie were the least known of the Iroquoian-speaking peoples who inhabited parts of Huronia. Up to the time of the dispersal, no white man—trader or priest—was known to have visited them, and no record of their culture or life style has been found although they are presumed to have lived much like their Huron relations. They were thought to have occupied the northwest shore of Lake Erie for many decades, but at the time of the dispersal they were actually living south and west of the lake with the Senecas hard on their eastern border. Just why they moved there is unknown. The warriors of the Erie were reported to number about 2,000, and they were noted among the other tribes as brave and disciplined fighters. Their diplomats were aggressive in dealing with the demands of the Iroquois confederacy, and the addition of refugees from the Huron, Petun, and Neutrals seems to have stirred up their willingness to go to war against their Seneca neighbors.

By the summer of 1654, it was becoming obvious to the Erie that they would be the next target of the Iroquois war machine. Reports reached them that the greatest native army ever raised in Iroquoia was about to descend upon them. More than 1,800 Iroquois warriors, now including warriors from all five members of their confederacy, were assembling. Part of this force, about 700 warriors, attacked the principal Erie town that summer. The Erie defended their palisades with great courage. In a scene better imagined to take place before a medieval European castle, the Iroquois built counter palisades and used scaling ladders to mount the defenses of the Erie. When the stockade was breached the Iroquois fell upon the Erie with unremitting fury, and those Erie who were not killed or captured, fled the region in haste.

Though small groups of the Erie fought on over the next few years, their tribal identity was just as surely destroyed by the Iroquois as had been that of the Huron, Petun, and Neutrals. Whereas a portion of the Huron–Petun who fled south toward the Ohio Valley became known as Wyandots (an archaic name for the Huron that had fallen into disuse), the Minguas (Mingos) who terrorized western Pennsylvania in the 18th century were undoubtedly the remnants of the Erie. Some of the Neutrals finally penetrated to the far south and may have become part of the Catawba nation of the Carolinas. The Petun refugees retained a far greater tribal identity than all the other dispersed nations by fleeing to the Ottawa and removing in stages to Green Bay. Thereafter, they reentered the history of the intertribal fur trade with the founding of Detroit almost a half century later.

As the dispersed tribes fled west, the Iroquois followed, but they could not spread their war of conquest with impunity. The tribes resident in the Green Bay area greatly feared the Siouan-speaking nations to their west. Even when faced with starvation, they did not choose to hunt in the Siouan borderlands, remaining instead near their villages to eke out a living by hunting small game. In the course of time, the Ottawa, their relations among the Ojibwa, and the remnant tribes—caught between the Iroquois hammer and a Siouan anvil—turned east in defense. They would ultimately drive the Iroquois out of all the territories they had conquered during the dispersal that were north of Lake Erie and west of present-day Cleveland.[30]

In 1653, more than 800 Iroquois cornered a mixed group of Huron, Petun, and Ottawa near Green Bay. For a while the Iroquois maintained their attack, but with the season growing late they became hungry and desired to go home. A truce was called and an agreement negotiated whereby the Green Bay tribes would provide food to the Iroquois in exchange for the release of some Huron captives they had among them. The Iroquois departed in two bands. The group that went home by the northern route across the lower peninsula of Michigan was attacked by a combined force of Chippewa and Mississauga, who defeated them and made captives of most of the survivors. The group taking the more southern route to Iroquoia pushed into the prairie country of the Illinois. Here they attacked a small Illinois village killing many of its inhabitants. A second band of Illinois warriors surprised these Iroquois in their retreat and overwhelmed them.

Meanwhile, a separate war band of Seneca had been raiding and killing in the territory of the Miami west of Lake Erie. It was reported that, "Every night as the Seneca traveled home, they killed and ate a Miami child. And every morning, they took a small child, thrust a stick through its head and sat it up on the path with its face toward the Miami town they had left." The Miami were thus greeted with grisly reminders of Seneca cruelty all along the trail as they pursued. The Miami ultimately outflanked the slow-moving Seneca column, which was heavily laden with plunder and captives. They set an effective ambush for the raiders from which only two Seneca escaped to tell the tale.[31]

Although they suffered several setbacks in trying to expand their war, by the end of the dispersal period, the Iroquois, and the Mohawk in particular, appeared to have attained most of their war aims with respect to Huronia. The Mohawk and the Seneca nations had shown how a series of single devastating blows, if struck against one target at a time, could defeat a wide array of potential enemies. As with the Mahican war, their unremitting focus and willingness to swallow their diplomatic pride for the moment in order to achieve a greater goal seemed to have served the Iroquois well.

The very nature of the Iroquois assault during the dispersal shaped the flight-response of the tribes that had been their targets. The remnants of the tribes—both Algonquian and Iroquoian—came to reside within a great inverted triangle of land in the Lake Michigan region that ran from Starved Rock in Illinois territory, to Sault Sainte Marie and Michilimackinac at the point where Lake Huron and Lake Michigan joined, to the west at Chequamegon Peninsula on Lake Superior. The region southeast of this area was abandoned as far as the Ohio River out of fear of the Iroquois.

The refugees severely disrupted the lives of the tribes that had traditionally occupied the land around Lakes Michigan and Superior. These included Chippewa, Fox, Sauk, Kickapoo, Miami, Illinois, Menominee, Winnebago, and others. The Ojibwa family alone was the most populous of all the Algonquian-speaking nations. It included the Ottawa, Chippewa, Mississauga, Potawatomi, and, of course, the Ojibwa. Many of these groups, weakened by disease and war, had no choice but to allow the unrelated refugees admittance to their lands.

Nonetheless, it has been noted that, "A common residence and a common enemy could not alone produce social bonds among the refugees; indeed, proximity and tension more often than not produced conflict." The host nations often viewed the refugees as treacherous. Yet, each group of refugees sought to form ties with the strangers; and the logic of tribal living brought those speaking common languages closer together. Within the commonality of language, the refugees formed a number of actual and symbolic kinship groups, inhabited neighboring villages, and began to intermarry. Some refugees, largely bereft of close relatives, took the decisive step of forming totally new clans with others in the same condition. This resulted in a merging of many previously unrelated peoples and the modification and reorganization of former patrilineal and matrilineal patterns into bilineal ones. The subsequent creation of multiple ties dissolved some social units and created others, and the conflicting networks of social and political loyalties largely destroyed the simple operative categories of Indian life such as tribe, village, and clan.[32]

Older notions of clan identity and tribal territoriality that had ruled the pre-dispersal world of the Great Lakes region were totally disrupted. The *pays d'en haut* triangle thereafter became a region of villages populated by misfits and multi-tribal bands rather than one of discrete nations (see Map 6). The nature of authority within any individual village differed significantly from that of its neighbor. "Nations shared a common language, culture, and ethnic identity, but the various villages of a nation did not necessarily share a common homeland. Whatever distinct homelands these villages had once possessed, the [dispersal] provoked by the Iroquois had made irrelevant." It was through the existence of this turmoil that the French government and the Catholic Church were able to make their inroads among the Indian nations.[33]

The French were quick to recognize the opportunities that this disorder created, and the Algonquian alliance they forged during this period was a product of both imperial and village politics. The village politics were often fragmented and unharmonious because a number of former tribal or clan leaders, each secure in their power in their own homeland, now vied for dominance among the refugees. The imperial politics of Europe, on the other hand, served to create a form of kinship between the refugees and the French that focused on the English and the Iroquois as enemies. The foundation of this alliance relied on a metaphorical relationship of the governor/father (Onontio) in Quebec and all his Indian/children. The French relieved the factionalism of village politics somewhat by recognizing a number of Alliance Chiefs who might represent their people outside the confines of the village "no matter what political or social position he held within his own society." These men mediated disputes among the allies and might act as a strategic counsel during military campaigns against outsiders. Although the Alliance Chiefs could be chosen to lead warriors in the field, they did not generally claim the power to command as a right.[34]

The One Longhouse

During the period of dispersal, the power of decision making had passed in large part from the Indians to the white colonials and traders. The Indians were largely unaware of the change. In the mist of the turmoil (1653), the governor of Quebec, Jean de Lauson, held a great peace council with the Iroquois nations, and the Jesuits agreed to establish a mission among the Onondaga, who had initiated the peace talks. Up to this time the French had refused to negotiate at Onondaga, forcing the Iroquois diplomats to come to Montreal or Quebec where all the Indian nations of the Northeast were equally disadvantaged. With time, Albany would become the place were treaty negotiations with the English would take place. Here the English and the Mohawks formed a special relationship. This circumstance placed the Mohawks, who were nearest to Albany, at a distinct advantage over the other member nations of the Iroquois Confederacy in terms of their influence.[35]

In the summer before this conference, a Mohawk war leader named Aontarisati, while on a war party against the Algonquian, had been captured by French-allied Indians. While he was being held prisoner by French authorities, Radisson reports, he was instructed in the Catholic faith, baptized, and immediately thereafter put to death. This so enraged the Mohawk that they refused to be a party to the treaty between the French and the Onondaga. A short time later, however, representatives of the Mohawk appeared at Quebec to protest the settlement of a mission among their brothers, the Onondaga, and asked that it be made among the Mohawk instead.[36]

According to the Jesuits in attendance at the meeting, the Mohawk diplomats described the Iroquois Confederacy in terms of the traditional longhouse in which they lived.

We, the five Iroquois nations, compose but one longhouse: we maintain but one fire; and we have, from time immemorial, dwelt under one and the same roof. Well then, will you not enter the longhouse by the door, which is at the ground floor of the house? It is with us Mohawk, that you should begin: whereas you, by beginning with the Onondaga try to enter by the roof and through the chimney. Have you no fear that the smoke may blind you, our fire not being extinguished, and that you may fall from the top to the bottom, having nothing solid on which to plant your feet?[37]

The sentiment expressed by the Mohawk was largely disingenuous. They feared that the advantage they had sought and won through hard-fought war was in danger of slipping away into the hands of the Onondaga. Nonetheless, it was from this speech that the imagery of a single longhouse came to represent the Five Nations of the Iroquois for Europeans. The general peace that ultimately resulted from this conference covered all of the northeastern fur country and allowed all five

The common arrangement of family cooking fires and smoke holes in the interior of a longhouse. The longhouse was a residence for a kinship group with individual families occupying the cubicles at the sides.

Iroquois nations to freely roam the St. Lawrence Valley to the discomfort of the resident Algonquians. The French, it appeared, were too well pleased with the removal of the Iroquois threat to their trade in furs to worry much as to the motives behind any Mohawk offering of peace.

Enter the Ottawa

In 1654, a great fleet of canoes filled with furs appeared on the Grand River bound for Montreal. This was manned largely by the ubiquitous Ottawas (aka, Outaouacs or Staring Hairs from their raised hair roaches). It was from this period that the Grand River of southern Canada became known as the Ottawa River. During much of the 17th century, *Ottawa* was a generic term used by the French for any western Indian who traveled east to trade at Montreal or Quebec. These often included, besides the Ottawa themselves, any of the Ojibwa, Nipissing, and Potawatomi. The Ottawa themselves seem to have been instrumental in putting these fur fleets together. The problem for the Ottawa was not in excluding other tribes from the fur fleets as had the Huron, but rather in recruiting them and holding them together in the face of the Iroquois threat.

A Jesuit observer noted, "All who go to trade with the French, although of widely different nations, bear the general name Outaouacs [Ottawa], under whose auspices they make the journey."[38]

The Mohawks were particularly taken aback by this event, but they were again buoyed in 1655 when there was no fur fleet at all. Nonetheless, in 1656, two French fur traders, Medard Chouart Des Groseilliers and his brother-in-law, Pierre-Esprit Radisson, appeared on the Ottawa River with 50 canoes loaded with furs and manned once again by Ottawa paddlers. This was to prove a fateful accomplishment. Groseilliers and Radisson had gone out into the northwest to collect the furs themselves. Never before had European traders gone into the interior to bring out furs without their first passing through the hands of an Indian middleman.

The joy at the breaking of the blockade was remarkable, and it was celebrated by both the French and the Indians. Montreal was filled with "Savage and Christian pageantry, high mass and dancers in worship of the bears, Jesuits sermons and Indian oratory, breechclouts and velvet breeches, nuns, war chiefs, woods-runners, ceremonious banquets, tribal debauches, the night crimson with fire, musical with river songs, hideous with the chanting and the yelping of the braves." The result was a mix of aboriginal and European glee that should have warned the Indians that they were being seduced by the fur traders.[39]

In 1656, the Mohawk attacked a grand convoy of 10 French soldiers, 4 Jesuit priests, and 2 lay brothers who were in the company of a mixed group of Huron, Onondaga, and Seneca Indians. Radisson placed the cause of this attack on Mohawk "jealousy for their brothers, the Onondaga" for they saw only too clearly that if French settled among the Onondaga, who lived between the Mohawk and the beaver country, all chance of Mohawk domination of the trade would be lost. The attack was generally bloodless with only one of the lay brothers being slightly wounded. The Onondaga protested being fired upon by their brothers, but the Mohawk blandly replied that they had mistaken them for Huron. This the Mohawk considered a purposeful insult. The convoy of canoes was allowed to proceed, but the attackers quickly made their way to the French mission and fort on Lake St. Louis where they attacked the Huron who lived nearby. The homes of these Huron were literally within range of the French guns at the fort, but the garrison dared not retaliate lest the whites in the area be made to suffer for it.[40]

In the next year, it was the Onondaga who violated their treaty obligation. Radisson, who was part of a large party making their way around the portage of the LaChine rapids, reported that a party of Iroquois warriors fell upon a large group of Huron men, women, and children accompanying Father Paul Ragueneau. Eight of the Huron men made a defensive stand around a large group of women who had "cowered together like a flock of sheep surrounded by wolves." The Iroquois initially offered no opposition to these men, and Ragueneau tried to reassure the unfortunate women. When all seemed calm, the Iroquois suddenly fell upon the Huron warriors killing all but one old man who in his time spared many Iroquois. "The Huron women were herded together and stood in deep silence with downcast eyes, blankets over their heads, while the Iroquois went about making camp and building fires to cook supper." Later that night, Ragueneau "borrowed three belts of wampum" from among the captives and strode into the Iroquois camp circle. He asked permission to speak, and made three demands—each punctuated with the presentation of a belt of wampum. He demanded in succession an end to the killing, a safe conduct for the Huron women and children, and the protection of his person, his baggage and that of the other Frenchmen in the party including Radisson. To these demands the Iroquois consented, and they accepted the belts of wampum as solemn symbols of their agreement.[41]

In 1658, the French policy of toleration for the antics of the Iroquois suddenly shifted under a new governor, Pierre d'Argenson. Immediately before his arrival at Quebec, three Frenchmen had been killed and their farms pillaged. Iroquois (presumably Onondaga) war parties were suspected, and Argenson immediately and personally led a company of troops into the forests in pursuit. Although he failed to run down his quarry, it was clear from his reactions thereafter that this governor was going to take steps to change the status quo with regard to the Iroquois. The Jesuit mission to the Onondaga at Ste. Marie de Gannentaha was hurriedly withdrawn, and Argenson ordered "the arrest, throughout the French settlements of all the Iroquois that should present themselves, from whatever quarter they might come." Among the first Iroquois seized were several Mohawk at Trois Riviers, who were sent to Quebec as prisoners.[42]

The Mohawk felt that the imprisonment of their men was unjust, and they would have gone to war with the French had any of them been executed as had Aontarisati five years early. Yet, the Seneca, who had been their main supporters in the recent wars of dispersion, had recently expressed to the Mohawk that they were war weary and unwilling to open a new conflict. Moreover, they feared attack from the Susquehannock to the south. Understanding that an attack on the French without Seneca aid was impractical, the Mohawk made a new agreement with the Dutch at Albany and reestablished the blockade of the Ottawa River.

The closing of the Ottawa River in 1658 was among the most effective trade blockades ever undertaken in all of history.[43] So effective were the Mohawk in suppressing the fur brigades that commerce in all of New France almost came to a halt. It was reported by a contemporary observer that of 360 canoes that attempted the run of the Mohawk gauntlet only 7 got through.[44]

Montreal was in a constant state of alarm as long as the Mohawk blockaded the Ottawa River. Small bands, breaking off from their watch of the river, would terrorize the French habitants by destroying their livestock and menacing solitary farmers. Killings were taking place at the very walls of French cities. In all the north country, not only was the fur trade interrupted, but settlement and agriculture were threatened. Plowmen were found scalped in their fields, and the bodies of engages were found floating in the river. In the winter of 1659–1660, a large number of Mohawk bands wintered on the Ottawa river, and the French, knowing the method of Iroquois strategy during the dispersal, apprehended an assault on their settlements in the spring.

The Defense of the Long Sault

In an attempt to avert the coming blow, Dollard des Ormeaux raised a band of young men and French Indians to ascend the Ottawa River and ambush the Iroquois as they passed. At the section of the river containing a series of rapids known as the Long Sault, Dollard and his men built a crude fortification—little more than an entrenchment strengthen by a few logs and piles of brush. Here they awaited the Iroquois. As the Indians shot down the rapids in their canoes, Dollard and his men opened fire upon them from the bank. The Iroquois were initially taken aback, but their increasing numbers forced Dollard and his men into the shelter of their fort. For eight days he and his little band of volunteers fought a savage defensive engagement. In the end, most of their Indian allies deserted them in ones and twos, and the whites were overpowered.

Those Frenchmen who were not killed in the battle were tortured and burned at stakes overlooking the river. Contemporary accounts record 17 hideous human monuments to this torture that the Mohawk left decorating the river bank at the Long Sault. When the Iroquois were confronted by the French with the facts of these murders, they arrogantly answered that because the French persisted in taking the Algonquian to their bosoms, they need not be surprised if blows struck in the direction of their Indian enemies sometimes struck Frenchmen. The governor could do little more than arrest a dozen Iroquois and hold them hostage.[45]

Nonetheless, Dollard's attempt to deter the Iroquois had been proactive, and it had inflicted so severe a loss upon the Iroquois that they withdrew into their own territory and left Montreal unmolested for some time. If 17 Frenchmen could hold off hundreds of Iroquois for several days from behind a breastwork of brush, how much better could the larger, armed forces of the colony do from behind the stone walls of Quebec or Montreal? Moreover, the defense had buoyed the local Algonquian-speaking peoples and increased their respect for the martial prowess of the French. After the Dollard massacre, the French policy of toleration for the aggressive methods of the Iroquois was largely superseded by a general hostility. It is widely supposed that the French would have countered the Iroquois victory at Long Sault with a large scale military stratagem of their own in 1661 except for the impending change in governors from the aggressive Argenson to the generally ineffective Baron Dubois D'Avaugour (1661–1663).

Removing the Mohawk Menace

In 1663, the colony of New France was placed under royal control, and a new form of government was initiated under the first Royal Governor, Chevalier de Mezy (1663–1665). Although De Mezy's administration was short-lived, the French were encouraged by the arrival of the Carignan-Salieres regiment of French regulars, who had gained great renown in the Turkish Wars. The employment of regulars was specifically designed to put an end to Iroquois aggression. The second royal governor, Daniel de Remy, Sieur De Courcelle (1665–1672), gave precedence to his military viceroy, the Marquis De Tracy, during the viceroy's stay in the colony, but De Courcelle chaffed when De Tracy did not immediately move to eliminate the Mohawk menace.

In 1666, De Courcelle led a raid of his own devising into Mohawk territory that badly misfired, but De Tracy led a better organized campaign in 1667 with a force of 1,100 men. He burned many Mohawk villages and destroyed their crops and orchards, but there was little loss of life as the occupants had prudently withdrawn. Nonetheless, the attack on the heart of Iroquoia had its desired effect. The Iroquois had never before been attacked by Europeans in this manner with their wives, children, and elders at risk. Dismayed by the specter of further disaster or impending starvation, the Mohawks joined with the other members of their confederacy in humbly seeking peace with the French. Notwithstanding doubts and suspicions on both sides, with great ceremony and the exchange of presents a solemn treaty was made at a great conference held at Montreal in 1667.

For more than two decades thereafter, the Iroquois remained at peace with the French. More importantly, with the Iroquois humbled, the whole north country was at peace for the first time in generations, and the fur trade was free to move forward unimpeded. Even the Mahicans, who had fought the Mohawks for several decades, succumbed to Iroquois diplomacy and formed a tenuous peace with them.

It would be an error to believe that the Iroquois had been forced into a one-sided peace agreement by French determination. Iroquois policies were rarely so straight-forward as to include a simple unilateral surrender. The Iroquois were well aware that the Dutch, at war with the English in Europe, were losing. Throughout the period, European observers seem to have failed to recognize the intricacies of intertribal diplomatic and economic manipulations or the sophistication of the Native American intelligence gathering resources.

It is certain that the Iroquois were responding to many circumstances when they made peace in 1667. The English had quietly displaced the Dutch in New Netherlands in 1664, and it was no accident that English sovereignty over New Netherlands and the Iroquois offer of peace took place almost simultaneously three years later. The removal of the Dutch, however, did not immediately eliminate the traders of that nation from competition, but with time they were replaced by the English, who had the potential to be more dangerous competitors in trade than the French. Yet, in the last quarter of the 17th century, the Anglo-colonials had not yet demonstrated the expansionism that would characterize England's policies in the 18th century.

Moreover, the Iroquois may have been responding to internal weaknesses. The *Jesuit Relations* reported an epidemic that had ravaged the villages of Iroquoia in the late 1660s and had killed many hundreds of warriors. Additionally, a coalition of northern tribes with the Abenaki had shown remarkable resistance to the Mohawk by "utterly destroying" a large party of their warriors in New England. These two circumstances may have left the Iroquois, who probably could field no more than 2,500 warriors in good times, in a diminished military condition. On the other hand, the Iroquois may simply have been repositioning themselves politically.

One person who understood the economic, political, and diplomatic sophistication of the Native Americans was Jolicoeur Charles Bonin, a French soldier serving in North America, who wrote, "The character of these people is a mixture of simplicity and trickery, nobility and meanness, vanity and politeness, good nature and treachery, valor and cowardice, humanity and barbarity."[46]

The Susquehannock Wars

Notwithstanding the ambiguity of the circumstances that led to peace in 1667, it seems certain that the Seneca were using the new found accord with the French Indians to prosecute a renewed war with their neighbors to the south, the Susquehannock.[47] The Susquehannock, an Iroquoian-speaking people, were noted as a redoubtable enemy of the Seneca, who had previously fought with them but had failed to achieve any decisive results. Although they inhabited a large region of present-day Pennsylvania, the Susquehannocks were a far-ranging people who sent hunting and war parties west into the Ohio River valley and well north of Lake Ontario. The Seneca and the Susquehannock continually annoyed one another during these small excursions in an attempt to patrol the borders of their respective territories and to stave off the likelihood of a clandestine buildup of invasion forces.

The Mohawk, reassured by their successes in the Beaver Wars of the 1640s, had ventured into the northern borderlands of Susquehannock territory in the winter of 1651–1652 to attack the village of the Atrakwaeronons, who may have been 1 of 20 bands associated with a loosely formed Susquehannock confederacy that dominated the mid-Atlantic region from the Potomac River in northern Virginia to the southern New York border with Pennsylvania. Although the Susquehannock maintained almost two dozen fortified villages and may have numbered between 5,000 and 7,000 persons, they took fright at reports of 500 to 600 captives being taken on their northern border by the Mohawk. They quickly began their own preparations for war with the Five Nations at that time. Periods of ill-feeling, discomfiture, and open conflict were to continue between the Susquehannocks and their northern cousins over the next quarter century.

Little is known of the First Susquehannock War. From 1652 until 1658, the Mohawk and the Susquehannock warred on each other by means of small itinerant raiding parties. The Mohawk failed to force either the surrender or the dispersal of the Susquehannock by these means, but the two nations joined together with the Dutch in 1660 to settle a dispute with the Esopus Indians of the Hudson Valley. It is quite certain that the Susquehannock were receiving firearms from the Swedish colonists in the Delaware Bay, and they were reported to have fitted their villages with several small cannons from this source. Nonetheless, when the Dutch conquered New Sweden in 1655, the Susquehannock became their customers, and active aggression between this nation and the Mohawks reportedly subsided.[48]

In 1663, however, more than 800 Iroquois warriors—drawn from the Senecas, Cayugas, and Onondagas—opened a fierce attack on the main stronghold of the Susquehannock. This was the first encounter of the Second Susquehannock War. Almost 700 Susquehannock, supported by 100 Delaware allies, massed to repel the attackers. If this attack was an attempt to do to the Susquehannock what had been done to the residents of Huronia during the dispersal, it did not work.[49]

The proximate cause of the outbreak of a second major conflict between the Senecas and the Susquehannocks in 1663 is obscured by the same lack of direct evidence that affects the study of all the intertribal wars of the 17th century. However, it seems clear that the causes of the conflict were rooted in the interdiction of the fur trade in the Susquehanna River valley. The importance of this war was that the English colonies of Maryland and Virginia took an active part in an intertribal trade conflict for the first time and significantly affected its outcome.

Throughout the 1660s, the Seneca had been increasingly harassed by the Susquehannock as they tried to move furs across the region that is now the New York–Pennsylvania border. The Seneca carried their beaver skins to Albany "with great inconvenience and by long and perilous routes" with the Susquehannock laying ambushes for them all along the way in a manner similar to that of the Mohawk along the Ottawa River. In order to defend their caravans, the Seneca were reported by the Jesuits to have devoted half their force in warriors as escorts.[50]

In the second war, the Susquehannocks were again supported by the firearms and small cannons formerly supplied to them by the colonials.

The cannons were not used tactically, but they were of great value strategically as a defense for the main Susquehannock village. Maryland initially sent gunpowder and 50 armed men to help defend the main Susquehannock village at Kanastoga (place of the great pole). Allied to the Susquehannocks were the remnants of the Erie, hereafter known as the Mingos, the Delaware, and the Shawnee—the last making their first appearance in the historical period as an aggressive force in intertribal warfare. The Shawnee at this time may have been members of a closely knit single tribe. However, in the 18th century, they represented a confederation divided into five semi-autonomous groups that included the Chillicothe, Hathawekela, Kispoko, Mequachake, and Piqua. The leadership of this confederation seems to have come from the first two of these groups.[51]

In an attempt to win concessions by diplomacy rather than might, the Seneca sent 25 representatives to the Susquehannock village to treat with the defenders. They were seized and burned at stakes raised upon the stockade in full view of the besieging Iroquois army. The Seneca retreated in frustration, but they were not alone in their adversity. The Cayuga, "younger brothers" of the Seneca, also seem to have suffered a great disaster at the hands of the Susquehannock at this time. Many of the Cayuga were driven north from their tribal lands into the now vacant region north of Lake Ontario. The Onondaga, who occupied the territory immediately adjacent to that of the Cayuga, felt constrained thereafter to take some part in the war. Ironically, the always perverse Oneida [fifth member of the Iroquois confederacy] initially refused to aid the Seneca and Cayuga in their hour of need.[52]

For several years, the Seneca continued the fight by promoting a continuous series of small raids. The Oneida finally joined them in 1664 and attacked the Delaware allies of the Susquehannock living on the Chesapeake Bay to the outrage of the Anglo-colonial officials in Maryland. Finally, Cayuga territory was again invaded by the Susquehannock, and a relief force of Seneca warriors was cut to pieces. Thereafter, it became evident that the Seneca simply could not deal with them. Repeated embassies were sent to the French to intervene, but the Comte de Frontenac, the royal governor at Quebec at the time, essentially refused to involve himself in the intertribal politics that surrounded the attacks.

Among the implications of these failed Iroquois attacks was the forging of an alliance between the Iroquoian-speaking Susquehannock and some of the Algonquian-speaking tribes of the mid-Atlantic region, particularly the Delaware. Some of these alliances were so strong that many Susquehannock families insisted on remaining with the Delaware even after a general peace had been constructed. Colonial authorities in Maryland and Virginia viewed these developments with ill-ease fearing that the balance of native power was shifting to their detriment.

Suddenly, in 1675, just as the Wampanoag rebellion known as King Philip's War was getting under way in New England, the Susquehannocks were reported to have been destroyed. The exact reasons for their demise were not clear but seemed to have included the involvement of the English colonials, who were greatly relieved by the development regardless of its origin. One scenario suggests that a force of Iroquois defeated the Susquehannocks in a major unrecorded battle and that the survivors fled south along the frontiers of Virginia and Maryland where they were exterminated or sold as slaves by whites. The ubiquitous Jesuits seemingly knew nothing of the details of the Susquehannock dispersion beyond the fact that they were gone, leaving their sudden disappearance an historical mystery. A few Susquehannock were still reported to be living in eastern Pennsylvania as late as 1763. These came to be called the Conestoga because they lived at Kanastoga (place of the great pole).

The sudden retirement of the Susquehannocks from their tribal territory has been explained in various ways.[53] The Iroquois were supposed to have badly beaten the Susquehannocks sometime between 1672 and 1675, although no historian has been able to identify the battle or the campaign that was supposed to have taken place, even in terms of a tribal tradition. It is altogether possible that a decisive battle between the Iroquois and Susquehannock in the wilderness might go unrecorded, yet, it is almost as certain that the reason for this is that the event "never happened."[54] The Iroquois themselves were uncharacteristically silent about any such victory. "Certainly, had it taken place, they would have bragged about it from Maryland to Maine."[55]

On the other hand, there is some evidence that the Susquehannock may have sought refuge in New York from the colonial governments of Maryland and Virginia, especially during the period of Bacon's Rebellion of 1676 when the Piscatawas and Mattawomans of the Delaware Confederacy had aided the colonial militia in the pursuit of a band of renegade Doeg Indians. Word of the near extermination of the followers of Metacomet (King Philip) in New England in that same year may also have caused the Susquehannock to seek a certain level of anonymity by residing among their Delaware neighbors. An Indian informant of the English noted, "The Susquehannocks laugh and jeer at the English saying they can do what mischief they please [because] the English can not see them."[56]

Meanwhile, Maryland's governor, Sir Charles Calvert called the surviving Susquehannock to a conference at Mattapinie (St. Mary's City) in the winter of 1675. To his surprise, a number of Susquehannock appeared, and after some tedious debate they agreed to remove their villages from Piscatawa to the general vicinity of present-day Washington, D.C. on the Potomac River. The colonial authorities were anxious that the Susquehannock remain apart from the Delaware lest they increase the power and influence of the latter. In 1677, most of these Susquehannock retired to Iroquoia to be under the protection of New York colony, but 26 families permanently joined the Delaware. This effectively destroyed the tribal integrity of the Susquehannock as a people, and gave the Delaware, due to their adoption of a majority of the tribe, command of the property rights below the falls of the Susquehanna River. The Iroquois seemingly received the remaining territorial rights of the Susquehannock above the falls. William Penn recognized these rights in 1683 when he purchased much of the region for the colony of Pennsylvania. The Susquehannock were thereafter "reduced to anonymity among their Iroquois and Delaware hosts."[57]

Delaware Grandfathers

The position and status of the Delaware nation during this and subsequent periods of colonial history is a topic of some debate. The Iroquois, when dealing with the whites, often referred to the Delaware as their "nephews" or as "women." Some historians have taken this as a symbol of Delaware subservience to the Iroquois. Furthermore, there is no record of the Delawares dealing independently with the colonial government of New York. Yet, the Delawares dealt with the officials of Pennsylvania independent of the Iroquois, and formulated agreements without asking their permission or sanction. On other occasions, the Delaware were openly regarded as the grandfathers of the Iroquois. Certainly, the Delaware were considered among the oldest of the Algonquian-speaking tribes. The confusion regarding their status appears to have arisen "among the interpreters rather than among the Indians" as they tried to make sense of the "bewildering nomenclature of fictive kinship and personal relations" for the whites in attendance at meetings and conferences. The term "nephew" may have been used in place of a phrase meaning *sister's children,* denoting high regard and close relationship, especially among nations of different linguistic stock. The term *woman* may have also been misinterpreted in the minds of whites. It must be remembered that women among the Iroquois were not held in contempt. They were instead the source of tribal power and leadership, the initiators of war and peace, and the mediators of internecine quarrels. Certainly, the Delaware had served as mediators time and again in disputes between neighboring tribes and between the tribes and the Dutch long before the British had come to know them.[58]

Among the plans devised to upset Dutch control of trade along the middle Atlantic seacoast of America in the spring of 1663, the English had proposed a war of conquest against the Delaware with whom the Dutch traders had become friendly. However, in November 1664, an English fleet had taken over New Netherlands and a peace between the two powers in Europe had made these plans redundant. The Duke of York's appointee as governor of the Dominion of New England, Sir Edmund Andros, was determined to stabilize English relations with the regional Indian populations. To that end, he sought out and won the friendship of the Delaware, who thereafter served as his mediators with other Indian nations. In the north, he placated the long-lived and turbulent situation between the

Iroquois and Mahicans by promising to protect both. In so doing, he set the boundary between New York and New England as the watershed between the valley of the Connecticut and Hudson Rivers at the suggestion of his Delaware advisors.

The End of Hegemony

In 1664, the Mohawks made an attack on the Sokoki tribe (possibly relations of the Mahicans) on the upper Connecticut River of Massachusetts. Ironically, the little-known Sokoki were able to repulse the Mohawk raiders sent against them. This assured the continued hostility of the New England tribes, particularly the Mahicans, to Mohawk attempts to enforce an Iroquois domination across all the Northeast woodlands. With the help of firearms supplied by the Puritans of Massachusetts, the New England tribes continued to wage an intermittent war on the Mohawk for control of the Hudson Valley.[59]

With the exception of some minor expeditions against the tribes to the west, by 1684, the Iroquois' attempt to achieve a fur trade monopoly was over. They had been wedded to the idea of trading furs at Albany throughout their struggles. When the English took possession of New Netherlands from the Dutch, the Iroquois skillfully switched their focus from one group of traders to the other. They also quickly saw that English goods were superior to those of the French and many times cheaper. However, the Indian nations of the Great Lakes could no longer be made to recognize the Iroquois as middlemen. The Five Iroquois nations, and the Mohawks in particular, had expended the lives of their young men in making war for an entire generation, and, ironically, had exhausted their ability to use war as a tool for economic success.

More importantly, by the last decades of the 17th century, Frenchmen had ascended the rivers and lakes into the interior to trade for furs directly with the native trappers thereby eliminating the middleman status that was the centerpiece of the Iroquois economic strategy. Medard Groseilliers and Pierre Radisson, Louis Joliet and Jacques Marquette, and particularly Robert Cavelier de la Salle had demonstrated the advantages to the Indians of dealing directly with the French. The active interposition of Frenchmen, or any Europeans, into the fur trade upset the underpinnings of the greater part of a century of intertribal trade wars and complicated the shape of the world for the Iroquois beyond their ability to refashion it more to their liking. Indian children, unborn when the Mohawk had begun their aggression against the Mahican, knew virtually nothing of peace and were now old men and women.

The Iroquois were astute politicians, subtle diplomats, and determined schemers who had proven that they would not give up at the slightest setback, but as the century turned they began to ponder a wiser policy. Might not the assumption of a great neutrality between the French and

English in the future better serve them than warfare? They had never before attempted to play one white competitor against the other, yet, this would be their position throughout most of the 18th century. This decision marked the end of the Iroquois attempt to gain a trading monopoly by purely military means, and it opened a new phase of carefully crafted diplomacy and brinkmanship.

Notes

1. Ian K. Steele, *Warpaths: Invasions of North America* (New York: Oxford University Press, 1994), 70–71.

2. Richard I. Melvoin, *New England Outpost, War and Society in Colonial Deerfield* (New York: W. W. Norton & Company, 1989), 28.

3. Melvoin, 47.

4. Contrary to opinions revolving around James Fennimore Cooper's use of the term *Mohicans* in the title of his most famous novel, both the terms Mahican and Mohican refer to the same people and are equally correct. The author has chosen the Mahican version of the term as it is most common in Dutch documents of the period. Conversely, the name Mohegan refers to a tribe living between the Connecticut and Thames Rivers who more closely tied to the Pequots of eastern Connecticut.

5. Shirley W. Dunn, *The Mohicans and their Land, 1609–1730* (Fleischmanns, NY: Purple Mountain Press, 1994), 233.

6. Dunn, 96–98.

7. As quoted by Dunn, 99. The observer, Domine Jonas Michaeleus, was lamenting the downturn in the volume of fur coming from the interior to New Amsterdam.

8. Dunn, 98.

9. Guy Omeron Coolridge, *The French Occupation of the Champlain Valley from 1609 to 1759* (Fleischmanns, NY: Purple Mountain Press, 1999), 11–12. For the use of the term "gladiatorial" see Steele, 66.

10. H. P. Biggar, ed., *The Works of Samuel de Champlain* (Toronto: The Champlain Society, 1933), vol. VI, 3.

11. Dunn, 99. The Mahicans of Massachusetts were later known as the Stockbridge Indians. Those who remained in New York were often called the Schagticoke or River Indians.

12. Francis Jennings, *The Ambiguous Iroquois Empire* (New York: W. W. Norton & Company, 1984), 113. See Dorothy V. Jones, *License for Empire: Colonialism by Treaty in Early America* (Chicago: University of Chicago Press, 1982).

13. George T. Hunt, *The Wars of the Iroquois, A Study in Intertribal Trade Relations* (Madison: University of Wisconsin Press, 1972), 32–35, 53.

14. Hunt, 55, 63.

15. Hunt, 96. The Neutrals were not inept with regard to canoes, but their territory in Huronia was devoid of the birch and elm trees needed to build them.

16. Hunt, 64.

17. Hunt, 59.

18. Hunt, 68.

19. Albert E. Stone, ed., *Letters from an American Farmer and Sketches of Eighteenth-Century America by J. Hector St. John de Crevecoeur* (New York: Penguin Classics, 1986), 378.

20. Jennings, 43.

21. Hunt, 72–73.

22. Hunt, 72–73.

23. Hunt, 74.

24. Hunt, 76.

25. Hunt, 92. Hunt is one of the few historians to report the details of this momentous event. Others dismiss the entire episode and its aftermath in a single paragraph.

26. Hunt, 93.

27. Quoting LaSalle in Richard White, *The Middle Ground, Indians, Empires, and Republics in the Great Lakes Region, 1650–1815* (New York: Cambridge University Press, 1991), 48–49.

28. Francis Parkman, *LaSalle and the Discovery of the Great West* (New York: The New American Library of World Literature, Inc., 1962), 54; White, 47–48.

29. Hunt, 98.

30. Jennings, 111.

31. White, 4–5.

32. White, 16–17.

33. White, 16–17.

34. White, 38–39.

35. Jennings, 166.

36. Stanley Vestal, *King of the Fur Traders, The Deeds and Deviltry of Pierre Esprit Radisson* (Boston: Houghton Mifflin Company, 1940), 67.

37. Elizabeth Metz, *Sainte Marie Among the Iroquois* (Syracuse, NY: Midgley Printing, 1995), 53. To complete the illusion, the Mohawks were the keepers of the eastern door, the Seneca that of the western door, and the Onondaga were the keepers of the central fire. These three were the older brothers of the confederacy with the Oneida and Cayuga being the younger brothers. All important Confederacy business was done at councils held at Onondaga.

38. White, 105–106.

39. Bernard DeVoto, *Course of Empire* (Boston: Houghton Mifflin, 1952), 97.

40. Vestal, 72–73.

41. Vestal, 76–77.

42. Metz, 105.

43. Vestal, 52.

44. Hunt, 104.

45. Vestal, 74.

46. Andrew Gallup, ed., *Memoir of a French and Indian War Soldier, Jolicoeur Charles Bonin* (Bowie, MD: Heritage Books, Inc., 1993), 216.

47. Hunt, 134–135.

48. Jennings, 110.

49. Jennings, 121.

50. Hunt, 139.

51. White, 192–193.

52. Jennings, 130.

53. Jennings, 141.

54. Jennings, 135.
55. Jennings, 136.
56. Jennings, 164.
57. Jennings, 159.
58. Jennings, 160–161.
59. Jennings, 129.

V

THE INDIAN FAMILY AS DIPLOMATS

12

Dispossessing the First Nations

At the time when the Swedes arrived, they brought land at a very inconsiderable price. For a piece of baize, or a pot full of brandy, or the like, they would get a piece of ground, which at present would be worth more than four hundred pounds, Pennsylvania currency.[1]

—Nils Gustafson, aged 91 in the year 1749

The land was filled with Ishmaels.

—William Brandon, historian

Sovereign Nations

It is certain that the native population felt the repercussions of European encroachment generations before the first settlers actually arrived in their country. European deep-sea fishermen had visited the New England coast since the early 1500s, and the Spanish and the French had begun settlements during the 16th century. The English had been active in Virginia since the 1580s, and the Dutch had sailed the Hudson River in 1609. Yet, the physical reality of meeting on the frontiers of civilization placed serious limitations on both the Indians and the settlers. The commonly held idea that colonists craved to own property and that Indians did not "distorts European notions of property as much as it does Indian ones."[2]

Both Indians and whites recognized ownership in terms of what could and could not be done with property as to its disposition. Both assigned boundaries to property possession, although those of the Indians were somewhat less definite than those of whites. And finally, both groups were granted their ownership of the land by some sovereign agency. In the case of the colonists, this was almost always directly from the Crown, or indirectly through the massive trading companies chartered by the crown. Among these were the Dutch West India Company, the Company of One Hundred Associates in French Canada, or the Plymouth or London companies set up to trade in Massachusetts or in Virginia.

For the Indians, land might be granted by their clan, their sachem, an overlord tribe, or one of the many confederacies that flourished in the region. Indians also occupied land as squatters through the sufferance of their native neighbors, who might actually claim it as their own. This type of occupation applied only to the use of the things of the land (the usufruct rights) such as the firewood, the plants, the water, the game, or the fish. Because this practice was so widespread, land ownership relations could become quite involved, and they were often misunderstood by whites.

The Iroquois of Central New York claimed sovereignty over much of the land to the south including that occupied by tribes in Pennsylvania, Delaware, Maryland, New Jersey, the Carolinas, all of the west bank of the Hudson River valley, and the western end of Long Island. The Canarsie of the western end of Long Island were a sub-tribe of the Delaware nation who may or may not have been subservient to the Iroquois, but the powerful Montauk of the eastern ends of Long Island viewed themselves as generally independent of any overlord. The remaining 10 or so tribes on Long Island viewed the Pequot of Connecticut across Long Island Sound as their overlords. Similarly, the Delaware of New Jersey, Pennsylvania, and surrounding areas considered themselves the Lenni-Lenapi (true men), yet, the Iroquois more than once called the Delaware "women" at grand councils implying to the whites present that they held sovereignty over them. Both the Delawares and many historians find this claim dubious.

The crux of the debate concerning sovereign and subservient nations seems to lie in the definition of a *tributary tribe*. To be a tributary tribe did not mean that the Indians were humiliated or denationized, but rather that they accepted, for example, the protection of the Iroquois and became loyal props to their stratagems and allies to their military operations. Moreover, they acknowledged relationship by token gifts of wampum or other signs of respect from time to time. Tributary nations were often called *younger brothers* or *children*, terms that connoted a protective familial relationship. The position of many tributary tribes was often closer to that of being given asylum as refugees than it was of being a conquered people. Protectors of long standing and close relationship were often called *uncles*, a term which also reflected a mutually respectful kinship-like relationship.

Shortly after the conquest of the Susquehannock (1675–1680), both the Conoy and Nanticoke of Maryland and the Delmarva Peninsula, respectively, became tributary tribes of the Iroquois Confederacy. These two

Algonquian-speaking tribes were closely related and may have once been a single political entity. When John Smith saw the Conoy in 1607, they were known as the Piscataway and lived on the lower Potomac River. In stages they moved north to southern Pennsylvania and finally to Chenango (near Binghamton, New York). Here, under the close scrutiny of their Iroquois uncles, they lost the last vestiges of their Conoy identity. Similarly, the Nanticoke ultimately moved away from the pressure of white encroachment to reside at Chenango. They were adopted into the Iroquios Confederacy as "children," but they were also accorded two positions as spectators at the Great Council Fire of the Iroquois at Onondaga.

The Tutelo, a Siouan-speaking people, lived in the piedmont of Virginia and were noted as brave and capable warriors, yet, they were "much knocked about by their neighbors, white and Indian." They were involved in a series of disastrous events in 1675 and 1676: attacked by the Susquehannock, allied to the wrong side in Bacon's Rebellion, and finally attacked by the resurgent forces of the governor of Virginia. Consequently, the number of surviving Tutelo were greatly diminished in just a short period of time, and they were forced from place to place during the next half century by the changing pressures that white settlement placed on them. In 1722, under the political sponsorship of the Cayuga of the Iroquois Confederacy, they moved into Pennsylvania. Their adoption as "younger brothers" of the confederacy coincided with the entry of the Nanticoke. By 1771, they had a settlement at the southern end of Cayuga Lake in New York.[3]

The Tuscarora were an Iroquoian people from North Carolina who maintained close ties with the central council fire in New York. The brief uprising known as the Tuscarora War of 1711–1712 was a direct result of white settlers occupying lands along the Pamlico, Roanoke, Tar, and Nuese Rivers that were in the domain of the Tuscarora. In 1711, itinerant Indians from another tribe attacked some isolated farms near New Bern, but the local white militias struck out in all directions without design or coordination. Once attacked by these whites, the Tuscarora retaliated, and more than 150 settlers perished in the more remote parts of the colony. Within a year, the North Carolina frontier was in ruins with entire regions totally abandoned by terrified whites. Shortly thereafter the Tuscarora were reported to have moved north, yet, they migrated slowly and only in small bands over the next 50 years. They were admitted to the longhouse "on the cradle board" (as a child), and their delegates to the council fire sat behind those of the Oneida and Seneca who spoke for them after a brief consultation. Nonetheless, in 1722 the Iroquois Confederacy went from being an alliance of five nations to that of six nations because of the incorporation of the Tuscarora. In 1765, the Iroquois Council sent representatives to North Carolina to bring away the last remnant of the Tuscarora people to New York.

The adoption of the Conoy, the Nanticok,e and the Tutelo as tributary tribes, and the incorporation of the Tuscarora as full members of a centuries old confederacy, underscores the importance of the Iroquois Confederacy in regional native politics, but it also makes clear that the adoptions were genuine. "The political agenda of the Iroquois tolerated, even fostered, the retention of tribal institutions among those minority bodies of natives who voluntarily came to ally themselves with the Longhouse, not withstanding the circumstances that they be of alien speech-stock and extraction." This form of institutional freedom added dignity as well as social and political equality to the tributary tribes of the Iroquois alliance.[4]

There were other refugee groups among the natives, most of them small and detached fragments of once important tribes, who sought the protection of more powerful neighbors. Among these were refugee Mahican from New York and surviving Wampanoag from New England who settled with the Delawares in Pennsylvania after having suffered severe defeats in war at the hands of the Iroquois and the English, respectively. The Wyandots and Minguas (Mingos) formerly the Huron and Erie, who were dispersed by the Iroquois, reappeared as allies of the Shawnee on the Ohio and Pennsylvania frontiers in the 18th century. The Iroquois had reluctantly allowed the Shawnees to move into southern Pennsylvania and had placed two Oneida chiefs (half kings) to oversee their behavior. Although these Shawnees numbered only 200 warriors at the time, they constantly involved themselves in disturbances with English traders because of their pro-French leanings. Ultimately, the pro-English Iroquois unceremoniously ordered them out of Pennsylvania, "back toward Ohio, the place from whence you came."[5]

After the Great Dispersal of the 17th century, Hurons and Ottawas moved westward to the upper Mississippi. Here they quarreled with the forest Sioux and ultimately drifted back toward Green Bay. The Ojibwa, armed with trade muskets, then waged a century long war with these same Sioux and pushed them out into the plains of Minnesota and Dakota. The Winnebago—who often go unnoticed for their fierceness—waged a crushing war with the Illinois, Potawatomi, and Miami displacing whole bands and driving the refugees to the French trading posts for succor. Northern Indians displaced by other native tribes drifted south, and refugees of the internecine wars in the South passed them on the trail moving north. "The land was filled with Ishmaels." The Shawnees, Mahicans, Wyandots, Mingos, and many other groups passed through different regions of the Northeast woodlands under similar circumstances leaving behind them a few abandoned villages and burial sites to plague the findings of future archeologists, as well as a vague anecdotal tradition of once having occupied particular places to frustrate the historians.[6]

The Indian concept of the ownership of land was rooted in its occupancy by a clan or chieftainship. Each group of villagers occupied and used the land on which they resided so long as they found it desirable. There are numerous indications in the archeological record of the intermittent occupation of even desirable locations and of migratory patterns among the native populations with different groups occupying the same spots at different times or seasons of the year. Most tribes would occupy a favorable location at one season of the year and move to another where food or shelter were more secure at some other season. Yet, the Indians had no intention of permanently abandoning their land when they moved.

Europeans comprehended the ownership of land in fee and believed that they had sole ownership without necessarily occupying a parcel until they sold or abandoned it. White settlers tended to remain on the land and wait out even the harshest conditions of weather and crisis for fear of losing it through abandonment. The Indians totally failed to comprehend the idea of absentee ownership. Yet, this is the common understanding of land ownership that we have today. Many persons own real estate that they have never seen or rarely visit. Much of the mistrust and hostility that developed among the natives toward the colonists was due to a mutual misunderstanding as to the permanent ownership and occupation of land.[7]

At the beginning of the 17th century, large divisions of the Delaware (Lenni-Lenape) confederacy occupied extensive territories from Maryland, Pennsylvania, and New Jersey to the Hudson River, and they generally remained at peace with the Europeans for more than 100 years. Numerically, the Lenni-Lenape were the most numerous of all the eastern Algonquians. Besides the regions already noted, their sub-tribes inhabited Staten Island and the western end of Long Island, but these were generally the eastern margins of their territory. Manhattan, the Bronx, and Westchester were occupied by members of another Algonquian-speaking sub-tribe of the Wappinger confederacy. To the east of the Wappinger nations and along the New England coast roughly from New York to Boston, the region was populated in turn by the Pequot and Mohegan of Connecticut, the Narragansett of Rhode Island, and finally the Wampanoag and Massachusetts nations. These were the principal nations of a region representing literally dozens of individual tribes, bands, and domestic groups, all of whom spoke Algonquian and had similar cultural characteristics and appearance.

The Dutch thought that the land surrounding present-day New York City belonged to the Weckquaesgeek (a sub-tribe of the Wappinger confederacy). This was an extensive tract that included much of the present-day Bronx, Yonkers, and Westchester County as far north along the Hudson River as Ossining. The island of Manhattan and most of Brooklyn belonged to the Canarsie (who were Lenni-Lenape). In fact the wooded island was occupied by a group known as Manhattans (Island People), but this name may have been descriptive of the place rather than the people. The Algonquian root *munnoh* or *manah* means *island*. There was also a native tradition that the region actually belonged to the Raritan (also Delaware), who had removed their entire population in the pre-contact period from Manhattan to New Jersey in what is today known as the

Raritan River valley. No reason was given for the move. Perhaps epidemic disease or fear of another tribe forced the Raritan to relocate. Nonetheless, the Manhattan, whoever they were, found the area abundant and capable of sustaining their families, and they moved on in.[8]

It should be noted that Native Americans rarely abandoned a region in the face of European advance, but many Indians believed that epidemics were due to the presence of evil manitou that could be avoided by moving away. The prosperous Matinecock of the Flushing area of Long Island, for instance, were virtually wiped out by a disease that they contracted from close contact with the surrounding white colonists, but they were hemmed in by Dutch lands that left them with nowhere to escape. The New England coastal region occupied by the Pilgrims at Plymouth was largely destitute of native people due to an epidemic that ravaged the Patuxet population in 1617, shortly before white arrival.

The French found the St. Lawrence River valley unoccupied by natives due in large part to the effects of recent intertribal warfare in the region. Nonetheless, there was a good deal of Indian movement along and behind the supposed border between settled and unsettled regions. "Even the Anglo-French frontier was not clearly defined as Indians traveled and traded back and forth among the French and the English."[9]

From the very beginning of the colonial period it was clear that the native inhabitants were being dispossessed of their land. To a greater or lesser degree, many Europeans wished to wrap their occupation of Indian lands in the cloak of legitimacy. The early Dutch and English settlers carefully purchased the land rights of tribes occupying coastal areas and recorded the deeds; the Moravian settlers of Pennsylvania conscientiously paid various Indian claimants for their lands several times. However, lands that appeared to be vacant were simply occupied by European immigrants. As late as the 18th century, a prominent officeholder in Pennsylvania determined that the colony was "quite destitute of Indians" and the land was thereby open to lawful settlement and occupation.[10]

Questions surrounding the property rights of the Native Americans were fundamental to the European concept of ownership and the European way of thinking concerning the disposition of property. Most believed that land could be claimed by right of discovery, and traditions dating to before the Crusades allowed Christians everywhere to dispossess non-Christians of their property. A second theory, based in Roman Law and called *vacuum domicilium,* allowed that land not occupied and settled was forfeit to those who took up residence and improved it. Thus, ownership of the land could be established at will if it were a wilderness, or if the original inhabitants had failed to build villages or had abandoned their fields. To the European mind, a land was unoccupied if it failed to exhibit structures such as buildings, fences, roads, and other characteristic works of civilization common to the European experience. Since the Native American culture eschewed such structures and favored moving between several fertile areas for seasonal, social, and subsistence purposes, the Europeans considered much of the land they saw uninhabited or abandoned in good conscience.

Even when whites attempted to do the right thing and purchase land from the Indians in the European sense, mutual misunderstandings, mistrust, and hostility developed. The Siwanoy of present-day Westchester County, New York claimed much of the mainland coast of Long Island Sound from the Norwalk archipelago in Connecticut to the mouth of the Bronx River, but they did not actually occupy the vast shoreline. The actual residents were generally migrant bands of fisher-folk, who annually moved from the interior to either Eastchester or Pelham Bay in order to harvest the abundance of clams, oysters, fish, and other seafood that could be found in the sheltered waters, extensive mud flats, and salt marshes.

In 1640, the Dutch in New Netherlands entered into a good-faith agreement with ambassadors of the Siwanoy to purchase the entire coastline west of Norwalk to the East River. The English at Norwalk made a similar agreement, at approximately the same time, with other chieftains of the Siwanoy living to the east of the Norwalk River (the New England side) for rights to overlapping portions of the same land. No one—not the Dutch, not the English, not the Indian chiefs who had received payments for the land—thought to inform the hapless natives that actually used the valuable seashore that their rights to be there had been bartered away.

"The effect of the dislodgement of the fishing population of the waters of the New York area, was to drive these people back into the forests, where their conditions of livelihood were radically changed." The level of "privation and hardship" that resulted from the loss of this source of seafood is unknown as most Indians were equally at home along the shore and in the upland forests. Nonetheless, when John Throckmorton, Anne Hutchinson, and their band of religious refugees from New England settled on a large piece of the disputed land along what is known today as Hutchinson's Creek (or River), they were attacked and raided as trespassers, their buildings burned, and their livestock slaughtered. "The Hutchinson family was massacred by Indians, whose grievance against them was founded on the agreement made at Norwalk with natives perhaps unknown to them and for considerations of which they received no part." Such outrages brought equally dreadful retribution on innocent Indians from whites, and the entire process—entered into in the best of good faith—destroyed the confidence and friendship of all the people residing in the region.[11]

Europeans who arrived in later centuries were favored with an unanticipated stroke of good fortune as migrating tribes, driven into the interior by apprehension of the Europeans in coastal settlements, established hunting trails, cleared land, and settled villages near water transportation in the wilderness. These they again lost to white intrusion as second generation settlers invaded the forests. For instance, the Piscataway Indians of Maryland, almost completely Christianized by the Roman Catholic Jesuit fathers, sought refuge from the Protestant government of the colony with the Delawares and the Iroquois of the north. Here they lost all distinction as a unique people. When white settlers pushed into these areas in the 18th century, they reaped the advantages of all the preparatory work done by the Piscataway in much the same way that the Pilgrims had occupied the fields of coastal New England left vacant by the disease-ridden Patuxet more than 100 years earlier.[12]

Many European explorers resorted to the expedient of claiming all the land drained by certain waterways by virtue of discovery. While they used rivers as gateways to the continent, beyond the fall line, which separated the coastal plain from the piedmont, the going was hard, and all semblance of absolute ownership became murky when the course of rivers and their watersheds were used as boundaries. In most cases, the European claimants to thousands of square miles of territory had not actually seen the land more then 20 paces beyond the banks of the nearest navigable body of water. The French, for instance, claimed all the land drained by the Ohio River and its tributaries. This region included the vast heartland of the present-day United States west of the Appalachian Mountains and east of the Mississippi River.[13]

Meanwhile, the English were content to establish their colonies on the more easily accessible Atlantic coastal plain, seemingly content to be hemmed in by the Appalachians. Nonetheless, colonial charters issued by English monarchs granted lands from the Atlantic coast inland without reference to any definitive western terminus other than the western (Pacific) ocean. Both Virginia and Pennsylvania claimed lands in the Ohio Valley under such charters. Under its royal charter, the Connecticut colony laid claim to lands in Ohio until after the American Revolution even though the colonies of New York and Pennsylvania intervened geographically. Such ad hoc methods established long-lasting competing claims for Native American lands among many colonies and served as points of dispute among Europeans of different nationalities as well as with the native population.

The first whites to breach the woodland frontiers were Dutch Boschlopers, British Longhunters, and French Coureurs de bois who followed Indian trails into the interior for their own economic purposes and who were tolerated, if not encouraged, by the natives for their own devious reasons. It is certain that the Iroquois, who stood sentinel on the threshold of the white frontier to the north, east, and south of Iroquoia, could have prevented the early seepage of white settlement had they so chosen. Indian politics seemingly played a larger part in opening many frontiers than did the pressure of white encroachment. No white settlements (with rare exceptions) were established prior to 1800 in the face of active opposition from any intact Indian nation. It may be for this reason that the first English settlements beyond the Appalachians were in the Kentucky and Ohio regions, which had been largely abandoned by the Indian nations.

The Purchase of Manhattan The exchange of 24 dollars (60 Dutch Gilders) worth of trinkets for the entire island of Manhattan is one of the most famous real estate transactions in history. The Dutch were business- and trade-oriented and never made extensive land claims in America. Peter Minuit, the Dutch governor of the tiny settlement of 32 Walloon families (Flemish Huguenots) at the southern end of Manhattan, arrived in New Amsterdam in 1624 to find the settlement in dire straits. The village was a minor outpost of the Dutch West India Company, whose main trading center was 100 miles up the Hudson River to the North at Fort Orange (Albany). Not long after his arrival, Minuit came to the realization that the future success of the colony on the island lay in attaining a tract of arable land, known as the Werpoes, near present-day City Hall Park. The company set strict rules for the purchase of land from the Indians because it did not want to alienate its potential partners in the fur trade among the natives. Minuit was constrained to follow these directives, and he set out to negotiate with the owners of the land parcel for its purchase.

The Werpoes was occupied at the time by members of the Canarsie tribe whose main strength was to be found in the western end of Long Island across the East River (Brooklyn). The Canarsies in the southern end of the Island of Manhattan shared its occupancy and presumably its ownership with the Weckquaesgeeks in the northern end with the dividing line beginning at the wide area of scrub forests, hills, and uncultivable land that includes present-day Times Square and much of Central Park. The Dutch seemingly failed to discover the extent of the native ownership situation with respect to the occupancy of the island before closing their deal.

In 1626, Minuit opened negotiations with several adult men of the nearby Canarsies for purchase of the Werpoes, but the Indians conveyed the notion that they would sell the entire Island of Manhattan to the whites and vacate their villages for an appropriate price. In this, the wily Indian leaders—a local sachem known as Meijeterma and a regional leader called Seyseys—were attempting a monumental land fraud of their own in securing for themselves alone all the goods that the whites offered for the island by cutting out their Wechquaesgeek neighbors to the north.

The Canarsie concluded the deal having received goods commensurate with what they were asked to concede, but valued by the Dutch at only 60 gilders (about $4,000 in present-day money). No detailed list of the items included in the transaction for Manhattan has survived, but, if the contract was similar to others of the same type and time, it can be concluded that it contained knives, axes, hoes, and other items made of metal; cloth, blankets, hats, or jackets; and at least some significant quantity of porcelain beads (highly valued as a replacement for Indian wampum). Of all the possessions available to the Indians from the whites, the iron implements most changed the everyday life of the natives, and caused them to immediately cast aside the stone tools that they replaced.

Immediately after concluding the transaction with Minuit, the Cansarie decamped for village sites on the opposite shore across the East River near their own relatives in Brooklyn. The only surviving contemporary account of the purchase transaction is a single sentence from a letter written at the time. "Our people...have bought the island of Manhattan from the Wild men for the value of sixty guilders."[14]

Relying upon the validity and scope of this agreement, the Dutch began to spread out toward the upper end of the island to inspect their new holdings. Here they found "the wide marshes of Harlem, the wooded ridges of Washington Heights, and the extensive fishing opportunities along the irregular shores of the Inwood district." The resident Wechquaesgeeks in the northern sections of the island were quite unwilling to abandon their "sheltered homes, their rich planting fields, their choice hunting grounds, and the graves of their ancestors." A second purchase from the Weckquaesgeeks was transacted. Almost forgotten and barely commemorated by a bronze plaque in Inwood park, this agreement seemingly settled only part of the dilemma between the Dutch and the actual owners of the land. As late as 1670, the Weckqauesgeeks were still laying claim to the middle of the island at Harlem even though they were confronted with a deed held by the English showing that the entire island had been bought and paid for almost a half century earlier by the Dutch.[15]

One of the problems that continued to surface with regard to land transfers between Indians and whites was that the Indians only dimly grasped the notion that Europeans could own large tracts of land that they did not occupy. Personal estates of 500, 1,000, and 10,000 acres were granted to European promoters who guaranteed to send out a certain number of settlers to improve the land. The Indians, dealing with the few hundred colonists that they saw, could not fathom such a mechanism for land ownership or the need for so few to own so much. The idea was completely foreign to their way of thinking.

The Pocumtuck Are No More

The Pocumtuck, an Algonquian-speaking people living among the great body of lesser known tribes, inhabited the westernmost parts of New England. Their place in the historical framework relies less on their significance as a discrete people than on the location of their 17th-century stronghold at Deerfield in Massachusetts. Anyone who has visited colonial Deerfield regards it as a special place, a historical place where one can imagine how the early colonial settlers of Massachusetts lived. Yet, here, before the English arrived, the Pocumtucks shared a lifestyle, language, and culture similar to that of the Mohicans, Wappingers, Abenaki, and Nipmucks that shared parts of the Connecticut River valley with them.

The size and strength of the Pocumtuck tribe defies precision, but they may have outnumbered their neighbors or may have been structured along the lines of a small confederacy of local bands. Historians disagree as to the absolutes, but the Pocumtucks seemingly numbered between 500 and 1,500 persons. One-third of these would have been warriors making them a formidable force militarily. As late as 1638, they seem to have been a healthy, strong, and generally amiable people who lived alongside their neighbors in a natural state of equilibrium.

Epidemic diseases were said to have ravaged the approximately 100,000 Amer-Indian inhabitants of New England during the first two decades of the 17th century. Contemporary reports of great mortality among the Indians to the contrary, the Pocumtucks, as a people, seem to have survived these outbreaks well enough. They provided hundreds of bushels of grain to the struggling white settlers of the lower valley throughout the 1640s and served as allies to the Narragansetts in a protracted struggle with the Mohegans some time in 1646. White contact in the Connecticut River valley did not take place until 1634. Over the next three decades, the Pocumtucks seem to have formed mutually advantageous partnerships in terms of land use and trade with the Europeans of several settlements in the lower valley.

The Pocumtuck villages lay along a wide plateau that rose in the middle of the Connecticut River valley. The site was ideal with its rich bottom lands, its peacefully flowing river with annual runs of salmon and shad, and its nearby forests filled with game. The surrounding mountains rose gently from the valley but close enough to keep out some of the snows that their neighbors received in winter and to moderate the summer heat. Corn rose head high by July and tobacco flourished in the extraordinarily fertile soil. Although others may have coveted the land, no one questioned who used it, maintained it, improved it, or owned it.

In 1664, the Pocumtucks hosted a great conference concerning Dutch and English trade that included representatives of the Mohawks and several local Algonquian tribes, including the Sokoki band of the Abenaki nation. During the conference, however, the Pocumtucks perceived that they were slighted, or openly insulted by the Mohawk diplomats. Feeling that they were powerful enough to avenge this wrong, the Pocumtuck and some warriors from among their Sokoki, attacked and murdered the entire Mohawk delegation of almost two dozen persons killing among them an important Iroquois leader named Saheda. In retaliation, the Mohawks sent a large war party to the Pocumtuck village at present-day Deerfield. As Europeans took no part in the conflict, no independent account of the ensuing conflict remains, but the result according to Indian tradition was that the Pocumtucks fell into a set-piece ambush and were utterly destroyed. The few survivors of the tribe scattered to be absorbed into other bands of Algonquian-speaking peoples, and their fertile and open lands lay abandoned and open to further English settlement.

Eleven years prior to King Philip's War (1675), which conflict is commonly cited by historians as the template for the extinction of Native

Americans by whites in New England, possibly the largest Indian force in the Connecticut Valley was no more. The agent of this change was neither contageous infection nor the unfettered greed of white expansionists, but rather the politics of submission, negoiation, alliance, and domination to be found among the Indians themselves. It can be argued that the demise and dispossession of the Pocumtucks was not typical, but the previous history and subsequent flow of intertribal affairs—particularly with respect to the policies and ambitions of the fierce and warlike Mohawks—suggests that this was not the case. "What happen to the Pocumtuck Indians was war with the Mohawks—and when the warring had ended, the Pocumtucks had been shattered forever."[16]

Within six years of the conflict between the Mohawks and the Pocumtucks, the English were farming Pocumtuck lands, and the colonial authorities had granted the settlement at Deerfield its official seal of approval. The story of how the Pocumtuck's were dispossessed of their land helps to show how the colonies expanded and how the English dealt with the Indians that they were dispossessing.

Ironically, the change in ownership at Deerfield was largely due to the religious dedication of Rev. John Elliot of Dedham more than 100 miles away near Boston. Elliot sought to bring Christianity to the Indians by engaging them more fully in a Christian way of living in a setting of villages built on the scale and pattern of the English countryside. In setting out his "praying towns," Elliot had the approval of the colonial government, but his town at Natick—1 of 14 in all—soon grew outside its grant of land to superimpose itself on land belonging to the township of Dedham. The Massachusetts General Court acknowledged the rights of the citizens of Dedham in this land dispute as early as 1650, but took no action to compensate them until 1663 when a group of surveyors were sent out to find a free, open, and desirable site to serve as fair compensation for the land occupied by the praying Indians at Natick.

Just six weeks after the Mohawks had destroyed the Pocumtucks, the selectmen arrived in the region and chose the former Indian lands for their own. Yet, they did so without unfairly dispossessing the miserable survivors of the tribe empowering Capt. John Pynchon to contact any of the Pocumtucks claiming rights to the property and buy their claims. The total cost was somewhat under £100 pounds, and the land was transferred so that the citizens of Dedham who chose to establish themselves at Deerfield might do so freely and with clear consciences. It seems in this case that the English were trying to follow the law, but the problem was that they were following English law as it pertained to Indian land ownership. The selling of land implied an acceptance of the English concepts of land ownership by the Indians that they had not confirmed. The English simply ignored the necessity of establishing this level of concensus by dictating their own sovereignty over the native population. Such arrogance could only come from a special sense of white ethnocentricity.[17]

The Pequot War

In the first years after their arrival, the English at Plymouth relied on the knowledge and help of the Indians for their survival. Among these were several tribes or sub-tribes spread along the New England coast from present-day Boston to New Haven. The Massachusetts, the Narrangsetts, the Wanpanoags, the Pequots, and the Mohegans were numbered among the major tribes. Among the leaders of the Wampanoag were Samoset, a local sachem, and Massasoit, who remained during their lives fast friends of the English. In the 1630s, however, New England experienced a vast influx of white settlers. A great Puritan migration from England began in 1630 when 700 colonists arrived. By 1640, more than 12,000 people had come to the shores of New England. Surrounded by available and generally vacant land, many Puritans began to move away from the centers of authority. They spread out along the Massachusetts coast or formed settlements along the rivers of Connecticut.[18]

In 1636, the Puritans of Massachusetts Bay launched a war against the strongest native military in the region, the Pequots. The tribe had used the preceding decades under their leader, Sassacus, to conquer their Indian neighbors and extend their influence along the coastline and into Long Island. Being on the border between the English and Dutch settlements, "Sassacus...played shifty politics with both, growing more and more arrogant and independent with everyone in sight as Pequot power increased." The excuse used by the whites for opening the war was a four-year-old murder charge against several Indians said to have killed a white trader. This reason has been described as "the flimsiest of pretexts" and "a matter of political and economic expediency." In June 1637, an English army of 200, fortified by 1,000 Narragansett and 70 Mohegan, attacked and destroyed the main Pequot town on the Mystic River and pursued the handful of survivors into the marshlands of southeastern Connecticut (at Southport) where they finished the slaughter. Thereafter, the Narragansett were left the strongest native tribe in the region. Sassacus fled to the Mohawks for sanctuary, but they found it politically expedient to kill him rather than court English enmity.[19]

In 1675, the governors of Plymouth opened a war of subjugation against the Wampanoag ruled by Metacomet, a son of Massasoit known as King Philip. The Narragansett, suffering under the growing suspicions of the English, threw in with the Wampanoag as did many other small tribes. The whites were aided in their war by 500 Mohegan under a sub-chief named Uncas, who held great enmity against Metacomet and entered the war as an English ally with great pleasure. With a white population now surpassing 50,000, the outcome of the war (King Philip's War) was unquestioned, yet, the conflict was the bloodiest in New England history. Metacomet was killed, and his hands and head were cut from his body. The head was impaled on a pike on the gateway wall of Plymouth Fort.

The survivors of alliance were scattered or hunted down and sold into slavery. Metacomet's widow, Nanuskooke, and his nine-year-old son were sent into slavery in Bermuda and never heard of again.

The Massachusetts General Court confiscated 7,000 acres of Wampanoag land as a partial repayment of the £100,000 that the war had cost. This was sold to a Boston syndicate for £1,000 and resold, in turn, to new settlers who named their town Bristol. In addition, the General Court determined to round up and sell 500 Indian slaves from among the remaining Wampanoag and Narragansett. By the 1770s, there were no more than a few dozen full-blooded Indians left in Providence Plantation, which included Bristol and Newport about 13 miles away. The two towns had entered the slave trade and would be second only to Charleston, South Carolina as a port of entry for black slaves from Africa in the 18th century.[20]

As a result of the wars against the Pequot, Wampanoag, and Narragansett almost all the land to the west of Narragansett Bay was opened to settlement as far as Iroquoia in New York with only the French-allied Abenaki of the northern woods to contest it. An alliance with the Abenaki, thereafter, became the focus of French diplomacy, and they became the scourge of British frontier settlements.

The Walking Purchase

The "Walking Purchase" negotiated between the Delaware tribe and William Penn in the 17th century encompassed all the land drained by the Delaware River from a certain point "back into the woods, as far as a man can go in a day and a half" and back to the river again. The Indians never meant the length of a day's journey inland to be a precise measurement; nor was it ever thought that the line would be paced off. Such accuracy did not figure in the Native American concept of land ownership. While the Delaware tribe meant to convey the use of a strip of land 30 miles long and a few miles deep along the river, in 1735, Penn's descendants took advantage of the lack of precision in the agreement to vastly expand the grant to the disadvantage of the native population.[21]

The Pennsylvania proprietors hired two agents, Timothy Smith and John Chapman, to clear the way for a monumental effort. A straight line path was cut through the forest prior to the measurement. Three walkers (Solomon Jennings, James Yates, and Edward Marshall) were engaged to travel this line in relays with horses and riders providing food and water. The day-and-a-half-long walk quickly turned into a 150-mile marathon that encompassed much of the Lehigh Valley. So extensive was the expansion of the original agreement, that the Delawares were left no land in the province of Pennsylvania at all. The Penn's thereby achieved one of the greatest land frauds in American history. Edward Marshall, one of the runners, thereafter lived on an island in the Delaware River near present day Marshall's Creek, PA where the Indians later took their revenge, killing his wife and son and wounding his daughter. Marshall escaped the raid without injury.[22]

Notes

1. Quoted in William Brandon, *Indians* (Boston: Houghton Mifflin Company, 1987), 166.

2. William Cronon, *Changes in the Land, Indians, Colonists, and the Ecology of New England* (New York: Hill and Wang, 1983), 69.

3. Paul A. W. Wallace, *Indians in Pennsylvania* (Harrisburg: Pennsylvania Historical and Museum Commission, 1986), 120.

4. Wallace, *Indians in Pennsylvania*, 117.

5. Wallace, *Indians in Pennsylvania*, 126.

6. Brandon, 195–196.

7. Reginald Pelham Bolton, *Indian Life of Long Ago in the City of New York* (New York; Harmony Books, 1934), 11.

8. Brandon, 167–168.

9. Colin G. Calloway, *The Western Abenakis of Vermont, 1600–1800: War, Migration, and the Survival of an Indian People* (Norman: University of Oklahoma Press, 1990), 17–19, 27.

10. Quoted in Gary B. Nash, *Red, White, and Black: The Peoples of Early America.* (Englewood Cliffs, NJ: Prentice-Hall, 1982), 98.

11. Bolton, 12–13.

12. Nash, 99.

13. Francis Jennings, *The Ambiguous Iroquois Empire, The Covenant Chain Confederation of Indian Tribes with English Colonies from its Beginnings to the Lancaster Treaty of 1744* (New York: W. W. Norton and Company, 1984), 27.

14. Bolton, 128.

15. Bolton, 128–129.

16. Richard I. Melvoin, *New England Outpost, War and Society in Colonial Deerfield* (New York: W. W. Norton & Company, 1989), 39.

17. Melvoin, 54–55.

18. Much of the native population of coastal New England had succumbed to disease brought from Europe by fisherman and traders leaving cleared field and untended orchards behind for the English to occupy.

19. Brandon, 172.

20. Robert Carse, *Ports of Call* (New York: Charles Scribner's Sons, 1967), 132.

21. Paul A. W. Wallace, *Conrad Weiser, Friend of Colonist and Mohawk: 1696–1760* (Lewisburg, PA: Wennawoods Publishing, 1996), 97.

22. Wallace, *Conrad Weiser*, 97–99.

13

The Indian Alliances

I shall be forced to take measures which will insure to our Canadiens and Indians treatment such as their zeal and services merit.
—Pierre de Vaudreuil, Governor of New France

New France

The history of Canada during the French Regime can be broken down into distinct phases. The period of French exploration was dominated by Samuel de Champlain who also served as the first governor-general (1633–1636) under the Company of One Hundred Associates, composed of investors who generally remained in France. It was understood that they would have a fur trading monopoly with the Indians and the right to govern the colony as they saw fit as long as they brought 4,000 colonists to settle there within 10 years. The proffered colonists failed to materialize, however, leaving the Frenchmen in Canada greatly outnumbered by the surrounding Indian nations. A determined attack would have certainly wiped out the French foothold in the northland.

The Company of One Hundred Associates was also required to support and defend the Catholic clergy and to establish missions to the Indians. This it did begrudgingly and not without a great deal of friction between the company officials and the ecclesiastics. The intertribal warfare that resulted in the dispersal of the Hurons and their allies from 1649 to 1653 changed the nature of the relationship between the French and their native allies, and the advantages of the fur trade in general tilted toward the whites. In 1663, the French colony came under royal control with a governor appointed by the Crown and supported by provincial troops supplied through the Ministry of Marine. Thereafter, the fur trade with the Indians was opened to any settler who wished to pursue it. This circumstance led many Canadiens to flee to the forests to live, trade, and marry among the Indians as coureurs de bois.

The fur traders were the first line of contact between the French regime and the Indians, but they were not considered colonists in the normal sense of the term. There were several categories of fur traders who worked under licenses from the company. The *marchand-voyageur,* or traveling merchant, was a licensed trader who did the actual buying and negotiating with the native trappers. From the beginning of the fur trade monopoly a number of woodsmen and guides were also kept on the company's payroll. These were the *engages,* who worked as paddlers, porters, and general laborers. The engages were young generally uneducated men, some in their teens, who signed a contract to remain employed in the colony for three years, but many remained in New France after their contracts ran out. Many engages bolted from their contracts to take up life in the wilderness as unlicensed fur traders. Individual settlers could find the fur trade quite lucrative, but only young and adventurous men could choose the harsh life of the frontier trader. Most tried fur trading for only a few years making one or two journeys into the interior before settling down and marrying.

The real colonists of French North America were the *habitants* (inhabitants), yet, for many decades after the founding of the colony they numbered only a few thousand. Living on farmsteads cut out of the forests along the rivers and streams of Canada, the habitants found little difficulty in making a living in the rich, virgin soil. Because of their small number and wide dispersion along the Canadian frontier, the habitants were openly terrorized by the New York Iroquois, but their small number also created less friction with the local Indians who were generally Algonquian.[1]

The influence of the French clergy among the Algonquian-speaking Indians vastly outweighed their small number, which was probably fewer than 100. Composed almost entirely of Jesuit priests before 1640, the French clergy tended to the spiritual wants of the colony. The Jesuit order was also specifically entrusted with the mission of converting the native population to Catholicism. The Father Superior of the Jesuits in Canada was thereby made a very influential person. The order seems to have had a genuine desire to establish firm foundations for the continued growth of the Catholic Church among the Native Americans. Nonetheless, the Jesuits seem to have attracted the enmity of many of the Iroquois, and members of their order were often detained, tortured, or killed when moving through Iroquois lands.

Onontio

The governors of New France were very important to its development of good relations with the Indians. While Acadia and Montreal each had a chief executive known as a governor, it was the Governor of Quebec who the Crown viewed as the governor-general of the entire colony. Under the One Hundred Associates there were six governors of Quebec. Samuel de Champlain (1633–1636) was the first and best known; but the second, Charles Huault de Montmagny (1636–1648), served the longest and may have been the most influential in establishing a working relationship with the Indians. It was Montmagny that the Indians first called *Onontio*, or "great mountain" in Algonquian, from the initial translation of his name *(mons magnus)* from French. Thereafter, *Onontio* became the commonly used term for "governor" used by Algonquians everywhere in the Northeast region.

The relationship formed between the governor-general of Canada and the Indians was largely modeled on the kinship structure of the native family, and references to this concept fill the written record of the period. The governor, Onontio, was the father, and the natives were his children. However, the familial model implied both subservience and obligations. In a report to his superiors, one French official noted, "You know ... that all the [Indian] nations of Canada regard the governor as their father, which in consequence, following their reasoning, he ought at all times to give them what they need to feed themselves, clothe themselves, and to hunt." At each French outpost, the commander, acting in the paternal role, saw to it that individual Indians regularly received gifts of powder, ball, and tobacco. On special occasions the governor-general distributed rations and special gifts to native leaders, such as muskets, medallions, and uniform coats. In turn, the Indians were required to behave as good and satisfied children and to obey and aid the governor when he was in distress. This often required them to go to war against the enemies of France.[2]

Frontenac

After the dissolution of the One Hundred Associates in 1663, the colony was run by a Royal Governor appointed by the king. The development of New France was particularly advanced by Louis de Buade, Comte de Frontenac et Pelluau, who served as Royal Governor twice: from 1672 to 1682 and again from 1688 to 1698. Frontenac was possibly the ablest governor of New France in the colonial era. In his first administration, Frontenac attempted to awe the Iroquois into submission by attacking their villages, and it was he who sent La Salle to explore the interior of the continent. Recalled to France in 1682, Frontenac was returned to Canada in 1688 because the Iroquois were again threatening the colonial frontiers. He again took up the task of securing New France with energy and ability. After the so-called LaChine raids of 1689, during which the Iroquois terrorized the colony, Frontenac sent three war parties composed of allied Algonquian warriors and a few Frenchmen from Montreal and Quebec to attack the British border settlements in New York and New England. This was the first time that Indians were set to war through the auspices of a European power, and it permanently changed the face of the frontier for both white and Indian families.

Under orders from Frontenac, transmitted through the Jesuits at the missions, the Abenaki and other allied Indians raided up and down the New England frontier during the period of King William's War (1688–1698). The French-inspired Indian raid against the British settlement at Schenectady in the dead of winter in 1690 was the first of its type, and it was particularly successful in creating panic among the British who general felt that the specter of Indian attack ended with the first snows of winter. The attacks on Salmon Falls in New Hampshire and Fort Loyal in Maine won many additional native tribes to the side of the French as the unfortunate white women and children who survived the trek to Quebec were ransomed by the sympathetic French governor. Thus began the first of a series of frontier wars between the French and British for control of the North American continent.

The menace of European inspired and coordinated Indian attacks on the frontier settlements would be considered a form of terrorism today. Nonetheless, the British, in their turn, embraced the idea and immediately began to negotiate with native tribes friendly to their cause to do the same. As there were fewer French settlements than British ones to attack, however, Indian raids were a far greater threat to Anglo-Americans than to Canadiens. Hundreds of miles of ever-shifting frontier settlements were not readily defensible against Indian raids, and the only effective strategy was thought to be a retaliation so brutal as to deter further incursions.

Encouraged by his initial success, Frontenac vigorously attacked the Mohawk in their own territory burning several of their major villages in 1693. These attacks on the Iroquoian homeland by native forces at the instigation of a European power changed the face of the frontier. The Mohawks, realizing that Frontenac was not a man to be taken lightly, sued for peace. Nonetheless, they were the very last of the major tribes of the Northeast woodlands to come to terms with the French in the 17th century.

Under Frontenac's administration, New France ceased to be a giant Catholic mission to the Indians, and the Indians became an extension of French imperialism. The Crown, however, always appointed two men to carry out any enterprise in the colony—one to act and the other to re-strict the action. This policy, which rears its head periodically throughout the history of New France, prevented any one person, such as Frontenac, from gaining total control of affairs or exercising absolute authority when important matters were at stake. Nonetheless, the Algonquians called Frontenac the "Great Onontio," a term of the highest respect, because he was able to overcome this systemic impediment. Francis Parkman noted,

"Frontenac…showed from the first a special facility of managing [the Indians]; for his keen, incisive spirit was exactly to their liking, and they worked for him as they would work for no man else."[3]

The Western Indian Alliance

The demands of maintaining an Algonquian alliance composed of dozens of disparate tribes continually challenged the French even as they attempted to preserve the integrity of New France. Indeed, bringing the Iroquois to the peace table again in 1701 (the Grand Settlement) had some unintended negative consequences for the government in Quebec. The fragile mosaic of Algonquian and Huron cooperation in the *pays d'en haut*, or upper country, was largely possible because the refugees of the Great Dispersal feared the Iroquois. This had caused them to cleave to the French missions for protection. Here the population densities approached 9 persons per 100 km². This was low by European standards, but the Indians considered this crowded because the average for the North American continent was only 2 persons per 100 km². With fear of the Iroquois removed, the unnatural Huron–Algonquian alliance began to break up. The Indian refugees spread out into the nearly empty lands in Ohio and western Pennsylvania. These promised better farming and more abundant game than the overpopulated Jesuit missions on the shores and islands of the Great Lakes, but the migration also removed them from the sphere of French influence and brought them closer to the English. The French immediately made plans to better secure the Ohio country.

The remnants of the Huron–Petun nations moved to Sandusky and proclaimed themselves Wyandot, and the Erie moved to western Pennsylvania to become known as the Mingo. It was during this period that the Shawnee quit the country of the Illinois entirely and moved east of the Appalachians; and the Miami, Potawatomi, and Mississauga moved closer to the St. Joseph's River region south and east of Lake Michigan. The interrelated Ottawa and Ojibwa once again became distinct groups with the Ojibwa of Chequamegon and Keweenaw emerging as an entirely separate group— the western Chippewa of western Lake Superior. Warfare between these Chippewa and the lake country Sioux on the upper Mississippi became a chronic conflict continuing for much of the 18th century (see Map 5). These changes were the products of peace, which was what everyone said they wanted. Yet, the prospect of peace generally weakened the Jesuit missions, made governance of the tribes more difficult, and brought many of the Algonquians into closer proximity to British traders arriving from over the Appalachian Mountains to the east.

In 1694, Frontenac sent a 36-year-old career army officer to command the vital post at Michilimackinac and the mission of St. Ignace. The officer, Antoine de la Mothe, Sieur de Cadillac, retained the position at Michilimackinac for three years and then returned to Quebec City a rich man having amassed a great profit by trading alcohol to the Indians for their furs. During his time in Quebec, Cadillac brought forward a well-considered plan for the establishment of a fortified post in the country of the Illinois. In 1699, Cadillac was given a royal mandate to build a fortified post called Fort Ponchartrain at Detroit on the St. Claire River. The post and settlement were meant to ensure that all the western tribes traded furs with the French rather than through the Iroquois to the British in the east.

Three years later, Cadillac closed the Jesuit mission at St. Ignace, moved the Michilimackinac garrison and clergy to Detroit, and consolidated the French presence in the Midwest. This left Detroit the major seat of French governance and trade in the lake country, and Cadillac hoped to draw the Algonquians to him so that he might serve as Onontio to the western tribes. In this he was successful, and the population density around Detroit rose to almost 12 persons per 100 km^2, six times the continental average. Unfortunately, the geographic isolation of the post also allowed it to become the scene of bitter conflicts among the native peoples as their bands were drawn to the region and population densities rose. Cadillac also failed to secure the fur trade between the western tribes and the French. His concept of trade had been geographic, while the actual flow of furs was largely influenced by the economics of price. The majority of western furs continued to pass through Iroquois middlemen to British and Dutch merchants at Albany who simply paid better than the French. In 1710, Cadillac left Detroit replaced by Joseph Guyon Dubuisson, a man of poor judgment and limited understanding of the Indian mind, who allowed the political and social issues among the Algonquians at the post to fester.

Philippe de Rigaud, Marquis de Vaudreuil, came to New France in 1687 as the commander of a detachment of marines. He had gained his military experience during 17 years of service in the King's musketeers in Europe where he rose to the rank of colonel. Vaudreuil was one of the first to react to the Iroquois attack on LaChine in 1689, and he prepared a brilliant defense of Montreal against further attacks by the Indians. He helped Frontenac defend Quebec during the British siege of the city in 1690, and he was made governor of Montreal when Louis Hector de Callieres was promoted Governor-General of Canada.

Vaudreuil succeeded Callieres as governor-general in 1703. His prudence and experience well suited him for the position during the trying years of Queen Anne's War (1702–1713). Vaudreuil was respected and feared by the Indians, and he constantly strove to strengthen the French alliance with them. During his administration, Fort Niagara, one of the most significant outposts and trading centers in the region, was built near the western end of Lake Ontario. A humane man, he was instrumental in ransoming hundreds of white captives from the natives during the war years even adopting one of them into his family to relieve her suffering.

During Vaudreuil's administration, quarrels among the Indians at Detroit broke into active intertribal warfare. Initially, the tensions were limited to troubles between the Ottawa and the Wyandots (former Huron-Petuns). However, in 1712, a major conflict among Algonquian peoples broke out as virtually all the natives from Peoria to Michilimackinac agreed to combine against the Fox and their allies, the Mascouten and the Kickapoo, who were living in the region surrounding Detroit. Based on their residence there before the Iroquois wars, the Fox claimed that they were the rightful masters of the region surrounding the post. Having more than 1,000 warriors, the Fox and their allies attempted to assert their claim by force, and soon rival hunters were murdering one another in the forests.

This brought the weight of internecine Algonquian warfare to focus on Detroit where the French had a poorly defended garrison of only 30 men. Dubuisson mistakenly identified the resulting crisis as a British–Fox plot to destroy his post, and he refused to protect the Fox or their allies when their enemies massed to attack them. When the carnage was over, more than 1,000 Fox, Mascouten, and Kickapoo (men, women, and children) were dead or taken prisoner. Many of the survivors were cruelly tortured. In fact, the Peoria tortured to death all the Fox warriors that they captured as a matter of course. In Peoria villages, the Jesuits reported that the charred and rotting bodies were left hanging from the X-shaped scaffolds where they had died. The remaining Fox allies either sought refuge among the Iroquois or continued sporadic revenge attacks on their enemies throughout the lake region. These now included any Frenchman unfortunate enough to come into contact with them.[4]

It seems unlikely that Vaudreuil believed that the disaster represented by the fate of the Fox was actually a product of British planning, but he did not hesitate to lay the blame at their door. For their part, the British were quite willing to use the disarray among France's Indian allies to renew their attempts to lure them away from the French sphere of influence. Vaudreuil used the Fox crisis as evidence that French presence in the west needed to be renewed and that the old Algonquian alliance needed to be reestablished. Gradually, all the old trading posts and missions closed or abandoned by Cadillac were restored. Michilimackinac, Green Bay, Chequamegon, Ouiatenon, Pimitoui, St. Ignace, and Saint Joseph were all reconstituted, a French officer was stationed among the Miami, and two additional missions were opened among the Illinois. This allowed the Indians easier access to French mediation, but it did nothing to rectify the blood debt of hundreds of Indian lives that lay between the Fox and Algonquian alliances.

Although Vaudreuil asserted that the foundation of his policy was to avoid French involvement in intertribal wars, the first stages of French mediation were obviously preparations for conflict in the Ohio country. Fort Chartres was constructed and garrisoned near the mouth of the Kaskaskia River, and Fort Vincennes was later built on the lower Wabash River. Oddly, it was the French governor of Louisiana who initiated these undertakings because he distrusted the ability of the government in Canada, which was thought to be too far removed from the scene of the crisis to be effective. Moreover, there were extensive kinship links between the native residents of Kaskaskia, particularly the Christianized Illinois, and the French voyageurs, soldiers, and habitants whose settlements adjoined one another in the midsection of the crisis area. Vaudreuil died in 1725, and his successor, Governor Charles de Beauharnois, abandoned any pretense at mediation among the tribes by launching a punitive Franco-Indian expedition against the Fox and their allies in 1728.[5]

Onontio, the Avenger

From 1715 to 1739 the French and British were ostensibly at peace, yet virtually all the upper country nations enlisted on the side of the French against the Fox in 1728. Yet, the decade-long attempt to force the Fox and their associates (which now included the Sauk) to submit only fed the unrest and drove them toward the British. When French policy evolved into a campaign of genocide in the eyes of their Indian allies, the united Algonquian front against the much-diminished Fox nation collapsed. The Indians believed that strong chiefs made distinctions between allies and enemies, but that weak chiefs viewed all outsiders as potential enemies. It was apparent to the native way of thinking that the French Onontio had pressed the war against the Fox only from the fear of being exposed as a weak chief. "The Fox wars were a cautionary lesson; they showed what happened when chiefs failed and when Onontio used violence against his own children."[6]

The French attempt to maintain a posture of force, when so many of the tribes in their alliance had decided against it, weakened their hold on the Indians during the 1730s. "Faced with Onontio the avenger, the Algonquians demanded the return of Onontio the mediator." Ottawa, Potawatomi, Menominee, and Winnebago all asked that the French grant the Fox peace, which the French finally did with great reluctance and with little grace. The French also lost status when their soldiers twice failed to intimidate the Natchez and the Chickasaw of Louisiana, who had destroyed a French settlement and made a pact with British traders. Moreover, the French made an unnecessarily strong show of force against the Weas, a tiny tribe living near the trading post at Ouiatenon, but it was clear to the Indian observers present that they were unable to make their threats effective.[7]

Rumors spread among several Indian groups that they would soon become the next victims of the French attempt at hegemony. "The French now seemed a greater danger than the Fox," and the Indians grew increasingly fearful of an increasingly militant France. This seemed especially true because the French, after more than two decades of virtual peace with the British, opened a new war (King George's War, approx. 1740–1748) with the British and began trolling once again for native allies to back them up. Yet, many Midwestern tribes had established fairly good relationships with the British at Albany or at Oswego during the interim. The Ottawa, Wyandots, and Ojibwa regularly traded with the British, and the Miami and the Weas had recently diverted nearly all of their furs to British traders who had appeared on the Ohio River. It was no longer in their interest to court only the favor of the French.[8]

Ironically, the French were at their strongest in terms of their influence on the Indians when they appeared to themselves to be at their weakest. This paradox was largely rooted in the Algonquian concept of patriarchy. When the French freely gave gifts and mediated quarrels, they acted as a father; but when they participated in the quarrels of their children, on one side or the other, according to Indian logic they lost their patriarchal status.[9]

Although Frenchmen and Indians fought side-by-side in the metaphorical sense, the Indians considered their war a twin set of parallel conflicts—one against the British, which they fought at the behest of the French, and the other against the Iroquois, which they fought to avenge very old wrongs. Moreover, many Indians believed that both the French and the British desired their lands. If the Indians could use the aid of the French to defeat and drive away the British (who they viewed as the weaker of the two), then they could deal with the French afterward as they pleased. While they fought for the French, they often did so in a lack-luster and ineffectual manner hoping all the time that the white men would eradicate each other in a face-to-face conflict. To this extent, the French diplomacy and expenditure on behalf of the Algonquian alliance had failed to firmly underpin Indian loyalty.

British Governance

The French claimed a great swath of the North American heartland as their own. Yet, they commanded the region from only two substantial colonial centers—one in Canada and one in Louisiana. British colonial governors attempted to replicate the relationship the French had with the Algonquian nations, but few were successful. The fault may reside in the fact that there were so many British governors, each pursuing policies for his individual colony that were sometimes at cross-purposes with his neighbors. This created for the Indian nations a complicated world requiring precarious diplomacy, careful management, and constant compromise with a great number of British "chiefs" who spoke with many voices, unlike the all-powerful and single-minded Onontio in Quebec. The success of William Johnson in bringing the Iroquois into an alliance with the British may reside in his insistence that only he speak as the agent of the government to the Indians—a point he argued vociferously on more than one occasion.

The French and Indian War in America, (1754–1763) began with a skirmish in the Ohio country—actually western Pennsylvania—between French colonial troops and Virginia provincial troops commanded by a young militia officer named George Washington. This war, named largely for the widespread participation of the native nations of the Northeast woodlands on the side of France, was the pivotal conflict in deciding the political fate of North America.

During much of the 17th and 18th centuries, the British had shown little interest in the trans-Appalachian west. The three periods of Anglo-French conflict between 1690 and 1750 had focused on Arcadia, Cape Breton Island, the coast of Maine, and the West Indies. Although the British colonials had seldom acted in concert during these previous crises, in the 1750s, the British colonial governors began to hold a series of conferences in New York, Pennsylvania, and Virginia to which they invited representatives of all the major tribes. During these meetings many presents were given and many promises were made. The British Crown also determined to establish Indian agents to deal with the Indians. Among these were George Croghan, James Adair, and William Johnson—possibly the most influential Anglo-colonial in all of North America with regard to the participation of Native Americans in the war. Moreover, these men peaked in terms of their influence over the tribes just as French influence was on the wane.

English traders had crossed the mountains and opened a trading post at Pickawillany on the Miami River. The post quickly took on the look of a fort, and more than a dozen traders worked there. They attracted more than 4,000 Indians per year, a volume of trade that dwarfed that at Detroit. In 1751, John Fraser opened a post at the confluence of French Creek and the Allegheny River in western Pennsylvania. The list of quality goods at low prices that these men brought over the mountain by pack horse was extraordinary. Pierre Pinchot, contemporary observer among the French noted:

The [English] goods for the Indian trade, are guns for hunting; lead, balls, powder; steel for striking fire; gun-flints, gun-screws; knives; hatchets, beads, men's shirts; cloths of blue and red for blankets and petticoats; vermilion and verdigris; red, yellow, green, and blue ribbons of English weaving; needles, thread, awls, blue, white, red, rateen for making moccasins; woolen blankets, of three points and a half, three, two, and one and a half of Leon cloth; mirrors framed in wood; hats trimmed fine, and in imitation, with variegated plumes in red, yellow, blue, and green; hoods for men and children of fringed rateen, galloons, real and imitation; brandy; tobacco; razors for the head; glass beads made after the fashion of wampum; black wines; paints, &c.[10]

The French viewed these developments with disquietude, and thereafter saw the British colonials as a united and devious foe bent on establishing themselves in the rich Ohio country where they could seduce the native tribes with a tidal wave of quality English goods at low prices. They immediately set out to drive British traders from these frontier regions, even ordering the murder of a Miami chief, Old Britain, who was thought to be leaning toward the British. The Indian leader was killed and eaten by his assassins.

More importantly, the French launched a program of fort building in the Ohio country. Governor Robert Dinwiddie of Virginia was very concerned when he learned that the French were building forts on the Allegheny River and Lake Erie, and he sent Major George Washington with a strongly worded message of protest to the French commander in the region.

The overland journey of Washington to the French post at Fort le Boeuf was more than 500 miles, and it was very difficult. Here Washington presented Dinwiddie's message to the commandant who promised to forward it to his superiors for their consideration. This brief exchange was followed by the arduous return of Washington to Williamsburg. The story of Washington's journey, published as quickly as the ink could dry, made him an overnight sensation in the colony. It was not surprising, therefore, that Dinwiddie placed Washington in charge of expelling the French from the Ohio country later that year. Dinwiddie gave Washington a regiment of 400 Virginians and attached them to two independent companies of regular troops and a few allied Indians to serve as guides and scouts. These set off to a wilderness rendezvous with a British detachment under Captain Trent who were already building a fort about 100 miles south of the point chosen by the French for their new post at the Forks of the Ohio. The British post was by no means complete.[11]

Meanwhile, the French governor sent his own aide, Captain Pierre de Contrecouer, with a force of 1,100 men to reinforce the western forts and to build a new post at present-day Pittsburgh to be called Fort Duquesne. Contrecouer, advised by friendly Indians that most of Washington's force was camped in the Great Meadows east of the Monongahela, forced Trent to retreat from his position. The French commander then chose Ensign Coulon de Jumonville de Villiers to lead a small group of soldiers to meet Washington en route and require him to leave the dominions of France. If he refused, Contrecouer promised to bring his entire force down upon them. That these two young men, de Jumonville and Washington, would meet in the wilderness of North America was fated to set almost all the kingdoms of Europe to war.

The night of May 27, 1754 was a rainy one, and de Jumonville and his small detachment had taken the opportunity offered by an overhanging cliff to spend the night out of the rain. Meanwhile, Washington, with a small group of soldiers and friendly Seneca Indians under the chief Monakaduto, had gone forward from the Great Meadows to attempt an observation of Contrecouer's camp at the forks. They accidentally found de Jumonville's camp. Washington placed his men around the campsite in a semicircle, and caught the French party totally unawares against the cliffside. A brief

fight ensued during which the French party suffered 8 dead and 21 captured. Two Frenchman escaped in the dark. At this point, Monakaduto
grabbed de Jumonville, who had surrendered, and murdered him with a
single blow of his hatchet to his skull. The British soldiers quietly watched
as the Seneca scalped the dead. Washington then retreated to the Great
Meadows and immediately began fortifying the camp. A rough stockade
was erected to house the sick and wounded, and the resulting structure
was named Fort Necessity.

Contrecouer, having learned of the murder of de Jumonville, immediately sent word to the young man's brother, Captain Coulon de Villiers,
to assemble a force of 1,400 French troops and Indian allies to attack
Washington's poorly constructed fort. On July 4, the French attacked. The
British were forced to keep under cover as the French and Indians peppered
their positions with musket shot and arrows from two nearby hills. By
nightfall, 30 of Washington's men were dead, and 70 were wounded. With
one quarter of his force as casualties and the situation becoming worse by
the moment, Washington chose to accept an offer to surrender.

The terms were very generous. Washington could retire with drums
beating and flags flying, but he was required to sign a statement to the
effect that he had "killed" de Jumonville. Jacob van Braam, Washington's
Dutch interpreter, translated the articles of surrender, which were in
French, for Washington. The section assigning responsibility for the death
of de Jumonville actually read—l'assassinat du Sieur de Jumonville—an as-
sassin. This was clearly untrue, and there is no evidence that Washington
had personally killed anyone.

The French used the time between the surrender of Washington and
the declaration of war in Europe to fill Quebec with reinforcements and
marshal their Indian allies. The French forts in the Ohio country and Fort
Duquesne were completed and garrisoned. Finally, a new and highly ex-
perienced officer was given command of all the French forces in America.
This was the Baron Ludwig August Dieskau, a professional soldier of
German birth who had learned his trade in the wars on the continent of
Europe. It was he that Montcalm would come to replace.

The British plan for the conflict in North America would require the
cooperation of the provincials and the Crown to a degree never before
experienced, but the regulars viewed the colonial volunteers as undisciplined, untrained, or worse. Two regiments of British regulars from
Ireland were transferred to Virginia. They were meant to ensure discipline
and order among the militia. Finally, Major General Edward Braddock
was made commander of all military affairs in North America so that the
colonials might come to learn how a war should be fought.[12]

Governor William Shirley of Massachusetts was made second-in-
command of all British forces. Although Shirley immediately began the
recruitment of forces, virtually no one in British North America was
prepared for the coming war. New France with its centralized authority,

well-trained and well-organized army, and a small but undivided peasantry had gained the allegiance of the majority of the Indian tribes.[13] As one of his first official acts, Shirley made a proclamation offering bounties of £20 to £50 for the capture or the scalps of the Indians allied to the French. "I do hereby require His Majesty's subjects...to embrace all opportunities of pursuing, capturing, killing, and destroying all and any of the aforesaid Indians."[14]

Braddock arrived in February 1755. By April, he had called upon several colonial governors to meet at Alexandria, Virginia to develop a strategy for the forthcoming campaign. Also in attendance was William Johnson, who had been given complete control of British Indian policy as Superintendent of Indian Affairs by King George II. The Alexandria meeting was historic.[15] The first proposal was for an expedition to secure the forks of the Ohio River and destroy Fort Duquesne. This operation was to be under the command of Braddock. The second was for the removal of all the French in Nova Scotia and the reduction of Fort Beausejour. This was the responsibility of the royal governor of Nova Scotia, Charles Lawrence, who would be aided by 2,000 colonial volunteers from Massachusetts. Shirley would lead an expedition to reinforce Fort Oswego before undertaking the reduction of the French post at Niagara. Finally, a colonial force was placed under the command of William Johnson who, with his Mohawks, was to attack the French post at Crown Point at the southern end of Lake Champlain; he was given the rank of major-general of provincial forces.[16]

Braddock set off into the wilderness building a road for his army ahead of him. The physical achievement of clearing this road exceeded any other road building project undertaken in North America to that time. Braddock's route ran from the Potomac River in Maryland along Nemacolin's Path, a route blazed by Christopher Gist and Thomas Cresap and authorized by the Ohio Company of Virginia in 1752. These frontiersmen had been assisted by a Delaware guide for whom the path was named. Finally, Braddock's route gradually wound passed the Great Meadow where Washington, now an aide to Braddock, had built Fort Necessity.[17]

The main strength of Braddock's command of 2,500 was the corps of regulars of the 44th and 48th of Foot commanded by Peter Halkett and Thomas Dunbar, respectively. These were filled out with companies of Virginia recruits. The rest of the force was made up of three companies of Virginia and Maryland rangers, two New York companies, a South Carolina militia unit, and teamsters and wagoneers for the baggage train. There were 86 officers, a mounted troop of 30 Virginia dragoons, and a small group of allied Indians.

Braddock's contempt for wilderness warfare can be seen in his attitude toward Britain's Indian allies. "These savages may, indeed, be a formidable enemy to your raw American militia but upon the King's regular and disciplined troops, sir, it is impossible they should make any impression."[18] Braddock dismissed all but 10 of his Indian scouts, relying instead on the ability of the colonial rangers to protect his column from surprise attack. Evidence suggests that he was almost as contemptuous of his ranger companies as he was of the Indians.[19]

Braddock's subsequent defeat at the Monongahela River was the most significant event in British colonial history to that time. One explanation for the defeat was based in the fact that 63 of the 86 officers involved in the action were casualties. Another explanation rests on the poor performance of the British regulars who were said to have panicked in fear of the French Indians and become hopelessly entangled with their fellows in the woods.[20] It seems from all accounts that a party of only 200 to 300 French and Indians led by Captain Hyacinth de Beaujeu was bent on combat despite its numerical inferiority with the enemy.[21]

It is certain that the French victory was largely attributable to the Indians. Captain Robert Orme, Braddock's aide, reported, "No sooner were the pickets upon their respective flanks...but we heard an excessive quick and heavy firing in the front."[22] A French observer reported, "The Indians...rushed upon them with their tomahawks, as did the French also when they disbanded, and a great massacre followed."[23] William Dunbar, a British Regular officer continued, "[W]e were alarmed by the Indian hollow [war cry] and in an instant found ourselves attacked on all sides...Our men [the regulars] unaccustomed to that way of fighting, were quite confounded and...were seized with the same panic and went into much disorder, some part of them being 20 deep."[24] Another British officer noted, "The men from what stories they had heard of the Indians in regard to their scalping...were so panic struck that their officers had little or no command over them."[25]

Washington was busy during the battle, but he later noted, "Many attempts were made to dislodge the enemy from an eminence on the right but they all proved ineffectual and fatal to the officers who by great exertions and good examples endeavored to accomplish it. In one of these the General received the wound of which he died...[I] placed the General in a small cart...and in the best order [I] could...brought him over the first ford of the Monongahela."[26] Washington continued. "At an encampment near the Great Meadows the brave, but unfortunate General Braddock breathed his last. He was interred with the honors of war, and...his remains, to guard against a savage triumph, if the place should be discovered, they were deposited in the road over which the army, wagons, etc. passed to hide every trace by which the entombment could be discovered. Thus died a man whose good and bad qualities were intimately blended."[27]

The defeat of General Braddock shocked the British public, which expected an immediate Indian uprising along the entire length of the frontier in its wake. "A whole army...routed and several hundred cut off by inhuman brutes perhaps scare a tenth of their number," wrote one editor. Another newspaper printed, "In consequence of this shameful defeat the frontiers of several southwestern provinces lay exposed to the enemy…[W]e have the highest reason to fear the worst."[28] General James Innes noted upon learning of Braddock's defeat, "Please God, I intend to make a stand here. It's highly necessary to raise the militia everywhere to defend the frontiers."[29]

The year 1755 was a bad one for the colonies. Besides Braddock's staggering defeat, William Shirley had delayed his advance on the French fort at Niagara, and the first signs of bad weather caused Shirley to cancel the operation. Shirley's failure to attempt the reduction of Fort Niagara damaged his otherwise good reputation.[30] Meanwhile, the provincials under Governor Lawrence had captured Fort Beausejour and were well forward in securing Nova Scotia. The defeat of the regulars at the Monogahela coupled with a provincial success in Nova Scotia left the redcoats with an extreme sense of frustration. One last operation of the four planned in Alexandria had yet to play out. It would provide a significant counterpoint to Braddock's defeat and reverse the tide of Franco-Indian relations.

The Crown Point Expedition

William Johnson opened a trading post in the Mohawk Valley in 1738 after emigrating from Ireland to manage the lands of his uncle. In less than two decades, he had become one of the most important men on the continent because he was beloved by the Iroquois. The Mohawk, in particular, trusted him and called him Warraghiyagey—He-Who-Does-Much. He had treated the natives fairly, learned their language, joined their war parties, taken one of their women as a wife, and fathered a number of Indian children. Johnson built a great stone house near present-day Johnstown, New York, which he called Johnson Hall. Here he entertained hundreds of Indians at a time, mostly at his own expense. No single person in North America had as much influence with the Iroquois.

At the Alexandria conference, Johnson had been assigned the campaign against Crown Point. The British received information that Crown Point was defended by only 800 Frenchmen and whatever Indians they could muster. The same spy brought word that the fort was in very good repair and defended by cannon. However, the French had word of Johnson's coming through the papers captured at the Monongahela, and would confront Johnson with 3,000 troops under the French commander-in-chief, Baron Dieskau.

In August 1755, Johnson disembarked his troops at the Great Carrying Place near the falls of the Hudson River. His entire Anglo-Indian force numbered about 2,900 men, but reinforcements were expected to follow. With him, Johnson had Captain William Eyre of the regular British artillery and 10 field pieces and the regulars to man them. Braddock had insisted that Eyre be attached to Johnson's command as he "did not choose to send an officer [Johnson] who had not seen service" alone into the wilderness in charge of an army. Such sentiments sounded hollow as part of Johnson's force was composed of a large contingent of several hundred Mohawk under the command of Tiyanoga, known as King Hendrick. It is noteworthy that the Iroquois, unlike their Huron cousins who quickly allied to their Algonquian neighbors, rarely fought a war with help from outside their own Five Nations confederacy.[31]

Leaving a skeleton force at the Carrying Place to build Fort Edward, Johnson moved to the southern shore of Lake St. Sacrament. He immediately renamed that body of water Lake George, for the British king. Of the Lake George site, Johnson wrote, "I found it a near wilderness, not one foot cleared. I have made a good wagon road to it from Albany, distance about 70 miles; never was house or fort erected here before. We have cleared land enough to encamp 5000 men. The troops now under my command and the reinforcements on the way will amount near that number."[32] A temporary camp was created on the lakeshore from brushwood and logs stacked among the stumps of the new-cut forest. The artillery pieces were emplaced to defend the breastwork and one field piece was very well situated on a small eminence on the flank. Johnson designated his partially completed post Fort William Henry after one of the king's grandsons.

Dieskau knew of Johnson's occupation of the Lake George shoreline and of the lightly held camp at Fort Edward. After ordering the initial construction of a fort at the strategic position known to the Indians as Ticonderoga, he quietly moved the French army up Lake George to within striking distance of Johnson's camp. Learning of the French approach on the morning of September 8, 1755, Johnson sent a large party of militia and friendly Mohawks back along the wagon road toward Fort Edward as a precaution. This detachment became known as the "Early Morning Scout." Johnson's own account of the battle of Lake George in the form of a dispatch was reported in the colonial newspapers less than a week later.

[I]n order to catch the enemy in their retreat from their camp...1,000 men were detached under the command of Col. [Ephraim] Williams...with upwards of 200 Indians...About an hour and a half afterwards we heard a heavy firing, and...I judged our people were retreating...About half an hour after 11 the enemy appeared in sight...made a small halt about 150 yards from our breastwork, when the regular troops (whom we judged to be such by their bright and fixed bayonets) made the grand and center attack. The Canadiens and the [French] Indians squatted and dispensed on our flank. The enemy's fire we received first from the regulars in platoons, but it did no great execution, being at too great a distance, and our men defended by the breastwork. Our artillery then began to play upon them, [and] the engagement now became general on both sides. The French regulars kept their ground and order for some time with great resolution, but the warm and constant fire from our artillery and troops put them into disorder...This was about 4 o'clock, when our men and Indians jumped over the breastwork, pursued the enemy, slaughtered numbers and took several prisoners, amongst whom was Baron de Dieskau...badly wounded in the leg and through both hips, and the surgeon fears for his life.

Dieskau died of his wounds in a few days.[33]

In the morning engagement the colonials had suffered their greatest losses of the battle. These included Colonel Williams, seven officers, and the Iroquois sachem, Tiyanoga. During the battle, Johnson received a wound in the thigh that was "very painful; the ball lodged and can not be got out." Nonetheless, one week later he was still planning to move against Crown Point. However, the expedition was fated to stall on the shores of Lake George.[34]

Several factors caused the Crown Point objective to be abandoned. Johnson's own wound was one. The death of many Indians, especially King Hendrick, caused the Mohawk to return home to mourn their dead, as was their custom. Finally, the colonial governments seemed satisfied to end the campaign with a victory over the main French force in hand rather than risk another engagement. Governor (Admiral) Sir Charles Hardy of New York wrote to the Board of Trade in January 1756, emphasizing the importance of Johnson's victory.

The advantages...are very considerable. Fort Edward stands at the Great Carrying Place on Hudson's River near 50 miles above Albany, and is the common passage from Canada to Albany, whether they come by Lake George, the South Bay [of Lake Champlain], or Wood Creek. Fort William Henry secures the pass[age] by Lake George to Hudson's River, Schenectady, and the Mohawk's country...By Fort William Henry...we shall be masters of the waters that lead to Crown Point and may facilitate any enterprise on that place or further up Lake Champlain should such be thought advisable.[35]

William Johnson's stature had never been higher. A Bostonian wrote, "This is the first time Mr. Johnson or any of his men ever fought an enemy...so that the...militia of New England have all the glory of the most obstinate and long engagement."[36] A Boston newspaper reported that the respect shown to Johnson "was equal to what might have been paid to a Marlborough on his return with victory from Flanders." His Royal Majesty, George II, made Johnson a baronet for life. He was thereafter Sir William Johnson.[37]

The New York Gazette reported of Sir William's arrival from Albany on January 5, 1756. "About six miles out of town, he was met by a considerable number of gentlemen on horseback, who conducted him to the King's Arms Tavern, where most of the principle inhabitants were assembled to congratulate him on his safe arrival. The ships in the harbor saluted him as he passed the streets, amidst the acclamation of the people. At night the city was beautifully illuminated."[38]

Meanwhile an unaccustomed quiet settled over the frontier. Both the British and the French had lost their principle military leaders, leaving their military organizations under the direction of seconds-in-command. More importantly for the frontier communities, the Indian nations began to vacillate in their traditional loyalties. Many hung back not knowing which way to jump. The initial reaction to Braddock's defeat was to attract many of the Indian nations that had formerly been neutral to the French, but Dieskau's defeat at the hands of the colonials and the Mohawk had made even the tribes closely allied to the French apprehensive.

The Mohawks were encouraged by the faith they had placed in their brother, Warraghiyagey. They chose to remain staunchly bound to the British. However, a delegation from the other four Iroquois nations went to Quebec during 1756 to reaffirm their friendship with the French. For most of the Iroquois, this was just good politics, but for the Seneca it was more. The fortified trading post built by the French at Niagara had attracted their trade, and even Johnson became unsure of their loyalty.[39] Shirley's failure to invest the place had left the Seneca unsure of British resolve. Sir Charles Hardy considered the reduction of Fort Niagara of the utmost consequence claiming that the loss of Niagara would "soon oblige the French to abandon their encroachments [in the Ohio country] as it will be scare possible for them to support those forts with garrisons or supply them with provisions."[40]

There were numerous calls for Johnson to supplant Shirley as commander of colonial forces, and the two men embarked upon a personal confrontation through the fall and winter of 1755–1756 over Sir William's authority as Indian agent. Johnson noted "the imperious style he [Shirley] writes to me since General Braddock's death...his threatening intimidations and his temper."[41] Johnson immediately requested that the Board of Trade clearly delineate his position. "Governor Shirley's interfering in the authoritative and ill-judged manner he has done, was injurious to the true system of Indian affairs, a violation of my commission and an arbitrary insult upon my character."[42]

Johnson ultimately received the support of the Board of Trade, which issued him a new royal warrant and a commission as colonel, agent, and sole superintendent of the affairs of the Six Nations and the northern Indians. Edward Atkins was made sole superintendent of the southeastern tribes. These events seem to have ended the influence with the Board formerly enjoyed by Shirley, but they failed to deter the interference of other British agents such as George Croghan—a Scots-Irish trader from the Ohio—and Andrew Montour—a Metis of Iroquois and French heritage who worked for the colonies of Pennsylvania and Virginia as his own interests dictated.[43]

Shirley's reputation was further damaged when word came in 1757 that the French and Indians had burned the British fort at Oswego. The post, which was actually two positions under the command of Colonel Hugh Mercer, was on Lake Ontario at the mouth of the Oswego River. The garrison of 1,600 men was composed largely of regular troops, but about a third were colonials. Oswego was important because it largely neutralized the French presence on the lake at both Fort Niagara and Fort

Frontenac. The French victory at Oswego "wrought marvels among the Indians, inspired the faithful, confirmed the wavering, and daunted the ill-disposed. The whole west was astir, ready to pour itself again in blood and fire against the English border."[44]

When Lord John Campbell, Earl of Loudoun, arrived in America in the summer of 1756 to replace Braddock as military commander, he blamed the loss of Oswego on Shirley's inaction and suggested the governor's recall to England. Thereafter, he dismissed all of Shirley's former plans and replaced them with his own schemes, which were directed once again at the Canadian Maritimes, specifically Fortress Louisbourg. Along with Loudoun came an influx of British officers into the colonies. Among these were several officers who would figure preeminently in the final stages of the war: Major-General James Abercromby, General Jeffrey Amherst, Brigadier General Lord Augustus Howe, and Major-General James Wolfe.

Montcalm

Louis Joseph, Marquis de Montcalm-Gozon de Saint-Veran, was a veteran soldier who had been under fire in Europe since he was 15 years old. In autumn 1755, Montcalm was made a major-general and given several battalions of regulars to bring with him to Canada where he was to prosecute the Seven Years War (French and Indian War) in the North American theater. Although Montcalm reported directly to the Minister of War, he would have to work closely with the French governor of Canada, Pierre Francois Rigaud, Marquis de Vaudreuil. Canadien by birth, Pierre was the son of Philippe de Vaudreuil, the former governor during Queen Anne's War (1701–1714). Pierre was the governor of New France during the entire period of the French and Indian War. Despite recent defeats in New York and Nova Scotia, he found it difficult to see why a general officer from France was now needed. For his part, Montcalm may initially have yielded to the governor's experience and knowledge of Canada and the Indians when formulating a strategy for the remainder of the war. In the subsequent series of engagements with the British, the Algonquian alliance became increasingly disenchanted with both Montcalm and the French governor. Although the French won as many battles as the British, they also suffered many disasters that proved decisive in breaking the Franco-Indian alliance.[45]

The governor had heretofore been considered the commander of the militia and the provincial companies. Previously, these and the allied Algonquian Indians were the only forces used to defend the colony, and they had done so effectively. Nonetheless, Vaudreuil wrote to the Minister of Marine in 1756, "I shall always maintain the most perfect union and understanding with M. le Marquis de Montcalm, but I shall be forced to take measures which will insure to our Canadiens and Indians treatment such as their zeal and services merit." Subsequent events were to make Pierre de Vaudreuil the last governor of New France.[46]

Montcalm liked the militia no better than he did the Indians. Yet, he understood the need to incorporate both the Canadiens and the Indian allies into his forces if he was to ensure the survival of New France. For their part, the Indians considered the French more formidable as forest fighters than the British, but the presence of French regulars with their continental ways did not encourage them. The Indians laughed at the useless parade ground maneuvers of which European commanders were so proud.

Unfortunately for French strategy, the heart of the Franco-Indian alliance was in the Great Lakes and the Illinois country, but the tactical focus of the war was to be on the Champlain–Richelieu channel though eastern New York (see Maps 4 and 5). The always faithful French-allied Abenaki on the New England border had been dealt a severe and unsettling chastisement by Rogers' Rangers at the mission of St. Francis early in the conflict. These had been the bulwark of French-Indian power in the east, and they were now hanging aloof licking their wounds. Many western tribes—the Ottawa, Menominee, Winnebago, Mississauga, Illinois, Huron-Petun, Potawatomi, and others—had to be drawn almost 1,000 miles to the French side in New York through the copious distribution of gifts and presents. Independent war belts from the Shawnee and the Delaware had been used to summon the Midwestern warriors to take up the hatchet. It was noted by a French observer that, "All the Indian nations were called together and invited to join and assist the French to repulse the British who came to drive them out of the land they were then in possession of."[47] However, if such considerations as gifts and promises alone determined the loyalty of the natives, as was seemingly the case, Montcalm feared that these Indian allies might be just as easily lured away by British bribes.[48]

Moreover, the direct clash of two European empires in the forests of North America threatened to rekindle many of the old and bitter rivalries among the tribes that had festered since the time of Cadillac, and bringing so many diverse peoples through the heart of Iroquoia racked the Algonquian alliance with discontent and apprehension. Montcalm was also visibly uncomfortable with the violence exhibited by the Indians when they engaged in battle, and he feared—correctly, as it turned out—that he could not control their savagery. Governor Beauharnois had previously noted that controlling the Indians on campaign required "mild and moderate means…on any occasion involving neither the honor of the French nation nor the King's arms." Montcalm had to tread a fine line when dealing with the Indians and use his power as a military commander sparingly and adroitly. However, he often attempted to treat the Indians as soldiers bound by military discipline rather than as individual warriors who generally acted as they pleased. This was a reality better understood by colonials than by European officers. At one point, Montcalm's relations with the Indians became so bad that Vaudreuil accused him of "wrecking the alliance."[49]

Forest Massacre

In July 1757, Montcalm gathered an army of 6,000 regulars and Canadiens, 2,000 Indians, and a large train of artillery at Ticonderoga. His objective was Fort William Henry, which stood on the Lake George battlefield. The fort's commander was Lt. Colonel George Munro, a hard-bitten Scottish veteran of the European wars. The small garrison of British redcoats, rangers, and Indian scouts had recently been enlarged to 1,500 with the arrival of provincial troops from New York, New Jersey, and New Hampshire. There were as well a large number of Anglo-American women and children seeking the security of the fort during the present crisis. The fort could house no more than 500 persons, however. Consequently, a fortified camp of ditches and brushwood was hastily established to accommodate most of them.[50]

General Daniel Webb was at Fort Edward within easy support of Munro. During the first three weeks of July, Munro sent out no fewer than six separate scouting parties, but the inability of the British to penetrate the screen of French-allied Indians along the lake proved frustrating. Finally, Colonel John Parker was ordered to undertake a reconnaissance in force. With five companies of New Jersey Blues and a few New York militiamen (about 350 men in total), Parker left the south shore of the lake in some two dozen whaleboats heading for the sawmill at the falls of the LaChute River near Ticonderoga almost 30 miles away.

Montcalm's Indians spied Parker's whaleboats traveling north just before nightfall and arranged an ambush at Sabbath Day Point on Sunday, July 24, 1757. Parker's troops included a number of experienced woodsmen, but they proved to be poor boatmen. They allowed the intervals between their boats to become irregular and sometimes very large. Three of the leading boats, much separated from the others, stumbled into the Indian ambush, and the noise of the initial encounter brought the other British vessels rushing to their aid just north of the point. Here the Indians, firing from the shore and launching their canoes into the lake, fell upon the detachment from all sides. All but four of the whaleboats were captured or overturned. In the attack, about 100 of Parker's men were shot, drowned, or hunted down in the forests to which they fled after reaching shore. Approximately 100 more, including Parker, retreated to Fort William Henry either by boat or on foot through the woods. The rest were taken prisoner and faced the threat of unimaginable tortures at the hands of the warriors.[51]

The Indians were overjoyed with their success. Montcalm almost immediately redeemed a number of the British captives from the Indians through the liberal distribution of gifts. In so doing, he spared many dozens of men a horrible fate, but his humanity was seen as weakness among some of the Indian allies. The next day, he sent out Brigadier de Levis with 3,000 men and an advanced party of Indians to march down the western shore of Lake George and prepare a fortified camp near present-day Bolton's Landing. Montcalm brought the rest of the army and the all-important siege artillery down the lake by boat. Once combined, the two forces moved to within three miles of Fort William Henry and nestled in a cove well-suited to the army's protection and security. Montcalm then initiated a formal siege with entrenchments, approaches, and parallels.

Six days of bombardment convinced Lt. Colonel Munro that further resistance was unless. Munro was brave enough, but the fort had not been built to withstand a classic artillery bombardment. Moreover, a letter from General Webb to Munro, intercepted by the French Indians, declared that no reinforcements from Fort Edward would be coming. Having been assured that help was impossible, Munro acceded to Montcalm's offer of an honorable surrender. It was agreed that the British would march out with the honors of war and be escorted to Fort Edward by a detachment of French troops.[52]

The British passed a troubled night in Fort William Henry as the Indians pillaged the fortified camp. When the British marched out on the morning of August 10, they were terrified that the French could not control the Indians. As the column of British at last began to move "the Indians crowded upon them, impeded their march, snatched caps, coats, and weapons from men and officers, tomahawked those that resisted, and, seizing upon shrieking women and children, dragged them off or murdered them on the spot... A frightful tumult ensued, when Montcalm, Levis and many other French officers, threw themselves among the Indians, and by promises and threats tried to allay their frenzy."[53]

Montcalm was said to have pleaded for the Indians to kill him and spare the British who seem to have been so stunned by the savagery of the attacks as to make little or no defense. The broken column straggled forward in disorder seeking the protection of the French advance guard who acted with unseemly detachment. Others retraced their steps to take refuge in the fort. The massacre ended in fits and starts with as many as 50 British dead. To his credit, Montcalm succeeded in ransoming about 400 British during the course of the day, but the Indians decamped in a body toward Montreal with about 200 captives.

Word came to Montcalm that a large reinforcement of troops to Fort Edward was expected shortly from Albany. This made an investment of that British post impossible. More importantly, since it was felt that successful war in the wilderness required the services of the Indians—and they had left—no further advance toward Fort Edward was possible. Montcalm, therefore, burned Fort William Henry and retired to Canada.

The Indians always maintained their own counsel with respect to the continuation of a campaign, but the massacre and the desertion of the warriors in the middle of an operation severely damaged their reputation in French eyes. In fact, it was not unusual for the Indians to decamp after a battle in order to mourn their dead or perform other cleansing rituals. The Mohawks had similarly abandoned William Johnson after the Battle of Lake George forcing him to abandon his own campaign against Ticonderoga in 1755.

Unfortunately, Indian strategic thinking was usually focused on the "now," and it did not necessarily include the prosecution of a long campaign in order to further what were clearly European aims. That they could follow a determined course of military operations had been shown in the 17th century when the Iroquois pursued a multi-year campaign of attacks and raids in order to drive their enemies from Huronia. Although both the French and the British supplied the Indian warriors with munitions and rations, their absence from their families for long periods on a European-style expedition meant a precipitous decline in the time they had for hunting. This might mean that their loved ones would starve during the next spring.

At Fort William Henry, the extent of the battle and the opportunities for captives to be made had not lived up to the expectations of the Indians. Through the use of promises and gifts the French had marshaled warriors from as far away as Green Bay for this particular campaign. Because the active operations had taken the form of a prolonged approach through the wilderness and a European-style siege carried out by sappers and artillerymen, the warriors—especially the young men—had not been given a sufficient chance to enhance their martial reputations. No enemy had made his presence known during the months that the French had taken to move south through the Lake Champlain–Lake George channel, and only a few skirmishes and ambushes had punctuated the tedious days before the battle. The Indians savored face-to-face and hand-to-hand confrontations, and the warriors found the firing of their muskets at militiamen hunkering behind the wooden palisades frustrating.

Moreover, the lack of personal contact limited the opportunity to take captives. The taking of captives was also a part of the native war culture. Captives were needed to "raise the dead" by adoption or to "cover the dead" through ransom or torture. Several warriors had been killed, especially at Sabbath Day Point, and Montcalm had frustrated the Indians by buying away many of the captives. The massacre of those who had surrendered at Fort William Henry—and in this case a massacre it was— might be defended as a form of blood revenge, but it was an aberration clearly outside the cultural norms of most tribes. Montcalm believed that the Indians had their blood lust up and were outside of his control, and he was probably correct in his conclusions.

A Winning Strategy

William Pitt became the Prime Minister of England in June 1757. His administration almost completely revitalized the British government, and he proposed a strategic plan for winning the war in North America. His initial strategic objectives were the three gatekeepers to Quebec—Fortress Louisbourg, Fort Carillon at Ticonderoga, and Fort Duquesne at the forks of the Ohio. Two of these had been the targets of colonial campaigns in the past, but the new fort at Ticonderoga had never before been tried. With the reduction of these posts accomplished, Pitt correctly reasoned that he could drive the French from Canada by taking the administrative center of French governance at the city of Quebec.

A long recitation of these events is beyond the scope of this discussion, but it should be noted that each victory recorded by the British further intimidated the Indian allies of the French. In 1758, Admiral Edward Boscawen landed a force of 12,000 British regulars under Generals Jeffery Amherst and James Wolfe in Louisbourg harbor. With the fortress besieged and with no hope of a relieving force breaking the blockade, the outnumbered French garrison surrendered within a few weeks. Amherst was thereafter called away with six regiments to support a planned operation against Ticonderoga, while Wolfe sought to press forward to Quebec. He wrote to Amherst, with whom he was on good terms, "An offensive, daring kind of war will awe the Indians and ruin the French...If you will attempt to cut up New France by the roots, I will come with pleasure to assist."[54]

Meanwhile, the attack on Ticonderoga in 1758 was entrusted to Major-General James Abercromby, who was considered inept and infirmed at age 51. Pitt had meant the command to go to Lord Augustus Howe, Brigadier General and second-in-command of the forces under Abercromby, but the old general had precedence.[55] Augustus Howe was a model soldier, young and highly regarded by the colonials. Howe placed himself in the hands of Robert Rogers and learned, first hand, his methods of woodlands warfare and ranger tactics. Had Howe's influence continued throughout the campaign it might have proved successful. Unfortunately, Howe, brave to the point of being oblivious to personal danger, went forward with a small party under provincial Major Israel Putnam to reconnoiter a possibly line of attack from the rear of Fort Carillon. Near the rapids of the LaChute River they encountered a detachment of French and Indians numbering about 350 whom Montcalm had sent to harass the British. A sharp fight ensued, and in the first moments Howe was killed by a shot to the chest. In that instant, the French had effectively overcome the British operation. Major Thomas Mante wrote, "In Lord Howe the soul of General Abercromby's army seemed to expire."[56] The British efforts under Abercromby to take the entrenchments around Fort Carillon by unremitting and seemingly senseless frontal assaults ended in a series of bloody repulses losing almost 2,000 men while Montcalm lost less than 400. Thereafter, the British army seems to have panicked somewhat in its retreat up Lake George leaving hundreds of barrels of provisions scattered along the shore, and it did not stop until it reoccupied the ground that held the burned ruins of Fort William Henry.[57]

Here they were greeted with glorious news. A colonial army of 3,000 men under the command of Lt. Colonel John Bradstreet had attacked and destroyed Fort Frontenac on the north shore of Lake Ontario. The colonials had then moved up to the site of Fort Oswego, burned the fort and the outbuildings, and captured the entire French lake fleet of nine armed vessels and scores of canoes. This effectively cut off the Great Lakes west to aid from Quebec or Montreal. Bradstreet then retired up the Oswego River to present-day Rome, New York where 1,000 men were detached to build a new British post named Fort Stanwicx right in the middle of Iroquoia. The advantages to the British wrought by this "All-American" victory were many. The French lost command of Lake Ontario and the supply line to their western forts, and the French-leaning Indians, initially buoyed in their alliances by a series of victories wrought by Montcalm, once again wavered.

In late autumn, 1758, Brigadier General James Forbes, with a force of 5,000 provincials and 1,500 Scots Highlanders, moved across Pennsylvania toward Fort Duquesne cutting a new road through the forests of the colony and leaving a series of fortified posts behind him. A detachment of 800 Highlanders, Royal Americans, and provincials under the command of Major James Grant advanced toward Fort Duquesne and were caught in a Franco-Indian ambush almost as fatal as that of Braddock years earlier. The entire affair was mismanaged by Grant who advanced his forces in separate detachments that were defeated in detail. The British lost almost 300 men before retiring. Two months later, when Forbes advanced toward Fort Duquesne with his main body, the French blew up their magazines and burned their own works, mainly because the Shawnee and Delaware warriors, who had been their most reliable allies, had abandoned them. Forbes, who was all but bed-ridden and near death, ordered a new fort built at the forks of the Ohio. This was named Fort Pitt in honor of the prime minister.

The Campaign of 1759

The French began the year of 1759 discouraged by the loss of many of their posts in the preceding year. Yet, they still held Fort Niagara at the western end of Lake Ontario, Fort Carillon at Ticonderoga, Crown Point, and the massive citadel of Quebec. The British campaign to reduce these important posts formed the core of British strategy in 1759. Brigadier General John Prideaux and Sir William Johnson would lead the attack on Fort Niagara. Jeffery Amherst would lead a renewed attack at Ticonderoga and Crown Point, and James Wolfe would attack Quebec.

The first two of these operations moved forward rapidly. By July, Amherst invested Fort Carillon with 11,000 men. Under orders from the governor of New France, the French left a force of only 400 at Carillon and withdrew the remaining forces to Montreal. Having no remaining Indian allies, the commandant abandoned the fort at Ticonderoga in the night, and

Amherst followed the retreating French to Crown Point, which was also found abandoned and destroyed.

Meanwhile, General Prideaux and Sir William Johnson had reached Niagara with their army in June. This force was made up of two regiments of regulars, a battalion of Royal Americans, and 3,000 provincials. Johnson had also attracted 900 Iroquois to the British for this offensive. This large turnout of Indians serves as a barometer of the war and shows how important the small British victories of the previous year really were. Early in the operation General Prideaux was killed, and Johnson assumed command of the operation. At this point, a French column of troops and Indians from the forts to the west approached to give Fort Niagara succor. Johnson and his Mohawks attacked this force and put it to rout. The survivors retreated all the way to Detroit burning many of their western posts and forts. Lacking the promise of reinforcement, Pouchot had no choice but to surrender. More importantly, French plans to counterattack the British at Fort Pitt collapsed when news that Niagara had fallen arrived. Ironically, the French posts in the west were like cannonballs supported by a very thin string of supplies. The capture of Niagara effectively cut off all of Canada to the west of Lake Ontario from the administrative heart of New France. The defeat also cut the heart out of the French-allied Indians who melted back into the forests.[58]

Bolstered by the successes at Louisbourg, Frontenac, Niagara, and Duquesne, General James Wolfe returned to Canada in 1759 to attack Quebec with a massive body of regular troops supported by 49 men-of-war. The French position atop the cliffs overlooking the river appeared impregnable, and the French would have to hold out just long enough to allow the Canadian winter to drive the British away. With great difficulty, Wolfe was able to erect batteries of artillery on Point Levis opposite the city. From here a brisk, if ineffective, fire was directed upon the city proper.

French Indians, sometimes accompanied by coureurs de bois, constantly raided the British outposts killing sentries and leaving behind the mutilated bodies of their victims. The American rangers seemed incapable of preventing these incursions. This caused a great deal of concern among the British troops, and the number of desertions consequently increased. Nonetheless, by mid-July a small number of British ships with part of Wolfe's army had slipped past the Quebec garrison and landed troops upstream of the city. This led to the immediate capture of the city. The fall of Quebec confirmed the victories of 1759 and led directly to the fall of Montreal and all of French Canada with it. The struggle for North America was over. In the Peace of Paris (1763), France lost almost all its possessions in North America.

Winning the Peace

The British won a great world-wide empire in the Seven Years War, but their grip on North America was a tenuous one. The accumulated effects of almost a century of colonial neglect, widespread prejudice against provincials, and a growing hatred of British regulars would cause the Anglo-American colonists to attempt to sever their ties with Britain in 1775.[59]

Throughout the French and Indian War, the Indians had maintained diplomatic relations with both sides correctly fearing that the Europeans fought only to decide who would plunder their lands. This alone attests to the sophistication of their politics. Yet, the Indians had always regarded the French as fathers, while the British were notably referred to as brothers. The fraternal kinship metaphors used by the Indian tribes toward the British indicate that they were viewed in a different light than the French. When the French surrendered Canada and Louisiana east of the Mississippi River to Britain in 1763, they also transferred all of Louisiana west of the river to Spain. The Indians were shocked that their father had abandoned them in such a fashion. This was not what a father was supposed to do. Observers noted that the singing and dancing common to the natives' villages suddenly ended as if all the people were in deep mourning.

Initially, the Indians envisioned the peace with the British in the same terms as those that had defined the alliance between the French and the medal chiefs, and the former members of the French alliance were seemingly willing to acknowledge at least a token Iroquois hegemony in the Northeast region. Yet, the British seemed incapable of fulfilling paternal obligations as the Indians viewed them, and they almost instantly asserted mastery over the Indians by building and garrisoning forts in Indian country in contravention of the propaganda they had disseminated among the tribes during the conflict. If the British did not act as fathers and had given up their role as truth-speaking brothers to act like conquerors, then they might very well be enemies capable of plotting the destruction of the Indians.

Keekyuscung, Tamaqua, and Shingas—three of the chiefs representing the residents of the area around Fort Duquesne (now Fort Pitt)—made it clear that they expected the British to go back over the mountains and take their people with them. An interpreter noted their words at a peace conference,

All the nations have jointly agreed to defend their hunting place at the Allegheny, and suffer no one to settle there; and as these Indians are very much inclined to the English interest, so they begged us very much to tell the governor [of Virginia], General [James Forbes], and all other people not to settle there. And if the English would draw back over the mountains, they would get all the other nations in their interest; if they stayed and settled there, all the nations would be against them; and they were afraid it would be a great war, and never come to a peace again.[60]

British agents—particularly William Johnson—tried to calm native fears with assurances and promises of reforms. Johnson and Atkins promised that the British soldiers occupying the forts would not attack the Indians and that they would work to alter those trade practices that had alienated the tribes. These would include the most common frauds and abuses of the British traders, who would now be uniformly regulated by the superintendents. In so doing, "the British would have to imitate the French by building a parallel infrastructure of forts, officers, gunsmiths, missionaries, medal chiefs, and annual presents."[61]

Croghan reported that an unnamed Shawnee diplomat was concerned that the British actions were creating a nostalgia for the French among the natives. Many longed for the return of Onontio, and those chiefs that negotiated with the British agents risked loosing influence among their own people. "All the Indian nations are very jealous of the English. They see that you have a great many forts in this country, and you are not so kind to them as they expected. The French were very generous to the Indians and always gave them clothing, and powder, and lead in plenty. But you don't do that brothers, and that is what makes the Indians so uneasy in their minds."[62]

Both George Croghan and Johnson felt that the subordination of the Indian nations of the Northeast was inevitable, but they also believed that the process could be peaceful and gradual. Croghan worried that British policies directed toward eliminating the French had done nothing toward conciliating the tribes. His answer was to win over the natives by the liberal distribution of presents. Montclam had used this policy to attract warriors for his campaigns, but the British Board of Trade acting from London was determined to eliminate this annual expense. Both Croghan and Johnson thought that use of annual presents to renew friendships and treaties might be difficult to eliminate. Johnson wrote that he was "apprehensive" lest the British be "premature in [their] sudden retrenchment of some necessary expenses, to which they [the Indians] have been always accustomed."[63]

The government decided to eliminate presents and coupled this with a renewed reliance on trade as the sole mechanism for exchanging European goods with the Indians. Regulations were put in place to ensure a fair and abundant trade free of a reliance on rum, but a policy of keeping the Indians short of powder and lead was also instituted. Lists of acceptable prices were published, and the trade in scalping knives, clasp knives, razors, tomahawks, flints, and fowling pieces was outlawed.

Neither Johnson or Croghan seriously questioned the measures taken in this regard. They simply criticized the speed with which they were implemented. With the banning of some of the most popular trade items, the traders almost immediately began to ignore the established price lists eliciting a general clamor among the Indians complaining of both high prices and the shortage of goods. A Delaware leader from Minisink on the Delaware River, Papoonhoal, complained of the deterioration of the relationship between the British traders and the natives.

Brother...you make it public that you will give a certain price for our skins, and that they are to be weighed and paid for at that set price according to their weight. Brother, there are two bad things in this way of dealing. You alter the price that you say you will give for our skins, which can never be right. God cannot be pleased to see the price of one and the same thing so often altered and changed. [Secondly] our young men finding that they are to receive for their skins according to their weight play tricks with them … to make them weigh more … Brother, you see that there is no love or honesty on either side.[64]

The Crown, nonetheless, was also quick to guarantee the protection of Indian lands. As part of a broader attempt at reform, the colony of Pennsylvania had renounced the purchase of the western lands made from the Iroquois at Albany in 1754, but it retained the first right to purchase any land that the Indians freely chose to sell. Moreover, in an attempt to improve or maintain their relations with the Indians, the government closed the trans-Appalachian lands to settlement in the Proclamation of 1763.

During the French and Indian War, General Edward Braddock built a wagon road from Virginia to the forks of the Ohio River, and General James Forbes built a road to the same place across the southern tier of Pennsylvania in 1758. These two roads were the greatest public works projects attempted in the British colonies in the period, and they provided improved access into the Indian lands. English traders, land speculators, and settlers began to pour into the Indian territory not only along the roads, but on every Indian trail and through every available mountain gap. This resulted in a breakdown of relations with the frontier tribes. "Indian people from Quebec and Maine to Georgia and Florida were complaining in vain to colonial authorities about trespasses on their land, and about schemes to get it." The British had spent seven decades wresting away the allegiance of the tribes from the French. The flood of settlers crossing the mountains, if undiminished, threatened to undo all the work of untold negotiations with the tribes and to make renewed warfare more likely.[65]

In order to limit friction with the Indian nations, King George III signed the Proclamation of 1763, which prohibited any white settlement west of the Appalachians and which required those already settled there to return to the east immediately. Yet, the line between the Indian lands and the colonies was "so hastily adopted" that it took no account of the settlements already made, nor of the royal lands granted to certain colonies and land companies in their charters. Not a single shilling of indemnification was offered to the colonials in the proclamation for the losses they would now sustain.[66]

The settlers that had taken the earliest steps on the frontiers were now those most disadvantaged. A contemporary observer noted that the frontiers had been "repeatedly attacked and ravaged by skulking parties of the Indians, who have with the most savage cruelty murdered men, women, and children without distinction, and have reduced near a thousand families to the most extreme distress."[67] A contemporary observer noted that the war waged by the Indians had already cost the lives of 2,500 British men, women, and children.[68] Many Anglo-Americans had invested both their labor and their scant capital in recently cleared fields, newly planted crops, and recently erected homes, barns, and fences. The potential economic hardship that they faced if they obeyed the proclamation and abandoned these holdings was staggering.[69]

In 1764, Matthew Smith and James Gibson responded to the proclamation in an open letter to Parliament. Called *A Remonstrance from the Pennsylvania Frontier,* the letter was published and widely read in the colonies. It stated in part, "It grieves us to the very heart to see such of our frontier inhabitants as have escaped savage fury with the loss of their parents, their children, their wives or relatives, left destitute by the public, and exposed to the most cruel poverty and wretchedness [by the government]."[70]

The real problem illustrated by the Proclamation of 1763 was that, given the reality of the colonial frontier at the time, the gradual elimination of the Native American population was as inevitable in the trans-Appalachian country as it had been in the east a century and a half earlier. It was all but impossible for the Crown to regulate trade with the Indians and to maintain its political alliances among the tribes without some military authority, whether imperial or local, appearing to impinge on the rights of either the Indians or the frontier population. In fact, the British army had erected no new forts, except one at Sandusky, choosing instead to simply garrison the posts and forts abandoned by the French. However, British policies that aspired to control the Indians were doomed to fail because of their inability to control the settlers. Increased regulation "only aggravated the tensions, alienated backcountry settlers and ensured that many of them would throw in their lot with the rebels once the Revolution began."[71]

Indian Insurgency

In 1764, a serious Indian uprising in the interior was undertaken by a coalition of tribal nations under the leadership of the Ottawa warrior, Pontiac. The history of this Indian uprising and the image of Pontiac as a merciless enemy is somewhat suspect because the documents from this period are overwhelmingly written from the British perspective. Moreover, the details have come down to us from two principle sources—Francis Parkman's *History of the Conspiracy of Pontiac* and Robert Rogers' *Ponteach: A Tragedy.* The racial struggle reported in these works reflected a European understanding of its own superiority and the inevitability of whites supplanting Indian everywhere. "Both Parkman and Rogers needed a chief [Pontiac] to symbolize a people. His fall would be his people's fall."[72]

Yet, Pontiac's was neither the first or last effort made by Native Americans to form a confederacy that would prevent whites, and particularly the British, from occupying their lands. Pontiac's revolt was built upon several such attempts that took place between 1760 and 1763, during which it became clear that the French had lost their place to the British but had not yet abandoned all their posts. No fewer than four sets of war belts were issued throughout the northern region prior to Pontiac's rebellion. Significantly, only one of these efforts—centering on the Catholic missions surrounding Montreal—was inspired by the French in a final attempt to defend Canada.

In 1760, Tamaqua tried to form a pan-Indian alliance centered among the Delawares and Shawnees, but it collapsed when the Iroquois notified the British of its existence. In 1761, the pro-French Chenussio Seneca, led by a chief named Kayashuta, attempted to form a confederation of western tribes (Seneca, Delaware, Shawnee, and Mingo) to deter the British from occupying Niagara, Detroit, and Pittsburgh. The wampum belts that carried the message of a new alliance were carried by the son of Chabert Joncaire, but the idea gained few adherents. The Detroit Indians—a loose confederacy of Potawatomi, Ottawa, Wyandot, and Ojibwa who feared the regional domination of the Senecas—betrayed the plan to William Johnson who grasped the opportunity to divide the western tribes from the influence of the pro-French Iroquois residing in the Jesuit missions. Johnson recognized the local Wyandot leadership with great effect. The Delaware symbolically abandoned their own pretensions to native leadership by bringing the embers of their own council fire at Detroit to the council house of the Wyandot and rekindling it there.[73]

The inability of the western tribes to unite in the face of the British military underscores the underlying divisions and realignments among the residents of the Great Lakes and Ohio country. These had continued to reverberate since the Great Dispersion of the 1650s had flooded the region with refugees. Without the fatherly guidance of Onontio, which had kept the Algonquian alliance focused on deterring the British, the short-term objectives of the tribes continually "collided and clashed." Consequently, they betrayed one another to the British in an attempt to gain influence among them. In 1762 alone, there were a number of planned insurgencies: the Detroit tribes laid plans to attack the Shawnee; the Ojibwa of Michilimackinac planned a war with the Menominee; and the Sauk girded themselves for war with the Illinois.[74]

During 1761 and 1762, crop failures, epidemics, and famine swept the Ohio country, and the Algonquians appealed to the British for assistance. The British largely failed to respond or took action with so little grace as to appear insincere. Sick Indians unable to hunt for their families appeared at posts throughout the region to beg for food as they had when they were controlled by the French. Yet, the British simply could not supply them, and the same poor scene was repeated at post after post. Nonetheless, Indians hunting on the upper Ohio found whites building cabins, cutting clearings in the woods, and hunting game that they considered their own; and although the redcoats drove the whites off, more settlers always appeared.

In the fall of 1762, Croghan received word that French provocateurs were among the Ottawa at Detroit where many of the chiefs and principal warriors of other nations had gathered for a secret council. The fact that the Ottawa now emerged as leaders in the rebellion movement was significant, and it was clear that they had taken some pains to keep the Delaware and the Iroquois of the Six Nations in the dark. The French agents assured the Indians that if they rebelled against the British, Onontio would return to support them. That winter the war belts circulated widely, and most of the experienced fur traders expected a crisis in the region.

In April 1763, the ideologies of rebellion by a multi-tribal force bore fruit at Detroit under the leadership of Pontiac. The Indians struck there first. Although the British garrison was able to drive them from the fort and withstand a siege, Captain Donald Campbell was seized by Pontiac while under a flag of truce and gruesomely tortured to death by an Ojibwa chief named Wasson some time later. The spark set at Detroit set other posts aflame. In June, Ottawas, Ojibwas, Wyandots, and some Senecas under Kayashuta took Fort Presque Isle and Fort Le Boeuf. The Weas, Miami, Potawatomi, and Mingo destroyed Fort Venango killing virtually all its inhabitants. Although the Ojibwas at Michilimackinac took the post at the Straits of Mackinaw, they denounced Pontiac and Kayashuta for the needless cruelties that they had allowed. At this point the revolt ended because several western tribes—chief among them the Menominee, Winnebago, Sauk, Fox, and Iowa—chose to defend the remaining British in the westernmost garrisons and escort them to safety in Montreal. The most dedicated among Pontiac's followers thereafter turned to the frontier where scores of traders and settlers were either killed or taken captive. By autumn, Pennsylvania alone had sustained 600 casualties. Nonetheless, the rebellion had collapsed from within and faltered.

General Amherst called on his troops to spare no Indian found in arms against British authority, and he approved a plan to spread blankets infected with smallpox among them. By the fall, Pontiac's alliance was falling to pieces. Wabbicomigot, a Mississauga chief, began to negotiate with the Detroit garrison for a truce, and some short time later Pontiac, himself, opened talks with Maj. Henry Galdwin, the commandant. Thereafter, the regulars of the Black Watch under Colonel Henry Bouquet, marching to relieve Fort Pitt, convincingly defeated a force of Delawares, Shawnees, and Mingos at the battle of Bushy Run in Pennsylvania. Word of this broke the back of the rebellion, but Galdwin assured Amherst that he would need at least 1,500 troops to police the region around Detroit alone.

Pontiac's Rebellion had many negative consequences for Native Americans. The effect of the uprising and of the intertribal wrangling can not be underestimated. The Grenville ministry had assured the Anglo-colonials that the red-coated regulars in garrison on the frontier would be "a thin red line between kidnap, scalping, and massacre" and would secure the white settlements now that the French were gone. However,

Pontiac's uprising seemed to validate many of the negative convictions held by the colonials with regard to the regulars. Every British garrison in the Great Lakes region was taken by the Indians save two, Fort Pitt and Fort Detroit, and the rebellion had just barely failed to evict the British from Niagara.[75]

Amherst was replaced by General Thomas Gage, who generally accepted the advice of William Johnson and George Croghan in attempting to repair British relations with the Algonquians. There were many among the British, particularly the Anglo-American colonists, who wanted the Algonquians punished by the might of British arms, but waging war in the Great Lakes west would be very difficult. An army of retaliation would simply drive the Indians further west into the arms of the French in the trans-Mississippi region and ruin the British fur trade, while those Indians out of its path could still fall upon the settlements.

Nonetheless, two parallel forces composed of redcoats and provincial troops raised in Virginia and Pennsylvania—one under Colonel John Bradstreet and one under Colonel Bouquet—were dispatched west along the north shore of Lake Erie and through the Ohio country, respectively. Yet, these did little more than burn thatch huts and cornfields causing some of the tribes to offer a truce. Johnson held several peace conferences during these operations, but with few exceptions, only those tribes that had refused to join Pontiac's uprising attended. Nonetheless, the Indians were aware that the British were willing to carry the conflict into their own country, and they hoped to reestablish the old French-style alliance of medal chiefs with them. Although the back of the Indian alliance was broken, the British army seems to have been unable to fully secure the frontiers until 1766.

Pontiac was the most famous Indian of the post-French and Indian War period, and he was impressed by his own success in bloodying the British nose. Yet, he was only a warrior, and he now tried to play the self-appointed role of a chief in making peace with the British proclaiming that he spoke for all the western tribes at a peace conference held in Ontario in 1766 by Johnson. This placed Pontiac in dangerous waters, and he found that his self-aggrandizement had displeased his own people. "British alliance chiefs, as Pontiac learned, could no more pretend to power than could French alliance chiefs." When he returned to his home among the Ottawa, many among the young warriors openly insulted and threatened him. On several occasions he was beaten. When he stabbed an Illinois diplomat at a peace conference in 1768, he became a man without a home, and he retired to the forests to hunt during 1768 and 1769. Finally, in the latter year, he reappeared in the French village of Cahokia accompanied by his two sons and a handful of loyal followers. While here, he was attacked by a warrior of the Illinois confederation seeking revenge who clubbed him from behind and stabbed him to death.[76]

The period from the end of Pontiac's Rebellion to the outbreak of the American Revolution was one during which the British Indian policy lost its center. Sir William Johnson, as sole Indian agent for the northern colonies, aspired to model the British Indian policy on the successful system used by the French. Yet, he could find no religious figures among the protestant missionaries to approximate the effect of the Jesuits, nor could he assemble bush rangers to move west and live among the Indians as had the French coureurs de bois.

Unlike the earlier Frenchmen, British colonials were settlers who did not believe that their lives depended on good relations with the Indians, neither did they look to live or seek refuge among them nor intermarry with them. On the contrary, the backwoods settlers were composed largely of Scotch-Irish immigrants from the borders of northern Britain and northern Ireland. They settled in the Appalachian backcountry from 1718 to 1775. On the frontier, the tough-minded Scotch-Irish pursued their own local interests by generally ignoring the English authorities. Unlike the Pennsylvania Quakers, who scrupulously paid for Indian land, the Scotch-Irish unabashedly believed that they were foreordained by Scripture to take their land from the Indians, by force if necessary. "On the frontier, the Scotch-Irish were hewing their way through the woods, killing Indians when it suited them, and developing a righteous indignation against the restraining orders which came from the government."[77]

Attempts to evict these settlers from Indian lands proved ineffectual. Even after the passage of the Proclamation of 1763, which restricted settlement west of the Appalachian Mountains, their numbers increased. The colonial governments showed little interest in evicting them, and even the redcoats under General Thomas Gage were unsuccessful in forcing them out. In 1767, the settlements on Redstone Creek and the Cheat River were literally burned out by British regulars, but within a few months they had reestablished themselves and doubled their number. Gage grew so disgusted that he thereafter refused to use the troops to halt Indian attacks on the settlers' cabins without direct orders from the king.

Meanwhile, the failure to remove the illegal settlers forced an expansion of military posts and garrisons in Indian territory; and the many frauds, injustices, and murders committed by them forced the British to cover the dead and compensate the Indians in order to maintain the fur trade. Both Johnson and Gage wanted to keep a clear dividing line between white and Indian lands, and the regulations issued by Johnson for the northern district in 1767 restricted trade to the military posts where commissioners, appointed by the Crown, could supervise it. "Unsupervised trade, Johnson contended, would lead only to widespread fraud. The Indians, who had no other recourse against fraud, would retaliate with robberies and murders. In the end, there would be war."[78]

Moreover, endless difficulties, internal jealousies, and unconditional greed quickly brought Johnson's entire plan to ruin. British traders, licensed by the commissioners, subverted the system by selling their furs to the French Metis on the upper Mississippi, Illinois, Wabash, and Ohio. The Metis then cooperated for a fee by sending them down river to New Orleans saving the British traders the cost of shipping the furs east. Croghan believed that all the British traders in the Illinois country sold their furs to the French, and Johnson thought that the rest would do the same if given the chance. Even Guy Carleton, governor of Canada, subverted the system by issuing passes to traders that allowed them to operate outside the system. Ostensibly, Carleton's passes were good only in the region north of Lake Superior, but once out from under the supervision of the commissioners, the traders essentially went wherever they chose. They openly flaunted the regulations, trading in liquor instead of blankets, and leaving the Indians discontented and impossible to control. This demonstrated to the Indians the inability of the British to control the frontiers as the French had done.[79]

Colonial confidence in British arms was severely shaken by the events of the Indian rebellion. The effectiveness of the Indian attacks had humiliated the British regulars and embarrassed the bureaucracy in London. Anglo-Americans soon began to realize that their own best interests were not always those espoused by the Crown. James Otis, writing from the perspective of the colonials, noted, "The late acquisitions [from the French] in America, as glorious as they have been, and as beneficial as they are to Great Britain, are only a security to these colonies against the ravages of the French and Indians. Our trade upon the whole is not, I believe, benefited by them one groat."[80]

The French and Indian War created a vast debt estimated by the British Exchequer at an unprecedented £150 million. An additional annual appropriation of almost £2 million was needed to provide for an army and navy to secure an empire that stretched from Hudson's Bay in Canada to Bombay in India half a globe away. Almost £350,000 of the annual expense was due to the administration of the American colonies. Although the Parliament expected to pay the lion's share of future expenditures, the Grenville ministry decided to extract at least some of the money— estimated at about £60 thousand in 1765—from the colonies in the form of a stamp tax. Although Americans were familiar with paying taxes, they had always come from the colonial assemblies. This plan misfired badly, and the tax was repealed. It seems that London miscalculated both the effect of the tax and the breadth of the reaction to it.

In response to the failure of the Stamp Act to provide revenue, the Board of Trade drastically cut its annual allowance for gifts to the Indians in order to save money. The attempt to enjoy the benefits of an Indian trade empire without sustaining its inherent costs destroyed the delicate balance between whites and Indians on the frontiers. The secretary of state, Lord Hillsborough, advised William Johnson to allow the disputes between the tribes and the settlers to work themselves out naturally. The Indians rightly judged that the abdication of the roles of mediator, diplomat, and enforcer indicated that the white settlers had won. Although London surrendered control over trade to the colonial legislatures, the colonials failed to regulate it at all, choosing instead to open a conflict with their mother country, the result of which would bring disaster to the Native Americans of the woodlands.

Notes

1. See W.H.P. Clement, *The History of the Dominion of Canada* (Toronto: William Briggs Publisher, 1897), chapter 4.

2. Richard White, *The Middle Ground, Indians, Empires, and Republics in the Great Lakes Region, 1650–1815* (New York: Cambridge University Press, 1991), 111–112.

3. Francis Parkman, *La Salle and the Discovery of the Great West* (New York: The Modern Library, 1999), 54.

4. White, 159.

5. White, 165.

6. White, 175.

7. White, 168–169.

8. White, 168–169.

9. White, 182–183.

10. James F. O'Neil, ed., *Their Bearing is Noble and Proud: A Collection of Narratives Regarding the Appearance of Native Americans from 1745–1850* (Dayton, OH: J.T.G.S., 1995), 20. Quoting Pierre Pinchot French commander at Niagara.

11. Washington wanted an appointment to the regulars, which was denied him largely because he was a colonial. This circumstance reinforces the idea that militia officers were held in contempt by the regulars and aids in understanding Washington's motivations for seeking high rank during the American Revolution.

12. The first quote is from a letter by St. Clair to Braddock on April 10, 1775. The second is from an unidentified British officer to his friends in London on April 8, 1755. Both can be found in Andrew J. Wahll, ed., *The Braddock Road Chronicles, 1755* (Bowie, MD: Heritage Books, 1999), 124.

13. Reported in Armand Francis Lucier, ed., *French and Indian War Notices Abstracted from Colonial Newspapers: 1754–1755* (Bowie, MD: Heritage Books, 1999), vol. 1, 282. See also Francis Parkman, *Montcalm and Wolfe,* (New York: Atheneum, 1984), 244.

14. Reported in Lucier, ed., 196–197.

15. Parkman, *Montcalm and Wolfe,* 244.

16. John Ferling, *Struggle for a Continent: The Wars of Early America* (Arlington Heights, IL: Harlan Davidson, 1993), 197. Also see Timothy J. Todish, *America's First World War: The French and Indian War, 1754–1763* (Ogden, UT: Eagle's View, 1987).

17. Louis M. Waddell and Bruce D. Bromberger, *The French and Indian War in Pennsylvania, 1753–1763: Fortification and Struggle During the War for Empire* (Harrisburg: Pennsylvania Historical and Museum Commission, 1996), 10–11.

18. Quoted in Francis Russell, *The French and Indian Wars* (New York: American Heritage Publishing, 1962), 94.

19. Braddock's general orders of April 8, 1755, found in Wahll, ed., 115.

20. See Waddell and Bromberger, 14–15.

21. The French have a few eyewitnesses. Monsieur Roucher was a French Canadian soldier at Fort Duquesne. Pierre Pouchot likewise left a memoir. Pierre de Contrecour and Jean-Daniel Dumas both commanded troops during the battle. Wahll, ed., 344.

22. Captain Robert Orme quoted in Wahll, ed., 345.

23. Quoting Monsieur Roucher and Ensign Godefroy in Wahll, ed., 367, 368.

24. Journal entries from William Dunbar found in Wahll, ed., 349.

25. Journal entries from an anonymous British officer found in Wahll, ed., 349.

26. Journal entries from Washington found in Wahll, ed., 348.

27. Journal entries from Washington found in Wahll, ed., 377.

28. Reported in Lucier, ed., vol. 1, 264–265.

29. A letter to an unknown addressee found in Wahll, ed., 377.

30. John A. Schutz, *William Shirley* (Chapel Hill: University of North Carolina Press, 1961), 198.

31. Major General Edward Braddock, May 17, 1755, to Major General Johnson found in Almon W. Lauber, ed., *The Papers of Sir William Johnson* (Albany: University of the State of New York, 1939), vol. 9, 171.

32. Major General Johnson, September 3, 1755, to the Board of Trade found in E. B. O'Callaghan, ed., *Documents Relative to the Colonial History of the State of New York* (Albany: Weed, Parsons and Co., 1855), vol. 6, 997.

33. A Boston newspaper account of Johnson's dispatch after the battle reported in Lucier, ed., vol. 1, 305–308.

34. Lucier, ed., vol. 1, 309.

35. Sir Charles Hardy, January 16, 1756, to the Board of Trade, O'Callaghan, ed., vol. 7, 4.

36. Reported in Lucier, ed., vol. 2, 29–30.

37. Reported in Lucier, ed., vol. 2, 3.

38. Reported in Lucier, ed., vol. 2, 7.

39. Lauber, ed., vol. 9, 785.

40. Governor Charles Hardy, January 6, 1756, to the Lords of Trade found in O'Callaghan, ed., vol. 6, 6.

41. Major-General Johnson, September 3, 1755, to Governor George Clinton found in O'Callaghan, ed., vol. 6, 996.

42. Major-General Johnson, September 3, 1755, to the Board of Trade found in O'Callaghan, ed., vol. 6, 991–996.

43. Secretary of the Board Pownall, December 2, 1755, to Major-General William Johnson found in O'Callaghan, ed., vol. 6, 1022.

44. Parkman, *Montcalm and Wolfe*, 271.

45. Parkman, *Montcalm and Wolfe*, 213.

46. Parkman, *Montcalm and Wolfe*, 269.

47. The French have a few eyewitnesses. Monsieur Roucher was a French Canadian soldier at Fort Duquesne. Pierre Pouchot likewise left a memoir. Pierre de Contrecour and Jean-Daniel Dumas both commanded troops during the battle. Wahll, ed., 344.

48. White, 175.

49. White, 246.

50. Ian K. Steele, *Betrayal, Fort William Henry and the "Masaacre"* (New York: Oxford UP, 1990), 97.

51. See Steele, *Betrayal,* 87–89; Parkman, *Montcalm and Wolfe,* 281–282.

52. Several historians claim that Daniel Webb, then holding the rank of general, refused to support Munro when requested, an infamous circumstance set in history over the intervening years and made a part of American folklore by James Fenimore Cooper and numerous Hollywood directors. The text of this letter was reported by Parkman in *Montcalm and Wolfe,* who claimed to have seen a complete copy in Colonel Joseph Frye's journal. The bloodstained original is reproduced in Steele, *Betrayal,* 103.

53. Parkman, *Montcalm and Wolfe,* 296–297.

54. Quoted in Parkman, *Montcalm and Wolfe,* 350.

55. Howe was the older brother of two men—William and Richard—who would appear in American history as the respective Army and Navy commanders of British forces during the American Revolution.

56. Putnam was to become an important general in the Continental Army in the American Revolution as was General John Stark who served as Rogers' second in command of the Rangers.

57. Robert Leckie, *A Few Acres of Snow: The Saga of the French and Indian Wars* (New York: John Wiley & Sons, Inc., 1999), 309–311.

58. White, 242.

59. See Dorothy Denneen Volo and James M. Volo, *Daily Life in the Age of Sail* (Westport, CT: Greenwood Press, 2001).

60. Quoted in White, 254.

61. White, 248.

62. Quoted in White, 268.

63. Quoted in White, 258.

64. Quoted in White, 264.

65. Colin G. Calloway, *Dawnland Encounters: Indians and Europeans in Northern New England* (Hanover, NH: University Press of New England, 1991), 23.

66. Samuel Eliot Morison, *Sources and Documents Illustrating the American Revolution 1764–1788 and the Formation of the Federal Constitution* (New York: Oxford University Press, 1965), 8.

67. Morison, 14.

68. Captain Dumas, commander of Fort Dusuesne, quoted in White, 244.

69. Morison, 10–11.

70. Morison, 11.

71. Calloway, *Dawnland Encounters,* 21.

72. White, 270.

73. See the note in White, 273.

74. White, 274.

75. White, 312.

76. White, 312–313.

77. Louis B. Wright, *The Atlantic Frontier: Colonial American Civilization, 1607–1763* (New York: Alfred A. Knopf, 1951), 224.

78. White, 318.

79. White, 322.

80. Morison, 7.

14

Fighting Back: The Dark and Bloody Ground

Thayendaneagea, of the martial brow,
Gayentwahga, Honeyawas, where are they?
Sagoyewatha, he is silent now;
No more will listening throngs his voice obey....
Gone are my tribesmen, and another race,
Born of the foam, disclose with plough and spade
Secrets of battlefield and burial place,
And hunting grounds, once dark with pleasant shade,
Bask in the golden light.

—Read at the Centennial Celebration of
Sullivan's Campaign against the Iroquois[1]

The Contest for the Frontiers

The American Revolution was a severe trial for British Indian policy. Almost from the onset of hostilities, the British military determined to wage war by inciting the Indians to attack the outlying settlements. Having abandoned the tribes to the ruthlessness of the settlers in the first half of the 1770s, the British scrambled in 1776 to create a wartime Indian alliance very much like the one that had formerly characterized French policy. Although British agents secured the unwavering support of four of the six confederated Iroquois nations and a few raiding parties from among the Shawnee, Mingos, and Potawatomis around Detroit, most other tribes remained neutral, were inconsistent allies, or proved unreliable on the battlefield. In 1781, British general Frederick Haldimand complained that there was "no dependence upon even those Indians who are declared in our favor...There has not been a single instance where the Indians have fulfilled their engagements but influenced by caprice, a dream or a desire of protracting the war, to obtain presents, have dispersed and deserted the troops."[2]

As in previous wars involving whites and Indians in the Northeast woodlands, the American Revolution was characterized by brutal and violent warfare on the frontiers. "The proximity and interconnectedness of Indian and colonial communities throughout large areas of North America gave the backcountry warfare of the Revolution a face-to-face nature that heightened its bitterness." This affected the Indian policy of the United States for decades thereafter.[3]

Initially, both loyalists and patriots put themselves forward as the legitimate heirs to the Native American alliances forged by the British during the French wars. The patriots faced a more difficult task in trying to bring the Indians to their side. Their agents came to the tribes too late and with too few presents to cement many friendships. British agents, already established among the Indian nations, were more successful than congressional ones in bringing the frontier tribes to their cause. Fortunately, the voice of William Johnson had been silenced by his death prior to the opening of hostilities. Nonetheless, the Americans constantly overestimated the number of Indians ranged against them. Although estimates grew as high as 8,500 warriors, there is little evidence that even half that number actually took the field in support of the British.[4]

Many tribes openly aligned themselves to the crown at the beginning of the conflict because they thought the British would quickly win the war or because they had formed a hatred of the patriot settlers in the previous decade. The Scotch-Irish settlers in particular had a long history of illegally occupying Indian land.[5] The frontier people "were Indian haters first, last, and always. For them, all Indians lived by murder and deserved death on sight."[6] Some settlers used the revolution as an excuse to continue their murderous ways under the guise of a crusade for political rights. Others genuinely believed that their actions were the only source of relief from the raids that continually plagued the back country.

The British agents reportedly did all in their power to "induce all the nations of Indians to massacre the frontier inhabitants of Pennsylvania and Virginia and paid very high prices in goods for the scalps the Indians brought in." From their base near Detroit, British agents Charles Langlade and Colonel Henry "Hair Buyer" Hamilton played a diplomatic tug-of-war over the Great Lakes tribes with the main American agent at Fort Pitt, Colonel George Morgan. At Fort Niagara, Sir Guy Johnson, nephew to Sir William, oversaw the effort to convince the Indians of western New York to take up arms against the patriots. With the added influence of his cousin, Sir John Johnson, and of the Mohawk war leader Joseph Brant, Sir Guy was able to bring four of the six nations of the Iroquois Confederacy to the British side.[7]

John Johnson, son of Sir William Johnson who had died in 1774, actively joined the Tories of his Royal Greens and Brant's Indians in the field. He was one of the most active loyalist leaders on the frontier. The father and son team of John and Walter Butler were also particularly active in harassing the settlements with their Tory Rangers. Dressed in short, dark green coatees, Indian leggings and moccasins, and carrying tomahawks and muskets, Butler's Rangers accompanied the Indians in raids throughout New York and Pennsylvania.[8]

The Crown's agents among the Indians were effectively opposed only by the Reverend Samuel Kirkland, a Congregational missionary to the Iroquois. An ardent patriot, Kirkland was able to win the help of the Oneida and Tuscarora for the patriots by appealing to them on religious grounds, suggesting that the Crown would force the Anglican religion upon them if the patriots lost.[9] With the exception of Kirkland's successful appeals, only by threatening the tribes with massive retribution could the agents of Congress hope to maintain Indian neutrality. Colonel Morgan told the tribes at Fort Pitt, "If the foolish people who have struck us so often, will grow wise immediately they may yet avoid destruction." Otherwise the patriot army would "trample them into dust." However, Morgan found that some of the tribes "were determined not to listen." They viewed his attempts to negotiate a neutrality "with increasing contempt."[10]

The Indians were assured by the British agents that they need not fear to "take up the hatchet against the Americans." Convinced that the redcoats would defeat the patriots as they had the French, the Indians undertook a series of frontier raids that demoralized the residents of the settlements. The attack on Wyoming Valley in Pennsylvania in July 1778, by Iroquois warriors and loyalist rangers under the command of Major John Butler, was one of the worst of these raids. This was closely followed by the burning of Cherry Valley in New York by a mixed force of Indians and loyalists under Captain Walter Butler. These attacks, in particular, seem to have been pivotal in moving Congress to action. Immediately thereafter, the Board of War of Congress concluded that a major operation against the Indians could not be avoided.[11]

Patriot Tribes

Certain tribes were friendly to the patriots, including a small number of Delawares, all the Stockbridge and Mohegan Indians, and many of the Abenakis of New Hampshire and Maine. While the loyalty of the Delawares was always suspect, that of the Stockbridge and Mohegan warriors of New England was not. Almost two dozen Stockbridge Indians were killed in a single encounter fighting for the patriots in the Bronx on a bluff overlooking the Van Courtlandt mansion.

The most crucial circumstance with regard to American Indian allies proved to be the wresting away of the Oneida and Tuscarora warriors from the Iroquois confederacy. Although the Six Nations reportedly could field 2,000 warriors, it was the Iroquois' failure to maintain their traditional tribal unity that proved most important in this instance. A firm stand by the confederacy in favor of the Crown would have posed an almost impossible strategic problem for the patriots as many neutral tribes were poised to follow their lead. It was particularly comforting to the patriots, therefore, that the Iroquois failed to provide a unified front in the Revolution.

The powerful Abenaki nation of New England had no great love for either "Britons or Bostonians."[12] Sir Guy Carleton, the British commander in Canada, seems to have underestimated the independent spirit of the Abenaki. He ordered them about in an arrogant and condescending manner and refused them presents of arms and ammunition unless they proclaimed undivided support for the crown. Nonetheless, Washington was surprisingly pleased when he was greeted by a delegation of Abenaki leaders at the camp at Cambridge overlooking Boston in 1775 pledging their services in the cause of liberty even before the British had evacuated the city. Abenaki warriors served as scouts for Benedict Arnold's expedition up the Kennebec River of Maine and were standing with the patriots in the Canadian snow before the walled city of Quebec in 1776. Congress responded to the Abenaki in the most positive terms possible, and the defeat of Burgoyne's army at Saratoga in 1777 helped immensely to cement good relations between the patriots and the tribe.

Joseph Louis Gill, the son of two whites adopted into the Abenaki nation during the French wars, proved an effective representative of the patriots among his people. Known as the "White Chief of the Saint Francis Abenaki," he seems to have formed around himself a hard core of native support for the patriots. Estimates of the number of Abenaki warriors available to prosecute a war vary widely from as few as 200 to as many as 2,000.[13] A company of Indian Rangers was formed under Gill, who was granted an officer's commission by Congress. These native rangers patrolled the northern forests along the border with Canada freeing the patriots of the task. However, as the war dragged on and the outcome grew less certain, Gill increasingly flirted with the British in Canada. This somewhat split Abenaki loyalty. Thereafter, groups of Abenaki scouts, ostensibly on opposite sides in the war, carefully avoided each other in the wilderness areas in the hope that at the end of the war the whole tribe might with some assurance gain an advantage from the ultimate winner of the conflict.[14]

The British Allies

Prominent among the allies of the British were those Iroquois who sought out arms and ammunition from the British at Fort Niagara. The Mohawks had always been staunch allies of the British, welded to them by their good will toward William Johnson. This loyalty they seem to have transferred more to his nephew, Guy, than to his son, John. The Seneca and Cayuga joined with the Mohawks almost immediately in a series of daring raids directed at the patriot settlements. The less decisive Onondaga Iroquois did not join them until 1779. The pro-British Iroquois warriors also attacked the villages of their pro-American kinsman, the Oneida and Tuscarora; and the Oneida, in turn, burned several Mohawk dwellings in retaliation. For the Iroquois, the Revolution was truly a war in which "brother killed brother," and the effect was to irreparably tear the kinship network among them asunder.[15]

The Seneca, who had joined Pontiac in 1764, placed many of their former hatreds aside and rejoined the redcoats because they clearly saw the American Revolution as a war in which to defend their homelands against white encroachment.[16] The great war leaders of the Seneca were Gayentwahga, known as Cornplanter, and Sayenqueraghta, a distinguished old warrior of 70 years known as Old Smoke. These men initially clung to a stubborn neutrality, but individuals and groups of Seneca warriors persisted in making "commitments [to the British] that undermined the consensus politics that traditionally guarded against rash decisions."[17] One Indian diplomat confided to an American agent that he could "no longer control [his] fighting men" who were turning " to the north" to join the British in Canada.[18]

The Neutral Nations

Many Indian nations tried to maintain neutrality in the white man's civil war, but the patriot militia on the frontier exhibited a peculiar disability for determining who among the native population were enemies and who were simply trying to remain neutral. Throughout the war many Indians "clung to a neutrality that cost them dearly."[19]

The Cherokees attempted neutrality and found themselves in the deplorable situation of being caught between loyalists and patriots who both assumed they were hostile.[20] As a consequence of their indecision, expeditions were undertaken in 1776, 1779, and 1781 against Cherokee villages.[21] These raids drove many of the Cherokees to seek help from the redcoats who largely failed to support them. The raids were timed to destroy the Indian harvests, leaving the women and children among the Cherokees little to eat for the winter. In 1782, a survivor of these outrages described the patriot raiders as "madmen."[22]

In 1777, a few patriots foolishly murdered an important diplomat named Cornstalk and thereby drove many formerly neutral Shawnee to the side of the British. The Onondaga Iroquois also struggled to maintain a neutrality until the patriots burned their crops in 1779. In 1780, a group of patriots attacked a Moravian town filled with neutral Delawares without provocation and killed 96 men, women, and children. Two years later, a similar attack took place on a Delaware village near Pittsburgh.

Some of the tribes of the trans-Mississippi west, including Sioux, Ojibwa, Fox, and Sauk warriors, initially rallied to the agents of the Crown because the patriots had no representatives in their villages. However, an ill-advised British attack on the Spanish town of St. Louis in 1780 ended in utter failure and caused the Crown to suffer a serious blow to its prestige among the Indians. This single failure seriously diminished the appetite of the western tribes for war against the patriots or their European allies thereafter.

Throughout the French and Indian War, the British government issued peace medals to the various chiefs in an attempt to imitate the relationship that the French had maintained with the chiefs of the Algonquian alliance. These medals had the image of George II on the front and a scene of a white man and an Indian in peaceful conference beneath a tree on the back with the dictum "Let us look to the most high who blessed our fathers with peace." During the revolution, and for some time thereafter, the Americans copied the British medals exactly in silver, bronze, and pewter for distribution among the tribes of western Pennsylvania. The engraver Edward Duffield included the 1757 date and the likeness of George II in order to symbolize the continuity of Anglo-American relationships with the Indians. Called the Quaker Peace Medals, they were among the first items struck by the U.S. Mint, and they continued to be distributed among Native American tribes until the dies failed in 1878.[23]

Joseph Brant

The Seneca leaders Cornplanter and Old Smoke "did not always enjoy a warm, working relationship" with the powerful Mohawk war leader Joseph Brant (Thayendaneagea) even though they belonged to the same Iroquois Confederacy. Brant, at age 32, was initially thought of as an upstart "with great pretensions, but little experience" in warfare, but he quickly came to be viewed as the foremost war leader among all the Iroquois. Brant left the Mohawk Valley in 1775 and traveled with Guy Johnson to Montreal where plans were made for the Iroquois to raise the King's standard across the frontier. Because he could speak the dialects of all the Iroquois nations and was noted for his devotion to the Johnson's, Brant was made Captain of the Six Nations Indian Department, but he failed, nonetheless, to influence the Oneida or Tuscarora warriors.[24]

Near Fort Niagara, Brant established a group of volunteers that included both Indians and whites, who the patriots considered renegades. He attracted most of his warriors from among the Mohawk. Moreover, although he was recognized as a senior war leader, he became easily embroiled in disputes with the leaders of the other Indian nations allied to the Crown. Nonetheless, Brant was "a man of exceptional ability, high character, and strong convictions."[25]

Brant distinguished himself throughout the revolution by leading numerous raids on patriot settlements. He was so active in pursuing the war in the New York and Pennsylvania border region that he was identified by eyewitnesses as simultaneously leading raids that were hundreds of miles apart—a physical impossibility ignored by many well-meaning but errant local historians. It has been determined, nonetheless, that his efforts were remarkably wide-ranging. Brant led several major raids in New York, on Cobleskill and Sharon (1778), on Springfield and Andrustown (1778), on German Flats (1778, and again in 1782), on Vrooman's Land (1780), on Harperfsield (1780), on Schoharie and Stone Arabia (1780), and on Ballston and Saratoga (1780). He also led the attack on the Minisink settlements in the Delaware Valley of Pennsylvania in 1779, and he helped, along with Cornplanter, to burn the Canajoharie district of New York in 1780.

Wyoming Valley

The British victory at Wyoming in June 1778 was overwhelming, but the atrocities performed upon the military and civilian captives by the Indians galvanized the frontier patriots. Those settlers, who were not caught unaware by Major John Butler's force of Indians and loyalist rangers, fled to the sanctuary of Forty Fort, one of the more substantial of several fortifications and blockhouses in the Wyoming Valley. The 24th Regiment of Connecticut militia assembled at the fort under Colonel Zebulon Butler and marched out to intercept the attackers with little comprehension of their actual number.[26] The engagement that followed, sometimes known as the "Battle of the Butlers," was decisive, and the British gave no quarter to the patriots. More than 300 of the residents were slain, and the valley was laid waste.[27] The inhabitants were made "totally dependent on the public, and...absolute objects of charity."[28] It was reported that the raiders "left about 230 women widows."[29]

Largely because of this attack, Washington determined to mount an offensive against the Indians and resolved "to carry the war into the heart of the country of the six nations; to cut off their settlements, destroy their next year's crops, and do them every other mischief of which time and circumstance will permit."[30] Congress agreed, thinking it more efficient to march 1,000 men, well led by a few determined officers, into Indian country and destroy it, rather than to "garrison the frontier settlements with three times their number."[31]

As a direct result of these decisions, Major General John Sullivan and Brigadier General James Clinton were directed to burn and plunder most of Iroquoia in 1779. While the continentals acted in the eastern villages, the militia and frontier volunteers of Colonel Daniel Brodhead mounted a separate operation from the west. The patriots attacked the towns of the Iroquois on the Mohawk River and those of the Delaware and the Muncee on the Allegheny.[32]

The Indian Campaign

The patriot strategy in the frontier war was aimed directly at the Indians rather than at the British. Their plan was to destroy the villages and burn the crops "late in the season when there was insufficient time for raising another crop before winter."[33] It was expected that the Indians would flee before the onslaught of the patriot forces, but with "nothing to subsist upon but the remains of last years corn" they would be forced to beg provisions from the British at Niagara.[34]

There was only one major military engagement during the Sullivan-Clinton campaign of 1779. This was at Newtown (Tioga), New York. The loyalist commander, Major John Butler, attempted to persuade his Indian allies to fall back before the weight of the patriot advance, but the Indians, led by Joseph Brant, stubbornly refused to budge. Butler then set his 800 men to work creating a fortification, "Having possession of the heights we would have greatly the advantage should the enemy direct their march that way." Sullivan's 3,200 troops, seeing the strength of Butler's position, attacked from both flanks and the center with infantry and light artillery. Meanwhile, the troops of generals Enoch Poor and James Clinton, overcoming serious topographical impediments, managed to almost encircle the less numerous British force, who, apprehending the danger, fled to the rear with their wounded and dying. "The battle of Newtown was so decisive that the panic-stricken enemy did not [thereafter] fire a single gun at the army on its march." Sullivan's expedition found nothing but empty villages along a 300 mile circuit through the Iroquois heartland, it being "impossible [for the British] to keep the Indians together."[35]

Sullivan crossed central New York and part of Pennsylvania in just 35 days and left behind a number of new-cut roads and new-built bridges, which helped to facilitate white settlement in the region after the war. In his official report to Congress, Sullivan noted that he had burned 40 Indian towns. "We have not left a single settlement or field of corn in the country of the [Iroquois], nor is there even the appearance of an Indian on this side of Niagara." The quantity of corn destroyed amounted to 160,000 bushels. The patriots also destroyed the plum, peach, and apple orchards of the Indians by cutting down or girdling the trunks of the trees. It would take decades to renew the agricultural produce of these trees.[36]

Colonel Daniel Brodhead, generally lacking restraint with regard to Indian fighting, set "a high standard for murder" during his phase of the operation.[37] Brodhead wrote to General Sullivan after several weeks of campaigning, "I think [the Indians] are willing by this time to make peace, but I hope it will not be granted them until they are sufficiently drubbed for their past inequities."[38] Brodhead's raids on the neutral Delaware villages at Coshicton and Lichtenau were particularly violent. In his official report, he noted, "The troops remained on the ground three whole days destroying the towns and cornfields. I never saw finer corn although it was planted much thicker than is common with our farmers."[39]

The murder of a Delaware leader, Red Eagle, and the execution of all the male captives over the age of 12 during Brodhead's operations, drove many of the neutral Indian nations into the arms of the British. The frontier militia became fearful of retaliation by the Indians and, recognizing their own excesses and believing that it was essential for the safety of their own families to return to their homes, began to desert Brodhead's command almost immediately.[40]

The Burning of the Valleys

In 1778, Joseph Brant established his headquarters at Onondaga, the ancestral center of the Iroquois Confederacy. From here he led more than 300 loyalists and Indians against the patriot settlements along the rivers and creeks that fed into the Mohawk River. Loyalists and Indians ranged throughout the New York frontier falling particularly on the old German and Dutch settlements in the Schoharie, Cobleskill, and Mohawk Valleys.

Brant burned the town of Cobleskill and plundered nearby Sharon in 1778. Ten houses and the patriot sulfur works at Sharon Springs were completely destroyed. Only by retreating to one of the three forts in the valley were the residents saved from destruction. A detachment of militia caught Brant's Indians in the open and engaged them with unforeseen results. Twenty-five patriots were killed and several were taken prisoner. Abraham Wemple, who later helped to bury the patriot dead, reported that one of the settlers was "butchered in the most inhumane manner...his body cut open and his intestines fastened around a tree several feet distant."[41]

The raid on nearby Cherry Valley a few months later was particularly violent. Many women and children were taken prisoner by the Indians, and many settlers were killed. Because some of these killings took place after the settlers had surrendered, the Cherry Valley raids were judged a massacre. Such reports completely terrorized the residents of the frontier region. More than 200 dwellings were burned during similar raids on German Flats, Vrooman's Land, Harperfsield, Schoharie, Stone Arabia, Ballston, and Saratoga in 1780. These tactical operations coordinated by British headquarters in Canada came to be known as "The Burning of the Valleys."[42]

The patriot governor of New York, George Clinton wrote with great foreboding of the results of these campaigns, "Schenectady may now be said to become the limits of our western frontier." Nonetheless, rather than increasing the support for the British among the residents of western New York, many loyalists took advantage of the opportunity afforded by these raids to abandon their homes and retreat with the Crown forces to Canada or Niagara. This left central New York with its potential to provide foodstuffs, forage, and raw materials for the Continental army almost completely in patriot hands.[43]

The War in the Ohio Country

In 1775, George Rogers Clark went to Kentucky from Virginia as a surveyor and land speculator. When the Indians sided with the British in 1776, he became the natural leader of the patriot forces who oppose them in the region. He was made a Lt. Colonel of provincial forces by the colony of Virginia and was authorized to raise troops to carry out his operations. In 1777, Clark repelled an Indian attack on Harrodsburg, sent out patrols to the Illinois country, and formulated plans for the conquest of the Ohio country. He also took measures to suppress the Indian attacks on the westernmost settlements. When his men faltered or hesitated to press their pursuit of the Indians, Clark "blackened his face" and in Indian fashioned "gave a war hoop" and marched off alone after them. This never failed to animate his men.[44]

Clark "hated Indians," and he believed that no punishment was too great for the Indians allied to the Crown. He told Henry Hamilton, the British governor of Detroit whom he had captured, that he hoped to see the entire race "extripated." He wrote, "To excel them in barbarity was and is the only way to make war upon Indians and make a name among them."[45] Clark reportedly said that, "he would never spare man, woman, or child of them on whom he could lay his hands." In one encounter, Clark personally bludgeoned to death with a tomahawk several Indian captives simply to fill the Native Americans of the region with fear.[46]

Having trained a body of men by summer 1778, he marched six days cross-country and surprised the British garrison at Kaskaskia on July 4. The French inhabitants of the region were happy to recognize the legitimacy of the patriot government, and the entire Illinois country was captured without the loss of a single man. Ironically, Clark, as a warrior, was a man that Indians could understand. "Blunt, remorseless, often cruel, and seemingly fearless, Clark swaggered and disdained his enemies." He was most successful in dealing with Indian leaders in this guise. Having dealt a staggering blow to the natives, he attempted a program of pacification among them, but this was complicated by his Indian hating and his natural tendencies toward violent action. When dealing with them as a representative of the Congress or as a diplomat he was largely out of his element.[47]

Clark was countered in his attempts at diplomacy by British Governor Henry "Hair Buyer" Hamilton. In 1779, Clark marched about 170 men through the swamps and tributaries of the Wabash River basin and appeared before the frontier headquarters of the astonished Hamilton at Vincennes in mid-winter demanding his surrender. By claiming that he had many more men than he really did, Clark overcame the willingness of the formidable British garrison to resist.

Only the small size of his actual force kept Clark from attacking Detroit directly. In 1780, he established Fort Jefferson near the mouth of the Ohio River and reached out from this post to defend his own outpost at Cahokia and the Spanish settlement at St. Louis. He then returned to Kentucky and gathered 1,000 men to invade and destroy the Shawnee villages in that region. In 1782, he led another force against the Indian villages on the Big Miami River. This was his last important service during the revolution. The hardships and exposure to cold and wet conditions during the war led to an infirmity in his middle years that crippled him before his time. His younger brother William was one of the leaders of the Lewis and Clark expedition that surveyed the Louisiana Territory in 1805.

Notes

1. Frederick Cook, *Journals of the Military Expedition of Major General John Sullivan Against the Six Nations of Indians in 1779 with Records of the Centennial Celebrations* (Auburn, NY: Knapp, Peck & Thompson, 1887), 529. The Mohawk Thayendaneagea (Joseph Brant), and the Senecas Gayentwahga (Cornplanter), Honeyawas (Farmer's Brother), and Sagoyewatha (Red Jacket) were all considered important Indian leaders against the patriots by those celebrating Sullivan's victories 100 years after the event. All the Senecas named were present during the Wyoming massacre.

2. Richard White, *The Middle Ground, Indians, Empires, and Republics in the Great Lakes Region, 1650–1815* (New York: Cambridge University Press, 1991), 367.

3. Colin G. Calloway, *The American Revolution in Indian Country, Crisis and Diversity in Native American Communities* (Cambridge, UK: Cambridge University Press, 1999), 4.

4. White, 368.

5. Louis B. Wright, *The Atlantic Frontier: Colonial American Civilization, 1607–1763* (New York: Alfred A. Knopf, 1951), 224.

6. R. Douglas Hurt, *The Ohio Frontier, Crucible of the Old Northwest, 1720–1830* Indianapolis: Indiana University Press, 1996), 67.

7. Howard Swiggett, *War Out of Niagara: Walter Butler and the Tory Rangers* (New York: Columbia University Press, 1933), 57.

8. Swiggett.

9. Hurt, 76.

10. Hurt, 76–77.

11. Hurt, 65.

12. Calloway, *The American Revolution*, 68.

13. Samuel Adams Drake, *The Border Wars of New England, Commonly Called King Williams's and Queen Anne's Wars*, (Williamstown, MA: Corner House Publishers, 1973), 150n.

14. For a more detailed account of Joseph Gill see John C. Huden, "The White Chief of the St. Francis Abenaki," *Vermont History* 24 (1956): 207, 337–338.

15. Calloway, *The American Revolution*, 34.

16. Hurt, 85. See also p. 78.

17. Gavin K. Watt, *The Burning of the Valleys: Daring Raids from Canada Against the New York Frontier in the Fall of 1780* (Toronto: Dundurn Press, 1997), 27.

18. Hurt, 66.

19. Calloway, *The American Revolution*, 39.

20. Calloway, *The American Revolution*, 58.

21. Calloway, *The American Revolution*, 49.

22. Calloway, *The American Revolution*, 50.

23. The die cracked in 1809, and those minted after this date clearly show the fault.

24. Watt, 26.

25. Barbara Graymont, *The Iroquois in the American Revolution* (Syracuse, NY: Syracuse University Press, 1972), 53.

26. Wyoming was then claimed by the state of Connecticut based on its original charter.

27. Thomas E. Byrne and Lawrence E. Byrne, eds., *The Sullivan-Clinton Expedition of 1779 in Pennsylvania and New York* (Elmira, NY: Chemung County Historical Society, 1999), 4.

28. Frederick Cook, 147.

29. Cook, 107–108.

30. Calloway, *The American Revolution*, 51.

31. The men referred to are General Armstrong (no first name) and Colonel Daniel Brodhead. Calloway, *The American Revolution*, 47–48.

32. Cook, 4.

33. Calloway, *The American Revolution*, 47.

34. Calloway, *The American Revolution*, 56.

35. Cook, 302.

36. Byrne and Byrne, 29. Sullivan resigned his commission upon his return to serve as a delegate to Congress.

37. Hurt, 85–86.

38. Letter of Daniel Brodhead to Major General John Sullivan, August 6, 1779; reported in Cook, 307.

39. Letter of Daniel Brodhead to General George Washington, September 16, 1779; reported in Cook, 308.

40. Hurt, 86.

41. Graymont, 166.

42. See Watt.

43. Graymont, 238–239.

44. White, 369.

45. Calloway, *The American Revolution*, 48.

46. Quoted in White, 368.

47. White, 371.

Epilogue: The Small Wars and Manifest Destiny

We will protect you against all future inconvenience. We wish to set aside a part of your territory for your nation, where you may live forever, you and your children.... [And] so that your children may become as intelligent as the whites, we wish to send to you teachers who will instruct them.

—The Fort Laramie Treaty, 1858[1]

Indian Life under the Great White Father

At the end of the Revolutionary War, many of America's Indian allies formed treaty relations with the United States while the Loyalist tribes generally passed to the west of the Appalachians or removed to Canada to take advantage of British protection. Other nations, which had attempted an uneasy neutrality during the revolution, viewed the new republic with cautious curiosity. American diplomats sent to the tribes attempted to resurrect the old ceremonial vocabulary of the "Great White Father" and his "Indian Children" formerly utilized by the British in forming treaties, with the president taking the place of the king. However, in the first decades of the 19th century the British retained control of Canada and much of the Great Lakes Region, and they willingly incited the Indians to cause trouble on the American frontier.

In the Proclamation of 1763, Britain had attempted to enforce a western boundary to white settlement along the Appalachian chain that generally favored the Indians. By comparison after the revolution, the independent-minded American states seemed weak and disorganized as white settlers and land speculators poured over the mountains and on to Indian land. The Mohawk war leader and British supporter Joseph Brant worked with native tribes throughout the Ohio country and the lakes region of Canada to create a Western Confederacy to coordinate a resistance to the United States and set the Ohio River as the border between Indian lands and those of the new republic. Americans claimed the entire Midwest and Great Lakes region and formed a political entity from it called the Northwest Territory because it was on the northwest margin of those lands recognized by treaty with Britain in 1783. Brant's confederacy thoroughly defeated two American armies sent to occupy the newly created Northwest Territory in 1790 and 1791, respectively. The latter force of 1,400 men led by Arthur St. Clair had more than 600 killed and 300 wounded making the defeat one of the worst proportionately ever visited on American troops in any war even into modern times. In response, a punitive force under General "Mad" Anthony Wayne won a battle with the tribes at Fallen Timbers, after which the British virtually abandoned the Indian survivors. This changed a minor victory by American arms into a huge diplomatic success with the Indians who yielded most of the Ohio country to white settlement. Wayne relied on the threat posed by a thinly spread series of forts from Cincinnati to Fort Wayne (Indiana) rather than diplomacy to bring the native leaders to the peace table.[2]

Throughout the crisis, the British feigned neutrality, but their agents assured the Indians of their support in terms of arms and ammunition. In 1794, the Jay Treaty required that the British abandon their western posts, but British pretensions to the Old Northwest were not truly eased until 1815, leaving the Indians to make the best deal with the United States that they could. During this crisis the tribes had gained the undying enmity of the western settlers, and most of the tribes abandoned the woodlands in the United States and sought refuge with the British in Canada. The tribes thereafter utilized the recognized border (medicine line) with the United States as an invisible, but effective, barrier to pursuit. The Oregon treaty line with Canada was not permanently settled at the 49th parallel until 1846, and it was used in a similar manner during the Plains Indian Wars of the second half of the century.

Among the major objectives of the Lewis and Clark Expedition (1803–1805) were efforts to make a show of American sovereignty over the Louisiana Territory after its purchase from France and to establish relations and treaties with the western tribes then living in the region. These had formerly owed allegiance to or recognized the British, French, or Spanish. Yet, from the inception of the United States, treaties and alliances between the federal government and the Indian nations were conveniently broken whenever coveting white settlers became numerous or aggressive enough to work their collective wills upon the politicians. The efforts of the Indian population to thwart white incursions into their lands often brought the government to intervene, usually on the side of the settlers and with devastating military force. Nonetheless, in 1809, federal troops forcibly removed 1,700 white squatters from Indian lands, but they were so quickly replaced by other intruders that, without a constant military presence, the policy seemed doomed to failure.

Indian policy at the federal level was initially crafted by George Washington's Secretary of War Henry Knox, and it was carried out by most of the administrations that followed. Knox envisioned a policy of "civilization" and "Christianization" for the tribes. He sought to teach the Indians to abandon their traditional gender-based communal economy of male hunting and warfare and female agriculture and childrearing for a Euro-American lifestyle of male-oriented farming and female domesticity that would allow the tribes to prosper on a much smaller land base. This, it was hoped, would open former Indian lands to white settlement without eradicating the Indians. Federal agents relentlessly pushed this civilization program, or a near facsimile, throughout the 19th century.[3]

The lands of the southeast quadrant of the present United States promised to be among the most productive in America. The dark, rich soils of Georgia, Alabama, and Mississippi initially attracted a scattering of pioneer farmers, many of them Scotch-Irish immigrants who passed through the established colonial settlements to carve out farmsteads on the frontier. The settlers thereby placed themselves in position to directly confront some of the fiercest warriors among the Indian tribes. Among them were the Creek, Cherokee, Choctaw, Chickasaw, and Seminole who resided in the heart of what would become cotton country in just a generation. The land was "perfectly suited to growing cotton, plenty of land for raising cattle, forests of elms and red oaks, peach trees, and magnolias." From 1810 to 1820, the region was flooded with white invaders many of whom would create the great plantations of antebellum society. They bought land for as little as $1.25 to $2.00 an acre.[4]

During Andrew Jackson's eight years as president (1828–1836), almost 100 Indian treaties were signed. Some of them were legitimate, and the tribes agreed to various amounts of just compensation to give up their lands and move west. Other agreements were questionable with agents misrepresenting the intent or meaning of the treaties or with tribes selling rights to lands that they did not possess. Some tribes went peacefully to the lands west of the Mississippi, but others dared to fight against the invaders. Chief among those who resisted white encroachment were the Muskhogean-speaking Lower Creek in the east, the Shawnee of the Midwest lake region, the fierce Dakotah (Sioux, Cheyenne, and related tribes) of the western plains, and the indomitable Apache and Comanche of the desert Southwest.

Manifest Destiny

Families are not normally considered agents of cultural change, but this was not the case in the early days of the United States. The simplest maps of the unknown interior spurred Americans to relocate to towns that existed nowhere except on land office surveys. Calling themselves settlers and emigrants, families from across the states began a march into the vaguely empty space west of the Appalachian Mountains and beyond. With them came the slaves, forced to emigrate sometimes in ways that forever broke black family ties. Before them stood the Indians and their families, aboriginal inheritors of the land, poised to be swept aside and dispossessed.

In July 1845, New York newspaperman John L. O'Sullivan wrote in the *United States Magazine and Democratic Review* that it was the nation's "manifest destiny to overspread and to possess the whole continent, which Providence has given for the development of the great experiment of liberty and self-government." The phrase *manifest destiny* caught the imagination of the country and came, thereafter, to stand for the entire expansive movement to the West. Yet, the slogan also coalesced a number of hazy images Americans had about themselves and the nation into a solid idea with purpose behind it. *Manifest destiny* was the one idea about the nation on which all sections in America could agree.[5]

For three decades (since 1803) the trans-Mississippi region of the Great Plains was considered a mere wilderness, tempting only to adventurers, land speculators, and fur traders. The 19th-century explorations of men such as Meriwether Lewis, William Clark, Zebulon Pike, John C. Fremont, and others hinted at the richness of the interior West, but only the Indian nations driven from the east by white encroachment settled there. Nonetheless, the exploration and domination of the North American continent was no haphazard series of fortuitous ramblings and random discoveries, but a careful process initiated by Thomas Jefferson in 1803 and programmed thereafter from the urban business centers of the East and Midwest, particularly Washington, D.C. and St. Louis. Armed at times with specific instructions, explorers, traders, artists, photographers, and soldiers were sent into the unfenced expanses of grass, the towering mountains, and the formidable deserts to gather information that would further the nation's plans for the development of the continent.[6]

Indian Removal

During the Creek War (1814–1815), Andrew Jackson led a force composed of militia and allied native warriors, but he came to believe that there was no real distinction between friendly and hostile Indians. In 1828, Jackson won the Presidency, and his populous attitudes toward Native Americans were swept into office with him. Ultimately, like some of his predecessors in office, particularly John Adams and James Monroe, President Jackson came to believe that the government should institute an Indian policy known as *forced relocation,* or *removal.* This policy would displace the remaining tribes of the Old Northwest to the great plains of the Dakotas, or to Minnesota, or to the area west of the Mississippi River now known as Oklahoma. Congressional debate between Whigs and Democrats questioned whether this was best for the Indians, but neither side suggested that the Indians retain their homelands or reestablish their former aboriginal lifestyle elsewhere. Realistically, the raids, hunting, and roaming associated with tribal existence in the past could no longer be accommodated within the boundaries of a developing United States.

The issue of removal was complicated by two additional facts. First, the five civilized nations of the Southeast—the Choctaw, Chickasaw, Creek, Cherokee, and Seminole—were settled in villages in this region and were using agricultural techniques that made them greatly more advanced than the western tribes. The Cherokee and the Creek mounted a particularly strong opposition to removal for this reason. Secondly, there had been intermarriage between the native peoples and both whites and blacks, producing many mixed race persons. The lifestyle adopted by these mixed race persons very closely resembled that of neighboring white farmers: dressing in the same style, following Christianity, and even owning slaves. Full-blooded Indians, however, tended to retain their tribal dress and customs. Only in Florida, among the Seminoles, did the native and black populations form an effective alliance against the white troops sent to suppress them.

Congressman Wilson Lumpkin of Georgia was determined to give the President of the United States the legal authority and the budget to clear out the Indians from the most desirable lands in America, especially the Cherokee of his own state of Georgia. In 1830, the Indian Removal Act was signed into law. The white population of the country had waited nervously for word of the act's fate in Congress, and many were shocked when they learned that it had passed. The whole American people had seemed to be against it. Now Jackson had signed the bill claiming that it said nothing about breaking old treaties with the tribes. The act empowered the states, if they so chose, to expel any of the native residents of a region by force exchanging land in the east for land in the west. The act provided for the compensation of any tribe relocated west of the Mississippi River, but Congress provided only half a million dollars for this purpose. The land that was being taken from the tribes was worth many times this amount.

The Native American was displaced by a numerically and technologically superior group of immigrants who transplanted their way of life, culture, religion, and language while dispossessing the Indian of his own. "The displacement of the native population in North America was accelerated by certain biological, technical, and cultural advantages enjoyed by European immigrants at the time of contact." Among these was a surplus white population in the cities that was prepared to emigrate; an acquired immunity to specific biological infections; the availability of sophisticated military weapons and tools; and an absolutist religious belief that the white race was meant by God to rule America.[7]

By the end of the 19th century, the original inhabitants of the area known as the Northeast woodlands were all but gone. They made up less than one percent of the population of the region and occupied little more than two percent of their original territory. Even this was allotted to them as reservations situated within a white nation that did not recognize them as citizens.

Notes

1. Alvin M. Josephy, Jr., *The Patriot Chiefs* (New York: The Viking Press, 1962), 283.

2. Daniel K. Richter, *Facing East from Indian Country, A Native History of Early America* (Cambridge, MA: Harvard University Press, 2001), 225.

3. Richter, 227.

4. Sean Michael O'Brien, *In Bitterness and in Tears: Andrew Jackson's Destruction of the Creeks and Seminoles* (Guilford, CT: The Lyons Press, 2003), 9.

5. William H. Goetzmann, *Exploration and Empire, The Explorer and the Scientist in the Winning of the American West* (New York: The History Book Club, 1966) ascribes the slogan *Manifest Destiny* to Jane McManus Storm.

6. See William H. Goetzmann, v–vi.

7. Bernd C. Peyer, *The Tutor'd Mind, Indian Missionary-Writers in Antebellum America* (Amherst: University of Massachusetts Press, 1997), 2.

Appendix: North American Indian Lifestyles

Native American Cultural Areas

In order to provide a comprehensive historical study rather than a vague "mile wide and inch deep" overview, this text has emphasized the family life and culture of the first nations inhabiting the Northeast woodlands. This was one of the largest, most populous, and most stable regions supporting Native American life. In the Northeast region, family structure, kinship, and social organization; material culture and religion; governance and economics; and the ways of war, peace, and diplomacy were fairly precise and well-defined, especially among the Iroquois. The region also had the largest number of literate observers in the 17th and early 18th centuries when Indian life was least contaminated by European contact. The Indians these writers saw were most like the way Indians actually were.

It is customary in studying Native Americans, however, to organize the totality of nations on the North American continent into several *cultural areas* in order to make convenient distinctions among discrete peoples. To a large degree, these geographical areas are an artificial construct, and some of the characteristics and distinctions attributed to the people living therein are arbitrary, if not transitory. Within the cultural areas, the diversity of traits was greater in the West and South than in the Northeast. Using the Mississippi River as a dividing line, the western half of the continent has seven areas while the eastern half has only two.

Depending on the degree of detail employed, ethnographers and social scientists have also identified dozens of distinct cultural subregions distinguished by geography or location, such as Mesa Verde, Danger Cave, or the Everglades. Nonetheless, the similarities found among the residents of the greater cultural areas usually outweigh any specific differences. Although each culture area was conceived as representative of a discreet type of Native American culture, the complex conditions of life and the ebb and flow of Indian nations are not easily adjusted to generalized types.

Many of these cultural areas can be combined within the continental United States into larger regions for further study. Besides the Northeast woodlands, there are the Southeast woodlands and Gulf Coast, the Southwest mesas and deserts, the Great Plains and the Plateau, and the California and Pacific Coasts. In this appendix, these will be emphasized.

The Indians of the Southeast Woodlands

The Southeast woodlands cultural area is most easily defined as that east of the Mississippi River to the Atlantic coastline and south of the Tennessee River to the Gulf Coast and Florida. As many as five different languages were spoken in the Southeast woodlands including Muskhogean, Iroquoian, Timucan, Siouan, and Caddo. In this area were found the Muskhogean (Upper and Lower Creek), the Choctaw, the Chickasaw, and the Seminole; the Iroquoian Cherokee, Tuscarora, and Savannah (Susquehannock); and also the Catawba, the Timuca, the Natchez, and the Yuchi.

Several small bands occupied the Atlantic coastal regions of South Carolina and Georgia, and they differed from other tribes in the area though their great reliance on aquatic food sources. As we have seen, the Tuscarora and the Susquehannock (known locally as the Savannah) were on the margins of the neighboring cultural area to the north, affecting the tribes therein and effected by them. The Timuca and the Seminole of the Florida borderland were intermediate types far less dependent on agriculture than the other major tribes. They were considerable users of aquatic resources and a bread-like starch taken from the root of the Coonti plant. They lived in circular shelters raised some small distance off the ground with comparatively open sides that may show some West Indian influence on their cultures.

The tribes most typical of the central region south of the Tennessee River valley—the Muskhogean, Cherokee, and Yuchi—shared several distinctive traits. Their homes were generally rectangular with curved roofs covered in bark or thatch. They also used a distinctive wicker-work lathe covered in mud-plaster for the sides. Their towns were well-fortified with palisades. Among other traits were a great use of vegetable food resources and intensive agriculture (maize, cane, pumpkins, watermelons, and tobacco). They hunted deer, bear, bison, turkeys, and other small animals. Their major weapon was the longbow. Fish were taken when convenient, but no great communal effort was put into developing an annual catch. Their use of bear oil, hickory nut and acorn nut oils, persimmon bread, and hominy was noteworthy but not dispositive of their identity. They built only dugout canoes because appropriate barks were not readily available.

Their costume was moderate and chiefly made of deerskins that were pounded in a mortar during the tanning process. This process was a distinction found nowhere else. The garments for men were shirt-like body coverings worn with a breechclout or wrap-around skirt, much like that of the women. The women used a toga-like upper body covering of deerskin. Outer clothing included bison robes, feather cloaks, finger-woven fabrics of bark fiber, and, in the western part of the area, some fabrics made of woven buffalo-hair. Their material culture evidenced no true sculpture and little metalwork, but they produced stonework (flint points, tools, scrapers, etc.) and pottery (coil process) of a high order. The women wove mats of cane and some of corn husks. They used cane and splints in their basketry and applied nicely wrought decorations to most of their basketry and woodwork. Stone knives and darts had both cane and bone handles.

There were also numerous small tribes living in the region. The Siouan-speaking Catawba attracted a nucleus of the small inland bands around them and formed an important pro-English confederacy in the early 18th century. The Yamasee were another weak confederacy, this time of small coastal bands. These initially supported the English but turned against them in the so-called Yamasee War of 1715. Soundly defeated by the colonials with help from the Lower Creek and the Chickasaw, the Yamasee removed to northern Florida, allied themselves to the Seminole, and continued sporadic raids into the Carolinas. It was in response to these raids and the Spanish presence that the colony of Georgia was established as a buffer in 1732.

The Natchez (Natchay) lived in 9 or 10 small villages near the present-day city on the Mississippi River that shares their name. In the 17th century, these villages supported a large indigenous population of related persons consolidated with refugees from Chickasaw aggression to their north. The Natchez were prominent as an example of a mound-building chiefdom with a royal lineage surviving into historical times. Among the Natchez, the women of the royal line could weld impressive power.

The Natchez and the Caddo-speaking tribes on the west bank of the Mississippi River may have had archaic connections to the culture of Mexico and middle America across the Gulf. Evidence suggests that in the 15th century a religious revival with Aztec-Mexican overtones reached the area bringing with it death cults and effigies of skulls, weeping faces, feathered serpents, and fat-lipped Eagle warriors carrying trophy heads more typical of Yucatan than North America. There is no evidence of a migration of people from Mexico, but rather there may have been an intrusion of ideas. The nearby Creek culture was seemingly less effected by the more gruesome aspects of this revival, which seems to have evaporated by the 16th century.

In general terms, the nations living in present-day Mississippi and the Gulf Coast shared some basic traits in their material culture that were observed in the historic period. They were hoe farmers; fished with similar tackle; hunted the same piney woods, cypress swamps, and cane breaks; and they used dugout canoes that they poled through the shallows and the bayous. All boiled the same type of corn soup, prepared the same hominy, and gathered the same nuts and berries. Their large towns with surrounding palisades and moats contained up to 300 family dwellings and served as defensive rallying points for outlying villages.[1]

In the 18th century, the English formed strong bilateral alliances with each of the so-called civilized tribes (Creek, Cherokee, Choctaw, and Chickasaw). Although the Choctaw and Chickasaw were hereditary antagonists, these alliances were maintained into the early 19th century. Nonetheless, the nearby influence of the French and Spanish kept the region in turmoil, and factions among the tribes were always in play. The Chickasaw were the most solid of the four English allies, and their territory, which bordered on the Mississippi, allowed them to harass the French voyagers going up and down the river. This constantly threatened the communications of the French in the Northeast and those in Louisiana and was effective in keeping the two isolated. The four civilized tribes never lost a major battle to an outside enemy from the time of Fernando De Soto in 1541 until the American Revolution. This included the destruction of a major Iroquois invasion force in 1732.

Of all the Native Americans in the Southeast, the four civilized tribes were most remarkable in terms of assuming white ways. They acquired livestock, undertook European farming techniques, married into leading families, and amassed political power as well as wealth. The Cherokee adopted white dress, built schools, roads, and churches; and the Cherokee scholar Sequoya developed a written alphabet for their language and created a native language press.

The Creek villages housed, besides their own people, fragments of many other tribes. Their confederacy of villages was itself in two parts seemingly divided into peace and war moieties with the peace towns (indicated by the color white) in the upper reaches of their territory and the war towns (red) in the lower. Traditionally, the principal chief of the confederacy was chosen from the upper towns, and the war chief was selected from the lower. The emergence of strong leaders among both the Upper and Lower Creek villages, however, caused a split in the tribe between the pro-French and pro-English factions. This broke largely along geographic boundaries with the Lower Creek leaning toward the French in nearby Mobile and New Orleans. To a lesser degree, the internal conflicts were between full-blooded Creek conservatives and the largely mix-blood progressives, particularly over the issue of the cession of land to the English. The unrest among the Creek transferred into the Federalist Era. Similar problems also beset the Choctaw, but they were not so marked.

The Muskhogean speaking Creek, Chickasaw, and Choctaw were often at odds among themselves, and the Iroquoian Cherokee argued with everyone. The Chickasaw and Choctaw were implacable rivals, and they were physically different suggesting a different genetic origin. The Chickasaw were tall, far-ranging, quarrelsome, and aggressive, while the Choctaw were quiet farmers of lesser stature who tended to stay near home and tend their garden plots. Moreover, the Chickasaw developed a statuesque and highly refined horse through careful breeding, and the Choctaw countered with a sturdy riding pony that admirers claimed was more horse for its height than any other. Finally, the Chickasaw, but not the Choctaw, sided with the Federal government in its operations against the Lower Creek and the British during the War of 1812.

From the inception of the United States, treaties and alliances between the federal government and the Indian nations were conveniently broken whenever coveting white settlers became numerous or aggressive enough to work their collective wills upon the politicians. The efforts of the Indian population to avoid removal and thwart white incursions into their lands often caused the government to intervene, usually on the side of the settlers, and sometimes with devastating military force.

In 1830, an Indian Removal Act was signed into Federal law in order to open the fertile Southeast region to white settlement. For the next 100 years, removal to reservations remained a basic Indian policy of the Federal Government. With the discovery of gold in Georgia on Cherokee land, further laws were passed that forbade any meeting of the tribal councils, but the Indians remained steadfast in their opposition to relocation. Alabama and Mississippi followed Georgia in passing laws requiring the Indians to comply. Most of the tribes in the region simply complied but not the Cherokee, who stood for their rights as a sovereign nation for almost a decade. In 1838, after the Cherokee had withstood court challenges, threats, bribes, confiscation of property, severed supplies, and other harassments to remain on their tribal lands, an escort of armed troops forced a great column of displaced Indian families westward to reservations in Oklahoma. Over a quarter of these Indians died on this journey, which came to be known among the Cherokee as the "Trail of Tears."

The Seminole—sometimes considered the fifth civilized tribe of the Southeast—suffered greatly at the hands of the Americans in the 19th century. Among the Seminole, the native, black, and mixed race populations of northern Florida formed an effective alliance against the white troops sent against them to force their removal. Fought almost constantly during the first half of the 19th century, the war with the Seminole is often considered the longest lasting continuous struggle between Indians and whites waged in America. An estimated 4,000 Seminole were ordered to leave Florida and remove to Oklahoma. Many refused when they discovered that any of them who had black blood would not be allowed to leave and might be sold into slavery. One of the reasons for the almost continuous prosecution of a long war against the Seminole was the refuge they afforded to runaway black slaves and their acceptance of blacks into their families and among their leadership. This fueled support for the war among the plantation owners and white yeomen farmers who lived in constant fear of slave revolts.

Osceola, one of the most important Seminole leaders, was encouraged to come to a peace conference in 1837, but was assaulted and bundled off to jail in Charleston, SC where he died.[2] After 1842, the government abandoned its focus on exterminating the Seminoles when some of the tribal leaders agreed to removal, but many mixed race Afro-Seminole continued to defend their families in the swamps. Raids and punitive expeditions continued back and forth. Moves to end the war by negotiation were met by cries of shame from white Floridians on the frontier; but Congressman Henry Wise complained that the "fatal, disastrous, disgraceful Seminole campaign" was being continued "without inquiry, and without discussion." Wise asked, "Would any corporation or company take 30 millions of dollars to pay the expenditures of this disgraceful Indian war?"[3] After several years of relative peace, in 1858, the federal government simply declared an end to the Seminole conflict. Throughout the Civil War about 120 Seminole remained behind quietly residing with their families on high ground in the swamps. In the end, the cost of Indian removal in the Southeast was approximately one white death for every three Indians transported to Oklahoma.

The Indians of the Plains and Plateau

The Plains tribes had first been encountered by the Lewis and Clark Expedition as it crossed the watershed of the Missouri River during their exploration of the Louisiana Purchase (1803–1805). These nations included many interrelated tribes and discrete bands, some of which were bitter enemies. These included Assiniboine, Mandan, Arapaho, Gros Ventre, Pawnee, Crow, Omaha, Osage, Cheyenne, Sioux, and other lesser known bands. It is difficult to systematically characterize each of the many migratory and nomadic tribes in this region in the same manner. From time to time, there were as many as 35 discrete tribes, groups, and subgroups on the plains. Many recognized bands were actually subdivisions of others. For instance, the original Sioux (Dakota) inhabitants of the plains included five major subgroups: Ogallala, Santee, Sisseton, Teton, and Yankton. The Blackfoot (Piegan, Brule, and Blood) were generally considered part of the Algonquian language family although they were politically and socially separated from those in the woodlands, and others like the Northern Comanche were generally consider a Southwestern tribe although they could be found most often roaming on the Plains in search of buffalo. The Nez Percé and Northern Shoshone exhibited strong Plains traits, but geographically they were residents of the Plateau cultural area.

In terms of their kinship systems, many of the tribes of the West were ambilineal, allowing individuals the option of choosing their lineage from either their father or mother. Although there could be more than one wife in a household (often sisters), the Plains Indians lived in matrilocal familial units, and the women owned the shelter and the few material objects that it contained. The men owned their horses, their personal weapons, and their regalia. At death, these were often placed with their bodies on a platform-style burial site with a favorite horse buried nearby.

Among the Plains tribes, both the Crow and Omaha were listed as archetypes in the kinship systems devised by Louis Henry Morgan in 1871 (*Systems of Consanguinity and Affinity of the Human Family*). Any subgroups of these archetypes were generally called "gens" or "sibs." The Omaha system was patrilineal with marriage promoted with cross-cousins found among the father's sister's children. It was matrilocal and emphasized a corporate affiliation to the familial kinship group including inheritance and tribute duties. The Crow system was both matrilocal and matrilineal with marriage partners found among their mother's brother's children. Like the Iroquois, the Crow emphasized the importance of clan identity and obligation. Most of the Western tribes fit into one or the other of these patterns to a greater or lesser extent.

The Plateau area joins the Plains on their western boundary, and its lack of a uniform topography and climate produced various lifestyles among the Native Americans living there. In eastern Oregon and Washington, southern Alberta and British Columbia, northern Idaho, and western Montana the land was moist and fertile in summer and cold and snow-filled in winter. The winters were very long. The southern part of the Plateau was a virtual desert. The Plateau people were on the boundaries of so many other cultural areas as to be effected by them all. Moreover, there were 16 or more dialect divisions among the bands resident in the region.

Meriwether Lewis left a wealth of miscellaneous information concerning the tribes of the northern Plateau. The traits that he noted can be summarized as: an extensive use of salmon, deer, roots (camas), and berries as food sources, and the storage of pulverized forms of these for winter use; semi-subterranean pit-like winter homes with a conical roof and a smoke hole entrance; and movable summer homes of reed- or mat-covered tents and pole-supported lean-tos. Other traits included poorly developed water transportation and the use of dogs (later horses) for moving possessions. Pottery was generally unknown, but the making of baskets, bags, and pouches was highly developed. The clothing was composed of deer-skin and furs. Stonework was limited to tools and projectile points, and their work in bone, metal, and wood was poorly developed. Remarkable traits included the use of handled digging sticks and cooking with hot rocks in holes and watertight baskets. Most Plateau tribes combined the traits of seed-gathers and buffalo hunters. Beginning about 1740, the

Plateau villagers began trading with the Plains tribes for horses; thereafter they became increasingly migratory.

The Nez Percé and Northern Shoshone were among the best known Plateau tribes. Other Shoshone bands lived in the more arid regions of western Utah and Nevada, but their material culture was essentially the same as their northern brothers. The Northern Shoshone lived in dome-shaped brush structures before they adopted the buffalo-skin teepee. They had no means of water transportation. Deer being scarce, they depended on small game, wild grass seeds, edible roots, and salmon. Like the Nez Percé, they generally came to depend on the buffalo once they took to the Plains. Shoshone warriors carried a Plains-like war shield, and their clothing was also very Plains-like. The Shoshone produced rabbit-fur blankets, good coil and twine baskets, and some undifferentiated jars and pots.

The Nez Percé lived in permanent double lean-to shelters made of poles and used a subterranean house as a young men's lodge or social club. Lodges and societies were formed around mutual interests such as war, medicine, or hunting, and they had initiation rights and member obligations. Their skin work was well-developed, but no effort was made toward the production of cloth. Their fish spears, hooks, traps, net bags, and wood work was much more advanced than any of the Plains tribes. They used sinew-backed bows, lances, clubs, and knives in war and used a heavy leather shirt reinforced with rod and slat armor. The Nez Percé women produced a highly refined form of basketry and very fine soft leather bags. Like the Shoshone, the Nez Percé became increasingly Plains-like once introduced to the horse.

The Plains nations lived in a great sea of grass. The Great Plains consisted of sprawling expanses of grassland up to 400 miles wide and more than 2,000 miles long extending from central Texas to Alberta. Today, 10 states and 3 provinces have been designated in this region. The grasses here were sometimes as tall as a person. The only consistent sources of potable water on the plains were marked by the sparse clumps of willow and cottonwood trees that lined the shallow streams and rivers. Firewood was at a premium, and the Indians commonly used dried buffalo dung (chips) or knotted grass twists as a source of fuel. Prairie fires were a great threat.

The chief cultural trait of the Plains nations was their single-minded dependence on the buffalo as a food source. These they hunted on foot with bows while disguised under a wolf-skin, or they drove whole groups of animals over cliffs to be killed or finished off with spears. Wolves were always prowling around the fringes of the herd, and the disguise allowed the hunter to get within the effective range of his weapon. The Plains nations, with limited exceptions, were entirely nomadic, living in buffalo-skin teepees for most or all of the year as they followed the buffalo herds in their north–south migrations across the Great Plains. Not until the 18th century did the horse become a mainstay of their culture.

Due to their mobile ways, the peoples of the Plains have a large number of nonconfirmatory (negative) characteristics. They lacked any form of agriculture, did not fish extensively, and had no form of water transportation. They did not produce pottery or basketry to any extent, had no true weaving, and only developed a weak ability to work in stone, wood, and bone. Nonetheless, they developed a highly regarded form of rawhide work, especially in their buffalo hide war shields of which the warriors were very proud. They also developed a special method of fashioning and decorating clothing from deerskins. These were described as "regal in their construction and decoration, requiring months for making."[4] The men wore breechclouts, leggings, moccasins, and simple shirts that sometimes reached to the knees. The moccasins were of decorated buffalo hide that had been fashioned by the women and softened by chewing the leather. Both men and women commonly kept their hair in two braids on either side of the face, and the eagle-feather headdresses of the men were distinctive. Some of the Plains peoples were semihorticultural, tapping a limited number of roots and berries and growing a little maize as added food resources, but most were wholly nomadic.

The Plains tribes developed a remarkable ability with horses, and their way of life became rooted in a *horse culture.* There were three primary uses among the Indians for horses: as riding animals during the hunt, as a tactical weapon of advantage in warfare, and as a burden bearer in moving camps. The Pawnee were known to hunt buffalo from horseback before 1700. They may have begun with long bows and lances as hunting weapons when afoot, but with the acquisition of horses they shortened their bows to about three feet to make them easier to use when mounted. Bows were still in use after guns were introduced to the Plains because firearms reloaded too slowly.

Undoubtedly, the hostile pressure of woodlands Ojibwa armed with firearms was a factor in moving the forest Sioux from Minnesota to the Dakotas, but once the Plains tribes had horses, the effect reversed itself even though the Sioux were unarmed in terms of guns. The woodland Ojibwa, thereafter, remained within the forest margins. An Ojibwa chief explained the military advantage of mounted warfare on the Plains. "While the Sioux keep to the plains with their horses we are no match for them; for we being footman, they could get upwind of us, and set fire to the grass; when we marched for the woods, they would be there before us, dismount, and under cover fire upon us. Until we have horses like them, we must keep to the woods, and leave the plains to them."[5]

Finally, the Indians were accustomed to the use of dogs as beasts of burden, and they quickly transferred their technology to use by horses by scaling up the travois. Whether the Indians first chose to use the horse as a form of transportation for goods, or for personal mobility is unrecorded. A number of Southwestern tribes at the beginning of the 18th century were known to transport their lodges by dog traction and to reserve their horses solely for warfare. This may have been due to the limited number of horses available to them at the time.

It should be remembered that the horse culture did not immediately make inroads into the vast entirety of the West. Its adoption was slowed by the availability of appropriate animals and the willingness of the tribes of the southern Plains to trade breeding stock, especially stallions, to the north. The native warrior reveled in his war stallion, and the Indians practiced no form of gelding (fixing). Indian warriors ridiculed white cavalry for riding geldings. Once present, the excellent range and abundant grasslands ensured a natural increase in the horse herds with relatively little care. A Blackfoot born on the plains of Canada in the 1720s might have seen the first horse acquired by his people as a child and lived to see the horse culture become stabilized among them at the turn of the century.

Horses diffused northward from the Spanish settlements from which they were initially traded, stolen, or driven. Thereafter, many tribes turned to secondary horse trading. The Pueblo revolt of 1680 against the Spanish estancias, rancheros, and missions was significant in that it threw almost all the horses in New Mexico onto the open Indian market. During the 18th century, the horse became a trading commodity among the tribes. Horses obtained by the Teton-Sioux from the Arikara were traded throughout the Dakota tribes. The Ute, and later the Comanche, became major suppliers to a secondary trading center among the Shoshone, while the Kiowa and Kiowa-Apache seem to have supplied horses as far away as the Upper Missouri. The Crow, who came late to the process, ultimately traded horses at a considerable profit all across the Plains. The Crow enjoyed stealing horses from their implacable enemy the Cheyenne. Cheyenne "Dog Soldiers," members of a warrior society that used Sirius (the Dog Star) as a totem, gladly retaliated. The profits to be had from horseflesh engendered a good deal of this intertribal raiding and rustling, and wealth, status, and marriage eligibility ultimately came to be measured in the number and quality of ones horses. The most significant period of Plains Indian Horse Culture was the first seven or eight decades of the 19th century. During this period, Native American horsemen ruled the Plains and formed possibly the best light cavalry in the world.

The eastern Plains tribes were the most sedentary. These included the Arikara, Hidatsa, Iowa, Kansa, Mandan, Missouri, Omaha, Osage, Oto, Pawnee, Ponca, Santee-Sioux, Yankton-Sioux, and the Wichita. These produced earth-covered lodges, some pottery and baskets, and circular skin boats. The western Plains tribes (Southern Shoshone, Ute, and Uinta) sitting on the edge of the plateau produced rather fine quality baskets, alternated between teepees and brush or woven mat covered shelters, and relied less on buffalo than they did on deer and small game. The northernmost members of the Plains community, particularly the Blackfoot and Assiniboine, exhibited many of the characteristics of the forest hunter blended with those of the Plains. By 1800, the Arapaho, Gros Ventres,

Crow, and Cheyenne, traditionally horticultural tribes, had all become no-madic hunters following the buffalo.

The most widely observed religious ritual on the Plains was the elab-orate and demanding Sun Dance, held at the summer solstice to thank the spirits (*wakan*), and the Great Spirit (*wakan tanka*), in particular, for the past year's success and to petition them for continued plenty in the coming year. The Siouan word *wakan,* the Iroquois word *orenda,* and the Algonquian term *manitou* seem to have been roughly equivalent in trying to represent the concept of spirit. The Sun Dance ceremony was held at a large circle of stones on the prairie and lasted for up to eight days. Many of these stone circles—actually thin lines of stone cobbles with a larger cen-ter pile—have been identified. The sacred circle was held to represent the repeating cycle of birth and death, and it often appears in Indian artwork, basketry, and rock paintings (petroglyphs). Most Western tribes also fol-lowed a "medicine bundle" and a "calumet" tradition.

The most historically colorful of the Plains tribes were the Sioux (Lakota or Dakota), who gave their name to two U.S. states. Their several bands generally followed the migrating herds of buffalo camping freely in Colorado, Wyoming, Nebraska, western Kansas, southern Montana, the Dakotas, and parts of Canada. The holy ground and cultural anchor of the Sioux was an area of Wyoming known as the Black Hills. When first con-tacted by Lewis and Clark, the Sioux were found to be so unfriendly as to be immediately labeled hostile, yet, they freely traded with the French, the agents of the British Hudson's Bay Company, and the mixed race Canadian Metis throughout the 18th century and early 19th centuries. From the time of Lewis and Clark (1805) until the establishment of the Oregon Trail (ap-prox. 1845), the tribes of the plains and Upper Missouri were visited only by trappers, traders, and a few artists and painters.[6]

The Indians of the Southwest Mesas and Deserts

The native residents of the Southwest were of two cultural types: the settled Indians of the pueblos (mud-brick or stone villages) and the no-madic tribes. On account of the highly developed state of their culture and their ancient antecedents, the sedentary pueblo dwellers seem to exhibit the traits of a single people and are sometimes incorrectly called the Pueblo. Yet, these cultures were far from unvaried. With minor differ-ences, the Indians of the pueblos fall into three geographical groups: the Hopi, the Zuni, and the Rio Grande. Each of these three had numerous Subgroups.

The pueblo cultures shared a number of characteristics besides housing: a dependence on maize and other cultivated foods, the use of irrigation, the domestication of turkeys, the weaving of cloth on upright looms, the art of masonry, the use of grinding stones for making corn meal rather than the mortar and pestle, the cultivation of cotton as a textile material, highly decorated pottery (some in color), and a unique building style that lends its name to the culture. There was some hunting of buffalo and deer with bows and throwing lances, but the most unique aspect of the hunt was a flat, curved hunting stick that could be thrown at small animals such as rabbits. The principal wild plant resource used for food was the piñon nut. The villagers sometimes wore deerskin clothing and buffalo robes, but woven clothing was more usual. Men wore an apron and a robe when needed, and women wore a woven garment reaching from the shoulder to the knees and fastened over the right shoulder only.

The earliest pueblo dwellers seem to have been the Anasazi, those whom the Navajo called the ancient ones. The center of their culture was in the present-day four corners of the Southwest where New Mexico, Arizona, Colorado, and Utah meet. The Anasazi were also known as the basket-makers from the extraordinary basketry that they produced, some so tightly wrought as to hold water for cooking with hot rocks. The Anasazi appear to have originally lived in houses built over a dug-down floor, but some time in the 7th or 8th century they began to build their home entirely above ground of logs and adobe mortar and then of stone. These were matrilocal clan dwellings with a mother, her married daughters, their hus-bands, and their children living together in a single structure with many rooms. Eventually, the entire village lived in multiroomed, multistoried buildings.

The Anasazi lived among the mesas (table-lands) and canyons of the region from about the 4th century to the 13th century. They may or may not be the direct ancestors of the pueblo tribes found by the Spanish three centuries after the end of this period. Certainly, the Hopi had lived in their three major mesa communities in Arizona for up to 1,500 years, and the Mesa Verde, Colorado complex of cliff pueblos, cave villages, and adobe structures were occupied for at least 1,000 years. Evidence suggests that the Anasazi moved, split, built and abandoned towns, and appeared and disappeared in many directions. Their square-shouldered petroglyphs are found over a wide area of the Southwest. There is no evidence of war, invasion, or physical conflict of any sort, however. Strangers may have entered the region and learned the peaceful and efficient Anasazi ways to become Anasazi themselves.

The Hopi, Zuni, and Rio Grande peoples may have been the product of this acculturation. The Hopi name for themselves was the "peaceful ones." The pueblo pit house *(kiva)*, a circular religious center with subter-ranean chambers, was entered through a hole in the roof. The interior of the kiva was decorated with symbolic likenesses of their spirits and dei-ties on the walls, and a mystical hole in the floor known as a *sipapu*. The pueblo Indians believed in spirits known as corn maidens and power-ful gods known as kachinas. The kachinas had supernatural powers over beasts, birds, trees, snakes, mountains, and stars. Pueblo dolls, known as kachina dolls, made of corn-husks, had the same square-shouldered look of Anasazi representations.

Among these pueblo peoples, kinship was divided between two moieties determined by birthright. The summer people and the winter people took turns running the towns for half the year. The men grew the corn, and the women ground it; men and women claimed ownership of homes, but the wife owned all that was in it. The man belonged more to his mother's house than his own, and he was the main tutor and advisor to his sister's children.

The Navajo were also residents of the Southwest. Their traditional territory was enclosed by four sacred mountains each in a different part of the four corner states: Tsisnaajini in the east (Colorado), Tsoodzil in the south (New Mexico), Doko'oosliid in the west (Arizona), and Dibe'ntsaaa in the north (also Colorado). Researchers and traditionalists argue about the origin of the Navajo. Scholars say the people migrated into the area from Canada with other Apachean peoples about A.D. 1000. The Navajo and Apache are related linguistically with several tribes of western Canada and the California coast who speak dialects of the Athapaskan (aka, Apachean) language group. The Navajo separated from the Apache just prior to contact with Spanish Europeans. The Navajo traditions have no record of such a movement from Canada. Instead, their religion suggests that they traveled through three or four underworlds beneath this one, exiting in the La Plata Mountains of southwestern Colorado. From here the gods created the four sacred mountains as a shelter for the people. The gods also established four rivers to serve as protective guardians. Among the mountain valleys and along these rivers, the Navajo hunted, gathered, and planted fields of corn, beans, and squash and pastured sheep that they had secured from their intercourse with the Spaniards. The San Juan River was a clear line of demarcation between the Navajo and their Ute neighbors, and both hotly defended the integrity of their territory. In the historic period, the Navajo were set upon by the Spanish, the Mexicans, the Mormons, and the American army. After the acquisition of parts of their territory in the Gadsden Purchase, the U.S. government forcibly removed up to 8,000 Navajo to Fort Sumner, New Mexico. This is known as the "Long Walk." A treaty ultimately allowed them to return to their lands. The Navajo reservation totally enclosed that of the Hopi.

The nomadic nations of the Southwest included a number of tribes and subtribes, particularly the Apache, Comanche, and Kiowa-Apache. The Southern Athapaskan language group is now generally called the Apachean language. It is definitely a linguistic as well as a geographic grouping. The Western Apachean was spoken by the San Carlos, the Chiricahua, and the Mescalero Apache, as well as the Navajo. Eastern Apachean was spoken by the Jicarilla, Lipan, and Kiowa-Apache. All except the Lipan and Kiowa-Apache were spoken in New Mexico, Arizona, and contiguous parts of Mexico. The Lipan was generally isolated in Texas and the Kiowa-Apache in western Kansas.[7]

The Comanche, Kiowa-Apache, and Apache defied the authority of both the Spanish and American governments and managed to delay white settlement of much of Texas, Arizona, and New Mexico for more than 100 years. The Comanche were originally residents of the Yellowstone region of Wyoming and Colorado where they split away from their Shoshone relatives after acquiring horses. The Kiowa were refugees from Teton Sioux aggression in the Black Hills. Besides these, there were five major divisions of the Apache, and these were separated into innumerable subtribes.

There were two types of Apache grouping: those based on territory and those based on kinship. There were more than 50 named clans with matrilineal–matrilocal bands composed of multiple households organized around a central woman, her husband, her married daughters, and their families. Although most marriages were monogamous, an individual man might be married at the same time to any number of sisters. Because the family lineage was based on the female and marriage was prohibited between closely related clans, kinship ties could be extremely complex. Apache men often sought eligible wives from among distant bands and were forced by the matrilocal family structure to reside away from their own clan.

Local leadership among the Apache was supplied through the family hierarchy, but tribal or band leaders rose to prominence through the force of their personality. Led in the second half of the 19th century by Mangas Coloradas, Cochise, Vitorio, Geronimo, and others, marauding bands of Apaches attracted few friends, Indian or white. They were tireless and implacable enemies when pursuing a vendetta. When on the prod they exhibited an uncanny slyness, a bottomless well of physical reserve, and a macabre and sometimes gruesome cruelty.

Since 1821, the Mexican government had followed an official policy of genocide regarding the Indians of the great Southwest, and the Treaty of Guadalupe Hidalgo that ended the Mexican-American War and the Gadsden Purchase had thrown much of the Southwest and much of the Indian problem into American hands. Initial contacts with the native tribes of the region were peaceful, but these soon became strained as America refused to recognize Indian rights and miners and settlers arrived in the territories. In a series of despicable incidents, Americans pretending friendship to the Indians killed or poisoned them, setting off a series of wars that lasted from 1850 until 1886.

Up to the time of the Mexican–American War of 1846, the Apaches reveled in attacking Spanish settlements and less aggressive tribes such as the pueblo tribes or the Navajo. The pueblo tribes and Navajo Indians were no complacent people—digger Indians as some whites called them. The pueblo tribes had staged a concerted rebellion against the Spanish in 1680, destroying virtually every mission in New Mexico and parts of

Arizona and treating the padres to some particularly gruesome deaths, but their time had passed. Few remained recalcitrant into the 19th century, and most had found life on federal reservations adequate if poor.

From their long exposure to the Catholic missionaries of Spain, it is not surprising to find that many southwestern bands were exclusively Christian, while others followed their traditional religion in part or in whole. Many spoke fluent Spanish, which facilitated communication and relieved misunderstandings somewhat. Yet, the bands railed under poor government treatment from both Mexico and the United States, and small groups of warriors regularly left the agencies and raised terror throughout the region.

The Chiricahau Apache gained in reputation and status in a series of strikes and counterstrikes against the whites during 11 years of war with the Americans (1861–1872). The entire Southwest was considered to be under threat from the Mescalero Apaches from 1866 to 1886. The Mescalero raided on both the Mexican and Texan sides of the Rio Grande. In 1874, the war chief named Geronimo (Goyathlay) was able to recruit a small band of Chiricahua Apache to raid across New Mexico and Arizona. He had a deep belief in the traditional Apache spirits and was seemingly entrusted by the other bands with avenging the many Apache deaths that had taken place over time. Geronimo acquired a recognition among his people as an intrepid and cunning fighter. He seemingly moved in and out of Mexico at will even though the American army and the Mexican Army were constantly tying to intercept him. When Geronimo finally surrender to General Nelson A. Miles in 1886, he was one of the best known Indian warriors in America. He and his people were sent to Florida with almost 500 other Apache and their families. In 1892, the Apache were removed to Oklahoma, where Geronimo sustained his family by ranching, farming, and selling autographed photographs of himself. He appeared at the St. Louis World's Fair and marched in Teddy Roosevelt's inauguration parade. The Apaches were released from confinement in Oklahoma by an act of Congress in 1913.

The Indians of California and the Pacific Coast

The Native American nations that resided in California can be divided into four or more subgroups, but those of the central region are the most typical. They included a number of Athapaskan speaking tribes: Yani, Yahi, Pomo, Patwin, Miwok, Maidu, Nisenan, Karok, Yurok, Wishosk, Shasta, and Hupa. Their main common characteristic was the use of an acorn meal as their chief food source. This was supplemented by wild seeds, small game, and fishing where possible. None of the Californian nations pressed oil from the acorns as did some tribes in the Southeast. Their temporary shelters were of brush, and more substantial structures were conical lean-tos supported by poles. There were no canoes, but rafts were used for water transportation. No pottery was in evidence, but basketry (both coil and twine) was highly advanced. Bags and mats were poorly crafted, and there was no true weaving. Work in skins was weak, cloth was minimal, and the feet were generally bare. Work in wood, bone, and metal was weak or nonexistent, and stone work was not highly advanced. The simple self-bow was their only weapon. These traits suggest a simple life in a pleasant environment that required little in the way of material culture for survival.

The southern California variants added to these traits the construction of plank canoes and some excellent work in stone and shell. Further south, these people disappear to be replaced by Yuman and Shoshonean tribes (Mohave, Yuma, Havasupai, Maricopa) with fine pottery, scandals rather than moccasins or bare feet, wooden war clubs, and curved rabbit sticks. All these seem to be intrusions. To the north was found coastal fishing, dugout canoes, the use of salmon as a supplemental food source, and rectangular plank houses with gables and circular doors. These all seem to be intrusions from the Pacific coast culture to the north.

Balanophagy, or acorn eating, was the most remarkable feature of the California nations, and it extended to wherever appropriate species of oak trees grew on the Pacific coast. When ordinary seeds or grains are used as food, some sort of grinding or pulverizing mechanism is needed to prepare them, but sweet acorn nuts can be eaten as easily as walnuts or almonds. The crux of the Californian acorn industry was the removal of objectionable levels of tannic acid from the more bitter nut varieties. The process of leaching the acids by soaking the shelled whole nut in water took months and was generally replaced by first pulverizing the nut-meat, and then boiling, leaching, and roasting it into an acorn meal. Sand-basin, twig (aka, bird's nest), and basket leachers were used. The California region seems to be one in which this advanced processing was independently invented. The fading distribution of acorn utilization as a food source roughly parallels the growing distribution of the use of sinew-backed bow and the wearing of moccasins.

The California tribes were among the first to feel the armed threat of white intrusion brought on by the discovery of gold in California. In the 1850s, the tribes that had resided in the Sierra Nevada were driven away from their hunting, fishing, and gathering grounds by the miners and lumberjacks. The native population of California decreased by as much as 70 percent in the decade before the Civil War.

The Northwest Pacific coast of Oregon and Washington states exhibited a strong material culture that featured a complexity that was as unique as it was rich. That the nations of this region were able to attain this high level is largely attributable to the amazing wealth of natural resources in their area. From the sea and rivers there were five species of fish—salmon, halibut, cod, herring, and smelt—that could provide food resources and one (the olachen or candlefish) that, when dried, burned like a candle. Some of these appeared seasonally, but they were all easily preserved. The sea also provided edible mollusks and a spectacular variety of marine game creatures such as sea otter, seals, porpoise, and whale. On land there was an abundance of game and berries, but vegetable foods were less plentiful. The forests made a number of easily worked woods available as raw materials.

The population included the Tlingit, Haida, Tsimshia, Kwakiutl, Chemakum, Quileute, Salish, Wakashan, and the Chinook. Further inland in the Oregon Territory, the extreme north of Montana and Idaho, and British Columbia were the Yakima, Walla Walla, Spokane, Wasco, Paiute, and Cayuse nations. The Chinook of lower British Columbia were among the most sophisticated because they served as middlemen in the native trade network both up and down the coast and into the interior making contact with many tribes.

The common traits of the culture can be summarized. Cooking was done with hot stones in boxes and baskets. The natives of the region developed large, ocean-going canoes made of dug-out logs and sometimes fitted with sails. There was no pottery or stone vessels, but basketry (twine, not coil) was highly developed. Mats of cedar bark and soft bags were present in abundance. There was no true loom, but some finger weaving was done downward from a hanging bar. Clothing was scanty, made chiefly of skins, and the feet were usually bare. Some moccasins and leggings were worn. The bow, club, and dagger were the only weapons. Stonework was rudimentary, and a hand-held stone hammer was used instead of a hafted one. Sculpture in wood, ivory, and bone was highly advanced.

Woodworking was highly developed and included the splitting and smoothing of planks. These were secured together by a unique method of hidden stitches. Large rectangular houses with gabled roofs were built of upright cedar planks. These were adorned with carved posts and totem poles. "The Northwest artists seemed to abhor blank surfaces and straight lines. Every inch of space was utilized to produce fantastic complexes of writhing, interlocked figures."[8]

The Northwest Pacific coast was also noted for the potlatch. This was the purposeful distribution by a person of food, gifts, and personal items to his neighbors, often to the extent of his own impoverishment. Potlatches were used to celebrate births, deaths, funerals, marriages, and many other events. They could include feasting, songs, dance, theatrical skits, and other entertainments as well as serious rituals and religious ceremonies. The host family showed its wealth by such distributions and gained social status thereby. The practical outcome was to raise the wealth of the lesser families in the community. Potlatches were often reciprocal events with the giver becoming a guest at those given by his neighbors.

The Oregon Territory became the destination for many white migrant families and Christian missionaries. The influx of intruders was not without turmoil. In 1847, Marcus and Narcissa Whitman, a married couple serving as missionaries to the Indians in Oregon for the American Missionary

Board, were killed along with 14 other whites by Cayuse Indians upset by the death of nearly all their sick children during a measles epidemic brought on by exposure to infected whites. Although the Whitman's administered to all the sick, only half of the infected white children had died. Subsequently, the militia counterattacked, escalating the incident into a war.

From 1851 to 1856, whites undertook a number of punitive raids against the Yakima, Walla Walla, and Cayuse nations. In 1855, Yakima attacks on parties of prospectors, brought in the U.S. regular army, which forced the Indians onto reservations. Not until the interposition of General William S. Harney did the raiding and counterraiding end. Harney, promoted to general and transferred from the Plains to the command of the Oregon Territory in 1858, used his understanding of the Indians to initiate a relatively peaceful settlement out of the ongoing troubles in the Northwest.

Recording Native America

In the early part of the 19th century, most of the North American continent west of the Mississippi River was largely an enigma thought to contain an unfamiliar and formidable geography, an undiscovered set of exotic flora and fauna, and a myriad of aboriginal tribes. Both Americans and Europeans were fascinated by the idea of recording what actually existed in the region beyond the Great Lakes, over the Rocky Mountains, and across the shifting border with British America.

Much of what we know about this part of America and its inhabitants has come down to us through the work of the naturalists, explorers, and artists/authors who visited there. "Even in its most primitive stage a cosmopolitan strain ran through the American borderland: it was a vastly thinned-out back yard of the world at large, where men of all nations and stations might meet and mingle in the course of their adventures."[9] These men traveled widely and lived for extended periods among the Indians, often in little known or uncharted regions, recording their impressions not only in the written word, but also in sketches, paintings, engravings, and lithographs. In the decades before the common use of the photographic camera, these artists made their images bristle with nervous energy and romantic fervor. In many cases, they captured actions and reactions on canvas that the slow-acting photographic processes of the day were incapable of recording.

No painter of the period is more closely associated with depicting the American Indian than George Catlin. In 1831, Catlin became acquainted with William Clark, the explorer of the Louisiana Purchase, who was himself the illustrator and map-maker of the official journal of the 1805 Lewis and Clark Expedition. It is uncertain how much Clark influenced his work, but during 1831 and 1832, Catlin ventured up the Platte River on two expeditions to make sketches of the Mandan Indians. He again ascended the Missouri River by steamboat and canoe in 1833 to finish the work he had begun. Catlin probably did not know that he was helping to document the culture of a vanishing people. The Mandan were decimated by disease and shortly thereafter ceased to exist as a separate identifiable culture having been absorbed into other related tribes.

Caitlin also visited a large Comanche village at the foot of the Wichita Mountains in 1834, and he made many sketches among the almost 800 skin-covered lodges that housed thousands of Indians. Catlin was not the most meticulous or most skilled of the artists that recorded the great horse cultures of the Plains peoples, but he was the first to expose them to the procedure of having their likenesses formally recorded—no small accomplishment among an unsophisticated and superstitious people. Even among the friendly Mandan, artists were occasionally subjected to threats and mistreatment. His initiation of the Indians to the protocols of sitting and posing no doubt made the work of those who followed him "more productive and less dangerous than [it] might otherwise have been."[10]

In 1838, Catlin offered his paintings for sale to Congress, but they were rejected. He then moved to Europe where his work was much more admired and profitable. Catlin benefited from the twin 19th-century movements of romanticism and scientific inquiry that valued recording aboriginal cultures before they were contaminated by civilization. Europeans, especially those in France and Germany, were intensely interested in America, and they consumed hundreds of journals, guides to immigrants, and novels illustrated with engravings and lithographs of the American frontier.

In 1844, Catlin wrote *Letters and Notes on the Manners, Customs, and Condition of the North American Indians,* an important documentary source for the study of the Native American people before they were completely contaminated by contact with the white man. In this work, Catlin correctly predicted, 50 years before the event, the destruction of the great buffalo herds of the American Plains. "The poor buffalo have their enemy man, besetting and besieging them at all times of the year and in all the modes that man...has been able to devise for their destruction. They struggle in vain to evade his deadly shafts."[11]

In the 1850s, George Catlin was hired by Samuel Colt to do a series of advertising prints for his firearms. The original oil canvases were to be of Colt firearms being used by Catlin himself in a number of exotic places. Six of the resulting works were lithographed in color and widely distributed. Yet, Catlin's rise to prominence was not without controversy because he showed the Indians and their family as people rather than as savages. Catlin's enthusiasm and respect for the Indian way of life was revealed in the journals of his travels published in 1867, *Life Among the Indians* and *Rambles Amongst the Indians of the Rocky Mountains and the Andes.*

Although Catlin is often the first name that comes to mind with regard to the painting of the American frontier, there were many other artists who traveled there. Titian Ramsay Peale accompanied an expedition to Florida in 1818 and made a record of the fauna and flora there. In the next year, as a member of Stephen Long's expedition along the South Platte River, he collected specimens and sketched birds, mammals, reptiles, fish, and insects found there. His work included more than 100 separate pieces of art.

Peter Rindisbacher was the first of many foreign-born artists to portray the U.S.–Canadian borderland to the world, and his work preceded that of other eminent artists by a decade. In 1821, the Red River region in which he lived was a wilderness made worse by the armed insurrection of the mixed race, French-speaking Metis Indians. For a decade, the colony had been on the verge of collapse, but Rindisbacher lost no time beginning his sketches once he reached America, first in pencil and pen and then in watercolors. His native subjects were primarily from among the Chippewa, Cree, Assiniboine, Winnebago, Sauk, Fox, and Sioux. He also recorded the activities of the Metis and British fur traders and the home life of the Swiss and Scottish settlers of the Red River colony.

In 1826, Rindisbacher moved to St. Louis, Missouri and produced a lithograph of one of his sketches, "A Sioux Warrior Charging." This stirring image first appeared in Baltimore in a new periodical, the *American Turf Register and Sporting Magazine*. The print was an instant sensation. Subsequently, nine more of his works were printed. In the last years of his life, he turned out his finest work dealing with the Indians, much of which revisited and improved on his earlier images.

When a minor German prince Maximilian von Wied traveled to the American West, he chose Charles (Carl) Bodmer, a Swiss painter, to make a pictorial record of his 1832 expedition to the upper Missouri. Bodmer made detailed illustrations of the life, habits, customs, and costumes of the Indians that they encountered through parts of present-day Nebraska, South and North Dakota, Montana, and Wyoming.

The subjects of Bodmer's work were largely portraits of individual Native Americans, but he did a number of river scenes, some of which included Indian villages. He was observant, and his work shows a conscious attention to detail. His meticulous painting of the interior of the pit house of a Mandan chief was the first of its kind to be published. Unlike many other artists of this genre, Bodmer made no attempt to romanticize his subjects. In 1834, he moved to France where he completed 81 paintings based on his sketches and watercolors. These he exhibited in a Paris art salon in 1836 opening a view of the American West to the world.

In 1846, Paul Kane, a wandering artist from Toronto, Canada, set out from Sault Sainte Marie for the farthest reaches of the Canadian West. Kane was determined to record the life of the North American Indians before the alcohol, gunpowder, and diseases of the white man changed them forever. He went all the way to the Pacific Ocean making sketches of Native Americans, their homes, villages, possessions, and cultural activities in Wisconsin, Alberta, British Columbia, and Vancouver. Along the way he also recorded the activities of the fur traders among the Indians in Saskatchewan and particularly at their post on the Columbia River. He drew a sketch of a minor eruption of Mount St. Helens in the Cascade Mountains of present-day Washington State, and he recorded the life of the people native to Idaho and the disputed Oregon border region. In 1847, Kane made final portraits of Reverend Whitman and his wife before their deaths. In 1848, Kane began transferring his sketches to canvas, thereby leaving a precise and detailed record of the region for future historians and ethnographers.

Heinrich Mollhausen made three trips to America from Germany as an artist/reporter and draftsman for the U.S. government. On his first trip, he joined the Rocky Mountain expedition of the German naturalist Prince Paul of Wurttemburg. These sketches were later lithographed. Some were made part of the official reports of the expeditions of Lt. A. W. Whipple and of Lt. J. C. Ives, who he accompanied from Arkansas to California and along the Colorado River, respectively. Like other artists, Mollhausen shared his work with an interested European public by writing journals and illustrating them with his own engravings and lithographs.

Alfred Jacob Miller was an American-born portrait painter selected to serve as an artist on a wagon expedition to the Rocky Mountains along the Oregon Trail. He sketched Native Americans and mountain men along the way, and he was the first to document the annual rendezvous of the fur traders in what is now southwestern Wyoming. Miller made 166 sketches that he turned into oil paintings upon his return to his studio in New Orleans. From 1840 to 1842, he also produced a portfolio of 83 small drawings and watercolors.

There were also a number of lesser known German authors/artists who traversed the United States in this period. In 1832, Tragott Bromme published a thorough account of Native American life among the peoples of the arctic circle (commonly known as Inuit or Eskimos) that included 80 engraved plates.

Charles Wimar came to America at age 15 and made friends with the Indians that lived on the outskirts of St. Louis. He retained a great love of the Native Americans, even after he returned to Germany in 1852, where he painted several studies of American Indians. His scenes were popular with early U.S. historians and novelists such as James Fennimore Cooper. One of his most famous works was "The Abduction of Daniel Boone's Daughter." This romanticized the actual woodland abductors into a noble Plains warrior astride a massive and well-muscled steed. This image was reproduced in many formats in subsequent years and helped to fix a sometimes inaccurate picture of the character of the Indian in the minds of Americans.

Notes

1. Alvin M. Josephy, Jr., ed., *The American Heritage Book of Indians* (New York: American Heritage Publishing, 1961), 144.

2. John Missall and Mary Lou Missall, *The Seminole Wars, American's Longest Indian Conflict* (Gainesville: University Press of Florida, 2004), 141.

3. Missall and Missall, 189.

4. Quoting newspaper correspondent Robert A. Strahorn in Jerome A. Greene, ed., *Battles and Skirmishes of the Great Sioux War, 1876–1877: The Military View* (Norman: University of Oklahoma Press, 1993), 14.

5. John C. Ewers, "The Horse Culture in Plains Indian History," in *The North American Indians, A Sourcebook*, ed. Roger C. Owen (Toronto: Collier-Macmillan Limited, 1971), 497–498.

6. John Young Nelson as told to Harington O'Reilly, *Fifty Years on the Trail: The Adventures of John Young Nelson* (Norman: University of Oklahoma Press, 1963), 104.

7. Harry Hoijer, "Indian Languages of North America," in *The North American Indians, A Sourcebook*, ed. Roger C. Owen (Toronto: Collier-Macmillan Limited, 1971), 77–78.

8. Josephy, Jr., ed., 295.

9. Marshall B. Davidson, "Carl Bodmer's Unspoiled West," American Heritage 14, no. 3 (April 1963): 48.

10. Davidson, 65.

11. George Catlin, *Letters and Notes on the Manners, Customs, and Condition of the North American Indians* (London: C. Adlard, Bartholomew Close, 1844), 31.

Maps

The Northeast Atlantic coast with some of the colonial place names used by Europeans for reference.

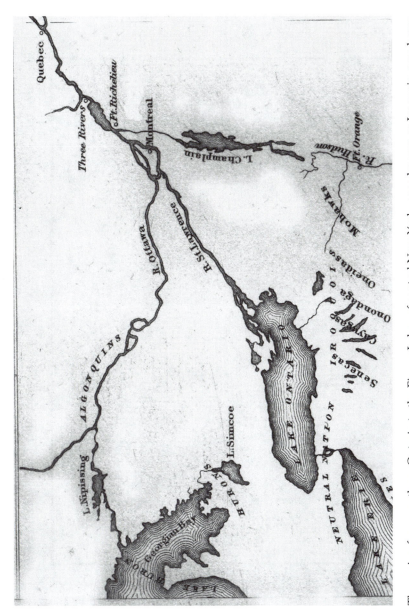

The region from southern Ontario to the Finger Lakes of central New York, once known as Iroquoia, was home to the Five (Six) Nations Confederacy (detail of Parkman Map).

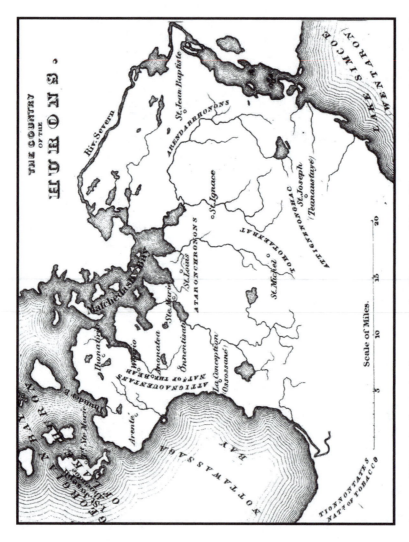

A map of Huronia, the region between Lake Simcoe and Lake Huron, which was the homeland of the Huron and their related cantons (detail of Parkman's map).

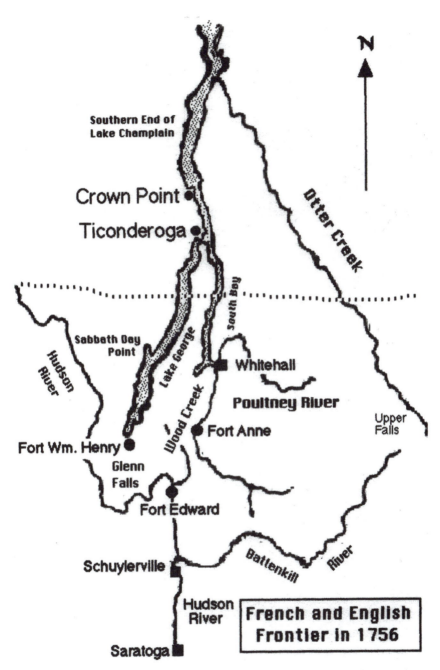

N

Southern End of
Lake Champlain

Otter Creek

Crown Point ●

Ticonderoga ●

South Bay

Sabbath Bay
Point

Hudson
River

Lake George

Whitehall

Poultney River

Upper
Falls

Wood Creek

Fort Anne

Fort Wm. Henry ●

Glenn
Falls

Fort Edward

Schuylerville

Battenkill River

Hudson
River

**French and English
Frontier in 1756**

Saratoga

The region surrounding the Ticonderoga peninsula may have been the most heavily fortified and strategically important position in all of North America in the 17th
and 18th centuries.

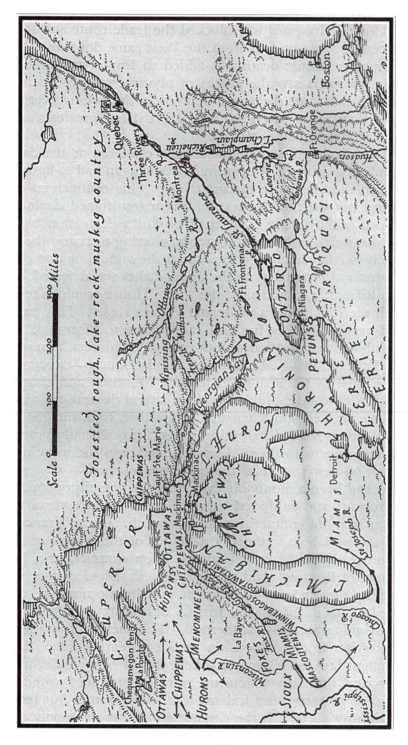

The Great Lakes region was at the cultural heart of the Northeast woodlands culture. This map from an early 19th-century school book locates a number of the western allied tribes before and after the dispersal.

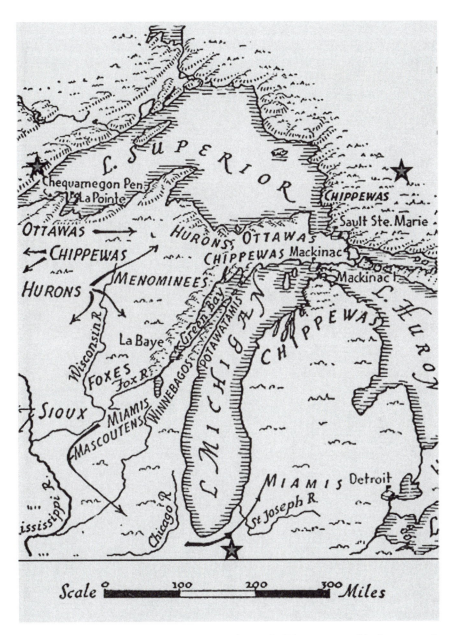

The Upper country, or *pays d'en haut*, in the mid-17th century with the approximate territories of its tribal residents. The stars serve as the points on the *pays d'en haut* triangle inside of which the bulk of the Great Lakes Indians lived.

Selected Bibliography

Bennett, Ralph, ed. *Settlements in the Americas: Cross-Cultural Perspectives.* Newark: University of Delaware Press, 1993.

Bolton, Reginald Pelham. *Indian Life of Long Ago in the City of New York.* New York: Harmony Books, 1934.

de Bougainville, Louis Antoine. *Adventures in the Wilderness. The American Journals of Louis Antoine de Bougainville.* Norman: University of Oklahoma Press, 1964.

Brandon, William. *Indians.* Boston: Houghton Mifflin Company, 1987.

Calder, Isabel M. *Colonial Captives, March, and Journeys.* Port Washington, NY: Kennikat Press, 1935.

Calloway, Colin G. *Dawnland Encounters: Indians and Europeans in Northern New England.* Hanover, NH: University Press of New England, 1991.

———. *New Worlds For All: Indians, Europeans, and the Remaking of Early America.* Baltimore: The Johns Hopkins University Press, 1997.

———. *The Western Abenakis of Vermont, 1660–1800: War, Migration, and the Survival of an Indian People.* Norman: University of Oklahoma Press, 1990.

Carver, Jonathan. *Travels Through the Interior Parts of North America in the Years 1766, 1767, and 1768.* Minneapolis: Ross & Hanes, 1956.

Cresswell, Nicholas. *The Journal of Nicholas Cresswell, 1774–1777.* New York: Dial Press, 1928.

Densmore, Frances. *How Indians Use Wild Plants for Food, Medicine and Crafts.* New York: Dover Publications, 1974; reprint of the 1928 edition.

Eckert, Allen W. *Wilderness Empire.* Toronto: Bantam Books: 1980.

Edmonds, Walter D. *The Musket and the Cross, The Struggle of France and England for North America*. Boston: Little, Brown and Company, 1968.

Ferling, John. *Struggle for a Continent: The Wars of Early America*. Arlington Heights, IL: Harlan Davidson, 1993.

Gallup, Andrew, ed. *Memoir of a French and Indian War Soldier, Jolicoeur Charles Bonin*. Bowie, MD: Heritage Books, Inc., 1993.

Hauptman, Laurence M., and James D. Wherry, eds. *The Pequots in Southern New England, The Fall and Rise of an American Indian Nation*. Norman: University of Oklahoma Press, 1990.

Hunt, George T. *The Wars of the Iroquois, A Study in Intertribal Trade Relations*. Madison: University of Wisconsin Press, 1972.

Jennings, Francis. *The Ambiguous Iroquois Empire, The Covenant Chain Confederation of Indian Tribes with English Colonies from its Beginnings to the Lancaster Treaty of 1744*. New York: W.W. Norton and Company, 1984.

Johnson, Michael G. *American Woodland Indians*. London: Osprey Publishing, 2000.

Josephy, Alvin M., Jr., ed., *The American Heritage Book of Indians*. New York: American Heritage Publishing, 1961.

Kalm, Peter. *Peter Kalm's Travels in North America*. New York: Dover Publications, 1964.

Karr, Ronald Dale, ed., *Indian New England, 1524–1674: A Compendium of Eyewitness Accounts of Native American Life*. Pepperell, MA: Branch Line Press, 1999.

Kupperman, Karen Ordahl. *Indians and English, Facing Off in Early America*. Ithaca: Cornell University Press, 2000.

Lauber, Almon W., ed., *The Papers of Sir William Johnson*. Albany: University of the State of New York, 1939.

Lucier, Armand Francis, ed., *French and Indian War Notices Abstracted from Colonial Newspapers: 1754–1755*. Bowie, MD: Heritage Books, 1999.

Mahon, John K. "Anglo-American Methods of Indian Warfare, 1674–1794." *The Mississippi Valley Historical Review* 45 (1958): 254–275.

Marshall, Ingeborg. *A History and Ethnography of the Beothuk*. Montreal: McGill-Queen's University Press, 1996.

McCallum, John H., ed. *Francis Parkman, The Seven Years War: A Narrative taken from Montcalm and Wolfe, The Conspiracy of Pontiac, and A Half-Century of Conflict*. New York: Harper Torchbooks, 1968.

McGee, Harold F., ed. *The Native Peoples of Atlantic Canada, A History of Indian-European Relations*. Ottawa: Carleton University Press, 1983.

Missall, John, and Mary Lou Missall. *The Seminole Wars, American's Longest Indian Conflict*. Gainesville: University Press of Florida, 2004.

O'Callaghan, E. B., ed., *Documents Relative to the Colonial History of the State of New York*. Albany: Weed, Parsons and Co., 1855.

O'Neil, James F., ed. *Their Bearing Is Noble and Proud: A Collection of Narratives Regarding the Appearance of Native Americans from 1740–1815*. Dayton, Ohio: J.T.G.S. Publishing, 1995.

Overton, Jacqueline. *Indian Life on Long Island*. Port Washington: Ira J. Friedman, Inc., 1963.

Owen, Roger C., ed. *The North American Indians, A Sourcebook*. Toronto: Collier-Macmillan Limited, 1971.

Parkman, Francis. *La Salle and the Discovery of the Great West*. New York: The Modern Library, 1999.

———. *Montcalm and Wolfe*. New York: Athenaeum, 1984.

Potter, Stephen R. *Commoners, Tribute, and Chiefs, The Development of Algonquian Culture in the Potomac Valley*. Charlottesville: University Press of Virginia, 1993.

Pouchot, Pierre. *Memoir Upon the Late War in North America Between the French and English, 1775–1760*. Roxbury, MA: E. Elliot Woodward, 1866.

Ritzenthaler, Robert E., and Pat Ritzenthaler. *The Woodland Indians of the Western Great Lakes*. Garden City, NY: The Natural History Press, 1970.

Romans, Bernard. *A Concise Natural History of East and West Florida*. Gainesville: University of Florida Press, 1962.

Russell, Howard S. *Indian New England Before the Mayflower*. Hanover, NH: University Press of New England, 1980.

Schoolcraft, Henry Rowe. *Algic Researches, North American Indian Folktales and Legends*. Minneola, NY: Dover Publications, Inc., 1999; reprint of the 1839 edition.

Seaver, James E. *A Narrative of the Life of Mrs. Mary Jemison*. Syracuse, NY: Syracuse University Press, 1990.

Smith, Richard. *A Tour of Four Great Rivers. The Hudson, Mohawk, Susquehanna and Delaware in 1769*. New York: Charles Scribner's Sons, 1906.

Steele, Ian K. *Warpaths: Invasions of North America*. New York: Oxford University Press, 1994.

Stone, Albert E., ed. *Letters from an American Farmer and Sketches of Eighteenth-Century America by J. Hector St. John de Crevecoeur*. New York: Penguin Classics, 1986.

Thwaites, Reuben Gold, ed. *The Jesuit Relations and Allied Documents*. Cleveland: Burrows Brothers, 1898.

Timberlake, Henry. *Lieutenant Henry Timberlakes's Memoirs*. Marietta, GA: Continental Book Co., 1948.

Vestal, Stanley. *King of the Fur Traders, The Deeds and Deviltry of Pierre Esprit Radisson*. Boston: Houghton Mifflin, 1940.

Volo, James M., and Dorothy Denneen Volo. *Daily Life on the Colonial Frontier*. Westport: Greenwood Press, 2002.

———. *Family Life in 17th- and 18th-Century America*. Westport: Greenwood Press, 2006.

Volwiler, Albert T. *George Croghan and the Westward Movement, 1742–1783*. Lewisburg, PA: Wennawoods Publishing, 2000.

Wacker, Peter O. *The Musconetcong Valley of New Jersey: A Historical Geography*. New Brunswick, NJ: Rutgers University Press, 1968.

Wallace, Paul A. W. *Conrad Weiser, Friend of Colonist and Mohawk: 1696–1760*. Lewisburg, PA: Wennawoods Publishing, 1996.

———. *Indians in Pennsylvania*. Harrisburg: The Pennsylvania Historical and Museum Commission, 1986.

Weber, David J. *The Spanish Frontier in North America*. New Haven: Yale University Press, 1992.

Weissman, Judith Reiter, and Wendy Lavitt, *Labors of Love, America's Textiles and Needlework, 1650–1930*. New York: Wing Books, 1987.

White, Richard. *The Middle Ground, Indians, Empires, and Republics in the Great Lakes Region, 1650–1815*. New York: Cambridge University Press, 1991.

Wilbur, C. Keith. *The Woodland Indians, An Illustrated Account of the Lifestyles of America's First Inhabitants*. Guilford, CT: The Globe Pequot Press, 1995.

Index

About the Authors

JAMES M. VOLO, Ph.D., has been teaching physics, physical science, and astronomy for the past 39 years. He received his bachelor's from City College in New York, his master's from American Military University, and his doctorate from Berne University. He has taught at the Graduate level for more than 15 years and authored several reference works regarding U.S. military, social, and cultural history. In addition, he has consulted on television and movie productions. Among his published works are *Blue Water Patriots: The American Revolution Afloat* (Greenwood, 2006), *Daily Life in Civil War America* (Greenwood, 1998), *Family Life in 19th-Century America* (Greenwood, 2007), *The Antebellum Period* (Greenwood, 2004), and the *Encyclopedia of the Antebellum South* (Greenwood, 2000), several of which were co-authored with his wife, Dorothy Denneen Volo. Presently, Dr. Volo teaches at Sacred Heart University in Fairfield, Connecticut.

DOROTHY DENNEEN VOLO is a math teacher at Norwalk Public Schools in Norwalk, Connecticut. She is co-author of *Family Life in 17th- and 18th-Century America* (Greenwood, 2006), *Daily Life during the American Revolution* (Greenwood, 2003), and many other Greenwood titles.